Introduction to Anglo-Saxon.

AN

ANGLO-SAXON READER,

WITH

PHILOLOGICAL NOTES, A BRIEF GRAMMAR,

AND A VOCABULARY.

By FRANCIS A. MARCH, LL.D.,

PROFESSOR OF THE ENGLISH LANGUAGE AND COMPARATIVE PHILOLOGY IN LAFAYETTE COLLEGE, AUTHOR OF "A COMPARATIVE GRAMMAR OF THE ANGLO-SAXON LANGUAGE," "METHOD OF PHILOLOGICAL STUDY OF THE ENGLISH LANGUAGE," ETC.

NEW YORK:

HARPER & BROTHERS, PUBLISHERS,

FRANKLIN SQUARE.

1872.

PREFACE.

It seems to be agreed that every English scholar ought to have some scholarly knowledge of the English language. Then every English scholar ought to study Anglo-Saxon. He ought to read representative passages in representative books of the literature thoroughly, dwelling on them line by line, and word by word, and making the text the foundation of general philological study. At least a daily lesson for one term ought to be given to this study in each of our colleges.

Enough such extracts for two terms' work are here given in a critical text. The notes contain, besides explanatory matter, outlines of the literature, biographical sketches of the authors, and bibliographical notices of manuscripts and editions. The author's Comparative Grammar opens with a history of the language, and illustrates the grammatical forms by those of the Sanskrit, Greek, Latin, Gothic, Old Saxon, Old Friesic, Old Norse, and Old-High German. It is part of the plan to give a full etymological vocabulary. Thus it is supposed that apparatus is provided for as thorough study of a portion of this tongue as can be given to Greek or Latin with our college text-books.

In this edition a brief grammar has been introduced, that it may be fitted for general use as an introduction to the study of Anglo-Saxon in High Schools and Academies where they might fear the Comparative Grammar. The etymological part of the Vocabulary is reserved for a future edition. It was thought best to make sure of the completeness of the list of words by working it over in class before giving it its final shape.

The selections were stereotyped, and the book and its plan announced in 1865.

F. A. M.

Easton, Pa., June, 1870.

CONTENTS.

I. READER.

NOTES,

CRITICAL, HISTORICAL, AND BIBLIOGRAPHICAL, pp. 71–93.

II. GRAMMAR.

III. VOCABULARY 149

ANGLO-SAXON READER.

[In pages 1-12, accent the first syllable of every word, unless an acute accent is printed over some other syllable. Words not in the Vocabulary are in the notes. §§ refer to the Author's Grammar.]

1. The Sower.

Luke, viii., 5–8.—Sum man his sæ̂d seôp: þâ hê þæt seôp, sum feôl piđ þone peg, and pearđ fortred′en, and heofenes fugelâs hit fræ̂ton. And sum feôl ofer þone stân, and hit forscranc′, forþam′-þe hit pæ̂tan næfde. And sum feôl on þâ þornâs, and þâ þornâs hit forþrys′môdon. And sum feôl on gôde eorđan, and porhte hundfealdne pæstm.

Mark iv., 3–9.—Ût eôde se sæ̂dere his sæ̂d tô sâpenne, and þâ hê seôp, sum feôl piđ þone peg, and fugelâs cômon, and hit fræ̂ton. Sum feôl ofer stân′-scyl′ian, þæ̂r hit næfde mycele eorđan, and sôna up eôde, forþam′ hit næfde eorđan þicnesse. Þâ hit up eôde, seô sunne hit forspæ̂l′de, and hit for-scranc′, forþam′ hit pyrtruman næfde.

---

1. *Sum*, a, § 136, 3, so English *some* in the plural; *man*, man, § 84; *his*, from *hê*, § 130; *sæ̂d, es*, n., seed, acc. sing.; *seôp*, sowed, imp. ind., from *sâpan*, imp. *seôp*, *seôpon*, p. p. *sâpen*, conj. 5, § 208; *þâ*, when; *þæt*, that, from *se*, § 133; *feôl*, fell, imp. ind. sing., 3d, from *feallan*, imp. *feôl*, *feôllon*, p. p. *feallen*, conj. 5, § 208; *piđ þone weg*, along the way, § 359; *pearđ fortred′en*, was trodden out, passive, imp. ind., sing., 3d., from *for-tredan*, imp. *-træd*, *-træ̂don*, p. p. *-treden*, conj. 1, § 199, *for-*, Ger. *ver-*, § 254; *heofenes*, heaven's, from *heofon*, § 79; *fugelâs*, fowls, from *fugol*, § 79; *hit*, it, from *hê*, § 130; *fr-æ̂ton*, ate up, imp. ind. pl., 3d, from *fr-etan*, imp. *-æt*, *-æ̂ton*, p. p. *-eten*, conj. 1, § 199, *fr-*<*for-*, § 254; *ofer þone stân*, over the stone, on the rock; *for-scranc′*, shrank away, imp. ind. sing., 3d, from *for-scrincan*, imp. *-scranc*, *-scruncon*, p. p. *scruncen*, conj. 1, § 201; *for-þam′-þe*, for this that, because; *pæ̂tan*, wet, moisture, from *pæ̂ta*, *n*, m., § 95; *næfde*, had not, *ne*+*hæfde*, imp. of *habban*, §§ 45, 222; *on þâ þornâs*, among the thorns, *þorn*, *es*, m., § 341; *for-þrys′môdon*, choked out, from *for-þrysmian*, imp. *-þrysmôde*, p. p., *þrysmôd*, conj. 6; *gôde eorđan*, good earth, sing. acc.; *porhte*, worked, produced, imp. sing., 3d, from *pyrcan*, imp. *porhte*, *porhton*, p. p. *geporht*, conj. 6, § 211; *hundfealdne pæstm*, hundred-fold fruit, *hundfeald*, adj., strong form, § 103.

Ût eôde, out yode, went forth, irreg. imp. of *gân*, § 208; *se sæ̂dere*, the sower, *sæ̂dere*, *s*, m.; *sæ̂d*, *es*, n.; *tô sâpenne*, to sow, gerund, §§ 173, 175, from *sâpan*, conj. 5, § 208, 2, to denote purpose, § 454; *cômon*, came, *cuman*, imp. *com*, *cômon*, p. p. *cumen*, conj. 1, § 200; *fugelâs*, *fræ̂ton*, see above; *stân-scylian*, stone-shelly place, *stân-scyli-e*, *-an*, f.; *mycele*, much, f. sing. acc. from *mycel*, § 104; *sôna up eôde*, soon up yode (sprang); *þicnesse*, sing. acc. from *þicnes*, *se*, f., thickness; *seô sunne*, *seô*, fem., from *se*; *hit for-spæ̂ldc*, swealed it away, parched it, *spæ̂lan*, imp. *spæ̂lde*, conj. 6; *for-scranc*, see above; *pyrtruman*, root, *pyrt*, wort,

And sum feôl on þornâs; þâ stigon þâ þornâs, and forþrys'môdon þæt, and hit pæstm ne bær.

And sum feôl on gôd land, and hit sealde, up stîgende and pexende, pæstm; and ân brohte þrŷtigfealdne, sum syxtigfealdne, sum hundfealdne.

Gehŷr'e, se þe eâran hæbbe tô gehŷr'anne.

---

2. Lord's Prayer.

Matthew, vi., 9–13.—Fæder ûre, þû þe eart on heofenum, sî þîn nama gehâl'gôd. Tô be-cum'e þîn rîce. Gepeorđ'e þîn pilla on eorđan spâ spâ on heofenum. Ûrne dæg'hpamlîc'an hlâf syle ûs tô dæg. And forgyf' ûs ûre gyltâs, spâ spâ pê forgyf'ađ ûrum gyltendum. And ne gelæ̂d' þû ûs on costnunge, ac âlŷs' ûs of yfle. Sôđlîce.

Luke xi., 2–4.—Ûre Fæder, þû þe on heofene eart, sî þîn nama gehâl'gôd. Tô cume þîn rîce. Gepeorđ'e þîn pylla on heofene and on eorđan. Syle ûs tô dæg ûrne dæg'hpamlîc'an hlâf. And forgyf' ûs ûre gyltâs, spâ pê forgyf'ađ ælcum þæ̂râ þe piđ ûs âgylt'. And ne læ̂d þû ûs on costnunge; ac âlŷs' ûs fram yfele.

---

plant, *truma, n*, m., trimmer, strengthener; *stigon*, stied, ascended, *stîgan*, imp. *stâh, stigon*, p. p. *stigen*, conj. 2, § 205; *þornâs, forþrysmôdon, pæstm*, see above; *bær*, bore, *beran*, imp. *bær, bæ̂ron*, p. p. *beren*, conj. 1, § 199; *sealde* (sold), gave, *sellan*, imp. *sealde*, conj. 6, § 209, *b; stîgende* (stying), springing, p. pr., neut. sing., nom., from *stîgan*, conj. 2, § 119, *a; pexende*, from *pexan*=*peaxan*, wax, grow, imp. *p(e)ôx, p(e)ôxon*, p. p. *pexen*, conj. 4; *ân*, one, some; *brohte*, brought, bore, *brengan*, imp. *brohte*, p. p. *broht*, conj. 6, § 209, *c; þrŷtigfealdne*, thirty-fold, from *þrŷtigfeald*, adj., m. sing. acc., with *pæstm*. *Ge-hŷr'e*, let him hear, subjunctive for imperat., § 421, 3, *ge-hŷr'an*, imp. *ge-hŷrde*, p. p. *ge-hŷred*, conj. 6; *se þe*, who, demon. *se* with relative sign *þe*, § 380, 3; *hæbbe*, subj. pres. of *habban*, §§ 169, 427; *tô ge-hŷr'anne*, to hear, gerund, § 452.

2. *Fæder*, father, sing. voc., §§ 87, 100; *ûre*, of us, our, plur. gen. of *ic*, § 130; *þû þe*, who, *þû*, thou, sing. nom., § 130, *þe* relative sign changing *þû* to a relative, §§ 134, 381, 2; *eart*, from *eom*, § 213; *heofenum*, heavens, pl. dat. of *heofon; sî gehâl'gôd*, be hallowed, passive, subj. pres. sing., 3d, from *hâlgian*, conj. 6, §§ 179, 187, subj. for imperative, § 421, 3; *Tô becume*, let come to us, subj., 3d, for imperative, *cuman*, imp. *com, cômon*, p. p. *cumen*, conj. 1, § 200; *þîn rîce*, thy reign, compare *-ric* in *bishopric; gepeorđ'e*, subj. for imperative from *ge-peorđan*, imp. *-pearđ, -purdon*, p. p. *porden*, Ger. *werden*, Old Engl. *worth*, be, be done; *eorđan*, sing. dat., from *eorđe; spâ spâ*, so so, as; *ûrne*, pron., poss. sing., acc. masc., from *ûre*, § 132; *dæg'-hpam-lîc'-an*, weak, sing. acc. masc., from *dæghpamlîc*, daily, §§ 105, 108; *hlâf*, loaf, bread; *syle*>sell, give, imperat., from *syllan*=*sellan*, conj. 6, § 188, *b; ûs*, pl. dat., from *ic*, § 297; *tô dæg*, to day, *tô*, prep., at, on, *dæg*, day, sing. acc. after *tô*, *tô þissum dæge* (on this day) has the same sense, § 352; *and*, general sign of connected discourse, § 463; *for-gyf'*, imperat., from *for-gifan*, conj. 1, § 199, *for-*, § 254; *gyltâs*, debts, guilt, pl. acc., from *gylt; pê*, we, from *ic*, § 130; *ûrum gyltendum*, our debtors, pl. dat. after *forgifađ*, § 297, *gyltend, es*, m.; *gelæ̂d'*, pres. imperative, from *gelæ̂dan*, § 185; *costnunge*, sing. acc., from *costnung, e*, f., temptation; *â-lŷs'*, imperat., from *â-lŷsan*, loose, release; *of*, from; *yfle*, sing. dat., from *yfel*, §§ 79, 301, 305, 348; *sôđlîce*, soothly, amen, interj.; *þæ̂râ*, of those, pl. gen. of *se*, § 133; *âgylt*, is indebted, ind. sing., from *â-gyltan*, imp. *-gylte*, p. p. *-gylt*, § 192.

3. The Good Samaritan.

Luke, x, 25–37.—Þâ ârâs′ sum ǣgleâp man, and fandôde his, and cpæđ: Lâreôp, hpæt dô ic þæt ic êce lîf hæbbe? Þâ cpæđ hê tô him: Hpæt ys geprit′en on þǣre ǣ? hû rǣtst þû? Þâ and′sparô′de hê: Lufâ Dryhten þînne God of ealre þînre heortan, and of ealre þînre sâple, and of eallum þînum mihtum, and of eallum þînum mægene; and þînne nêhstan spâ þê sylfne. Þâ cpæđ hê: Ryhte þû and′sparô′dest: dô þæt, þonne lyfâst þû. Þâ cpæđ hê tô þam Hǣlende, and polde hine sylfne geriht′pîsian: And hpylc ys mîn nêhsta? Þâ cpæđ se Hǣlend, hine up beseônd′e: Sum man fêrde fram Hier′usal′em tô Hiericho, and becom′ on þâ sceađan, þâ hine bereâf′edon, and tintregôdon hine, and forlêt′on hine sâm′-cuc′ene. Þâ gebyr′ede hyt þæt sum sacerd fêrde on þam ylcan pege; and þâ hê þæt geseah′, hê hine forbeâh′. And ealspâ se diâcon, þâ hê pæs piđ þâ stôpe, and þæt geseah′, hê hyne eâc forbeâh′. Þâ fêrde sum Samar′itân′isc man piđ hine: þâ hê hine geseah′, þâ peard hê mid mild′-heort′nysse ofer hine âstyr′ed. Þâ geneâ′lǣhte hê, and prâđ his pundâ, and

3. *Â-râs′*, arose, *â-rîs′an*, imperf. *-râs′*, *-ris′on*, p. p. *-ris′en*, conj. 2, *ǣ-gleâp*, law-clever; *fandôde*, tried, examined, *fandian*, imperf. *fandôde*, p. p. *fandôd*, akin to *findan*, find; *his*, genitive after *fandôde*, § 315, III.; *cpæđ*, quoth, *cpeđan*, imperf. *cpæđ*, *cpǣdon*, p. p. *cpeden*, conj. 1, § 197; *lâreôp*, teacher, from *lâr*, lore; *dô*, shall do, subj. pres. sing., 1st, from *dôn*, imperf. *dide*, p. p. *dôn*, irreg., § 213; *ê-ce* (for *aye*), everlasting; *hæbbe*, subj. pres.; *ys*=*is*; *ge-prît′an*, imperf. *ge-prât′*, *ge-prit′on*, p. p. *ge-prit′en*, conj. 2; *ǣ*, law, f. ind., § 100; *rǣtst*, readest, *rǣdan*, imperf. *rǣdde*, p. p. *rǣded*, *rǣd*, conj. 6, *rǣdest*>*rǣtst*, irreg. like *bintst*, § 192; *lufâ*, impera. of *lufian*; *of*, out of, from, with dative of source; *nêhsta*, *n*, m., superlative of *neâh*, nighest one, neighbor; *þê*, acc. of *þû*; *sylf*, self, declined like an adjective, § 131; *ryhte*, adv., =*rihte*; *dô*, imperat.; *þonne*, then; *lyfâst*, pres. for fut., from *lifian*, conj. 6, §§ 222, 413, 4. *Hǣlende*, Savior, healing one; *polde*, would, *pillan*; *ge-riht′-pîs-ian*, justify, conj. 6; *riht-pîs*, wise in right, Engl. righteous; *hpylc*, which, who=*hpâ-lîc*, Latin *qua-lis*; *hine up beseônd′e*, looking up at him, a translation of Latin *suspiciens*, which some copies have for *suscipiens*; *seônde*, p. pr., from *seôn*, imperf. *seah*, *sǣgon*, p. p. *ge-sep′en*, conj., §§ 197, 199; *fêrde*>*fêran*, fare, go; *Hier′usal′em*, *es*, m., but here dative undeclined; *Hiericho*, acc., undeclined; *be-com′*, came, *becum′an*; *on þâ sceađan*, among the thieves (those who *scathe*), § 341, II.; *be-reâf′edon*, bereft, stript, *be-reâf′ian*, imperf. *-reâf′ede*, p. p. *-reâf′ed*, conj. 6; *tintregôdon*, tormented, *tintreg-ian*, imperf. *-ôde*, p. p. *-ôd*, conj. 6; *for-lêt′on*, left, *for-lǣt′an*, imperf. *-lêt′*, *-lêt′on*, p. p. *-lǣt′en*, conj. 5, *for-*, Ger. *ver-*, as in *for-sake*, *for-bid*, § 254; *sâm-cucene* (semi-quick), *cucene* for *cucenne*, acc. of *cucen*=*cpicen*, §§ [illegible], 119, *c*; *gebyr′ede hyt*, it was brought about, *ge-byr′ian*, imperf. *-byr′ede*, p. p. *byr′ed*, conj. 6, akin to *beran*, bear, *hyt*, bad spelling for *hit*; *sacerd*, *es*, m., priest, from Latin *sacerdos*, akin to *sacred*, *sacerdotal*; *fêrde*, *fêran*, conj. 6; *ylcan*, same, weak decl., § 133, 3; *ge-seah′*, saw, *ge-seôn′*, imperf. *-seah′*, *-sǣg′on*, p. p. *-sep′en*, conj. 1, § 199; *hine for-beâh′*, turned away from him, *for-bûg′an*, imperf. *-beâh′*, *-bug′on*, p. p. *-bug′en*, conj. 3, Engl. bow; *eal-spâ*, all so, also; *diâcon*, *es*, m., deacon, Levite; *hê*, repeated subject, § 287; *hyne*=*hine*, bad spelling; *eâc*, Ger. *auch*, Engl. *eke*, also; *piđ* (with), beside; *þâ . . . þâ*, when . . . then; *peard â-styr′ed*, imperf. passive *â-styr′ian*, imperf. *-styr′ede*, p. p. *-styr′ed*, stir, conj. 6; *mild-heortnys*, *se*, f. (mild-heartedness), compassion; *geneâ′lǣhte*, drew nigh, *ge-neâ′-lǣcan*, imperf. *-lǣhte*, p. p. *lǣht*, conj. 6; *prâđ*, bound up, *prîđan*, wreathe, imperf. *prâđ*, *priđon*, p. p. *priđen*,

on-âgeât' ele and pîn, and hine on his nŷten âset'te, and gelǽd'de on his lǽce-hûs, and hine gelâc'nôde, and brohte ôðrum dæge tpegen penegâs, and sealde þam lǽce, and þus cpæð: Begŷm' hys; and spâ-hpæt'-spâ þû mâre tô ge-dêst', þonne ic cume, ic hit forgyld'e þê. Hpylc þǽrâ þreôrâ þyncð þê þæt sig þæs mǽg þe on þâ sceaðan befeôl'? Þâ cpæð hê: Se þe hym mild'-heort'nysse on dyde. Þâ cpæð se Hǽlend: Gâ, and dô ealspâ.

4. The Lord's Day.

Matthew, xii., 1–13.—Se Hǽlend fôr on reste-dæg ofer æcerâs; sôðlîce his leorning-cnihtâs hingrede, and hig ongun'non pluccian þâ ear and etan. Sôðlîce þâ þâ sundor-hâlgan þæt ge-sâp'on, hî cpǽdon tô him: Nû þîne leorning-cnihtâs dôð þæt him âlŷf'ed nis reste-dagum tô dônne. And hê cpæð tô him: Ne rǽdde gê hpæt Dauid dyde þâ hine hingrede, and þâ þe mid him pǽron, hû hê in-eô'de on Godes hûs, and æt þâ offring-hlâfâs þe nǽron him âlŷf'ede tô etanne, ne þâm þe mid him pǽron, bûton þâm sacerdum ânum? Oðde ne rǽdde gê on þǽre ǽ, þæt þâ sacerdâs on reste-dagum on þam temple gepem'mað þone reste-dæg, and

conj. 6, § 205; *pund, e*, f., wound; *on âgeât'*, poured in, *â-geôt'an*, imperf. *-geât'*, *-gut'on*, p. p. *-gut'en*, conj. 3, akin to *gush, guzzle; nŷten*, beast, akin to *neat; â-set'te*, set, *âsett'an*, conj. 6; *lǽce-hûs, es*, n., leech house, hospital, hotel; *ge-lâc'nôde* (leeched), doctored, *ge-lâc'nian*, imperf, *-lâc'nôde*, p. p. *lâc'nôd; brohte* < *brengan*, conj. 6, § 209; *ôðrum* < *ôðer*, other, second, next, dative of time, § 304; *penegâs, peneg, es*, m., penny, stamped money, akin to *pawn*, Latin *pannus; sealde*<*sellan*, conj. 6, § 209; *lǽce, s*, m., leech; *cpæð*, quoth, <*cpeðan*, conj. 1; *be-gŷm'*, imperat. *be-gŷm'an*, imperf. *-gŷm'de*, p. p. *-gŷm'ed*, conj. 6; *hys*, bad spelling for *his*, genitive after *begŷm*, § 315; *mâre*, neuter acc. with *spâ-hpǽt'-spâ; tô ge-dêst'*, doest to him, *ge-dôn'*, irreg. § 213; *cume, forgyld'e*, pres. for future, § 413; *þyncð*, seemeth, *þyncan*, imperf. *þuhte*, p. p. *geþuht'*, conj. 6, § 211; *þæt*, that, conjunction; *sig* for *sî*, may be < *eom; þæs mǽg*, the kinsman of him; *þe*, that, who; *mild-heortnysse*, acc., see above; *on dyde*, did, showed, from *dôn*. *Gâ*, go, *gân*, irreg., imperf. *eôde*, p. p. *gân*, § 213; *dô* < *dôn*, § 213; *eal-spâ*, all so, likewise.

4. *Fôr* < *faran*, imperf. *fôr, fôron*, p. p. *faren*, conj. 4, fare, go, in fare-well; *reste-dæg, es*, m., rest-day, dative irreg., § 71; *æcerâs*<*æcer*, acre, Lat. *ager*, Gr. ἀγρός, Ger. *acker*, field; *leorning-cnihtâs*, learning knights, disciples, Ger. *knech't*, servant, *-cniht, es*, m.; *hingrede*, it hungered, impersonal imperf. of *hingrian* (*y* > *i*), conj. 6, governing the acc. of the persons hungering, § 290, *c; on-gun'non*, imperf. of *on-ginn'an*, conj. 1; *pluccian*, pluck, imperf. *pluccôde*, p. p. *pluccôd*, from Romanic *piluccare*, Lat. *pilus*, hair; *ear, es*, n., ear; *þâ þâ*, when the; *sundor-hâlga, n*, m. (sundered holy), Pharisees; *ge-sâp'on*<*ge-seôn'*, *-seah'*, *-sâp'on*, p. p. *sep'en*, conj. 1; *cpǽdon*<*cpeðan*, § 197; *dôð*<*dôn*, irreg., § 213; *þǽt*, what; *nis* = *ne* + *is*, § 213; *tô dônne*, gerund <*dôn; Ne rǽd'de gê*, read ye not, *rǽdan*, read, imperf. *rǽd'de*, conj. 6, *rǽdde* for *rǽddon* before the subject, § 170; *pǽron*, § 213; *in-eô'de*, in yode, entered, irreg., from *in-gân'*, § 213; *æt* < *etan; offring-hlâf, es*, m., offering-loaves, show-bread; *nǽron*=*ne*+*pǽron*, were not, § 213; *sacerdum*, plur. dat. *sacerd, es*, m.<Lat. *sacerdos*, priest, akin to sacred, sacerdotal; *ânum* < *ân*, alone; *ǽ*, f. indec., law; *ge-pem'man*, pro-

synd bûton leahtre? Ic secge sôđlîce eôp þæt þes is mǽrra þonne þæt templ. Gif gê sôđlîce piston hpæt is, Ic pille mild-heortnesse and nâ on-sægd'nesse, ne geniđ'râde gê ǽfre un'scyldig'e. Sôđlîce mannes sunu is eâc reste-dæges hlâford.

9. Þâ se Hǽlend þanon fôr, hê com in tô heorâ gesom'nunge; þâ pæs þǽr ân man se hæfde for-scrunc'ene hand. And hig âcsôdon hine, þus cpeđende: Is hit âlŷf'ed tô hǽlanne on reste-dagum? þæt hig prehton hine.

Hê sǽde him sôđlîce: Hpylc man is of eôp, þe hæbbe ân sceâp, and gif þæt âfylđ' reste-dagum on pyt, hû ne nimđ hê þæt, and hefđ hit up? Þitodlîce miclê mâ man is sceâpe betera; pitodlîce hit is âlŷf'ed on reste-dagum pel tô dônne. Þâ cpæđ hê tô þam men: Âþen'e þîne hand. And hê hî âþen'ede; and heô pæs hâl gepord'en spâ seô ôđer.

5. The Sower.

Matthew, xiii., 4–8.—Sôđlîce, ût eôde se sǽdere his sǽd tô sâpenne: and þâ-þâ hê seôp, sume hig feôllon piđ peg, and fuglâs cômon and ǽton þâ.

Sôđlîce sume feôllon on stǽnihte, þǽr hit næfde mycle eorđan, and hrædlîce up sprungon, for-þam'-þe hig næfdon þǽre eorđan

fane, imperf. *-pem'de*, p. p. *-pemm'ed*, conj. 6; *synd<eom*, § 213; *leahtre*, dative from *leahtor*, *es*, m., blame, crime; *þes*, this man; *mǽrra*, adj. comp. masc.=*mâra* (more), greater; *templ* =*tempel*, § 73, 6; *piston*, irreg. <*pitan*, know, Engl. wit, wist, § 212; *mild-heortnes*, *se*, f., mercy; *on-sægd'nes*, *se*, f., sacrifice, akin to *say*, as that which is vowed, dedicated; *ge-niđ'râde*, imperf. subj. plur. *-de* for *-don* before *gê*, § 170, *ge-niđ'rian*, imperf. *-niđ'râde*, p. p. *niđ'râd*, conj. 6, humiliate, condemn, from *niđer*, nether, beneath; *un'-scyldige*, adj. plur., the guiltless, *scyldig*, Ger. *schuldig*, akin to *shall*, owe, § 212; *hlâf-ord*, *es*, m., lord, loaf-master, *-ord* akin to Ger. *wirth*, Fries. *werda*, host, housekeeper; *com<cuman; ge-som'nung*= *ge-sam'nung*, assembly, akin to *sam*, same; *for-scrinc'an*, imperf. *-scranc'*, *-scrunc'on*, p. p. *-scrunc'en*, shrunken away; *hig* < *hî*, they; *tô hǽlanne*, gerund from *hǽlan*, imperf. *hǽlde*, p. p. *hǽled*, heal, akin to *hâl*, hale, whole; *prehton*, subj. imperf., from *preccan*, attack, conj. 6, § 209, akin to wreak; *sǽde*<*secgan*, imperf. *sægde*>*sǽde*, p. p. *sægd*, *sǽd*, conj. 6, § 209; *âfylđ'*, falleth, pres., *â-feall'an*, imperf. *-feôl'*, *-feôll'on*, p. p. *-feall'en*, conj. 5, § 208; *pyt*, *es*, m., pit, from Lat. *put-eus; hû*, inter. sign, § 397, *b; nimđ*<*niman*, take; *hefđ*, heaveth, *hebban*, § 207; *pitodlîce*, verily, so then; *miclê mâ*, more by much, § 302, *d; sceâpe*, dat. after comp. *betera*, § 303; *men*, dat. of *man*, § 84: *â-þen'ê*, stretch forth, *â-þen'ian*, imperf. *-þen'ede*, conj. 6, akin to Lat. *tendo; hî*, acc. sing. fem. of *hê*, § 130; *ge-pord'en*, p. p. from *gepeorđ'an*.

5. For unexplained words, see pp. 1–2.—*Sôđlîce* (soothly), truly, lo! interj.; *þâ-þâ* (then when), when; *hig*=*hî*, *g*, dissimilated, § 27; *sume hig*, some they fell=some of them fell, appositive for partitive, § 287, *c; þâ*, them, plur. acc. from *se; sôđlîce*, and, but, general connective, § 463, 8; *stǽnihte*, acc. sing. *stǽniht*, *e*, f., stony ground; *þǽr hit næfde*, where it had not, careless for *hig næfdon*, *sǽd* might be either sing. or plur.; *hrædlîce*, quickly, akin to Engl. *rath*, rather; *sprungon*, sprang, *springan*, imperf. *sprang*, *sprungon*, p. p.

dŷpan: sôđlîce, up âsprung'enre sunnan, hig âdrup'edon and forscrunc'on, for-þam'-þe hig næfdon pyrtrum:

Sôđlîce sume feôllon on þornâs, and þâ þornâs peôxon and forþrys'môdon þâ:

Sume sôđlîce feôllon on gôde eorđan, and sealdon pæstm, sum hundfealdne, sum syxtigfealdne, sum þrittigfealdne.

---

6. Trust in God.

Matthew, vi., 26–33.—Beheald'ađ heofenan fuglâs: forþam'þe hig ne sâpađ, ne hig ne rîpađ, ne hig ne gaderiađ on berne; and eôper heofonlîca Fæder hig fêt. Hû ne synd gê sêlran þonne hig? Hpylc eôper mæg sôđlîce geþenc'an þæt hê ge-eâc'nige âne elne tô his anlîcnesse?

And tô hpî synd gê ymb'-hŷd'ige be reâfê? Besceâp'iađ æceres lilian, hû hig peaxađ; ne spincađ hig, ne hig ne spinnađ: ic secge eôp sôđlîce, Þæt furđon Salomon on eallum hys puldre næs oferprig'en spâ spâ ân of þysum.

Sôđlîce, gif æceres peôd, þæt þe tô dæg ys, and byđ tô morgen on ofen âsend', God spâ scrŷt, eâlâ gê gehpǽd'es geleâf'an, þam myclê mâ hê scrŷt eôp.

Nellen gê eornostlîce beôn ymb'-hŷd'ige, þus cpeđende, Hpæt ete pê? ođđe hpæt drince pê? ođđe mid hpam beô pê oferprig'ene? Sôđlîce ealle þâs þing þeôdâ sêcađ: pitodlîce, eôper Fæder pât þæt gê ealrâ þyssâ þingâ beþurf'on.

Eornostlîce sêcađ ǽrest Godes rîce and his riht'pîs'nesse, and ealle þâs þing eôp beôđ þǽrtô ge-eâc'nôde.

---

sprungen, conj. 1; *dŷpa, n*, m. acc., depth; *â-sprung'enre*, p. p. sing., f., dat. absolute from *âspring'an*, conj. 1, the sun having (sprung up) risen, § 304, *d; âdrûp'edon*, dried, *â-drup'-ian*, imp. *-ede*, *-edon*, p. p. *-ed*, conj. 6; *pyrtrum*, *es*, m.=*pyrtruma*, see page 1.

6. *for-þam'-þe*, for this that, for; *sâpan*, sow, imp. *seôp*, *seôpon*, p. p. *sâpen*, conj. 5; *ne ne*, emphatic, § 400; *rîpan*, reap, imp. *râp*, *ripon*, p. p. *ripen*, conj. 2; *bern*, *es*, n., barn, <*ber-ern*, barley house, § 229: some texts read *ber-ern*, acc. plur. like the Greek; *fêt*<*fêdeđ*, § 194, 36, 5; *synd*=*sind*, from *eom*, § 213; *sêlran*<*sêl*, §§ 123, 128; *eôper*, §§ 130, 312; *mæg geþenc'an*, § 176, *ge-eâc'n-ian*, imp. *-ôde*, p. p. *-ôd*, conj. 6, add, eke, *-ige*, subj., §§ 184, 425; *eln*, *e*, f., Lat. *ulna*, ell; *anlîcnes*, *se*, f., likeness, stature; *tô hpî*, to what end, wherefore, § 352, IV., 135; *ymb'-hŷd'ig*, adj., anxious about, worried; *be-sceâp'ian*, imp. *-ôde*, p. p. *-ôd*, behold (*sceâp*>*show*), conj. 6; *lili-e*, *-an*, f., lily; *spincan*, imp. *spanc*, *spuncon*, p. p. *spuncen*, conj. 1, Old Engl. swink, toil; *spinnan*, spin, imp. *span*, *spunnon*, p. p. *spunnen*, conj. 1, § 201; *ofer-prîh'an*, imp. *-prâh'*, *-prig'on*, p. p. *-prig'en*, conj. 2, § 205, cover over, dress (rig); *peôd*, *es*, n., weed; *þæt þe*, that that, which, § 380; *âsend'*, p. p., § 190; *scrŷt*<*scrŷdan*, §§ 192, 36, 5, akin to *shroud; gehpǽd'e*, adj., little; *þam miclê mâ*, more by much than that, §§ 303, 302, *d; ete*<*etađ*, § 165; *þingâ*, gen., § 317, *b; riht'pîs'nes*, *se*, f., righteousness; *ge-eâc'nian*, conj. 6, add, see over.

7. The Prodigal Son.

Luke, xv., 11–32.—11. Sôđlîce
sum man hæfde tpegen sunâ.

12. Pâ cpæđ se gingra tô his fæder, Fæder, syle mê mînne dæ̂l mînre æ̂hte þe mê tô gebyr'eđ. Pâ dæ̂lde hê hym hys æ̂hte.

13. Pâ, æfter feâpa dagum, ealle his þing gegad'erô'de se gingra sunu, and fêrde præclîce on feorlen rîce, and forspil'de þâr his æ̂htâ, lybbende on his gæ̂lsan.

14. Pâ hê hig hæfde ealle âmyrr'ede, þâ peard mycel hunger on þam rîce; and hê peard pædla.

15. Pâ fêrde hê and folgôde ânum burh'-sitt'endum men þæs rîces: þâ sende hê hine tô his tûne, þæt hê heôlde hys spŷn.

16. Pâ gepil'nôde hê his pambe gefyll'an of þâm beân'-codd'um þe þâ spŷn'æ̂ton; and him man ne sealde.

17. Pâ beþoh'te hê hine, and cpæđ, Eâlâ hû fela yrđlingâ on mînes fæder hûse hlâf genôh'ne habbađ, and ic hêr on hungre forpeorđ'e!

18. Ic âris'e, and ic fare tô mînum fæder, and ic secge him,

19. Eâlâ fæder, ic syngôde on heofenâs, and befor'an þê, nû ic neom pyrđe þæt ic beô þîn sunu nemned: dô mê spâ æ̂nne of þînum yrđlingum.

20. And hê ârâs' þâ, and com tô his fæder. And þâ gyt, þâ hê pæs feor, his fæder hê hyne geseah', and peard mid mild'-heort'nesse âstyr'ed, and âgên'

---

12. *gingra*, comparative of *geong*, young, § 124; *æ̂hte*, akin to *âgan*>Engl. *owe, own; gebyr'eđ*, from *ge-byr'ian*, imp. *ge-byr'ede*, p. p. *ge-byr'ed*, conj. 6, be-falleth, akin to *bear, is borne; dæ̂lde*, dealt; *hym, hys*, bad spelling for *him, his.*

13. —*feâpa*, few, here undeclined, dat. plur., *feâpum, feâum, feâm*, are the common forms; *gegad'erian*, imp. *gegad'erôde*, p. p. *gegad'erôd*, conj. 6, gather; *præc-lîce*, adv., exile-like, abroad, akin to *wretch; feor-len*, adj., far; *rîce*, Engl. *-ric*, Ger. *reich; for-spill'-an*, spill away, destroy, imp. *spil'de*, p. p. *-spill'ed*, conj. 6; *lybbende*, bad spelling for *libbende*, living; *gæ̂lsan*, riotousness, luxury, Ger. *geil-heit*, akin to Engl. gala, *gæ̂lsa, n*, m.

14. —*hig*<*hî*, plur. of *hê*, them; *â-myrr'an*, imp. *-myrr'ede*, p. p. *-myrr'ed*, destroy, dissipate, akin to Engl. *mar; peard*<*peordan; hunger, es*, m.; *pædla, n*, m., pauper, vagabond, akin to *padan*, go about>wade, waddle.

15. —*burh'-sitt'endum*, borough-sitting, dat. sing. from *burh'-sitt'ende*, adj.; *men*, dat. sing. of *man*, § 84; *tûne*, dat., § 352 (town), inclosure; *healdan*, imp. *heôld, heôldon*, p. p. *healden*, conj. 5, *heôlde*, subj. imp., might (hold) keep; *hys spŷn* (*y, ŷ* for *i, î*).

16. —*pamb, e*, f., Engl. *womb*, belly; *beân'-cod, des*, m., bean cod, husk; *man*, (indefinite) one, § 136, 2; *sealde*<*sellan.*

17. —*beþoh'te*, bethought, *be-þenc'an*, imp. *-þoh'te*, p. p. *-þoht'*, conj. 6, § 209; *hine*, himself, § 131; *fela*, many, indecl., Ger. *viel*, Gr. πολύς, akin to *full; yrđlingâ*, gen. plur. partitive, Engl. *earthling; hlâf*>*loaf; genôh'ne*, acc. sing. of *ge-nôh'*, adj., enough; *hungre*, see over; *forpeorđ'an*, be away, perish, imp. *-peard'*, *-purd'on*, p. p. *-pord'en*, conj. 1, Ger. *werden*, O. E. *worth, for-*, Ger. *ver.*, as in *forsake*, § 254.

18. —*âris'e*, pres. for future, § 413.

19. —*syng-ian*, sin, imp. *-ôde*, p. p. *-ôd*, conj. 6, imp. for perf., § 414; *neom=ne+eom*, am not, § 213; *pyrđe*, worthy; *dô*, imperat. of *dôn*, do, make; *mê*, acc.

20. —*ârâs', âris'an; þâ*, then; *com*, from *cuman;* and then yet, when; *feor*, prep., far from, § 336; *hê*, § 288, *b; hyne*, bad spelling for *hine; geseah'*<*geseôn'; peard*<*peordan; â-styr'-ian*, imp. *-ede*, p. p. *-ed*, conj. 6, stirred; *mild'-heort'nes, se*, f., mild heart, compassion;

hine arn, and hine beclyp'te, and cyste hine.

21. Pâ cpæđ his sunu, Fæder, ic syngôde on heofen, and befor'an þê, nû ic ne eom pyrđe þæt ic þîn sunu beô genem'ned.

22. Pâ cpæđ se fæder tô his þeôpum, Bringađ rađe þone sêlestan gegyr'elan, and scrŷdađ hine; and syllađ him hring on his hand, and gescŷ' tô his fôtum;

23. And bringađ ân fæt styric, and ofsleađ'; and uton etan, and gepist'full'ian:

24. forþam' þes mîn sunu pæs deâd, and hê ge-ed'cucôde; hê forpearđ', and hê ys gemêt'. Pâ ongun'non hig gepist'lǣc'an.

25. Sôđlîce his yldra sunu pæs on æcere; and hê com: and þâ hê þam hûse geneâ'lǣh'te, hê gehŷr'de þone spêg and þæt pered.

26. Pâ clypôde hê ǣnne þeôp, and âcsôde hine hpæt þæt pǣre.

27. Pâ cpæđ hê, Pîn brôđer com, and þîn fæder ofslôh' ân fæt cealf; forþam' þe hê hine hâlne onfêng'.

28. Pâ gebealh' hê hine, and nolde in gân': þâ eôde his fæder ût, and ongan' hine biddan.

29. Pâ cpæđ hê, his fæder and'spariend'e, Efne, spâ fela gearâ ic þê þeôpôde, and ic nǣfre þîn gebod' ne forgŷm'de,

---

âgên'=ongeân', against, towards; *irnan*, imp. *arn*, *urnon*, p. p. *urnen*, metathesis for *rinnan*, run, conj. 1, § 204; *be-clypp'an*, imp. *beclyp'te*, p. p. *be-clypt'*, conj. 6, § 189; *be-clip*, embrace; *cyssan*, imp. *cyste*, p. p. *cyst*, conj. 6.

21. —See verse 19.

22. —*þeôp*, O. Engl. *thew*, servant, akin to Ger. *dienst*, *dirne*, O. Engl. *therne; bringan*, imp. *brang*, *brungon*, p. p. *brungen*, conj. 1, bring; *rade>rathe*, Bring the *rathe* primrose, Milton, Lycidas, 142, comp. *rather*, sooner; *sêlestan*, superl. of *sêl*, good, akin to Ger. *seelig*, O. Engl. *seely*, Engl. *silly; ge-gyr'ela*, *n*, m., robe, akin to *gear*, *garb; scrŷdan*, akin to shroud; *hring*, *es*, m., ring, Ger. *ring*, Lat. *circus*, Gr. κίρκος; *fôt*, Ger. *fusz*, Lat. *pes*, Gr. πούς, declension, § 84.

23. —*fæt*, *te*, adj., fat; *styric*, *es*, m., sturk, calf, Ger. *sterke*, akin to *steer*, Ger. *stier*, Lat. *taur-us*, Gr. ταῦρος, Sansk. *sthûra-s; of-sleâđ'* <*of-sleân'; uton*, subj. of *pîtan*, go, §§ 176, 224, 443, like Lat. *eamus*, Fr. *allons*, let us (go to) eat; *ge-pist'-full'ian*, imp. *-ôde*, p. p. *-ôd*, conj. 6, *pist*, existence, victuals, from *pesan*, be, *pist'-fullo*, fulness of victuals, a feast, *gepist'full'ian*, to feast, be merry.

24. —*ge-ed'-cuc'-ian*, imp. *-ôde*, p. p. *ôd*, conj. 6, *ed'-*, §§ 15, *a*, 254, back, again, *cuc* < *cpic*, quick, alive, Lat. *viv-us*, Gr. βίος, Sansk. *g'îv-a-s; for-pearđ'*, see verse 17; *ys*, bad for *is; ge-mêt'-an*, imp. *-mêtt'e*, *-mêt'ed*, p. p. *-mêt'*, met, found; *on-ginn'an*, begin; *gepist'-lǣc'an*, *-lǣh'te*, *-lǣht'*, conj. 6, see verse 23, *lâc*, *lǣcan*, akin to *-lock*, *wed-lock*, §§ 229, 233, 250.

25. —*yldra*, comp. of *eald*, old, § 124; *æcere*, see over; *geneâ'læh'te*, *geneâ'lǣc'an*, come near; *spêg*, akin to *sough*, and to Ger. *schwegelpfeife; pered*, company, akin to *per*, man, Goth. *vair*, Lat. *vir*, Sansk. *vîra*.

26. —*clyp-ian*, imp. *-ôde*, p. p. *-ôd*, conj. 6, O. Engl. *clepe*, *yclept*, in heaven *yclept* Euphrosyne, Milton, L'Al., 12; *âcsôde* > asked, metathesis; *pǣre*, subj., < *pesan*, §§ 423, 425.

27. —*of-sleân'*, imp. *-slôh'*, *-slôg'on*, p. p. *-slag'en*, conj. 4, § 207; *hâlne*, acc. of *hâl*, (w)hole, hale, Ger. *heil*, Gr. καλός; *on-fôn'*, imp. *-fêng'*, *-fêng'on*, p. p. *-fang'en*, conj. 5, §§ 208, 216, Ger. *fangen*, fang, catch, receive.

28. —*gebealh' hine*, swelled himself, was angry, § 290, *d*, *ge-belg'an*, imp. *-bealh'*, *-bulg'on*, p. p. *-bulg'en*, conj. 1, akin to bulge, belly, bellows; *nolde=ne polde* < *pillan*, § 212; *gân*, imp. *eôde*, p. p. *gân*, irreg. go, (yode) went, gone, § 213; *biddan*, Ger. *bitten*, bid, ask.

29. —*and'spariend'e*, answering, *and'-*, § 15, *a*, Lat. *ante-*, Gr. ἀντί-, in return, § 254, *sparian*, swear, speak emphatically; *efne*, akin to *efen*, even, § 263; *fela*, so many of years, see verse 17; *þeôpôde* < *þeôpian*, see *þeôp*, verse 22, *gebod'*, from *beôdan*, Ger. *bieten*, bid, order, *beôdan* and *biddan* (see verse 28) unite in Engl. *bid*, akin to *bead; for-gŷm'-an*, imp. *-gŷm'de*, p. p. *-gŷm'ed*, Goth. *gâumjan*, Ger. *gaumen*, O. Engl. Scot. *yeme*, *goam*, to see,

and ne·sealdest þû mê nǽfre ân ticcen, þæt ic mid mînum freôndum gepist'fullôde;

30. ac syđđan þes þîn sunu com, þe his spêde mid mylt'ystrum âmyr'de, þû ofslôg'e him fæt cealf.

31. Pâ cpæđ hê, Sunu, þû eart symle mid mê, and ealle mîne þing synd þîne: þê gebyr'ede gepist'full'ian and gebliss'ian: forþam' þes þîn brôđer pæs deâd, and hê ge-ed'cucôde; hê forpearđ', and hê ys gemêt'.

8. Love your Enemies.—*Matthew*, v., 38–48.

ANGLO-SAXON.

38. Gê gehŷr'don þæt gecped'en pæs, Eâge for eâge and tôđ for tôđ,

39. Sôđlîce ic secge eôp, Ne pinne gê ongên' þâ þe eôp yfel

GOTHIC OF ULPHILAS.

38. Hâus'idêd'uþ þatei kviþan ist, Âugô und âugin, jah tunþu und tunþâu.

39. Iþ ik kviþa izvis ni and'stand'an allis þamma un'sêl'jin;

---

8. This extract is prepared to give definite knowledge of the relation between the·Gothic of Ulfilas and the Anglo-Saxon, and for introduction to Comparative Grammar, especially to etymology and phonology. Each Gothic word is first turned into an English word of the same root, so far as may be. These are helped out by other words in italics, so as to form a sort of translation to one who knows the meaning of the passage. The words are then explained, and laws of change referred to as given in the Grammar. Grimm's law applies to almost every word, and is here referred to once for all, §§ 18, 41.

care for; *ticcen, es*, n., kid, Ger. *zicke*, kid, *ziege*, goat; *freônd*, Ger. *freund* <*freôn*, to love; *gepist'fullôde*, see verse 23.

30. —*ac*, but, § 262; *siđđan* (since), as soon as; *spêd*>Engl. *speed*, haste, success, wealth; *myltystr-e, an*, f., harlot, from *myltan*, melt, yield (in virtue), *-estre*, §§ 228, 232; *âmyr'de* =*âmyrr'ede*, see verse 14; *ofslôg'e*, verse 27.

31. —*symle*, always, akin to *same*, Lat. *simul, semper; mid*, Ger. *mit*, Gr. μετά, § 254; *þê gebyr'ede*, it became thee, see verse 12; *gepist'full'ian*, see verse 23; *ge-bliss'-ian*, imp. *-ôde*, p. p. *-ôd*, conj. 6, be blissful, akin to *bless; ge-ed'cucôde*, see verse 24; *forpearđ'*, *gemêt'*, verse 24.

8.—38. Hear-did-ye that-*which* queth-en is, Eye *for* eye, *and* tooth *for* tooth. *Hâusi-dêduþ* =*hŷr-don, hâusjan*, A.-S. *hŷran*>hear, Ger. *hören, âu*>*eâ*>*ê, ŷ*, §§ 18, 38, *s*>*r*, § 41, 3, *b*, *-dêduþ*, A.-S. *-don*, did, Ger. *-te*, weak inflection, § 168; *þat*-ei, A.-S. *þæt*>that, Ger. *das*, *-ei*, § 468; *kviþan*, A.S. *cpeđen*>O. E. quethe, be-queath, quoth, O. H. G. *chedan;* § 197; *ist*, A.-S. *is*>is, Ger. *ist*, Lat. *est*, Gr. ἐστί, Sansk. *ásti*, § 213; *pæs*>was, Goth. *vas*, Ger. *war*, § 213, 41, 3, *b; âugô*, A.-S. *eâge*>eye, Ger. *auge*, vowel change, §§ 18, 38, declension, § 95; *und*, A.-S. *ôđ*, Ger. *unt*, § 254; *for*, Goth. *faur*, Ger. *für*, § 254; *ja-h*, and, A.-S. *ge*, O. H. Ger. *jo-h*, Lat. *ja-m*, § 262; *tunþu*, A.-S. *tôđ*>tooth, Ger. *zahn*, Lat. *dent-is*, Gr. ὀ-δόντ-ος, Sansk. *dant-as*, § 37, declension, §§ 86, 93.

39. *But* I queth *to*-you not *to*-stand-*against at*-all the unseely; *but* if *any-one*-who-*ever* thee *strike* by dexter thine chin, wind *to*-him *also* the other. *Iþ*, but, A.-S. *ed-, ođ-đe*, O. H. G. *ed-*, Lat. *at*, § 262; *ik*, A.-S. *ic*>I, Ger. *ich*, Lat. *ego*, Gr. ἐγώ, Sansk. *aha'm*, § 130; *kviþa*, verse 38, inflection, § 165; *secge*>say, Ger. *sagen; izvis, eôp*>you, § 130; *ni*, A.-S. *ne*, n-ot, O. H. G. *ni, ne*, Lat. *ne*, Gr. νη-, Sansk. *na*, § 254; *and'-stand'an, and-*, A.-S. *and-*> an, in an-swer, Ger. *ant-*, Lat. *ante*, Gr. ἀντί, Sansk. *ánti*, § 254, *standan*, A.-S. *standan*> stand, Ger. *stehen*, Lat. *sta-re*, Gr. ἵ-στη-μι, Sansk. *sthâ*, § 216; *pinne*<*pinnađ* before *ge*, § 165; *ongên'* for *ongeân'*, Ger. *ent-gegen*, § 251; *allis*, A.-S. *ealles*, Ger. *alles*, § 251;

dôđ; ac gyf hpâ þê sleâ on þîn spŷđre penge, gegear'pâ him þæt ôđer.

40. And þam þe pylle on dôme pid þê flîtan, and niman þîne tunecan, lǽt him tô þînne pæfels.

41. And spâ-hpâ'-spâ þê genŷt' þûsend stapâ, gâ mid him ôđre tpâ þûsend.

42. Syle þam þe þê bidde, and þam þe æt þê pille borgian ne pyrn þû him.

43. Gê gehŷr'don þæt ge-

ak jabâi hvas þuk stâutâi bi taihsvôn þeina kinnu, vandei imma jah þô anþara.

40. Jah þamma viljandin miþ þus stâua jah pâida þeina niman, aflêt' imma jah vastja.

41. Jah jabâi hvas þuk ananâuþ'jâi rasta âina, gaggâis miþ imma tvôs.

42. Þamma bidjandin þuk gibâis, jah þamma viljandin af þus leihvan sis ni us'vand'jâis.

43. Hâus'idêd'uþ þatei kviþan

þamma, A.-S. *þam*, him, Ger. *dem*, Gr. τῳ, Sansk. *tá-smâi*, § 104; *þâ þe*, § 104; *yfel*, verse 45; *un'sêljin*, *un-*, § 254, *sêls*, A.-S. *sêl*, *sǽlig* > seely, silly, Ger. *selig*, akin to Lat. *salvus*, Gr. ὁλοός, declension weak, § 107; *ak*, A.-S. *ac*, O. H. G. *oh*, but, § 262; *jabai*, A.-S. *gif* > if, O. H. G. *ibu*, § 262; *hvas*, A.-S. *hpâ* > who, Ger. *wer*, Lat. *qui-s*, Sansk. *kas*, § 135; *þuk*, A.-S. *þec* > thee, Ger. *dich*, Lat. *tê*, Gr. τέ, Sansk. *tvâ*, § 130; *stâut-ai*, Ger. *stossen*, Lat. *tund-o*, Gr. Τυδ-εύς, Sansk. *tud; sleâ* < *sleân* > slay, Ger. *schlagen*, Goth. *slahan; bi*, A.-S. *bî*>by, Ger. *bei*, § 254; *taihsvôn*, Lat. *dexter; spŷđre*, right, comp. of *spîđ*, strong; *þeina*, A.-S. *þîn*>*thine*, Ger. *dein*, Lat. *tuus*, § 132; *kinnu*, A.-S. *cinne* > chin, Ger. *kinne*, Lat. *gena*, Gr. γένυ-ς, declension, § 93; *penge*, *s*, n., wang, cheek, Ger. *wange; vandei*, *vandjan*, A.-S. *pendan* > wend, Ger. *wenden; imma*, A.-S. *him* > him, Ger. *ihm*, § 130; *þâ anþara*, A.-S. *þæt ôđer* > that other, Ger. *die andere*, Gr. ἕτερος, Sansk. *antará*, § 126.

40. *And the*-one willing *with* thee *a-law-suit* and *tunic* thine *to*-him, let off *to*-him *also* vest. *Jah*, verse 38; *þamma*, verse 39; *viljandin*, p. pr. *viljan*, A.-S. *pillan*>will, Ger. *wollen*, Lat. *volo*, Gr. βούλομαι, Sansk. *var*, *val*, § 212; *miþ*, A.-S. *mid*, Ger. *mit*, Gr. μετά, Sansk. *mi-thás*, § 254; *piđ*>with, Goth. *viþra*, Ger. *wider*, § 254; *þus*, see *þuk*, verse 39; *stâua*, judge, judgment, Grimm says from *stabs*, A.-S. *stæf* > staff, Ger. *stab*, and so *staff-bearer; jah*, verse 38; *pâide*, A.-S. *pâd*, Ger. *pfeit*, Gr. βαίτη, a borrowed word, akin to *pǽd* > weeds, O. H. G. *wât; tunec-e*, *-an*, f., from Lat. *tunica; þeina*, verse 39; *niman*, A.-S. *niman*>nim, Ger. *nehmen*, take, § 165; *af-*, A.-S. *of-* > off, of, Ger. *ab-; lêtan*, A.-S. *lǽtan*>let, Ger. *lassen; imma*, verse 39; *jah*, verse 38; *vastja*, Lat. *vest-is*, vest, Gr. ἔσθης, A.-S. verb *perian*>wear (*s*>*r*, § 41); *pæfels*, better *pefels*<*pefan*, weave.

41. And if *any-one*-who-*ever* thee need rest one, go *with* him two. *ana-nâuþjâi*, *ana*, verse 45, *nâuþjan*, A.-S. *nŷdan* > need, Ger. *noth; ge-nŷt'*<*ge-nŷdan*, compel, inflection, §§ 170, 192; *rasta*, A.-S. *reste*>rest, Ger. *rast*, resting-place, mile; *þûsend*>thousand, Ger. *tausend*, Goth. *þusundi*, § 159; *stæpe*, *s*, m.> step; *âina*, A.-S. *ân* > one, an, a, Ger. *ein*, Gr. ἕν-ος, Lat. *un-us*, § 139; *gaggâis*, A.-S. *gâ* >go, Ger. *gehen*, § 213; *tvôs*, A.-S. *tpâ*>two, Ger. *zwei*, § 139.

42. *To*-the-*one* bidding thee give, *and from*-the-*one* willing of thee *to-take-a*-loan *self* not wend. *Bid-jandin*, p. pr. *bidjan*, A.-S. *biddan* >bid (ask), Ger. *bitten; gib-âis*, A.-S. *gifan* >give, Ger. *geben; syle*>sell; *leihvan*, A.-S. *lîhan*, Ger. *leihen* > *lǽn* > loan; *borgian* > borrow, Ger. *borgen*, to give on *borowe*, security < *beorgan* > bury, secure; *sis*, dative of *seina*, A.-S. *sin*, Ger. *sich*, self, § 131; *us'vand'jais*, Ger. *abwenden*, *us-*, A.-S. *or-*, Ger. *ur-*, away, *vandjan*, verse 39; *pyrnan*, imp. *pyrnde*, p. p. *pyrned*, conj. 6, warn off, repel, deny, akin to *parnian*, Ger. *warnen*, warn.

43. Hear-did-ye that-*which* queth-en is, *be*-Friend nighest thine, *and be*-foe fiend thine. *Hâus'idêd'uþ —ist*, verse 38; *fri-jos*, A.-S. *freôgan*, Ger. *freien*, love, kiss, woo, Sansk. *pri*, Gr. πρᾷ-ος, hence *freônd* > friend, Ger. *freund*, p. pr.; *lufan*, Goth. *liuban*, Ger. *lieben*, Lat. *lubet*, *libet*, Gr. λίπ-τομαι, Sansk. *lubh; nêh-*, A.-S. *nêh-stan*, *nêxtan*, Ger. *nähst*,

cped'en pæs, Lufâ þînne nêxtan, and hatâ þînne feônd:

44. Sôđlîce ic secge eôp, Lufiađ eôpre fŷnd, and dôđ pel þâm þe eôp yfel dôđ, and gebidd'ađ [for eôpre êhterâs and] tǣlendum eôp;

45. þæt gê sîn eôpres Fæder bearn þe on heofonum ys, se þe dêđ þæt hys sunne up âspringđ' ofer þâ gôdan and ofer þâ yfelan, and hê lǣt rînan ofer þâ riht'-pîs'an and ofer þâ un'rihtpîsan.

ist, Frijôs nêhvundjan þeinana, jah fiâis fiand þeinana:

44. aþþan ik kviþa izvis, Frijôþ fijands izvarans [þiuþjâiþ þans vrikandans izvis] vâila tâujâiþ þâim hatjandam izvis, jah bidjâiþ bi þans us'þriut'andans izvis;

45. ei vairþâiþ sunjus attins izvaris þis in himinam, untê sunnôn seina ur'rann'eiþ ana ubilans jah gôdans, jah rigneiþ ana ga-raiht'ans jah ana in'vind'ans.

---

nearest; *fiâis*, hate, *fijan*, A.-S. *fian*, O. H. G. *fiên* > *fiand*, A.-S. *feônd* > fiend, Ger. *feind*, p. pr., hating, used as a substantive; *hat-ian*, imp. *-ôde*, p. p. *-ôd*, conj. 6, hate, Goth. *hatan*, Ger. *hassen*, perhaps akin to Lat. *odi.*

44. *But*-then I queth *to*-you, be-Friend fiends yours, bless those wreaking *on*-you, well do to-them hating you, and bid by those out-*thrusting* you. *aþ-þan*, Lat. *at*, but, see verse 39 and § 262, *-þan*, demons. particle, § 262; *þiuþjâiþ—izvis*, εὐλογεῖτε τοὺς καταρωμένους ὑμᾶς, is omitted in the Latin, and so in the Anglo-Saxon; *þiuþjan*, do good, bless <*þiuþ*, good, not in other tongues, root *þiv*, grow, akin to A.-S. *þeôp*, *þipe*, boy, servant; *þans*, acc. plur. of demons., §§ 104, 107; *vrikandans*, cursing, *vrikan*, A.-S. *precan* > wreak, Ger. *rächen; vâila*, A.-S. *pel* > well, Ger. *wohl; tâu-jâiþ*, A.-S. *tapian* > taw, Ger. *zauen*, make, equip, do, a kindred stem to *dôn* > do, Ger. *thun*, Gr. θε, τί-θη-μι, Sansk. *dhâ; þâim*, dat. plur., A.-S. *þâm* > them, Ger. *dem; hatjandam*, verse 43; *biddan*, verse 42; *us'þriut'-andans*, p. pr., *us-*, verse 42, *þriutan*, A.-S. *þreôtan*, Ger. *ver-driessen*, Lat. *trudo*, extrude; *êhtere*, *s*, m., persecutor; *tǣlendum*, p. pr., *tǣl-an*, imp. *-de*, p. p. *-ed*, conj. 6, speak evil, akin to Gothic *taljan*, A.-S. *tellan* > tell, Ger. *zählen*, tale, tally.

45. *That you-may*-worth sons *of-Father* your the-*one* in *heavens*, *since* sun *his* up-runneth on evil *and* good, *and he*-raineth on righteous *and* on in-wound. *Ei*, that, if, pronominal, probably from relative *ja*, and so akin to Gr. εἰ, Lat. *s-i*, § 262; *vâirþ-âiþ*, A.-S. *peorđan* > O. E. worth, be, Ger. *werden; sunus*, A.-S. *sunu* > son, Ger. *sohn*, Gr. υ-ιός, Sansk. *sû-nus* < *su*, bear; *bearn* > bairn, Goth. *barn* < Goth. *bairan*, A.-S. *beran* > bear, Ger. *ge-bähren*, Lat. *fero*, Gr. φέρω, Sansk. *bi-bhár-mi; attins*, father, O. H. G. *atto*, Ger. child-speech *ette*, Sansk., Gr., Lat. *atta*, similar words far and wide beyond the Indo-European tongues, so as to suggest that they are interjectional. The linguals in this use are as common as the labials *pâ-pâ*, *ab-bâ*, *mâ-mâ; dâ-dâ* > Engl. dad, is wide-spread; *þis*, genitive of article, verse 39, § 104; *in*, A.-S. *in* > in, Ger. *ein*, Lat. *in*, Gr. ἐν, Sansk. *aná*, § 254; *himinam*, plur. dat. of *himins*, declined as in § 70, Ger. *himmel*, and in the other Teutonic tongues except A.-S., from root *him*, cover, and so analogous to Low Ger., O. Sax., A.-S., *heofon* > heaven, root *hib* > heave; *untê*, O. H. G. *unza*, unto, until, since, compare *und*, verse 38; *sunnôn* < *sunnô*, f., § 95, *c*, A.-S. *sunne* > sun, Ger. *sonne*; *sein*, A.-S. *sîn*, Ger. *sein*, his, § 132; *ur'-rann'eiþ*, *ur-* = *us-*, verse 42, *rannjan*, cause to rain, *rann-eiþ* = *-jiþ*, 3d sing., § 165, *d*, < *rinnan*, imp. *ran*, A.-S. *rinnan* > run, Ger. *rinnen; â-spring'an*, conj. 1; *ana*, A.-S. *an*, *on* > on, Ger. *an*, Gr. ἀνά, Lat. *an-*, Sansk. *aná*, § 254; *ubilans*, declension, § 107, A.-S. *yfelan* > evil, Ger. *übel; gôd-*, A.-S. *gôd* > good, Ger. *gut; rigneiþ* < *rignjan*, inflect., § 165, *a*, A.-S. *rînan* > rain, Ger. *regen*, Lat. *rigo*, Gr. βρέχ-ειν, root *vragh*, Sansk.; *ga-raiht'-ans*, declension, § 107, A.-S. *riht-pîs* > righteous, Ger. *recht*, Lat. *rect-us*, root *rg'*, Gr. ὀρέχ-ειν, Lat. *reg-o*, Goth. *rakjan*, A.-S. *rǣcan* > reach, Ger. *reichen; in'-vind'-ans*, § 107, *in-*, see over; *vindan*, A.-S. *pindan* > wind, Ger. *winden*, twisted, perverted, wrong; *un'-riht-pîs*, adj., unrighteous.

46. Gyf gê sôđlîce þâ lufiađ þe eôp lufiađ, hpylce mêde habbađ gê: hû ne dôđ mânfulle spâ?

47. And gyf gê þæt ân dôđ þæt gê eôpre gebrôđ'ra pylcumiađ, hpæt dô gê mâre? hû ne dôđ hæđene spâ?

48. Eornostlîce beôđ fulfrem'ede, spâ eôper heofonlîca Fæder is fulfrem'ed.

46. Jabâi âuk frijôþ þans frijôndans izvis âinans, hvô mizdônô habâiþ? niu jah þâi þiudô þata samô tâujand?

47. Jah jabâi gôleiþ þans frijônds izvarans þatâinei, hvê managizô tâujiþ? niu jah môtarjôs þata samô tâujand?

48. Sijâiþ nu jus fullatôjâi, svasvê atta izvar sa in himinam fullatôjis ist.

---

46. If eke *you-be*-friend those *be*-friending you *al*-one, what mede have-*you*? *Do*-not they *also* of-the-dutch that same do? *âuk*, A.-S. *eâc* > eke, Ger. *auch*, § 254; *frijôþ*, verse 43, inflect., § 165, *d*; *âinans*, acc. pl., verse 41; *hvô*, verse 39; *hpylc*<*hpâ-lîc*, Ger. *welch*, which, § 135; *mizd-ônô*, gen. pl. of *mizdô*, decline, § 95, A.-S. *meord*, Gr, μισθ-ός, akin to A.-S. *mêd*, *e*, f. > meed, Ger. *miethe*; *habâiþ*, inflect., § 170, A.-S. *habbađ*, have, Ger. *haben*, akin to Lat. *habeo*; *ni-u*, A.-S. *ne*, not, verse 39, *hû ne*, emphatic interrog., §§ 252, 397; *þâi*, they, § 104; *þiudô*, gen. plur. < *þiuda*, declens., § 88, A.-S. *þeôd* > O. Engl. thede, people, O. H. G. *diota*, akin to A.-S. *þeodisc*, people, Ger. *deutsch*>Dutch; *mânful*, adj., sinful, *mân*, sin, akin to *mæne*> mean, Goth. *ga-mâins*, Ger. *ge-mein*, common, *ful* > full, Goth. *fulls*, Ger. *voll*, Gr. πλέος, Lat. *ple-nus*, Sansk. *pûr*, § 229; *samô*, A.-S. *same*>same, O. H. G. *samo*, Lat. *sim-ilis*, Gr. ὁμ-ός, Sansk. *sam-as*, see *sam-*, § 254; *spâ*, § 252; *tâujand*, 3d plur., inflect., § 165, verse 44.

47. *And* if *you-greet* those friends yours that-*al*-one, what more do-*ye*? *Do*-not *also* meters that same do? *gôleiþ*, *gôljan*, greet, akin to A.-S. *gâl* > O. Engl. gole, glad, Ger. *geil*, Goth. *gâiljan*, rejoice, and perhaps to A.-S. *galan*>*-gale*, nightin-gale, Ger. *gellen*, yell, cry; *pyl-cumian*, imp. *-ôde*, p. p. *-ôd*, conj. 6, Ger. *willkommen*, welcome<*pil-cuma*, a wished-for comer, *pillan*, verse 40, *cuman* >come, Goth. *kviman*, Ger. *kommen*, Sansk. *gâ* > *gvâ* > *va*, Lat. *ve-nio*, *βa*, Gr. ἔ-βη-ν, parasitic *v* and Grimm's law, § 33; *managizô*, comp. of *manags*, much, many, A.-S. *maneg* > many, Ger. *manch*, comparative endings, § 123, *a*; *mâre* > more, Goth. *mâiza*, Ger. *mehr*, Lat. *major*, Gr. μεῖζων. Sansk. *mâhîjãs* (§ 123, *a*); *môtarjôs* < *môta*, Ger. *maut*, tax, Grimm says akin to *mêde*, verse 46; *hæđen* > heathen, Goth. *hâiþnô*, Ger. *heiden* <A.-S. *hæđ*>heath, Goth. *hâiþi*, Ger. *heide*, dwellers on the heath, compare *pagan* < *paganus*.

48. *Be* now you full-done, so-so *Father* your the in *heavens* full-done is. *sijâiþ*, 2d plur., pres. subj. of the verb to be, A.-S. *sîn*, §§ 213, 170; *nu*, A.-S. *nû* > now, Ger. *nu-n*, Gr. νύ, Lat. *nunc*, Sansk. *nu*, § 252; *jus*, § 130; *fulla-tôjâi*, *fulls*, verse 46, *tôjâi*, do, akin to *tâu-jan*, verse 44; *svasvê*, A.-S. *spâ* > so, Ger. *so*, § 252; *sa*, A.-S. *se*, Sansk. *sa*, Gr. ὁ, article, § 104.

---

9. The Lord's Prayer in Gothic.

Matthew, vi., 9–13.—*Atta unsar þu in himinam, Veihnâi namô þein. Kvimâi þiudinassus þeins. Vairþâi vilja þeins, svê in himina jah ana airþâi. Hlâif unsarana þana sinteinan gif uns himma daga. Jah aflêt' uns þatei skulans sijâima, svasvê jah veis aflêt'am þâim skulam unsarâim. Jah ni briggâis uns in frâistubnjâi, ak lâusei uns af þamma ubilin; untê þeina ist þiudangardi jah mahts jah vulþus in âivins. Amên.*

THE next part of the Reader is prepared on a plan somewhat like that proposed by Thomas Jefferson to the University of Virginia. Facing each page of Anglo-Saxon will be found its counterpart in a sort of English. Each word is changed into the form which it took when the inflections weakened and it became English. Many are long since obsolete. Such are explained in the foot-notes. A good deal of knowledge of Anglo-Saxon and of the growth of English may be gained very fast and very easily by such apparatus.

In the translation, words in italics are not of the same root as the Anglo-Saxon which they represent, or are added.

In the foot-notes—

(Ch.) means that the word before it is in Chaucer.

(H.) Halliwell's Dictionary of Archaic and Provincial Words.

(P. P.) Piers Ploughman.

(S.) Stratmann, Dictionary of the English of the 13th, 14th, and 15th Centuries.

(Wycl.) Wycliffe.

(?) not found by me as yet.

When there is no sign of this sort the word is in Webster's Dictionary. Look for parts of compounds; especially drop *i-*, *be-*, and the like. If the proper meaning is not seen in Webster, look at what he says in the etymology, or look at the Vocabulary of this Reader.

Two pages of poetry (p. 52*, 53*) are prepared in the same way.

DIALOGUES OF CALLINGS.

1. Teacher and Scholar.

The learner saith:

We childer[1] bid[2] thee, O lo lore-*master*, that thou teach us to-speak in Latin i-rerd[3] rightly, forthat[4] un-i-lered[5] we are, and i-wemmedly[6] we speak.

The lore-*master* answereth:

What will ye speak?

S. What reck we what we speak, but[7] it right speech *be*, and behoove-*full*, not idle or frakel[8]?

T. Will ye be (be-)swinged on learning?

S. Liefer[9] is to-us to-be (be-)swinged for lore, than it ne[10] to-ken; ac[11] we wit thee bile-whit[12] *to-be*, and to-nill[13] (on-bi-)lead[14] swingels[15] on-us, but[16] thou be to-i-needed[17] from us.

T. I ax[18] thee, what speakest thou? What hast thou of work?

S. I am monk, and I sing each day seven tides[19] mid[20] i-brothers, and I am busied in reading and in song, ac[11] though-whether[21] I would between learn to-speak in Latin i-rerd[3].

T. What ken these thy i-feres[22]?

S. Some are earthlings[23], some shepherds, some oxherds, some eke[24] so-like[25] hunters, some fishers, some fowlers, some chapmen[26], some shoe-wrights, some salters, some bakers.

2. Teacher and Ploughman.

T. What sayest thou, earthling[23], how bi-goest[27] thou work thine?

Pl. O lo, lief[28] lord, thraly[29] I derve[30]; I go out on day-red[31], thewing[32] oxen to field, and yoke hem[33] to sull[34]; nis[35] it so stark[36] winter that I dare lout[37] at home for awe of lord mine; ac[11] yoked[39] oxen[39], and i-fastened[39] share[39] and coulter mid[20] the sull[34], each day I shall ear[38] full acre or more.

---

[1] children (Ch.). [2] pray. [3] language (H.). [4] because. [5] unlearned (S.). [6] corruptly; *wem*, a spot. [7] if only. [8] vile (S.). [9] pleasanter. [10] not. [11] but (S.). [12] gentle (S.). [13] not wish. [14] inflict (?). [15] blows. [16] unless. [17] compelled (S.). [18] ask. [19] times. [20] with (P. P.). [21] whether or no, notwithstanding. [22] comrades (S.). [23] ploughmen. [24] also. [25] likewise. [26] merchants. [27] practisest (H.). [28] dear. [29] hard (H.) [30] toil (S.). [31] dawn (S.). [32] driving (S.). [33] 'em, them (Ch.). [34] plow. [35] is not. [36] severe. [37] loiter, lurk (Ch., P. P.). [38] plough. [39] dative absolute, § 304, *d.*

DIALOGUES OF CALLINGS.

---

1. Teacher and Scholar.

Se leornere segeð:

Ƿê cildru biddað þê, eâlâ lâreôp, þæt þû tǽce ûs sprecan on Ledenê gereordê rihte, forþam ungelǽrede pê sindon, and gepemmedlîce pê sprecað.

Se lâreôp andsperâð:

Hpæt pille gê sprecan?

Le. Hpæt rêce pê hpæt pê sprecân, bûtan hit riht sprǽc sî, and behêfe, næs îdel oððe fracoð?

Lp. Ƿille gê beôn bespungen on leornunge?

Le. Leôfre is ûs beôn bespungen for lâre, þænne hit ne cunnan; ac pê piton þê bilepitne pesan and nellan onbelǽdan spinglâ ûs, bûtan þû beô tô-genŷded fram ûs.

Lp. Ic âxie þê, hpæt spricst þû? Hpæt hæfst þû peorces?

Le. Ic eom munuc, and ic singe ælcê dæg seofon tîdâ mid gebrôðrum, and ic eom bysgôd on rǽdinge and on sangê; ac þeâhhpæðere ic polde betpeônan leornian sprecan on Ledenê gereordê.

Lp. Hpæt cunnon þâs þîne gefêran?

Le. Sume sind yrðlingâs, sume sceâphirdâs, sume oxanhirdâs, sume eâc spylce huntan, sume fiscerâs, sume fugelerâs, sume cŷpmen, sume sceô-pyrhtan, sume sealterâs, sume bæcerâs.

---

2. Teacher and Ploughman.

Lp. Hpæt segst þû, yrðling, hû begǽst þû peorc þîn?

Y. Eâlâ, leôf hlâford, þearle ic deorfe; ic gâ ût on dægrêd, þŷpende oxan tô feldâ, and geocie hî tô sulh; nis hit spâ stearc pinter, þæt ic durre lutian æt hâm for egê hlâfordes mînes; ac geocôdum oxum, and gefæstnôdum scearê and cultrê mid þǽre sulh, ælcê dæg ic sceal erian fulne æcer oððe mâre.

Lp. Hæfst þû ǽnigne gefêran?

Y. Ic hæbbe sumne cnapan þŷpendne oxan mid gadîsenê, þe eâc spylce nû hâs is for cŷlê and hreâmê.

Lp. Hpæt mâre dêst þû on dæg?

Y. Gepislîce þænne mâre ic dô. Ic sceal fyllan binnan oxenâ mid hîgê, and pæterian hî, and scearn heorâ beran ût.

Lp. Hîg! hîg! Micel gedeorf is hit!

Y. Gea, leôf, micel gedeorf hit is, forþam ic neom freô.

3. Teacher and Shepherd.

Lp. Hpæt segst þû, sceâphirde? Hæfst þû ǽnig gedeorf?

S. Gea, leôf, ic hæbbe; on forepeardne morgen ic drîfe sceâp mîne tô heorâ læse, and stande ofer hî on hǽte and on cŷlê mid hundum, þŷ læs pulfâs forspelgen hî, and ic ongeân lǽde hî tô heorâ loca, and melce hî tpeôpa on dæg, and loca heorâ ic hebbe þǽrtô, and cêse and buteran ic dô, and ic eom getrŷpe hlâforde mînum.

4. Teacher and Oxherd.

Lp. Eâlâ, oxanhirde, hpæt pyrcst þû?

O. Eâlâ, hlâford mîn, micel ic gedeorfe: þænne se yrđling unscenđ þâ oxan, ic lǽde hî tô læse, and ealle niht ic stande ofer hî paciende for þeôfum, and eft on ǽrmergen ic betǽce hî þam yrđlinge pel gefylde and gepæterôde.

Lp. Is þes of þînum gefêrum?

O. Gea, hê is.

5. Teacher and Hunter.

Lp. Canst þû ǽnig þing?

H. Ânne cræft ic can.

Lp. Hpilcne?

H. Hunta ic eom.

Lp. Hpæs?

H. Cyninges.

Lp. Hû begǽst þû cræft þînne?

H. Ic brede mê max, and sette hî on stôpe gehæpre, and ge-

T. Hast thou any i-fere[1] ?

Pl. I have some[2] knave[3] thewing[4] oxen with gad-iron, that eke[5] so-like[6] now hoarse is for chill and ream[7].

T. What more doest thou a[8] day ?

Pl. I-wis[9] then more I do. I shall fill bins of oxen mid[10] hay, and water hem[11], and shern here[12] bear out.

T. Hi! hi! Much derf[13] is it!

Pl. Yea, lief[14], much derf[13] it is, forthat[15] I nam[16] free.

3. Teacher and Shepherd.

T. What sayest thou, shepherd? Hast thou any derf[13] ?

S. Yea, lief[14], I have; on forward[17] morning I drive sheep mine to here[12] lease[18], and stand over hem[11] on heat and on chill mid[10] hounds, the less[19] wolves for-swallow[20] hem[11], and I again lead hem[11] to here[12] locks, and milk hem[11] twice a[8] day, and locks here[12] I heave thereto[21], and cheese and butter I do[22], and I am true to-lord mine.

4. Teacher and Oxherd.

T. Oh, lo, oxherd, what workest thou ?

O. Oh, lo, lord mine, much I derve[13]: then[23] the earthling[24] unsheneth[25] the oxen, I lead hem[11] to lease[18], and all night I stand over hem[11] watching for thieves, and after on ere-morning[17] I beteach[26] hem[11] to-the earthling[24] well i-filled and i-watered.

T. Is this of thy i-feres[1] ?

O. Yea, he is.

5. Teacher and Hunter.

T. Kenst thou any thing?

H. One craft I ken.

T. Which?

H. Hunter I am.

T. Whose?

H. King's.

T. How bi-goest[27] thou craft thine?

H. I braid me meshes, and set hem[11] on a stow[28] i-happy[29], and

[1] fere, comrade. [2] a. [3] boy. [4] driving (S.). [5] also. [6] likewise. 7. shouting (S.). [8] on. [9] certainly, I wis. [10] with (Ch.). [11] them (Ch.). [12] their (Ch.). [13] toil (S.). [14] dear, sir. [15] because. [16] am not (Ch.). [17] early. [18] leasow, pasture. [19] less for that, lest. [20] for-, Germ. ver-, § 254, 2 (S.). [21] also I move their folds. [22] make. [23] when. [24] ploughman. [25] unyokes (?). [26] assign (Ch.). [27] practice (Ch.). [28] place (S.). [29] fit.

i-tyht[1] hounds mine, that wild-deer[2] hi[3] egg[4], till-that-that hi[3] come to the nets un-fore-show-edly[5], that hi[3] so be be-grined[6], and I off-slay hem[7] on[8] the meshes.

T. Ne[9] canst thou hunt but mid[10] nets?

H. Yea, but[11] nets hunt I may.

T. How?

H. Mid[10] swift hounds I be-take[12] wild-deer.[2]

T. Which wild-deer[2] swithest[13] i-fangest[14] thou?

H. I i-fang[14] harts, and boars, and roe*bucks*, and roes, and whilom hares.

T. Wert thou to day on hunting?

H. I nas[15], forthat[16] Sunday is, ac[17] yester day I was on hunting.

T. What i-latchedst[18] thou?

H. Twain harts and one boar.

T. How i-fangest[14] thou hem[7]?

H. Harts I i-fang[14] on[8] nets, and boar I off-slew.

T. How wert thou dursty[19] to-off-stick boar?

H. Hounds (be-)drove him to me, and I there, to-gainst[20] standing, ferly[21] off-stuck him.

T. Swithy[22] thristy[23] thou wert then?

H. Ne[9] shall hunter fright-full be, forthat[16] mis-like[24] wild-deer[2] won[25] in woods.

T. What dost thou by[26] thy hunting?

H. I sell[27] to-king so-what-so[28] I i-fo[14], forthat[16] I am hunter his.

T. What selleth[27] he thee?

H. He shrouds[29] me well and feeds, and whilom he selleth[27] me horse or badge[30], that the more lustily craft mine I be-go[31].

6. Teacher and Fisher.

T. Which craft kenst thou?

F. I am fisher.

T. What (be-)gettest thou of thy craft?

F. Bi-live[32], and shroud[29], and fee[33].

T. How i-fangst[14] thou fishes?

F. I a-sty[34] my ship, and werp[35] meshes mine on[8] ac[36], and angle I werp[35] and spirt-*net*[37], and so-what-so[28] hi[3] i-haft[38], I nim[39].

T. What if it unclean fishes be?

---

1 educate, train (S.). 2 beasts. 3 they (P. P.). 4 pursue. 5 unexpectedly. 6 taken in a *grin*, or snare. 7 them (Ch.). 8 in. 9 not. 10 with (Ch.). 11 without. 12 catch. 13 most (Ch.). 14 take (S.). 15 was not (Ch.). 16 because. 17 but (P. P.). 18 took. 19 daring (S.). 20 against (?). 21 suddenly (S.). 22 very (Ch.). 23 bold (Orm.). 24 unlike, various. 25 live. 26 with. 27 give. 28 whatsoever. 29 clothes. 30 ring, bracelet. 31 practice (Ch.). 32 victuals (P. P.). 33 money. 34 mount. 35 throw (S.). 36 water, river (S.). 37 fishing-net (H.). 38 catch (?). 39 take.

tyhte hundâs mîne, þæt pildeôr hî êhtân, ôđ-þæt-þe hî cumân tô þâm nettum unforesceâpôdlîce, þæt hî spâ beôn begrinôde, and ic ofsleâ hî on þâm maxum.

Lp. Ne canst þû huntian bûtan mid nettum?

H. Gea, bûtan nettum huntian ic mæg.

Lp. Hû?

H. Mid spiftum hundum ic betæce pildeôr.

Lp. Hpilce pildeôr spîđôst gefêhst þû?

H. Ic gefô heortâs, and bârâs, and rân, and rǣgan, and hpîlon haran.

Lp. Þǣre þû tô dæg on huntnôđe?

H. Ic næs, forþam sunnan dæg is, ac gystran dæg ic pæs on huntunge.

Lp. Hpæt gelæhtest þû?

H. Tpegen heortâs and ânne bâr.

Lp. Hû gefênge þû hî?

H. Heortâs ic gefêng on nettum, and bâr ic ofslôh.

Lp. Hû pǣre þû dyrstig ofstician bâr?

H. Hundâs bedrifon hine tô mê, and ic þǣr, tôgeânes standende, fǣrlîce ofsticôde hine.

Lp. Spîđe þrîste þû pǣre þâ.

H. Ne sceal hunta forhtful pesan, forþam mislîce pildeôr puniađ on pudum.

Lp. Hpæt dêst þû be þînre huntunge?

H. Ic sylle cyninge spâ-hpæt-spâ ic gefô, forþam ic eom hunta his.

Lp. Hpæt sylđ hê þê?

H. Hê scrŷt mê pel and fêt, and hpîlum hê sylđ mê hors ođđe beâh, þæt þŷ lustlîcôr cræft mînne ic begange.

---

6. Teacher and Fisher.

Lp. Hpilcne cræft canst þû?

F. Ic eom fiscere.

Lp. Hpæt begytst þû of þînum cræfte?

F. Bigleofan, and scrûd, and feoh.

Lp. Hû gefêhst þû fiscâs?

F. Ic âstîge mîn scip, and peorpe max mîne on eâ, and angel ic peorpe and spyrtan, and spâ-hpæt-spâ hî gehæftađ, ic genime.

Lp. Hpæt gif hit unclǣne fiscâs beôđ?

F. Ic peorpe þâ unclǣnan ût, and genime mê clǣne tô mete.

Lp. Hpǣr cŷpst þû fiscâs þîne?

F. On ceastre.

Lp. Hpâ bygđ hî?

F. Ceasterpare. Ic ne mæg spâ fela gefôn spâ-fela-spâ ic mæg gesyllan.

Lp. Hpilce fiscâs gefêhst þû?

F. Ǣlâs and hacodâs, mynâs and ǣlepûtan, sceôtan and lampredan, and spâ-hpylce-spâ on pætere spimmađ.

Lp. For hpŷ ne fiscâst þû on sǣ?

F. Hpîlum ic dô, ac seldon, forþam micel rêpet mê is tô sǣ.

Lp. Hpæt fêhst þû on sǣ?

F. Hæringâs and leaxâs, merespîn and styrian, ostran and crabban, musclan, pinepinclan, sǣcoccâs, fagc, and flôc, and lopystran, and fela spilces.

Lp. Pilt þû fôn sumne hpæl?

F. Nic.

Lp. For hpŷ?

F. Forþam plihtlîc þing hit is gefôn hpæl. Gebeorhlîcre is mê faran tô eâ mid scipe mînum, þænne faran mid manigum scipum on huntunge hranes.

Lp. For hpŷ spâ?

F. Forþam leôfre is mê gefôn fisc þæne ic mæg ofsleân, þænne þe nâ þæt ân mê, ac eâc spilce mîne gefêran mid ânê slegê hê mæg besencan ođđe gecpylman.

Lp. And þeâh, manige gefôđ hpælâs, and ætberstađ frêcnessâ, and micelne sceat þanon begitađ.

F. Sôđ þû segst, ac ic ne geþrîstige for môdes mînes nŷtenysse.

---

7. Teacher, Fowler, and Hunter.

Lp. Hpæt segst þû, fugelere? Hû bespîcst þû fugelâs?

Fug. On fela pîsenâ ic bespîce fugelâs; hpîlum mid nettum, hpîlum mid grinum, hpîlum mid lîmê, hpîlum mid hpistlunge, hpîlum mid hafocê, hpîlum mid treppan.

Lp. Hæfst þû hafoc?

Fug. Ic hæbbe.

Lp. Canst þû temian hî?

Fug. Gea, ic can. Hpæt sceoldon hî mê, bûtan ic cûđe temian hî?

F. I werp[1] the unclean out, and i-nim[2] me clean to[3] meat.

T. Where chopst[4] thou fishes thine ?

F. On Chester[5].

T. Who buyeth hem[6] ?

F. Chester-were[7]. I ne[8] may so fele[9] i-fon[10] so-fele-so[9] I may i-sell.

T. Which fishes i-fangst[10] thou ?

F. Eels and haked[11], minnows and eel-pouts, shot[12] and lampreys, and so-which-so[13] on water swimmeth.

T. For why ne[8] fishest thou on sea ?

F. Whilom I do, ac[14] seldom, forthat[15] much rowing to-me is to sea.

T. What fangst[10] thou on sea ?

F. Herrings and laxes[16], mere-swine[17] and sturgeons, oysters and crabs, muscles, pinewincles, sea-cockles, fadge, and flowks, and lobsters, and fele[9] of such.

T. Wilt thou fon[10] some whale ?

F. Not I.

T. For why ?

F. Forthat plightly[18] thing it is to-ifon[10] whale. I-burg-lier[19] is to-me to-fare[20] to ae[21] mid[22] ship mine, than to-fare[20] mid[22] many ships a hunting of grampus.

T. For why so ?

F. Forthat[15] liefer[23] is to-me to-ifon[10] fish that I may off-slay, than that no[24] that one[24] me, ac[14] eke[25] such[25] my i-feres[26] mid[22] one sley[27] he may (be-)sink *or* i-quell[28].

T. And though[29] many i-fo[10] whales, and at-burst[30] frecness[31] and much scot[32] thence (be-)get.

F. Sooth thou sayest, ac[14] I ne thristy[33] for mood's mine ne-wit-iness[34].

---

7. Teacher, Fowler, and Hunter.

T. What sayest thou, fowler ? How be-swikest[35] thou fowls ?

F. On fele[9] wise[36] I be-swike[35] fowls ; whilom with nets, whilom with grins, whilom with lime, whilom with whistling, whilom with hawk, whilom with trap.

T. Hast thou hawk ?

F. I have.

T. Canst thou tame hem[6] ?

F. Yea, I can. What should hi[37] me, but[38] I could tame hem[6] ?

---

[1] throw (S.). [2] take. [3] as, for. [4] sell. [5] city ; compare West-*chester*. [6] them (Ch.). [7] Citizens ; compare *were*-wolf. [8] not. [9] so many as. [10] take. [11] pike. [12] trout. [13] such as. [14] but (P. P.). [15] because. [16] salmon. [17] porpoise. [18] perilous (?) [19] safer, *iboruwen*, safe (S.). [20] go. [21] river (S.). [22] with (Ch.). [23] preferable. [24] not only. [25] likewise, also. [26] comrades. [27] blow (S.). [28] kill. [29] yet. [30] escape (S.). [31] danger (?). [32] money. [33] dare (compare adj., S.). [34] dullness (?). [35] catch. [36] ways. [37] they (profit) (P. P.). [38] unless.

H. Sell[1] me a hawk.

F. I sell[1] lustliche[2] if thou sellest[1] me a swift hound. Which hawk wilt thou have, the more[3], whether-the[4] the less?

H. Sell[1] me the more[3].

T. How (a-)feedest thou hawks thine?

F. Hi[5] feed hem[6]-selves and me on winter, and on lent[7] I let hem[6] (at-)wind[8] to wood, and i-nim[9] me birds[10] on harvest, and tame hem[6].

T. And for why (for-)lettest thou the i-tamed (at-)wind[8] from thee?

F. For-that[11] I nill[12] feed hem[6] on summer, for-that[11] that hi[5] thraly[13] eat.

T. And many feed the i-tamed over summer, that eft[14] hi[5] *may*-have yare[15].

F. Yea, so hi[5] do, ac[16] I nill[12] oth[17] that one[18] derve[19] over hem[6], for-that[11] I can others, no[20] that one[18], ac[16] eke so-like many, i-fon[21].

---

8. Teacher and Merchant.

T. What sayest thou, monger[22]?

M. I say that behoove*full* I am ye[23] to-king, and aldermen, and wealthy, and all folks.

T. And how?

M. I (a-)sty[24] my ship mid[25] lasts[26] mine, and row over sea-like deals[27], and chop[28] my things, and buy things dear-worth[29], that on this land ne[30] be a-kenned[31], and I it to i-lead[32] you hither mid[25] mickle[33] plight[34] over sea, and whilom[35] forlideness[36] I thole[37] mid[25] loss of-all things mine, uneath[38] quick[39] at-bursting[40].

T. Which things (i-)leadest[32] thou to-us?

M. Palls[41] and silks, dear-worth[29] gems, and gold, selcouth[42] reef[43] and wort-i-mang[44], wine, and oil, elephant's bone, and maslin[45], *bronze*, and tin, sulphur, and glass, and of-the-like fele[46].

T. Wilt thou sell things thine here, all so[47] thou hem[6] i-broughtest there?

M. I nill[12]. What then me framed[48] i-derf[49] mine? Ac[16] I will hem[6] chop[28] here lovelier[50] than I buy there, that some i-strain[51] me I may-(be-)get, thence[52] I me (a-)feed, and my wife, and my son.

---

[1] give. [2] with pleasure (S.). [3] larger. [4] or (S.). [5] they (P. P.). [6] 'em, them (Ch.). [7] spring. [8] fly off (S.). [9] take. [10] young. [11] because. [12] will not. [13] very much (H.). [14] after. [15] ready, trained. [16] but (P. P.). [17] for (?). [18] alone. [19] toil (S.). [20] not that only, but likewise also many. [21] catch (S.). [22] merchant. [23] both (?). [24] ascend. [25] with (P. P.). [26] loads (Ch.). [27] parts, regions. [28] sell. [29] of great worth (S.). [30] not. [31] produced, kinded (S.). [32] bring to (S.). [33] much. [34] danger. [35] sometimes. [36] wreck (?). [37] suffer. [38] not easily. [39] alive. [40] escaping (S.). [41] purple cloth. [42] seldom seen, rare. [43] robes. [44] spices (?). [45] brass. [46] many (P.P.). [47] at the same price. [48] profited (S.). [49] toil (S.). [50] dearer (?). [51] gain (S.). [52] whence.

H. Syle mê ânne hafoc.

Fug. Ic sylle lustlîce, gif þû sylst mê ânne spiftne hund. Hpilcne hafoc pilt þû habban, þone mâran, hpæđer þe þone læssan?

H. Syle mê þone mâran.

Lp. Hû âfêst þû hafocâs þîne?

Fug. Hî fêdađ hî selfe and mê on pintrâ, and on lencten ic læte hî ætpindan tô pudâ, and genime mê briddâs on hærfeste, and temige hî.

Lp. And for hpŷ forlætst þû þâ getemedan ætpindan fram þê?

Fug. Forþam ic nelle fêdan hî on sumerâ, forþam þe hî þearle etađ.

Lp. And manige fêdađ þâ getemedan ofer sumor, þæt eft hî habbân gearpe.

Fug. Gea, spâ hî dôđ, ac ic nelle ôđ þæt ân deorfan ofer hî, forþam ic can ôđre, nâ þæt ânne, ac eâc spilce manige, gefôn.

---

8. Teacher and Merchant.

Lp. Hpæt segst þû, mangere?

M. Ic secge þæt behêfe ic eom ge cyninge, and ealdormannum and peligum, and eallum folce.

Lp. And hû?

M. Ic âstîge mîn scip mid hlæstum mînum, and rôpe ofer sælîce dælâs, and cŷpe mîne þing, and bycge þing deôrpyrđe, þâ on þissum lande ne beôđ âcennede, and ic hit tôgelæde eôp hider mid miclum plihte ofer sæ, and hpîlum forlidenesse ic þolie mid lyrê ealrâ þingâ mînrâ, uneâđe cpic ætberstende.

Lp. Hpilce þing gelædst þû ûs?

M. Pællâs and sîdan, deôrpyrđe gimmâs, and gold, selcûđe reâf, and pyrtgemang, pîn, and ele, ylpes bân, and mæsling, ær, and tin, spefel, and glæs, and þylces fela.

Lp. Pilt þû syllan þing þîne hêr, eal spâ þû hî gebohtest þær?

M. Ic nelle. Hpæt þænne mê fremôde gedeorf mîn? Ac ic pille hî cŷpan hêr luflîcôr þænne ic gebycge þær, þæt sum gestreôn mê ic begite, þanon ic mê âfêde, and mîn pîf, and mînne sunu.

---

9. Teacher and Shoemaker.

Lp. Pû, sceô-pyrhta, hpæt pyrcest þû ûs nytpyrđnesse?

S. Is pitodlîce cræft mîn behêfe þearle eôp, and neôdþearf.

Lp. Hû?

S. Ic bycge hŷdâ, and fel, and gearcie hî mid cræfte mînum, and pyrce of him gescŷ mislîces cynnes; spiftlerâs, and sceôs, leđer-hosan, and butericâs, bridel-þpangâs, and gerǣdu, and flaxan, and higdifatu, spurleđeru, and hælftrâ, pusan, and fætelsâs, and nân eôper nele oferpintran bûtan mînum cræfte.

---

10. Teacher and Salter.

Lp. Eâlâ, sealtere, hpæt ûs fremâđ cræft þîn?

Sealt. Pearle fremâđ cræft mîn eôp eallum: nân eôper blisse brŷcđ on gereordunge, ođđe metê, bûtan cræft mîn gistlîđe him beô.

Lp. Hû?

Sealt. Hpilc mannâ peredum þurhbrŷcđ mettum bûtan spæcce sealtes? Hpâ gefyldđ cleôfan his, ođđe hêdernu, bûtan cræfte mînum? Efne, butergeþpeor ælc and cŷsgerun losađ eôp, bûton ic hyrde ætpese eôp, þe ne furđon pyrtum eôprum, bûtan mê, brûcađ.

---

11. Teacher and Baker.

Lp. Hpæt segst þû, bæcere? Hpam fremâđ cræft þîn, ođđe hpæđer bûtan þê pê mâgon lîf âdreôgan?

B. Gê mâgon pitodlîce þurh sum fæc bûtan mînum cræfte lîf âdreôgan, ac nâ lange, ne tô pel; sôđlîce bûtan cræfte mînum ælc beôd æmtig biđ gesepen, and bûtan hlâfe ælc mete tô plǣttan biđ gehpyrfed. Ic heortan mannes gestrangie; ic mægen perâ eom; and furđon lytlingâs nellađ forbŷgean mê.

---

12. Teacher and Cook.

Lp. Hpæt secgađ pê be coce? hpæđer pê beþurfon on ǣnigum cræfte his?

C. Gif gê mê ût-âdrîfađ fram eôprum gefêrscipe, gê etađ pyrtâ

9. Teacher and Shoemaker.

T. Thou, shoe-wright, what workest thou us of nut-worth-ness[1]?

S. Is witterly[2] craft mine behoove*full* thraly[3] to-you, and need-tharf[4].

T. How?

S. I buy hides and fells, and yark[5] hem[6] mid[7] craft mine, and work of hem[6] (i-)shoes of mis-like[8] kind; swiftlers[9], and shoes, leather-hose, and bottles, bridle-thongs, and i-readies[10], and flasks, and *heedy*-fats[11], spur-leathers, and halters, purses and pouches, and none of you nill[12] over-winter but[13] my craft.

10. Teacher and Salter.

T. O lo, salter, what us frameth[14] craft thine?

S. Thraly[3] frameth[14] craft mine you all: none of-you bliss brooketh[15] on i-rerding[16], or meat[17], but[18] craft mine guestly[19] to-him be.

T. How?

S. Which of men wered[20] through-brooketh meats but[13] swack[21] of-salt? Who i-filleth cleve[22] his, or heed-erne[23], but[13] craft mine? Even[24], butter-thwer[25] each and cheese-i-runnet loseth to-you, but[18] I herd[26] at-be to-you, that[27] ne[28] forthen[29] worts[30] your, but[13] me, brook[15].

11. Teacher and Baker.

T. What sayest thou, baker? Whom frameth[14] craft thine, or whether but[13] thee we may life (a-)dree[31]?

B. Ye may witterly[2] through some fac[32] but[13] my craft life (a-)dree[31], ac[33] no[34] long ne[35] too[36] well; soothly[37] but[13] craft mine each bode[38] empty beeth[39] seen[39], and but[13] loaf each meat to wlating[40] beeth i-warped. I heart of-man i-strengthen; I main[41] of-were[42] am; and forthen[29] littlings[43] nill[44] for-bug[45] me.

12. Teacher and Cook.

T. What say we by[46] cook? Whether we be-tharf[47] in any *respect* craft his?

C. If ye me out-a-drive from your i-fere-ship[48], ye eat worts[30]

---

[1] usefulness (see *nut*, use, S.). [2] certainly (P.P.). [3] very much (H.). [4] needful (tharf=need, Ch.). [5] prepare (H.). [6] 'em, them (Ch.). [7] with (P.P.). [8] unlike, various (S.). [9] slippers. [10] trappings. [11] bath-buckets (?). [12] wish not to pass the winter. [13] without (S.). [14] profiteth (H.). [15] enjoyeth. [16] luncheon (?). [17] dinner. [18] unless. [19] hospitable. [20] sweet, fresh meats thoroughly enjoys (S.). [21] taste (?). [22] cellar (S.). [23] pantry. [24] aye. [25] churning (?). [26] keeper, preserver. [27] who, *i. e.*, you. [28] not. [29] furthermore (S.). [30] vegetables. [31] endure. [32] time (?). [33] but (P. P.). [34] not. [35] nor. [36] so. [37] in truth. [38] table (H.). [39] seems. [40] loathing (S.). [41] strength. [42] men; compare *were*-wolf. [43] children. [44] will not. [45] shun (S.). [46] about. [47] need (tharf=need, Ch.). [48] company (see i-fere, S.).

your green, and flesh-meats your raw, and ne[1] forthen[2] fat broth ye may but[3] craft mine have.

T. We ne[1] reck by[4] craft thine, ne[5] he[6] to-us need-tharf[7] is, forthat[8] we-selves may seethe the things that to seethe are, and brede[9] the things that to brede[9] *are.*

C. If ye for that me from-a-drive[10], that ye thus do, then be ye all thralls, and none of-you ne[1] beeth lord; and, though-whether[11] but[3] craft mine ye ne[1] eat.

---

13. Teacher and Scholar.

T. O lo! thou monk, that me to speakest, even[12] I have a-found thee to-have good i-feres[13], and thraly[14] need-tharf[7]; and I ask[15] them.

S. I have smiths, iron-smiths, gold-smith, silver-smith, ore[16]-smith, tree-wright[17], and many other of-mis-like[18] crafts be-gangers[19].

T. Hast thou any wise i-thought-*full*[20] *one?*

S. I-wisly[21] I have. How may our gathering but[3] i-thinking[20] *one* be wissed[22]?

---

14. Teacher, Counselor, Smith, and others.

T. What sayest thou, Wise? Which craft to-thee is[23] i-thought[23] betwixt[26] those further[24] *to be?*

C. I say to thee, to-me is i-thought[23] God's thewdom[25] betweoh[26] those crafts eldership to-hold, so so it is (i-)read on gospel, Foremost seek riche[27] God's, and righteousness his, and those things all be to-i-eked[28] to-you.

T. And which to-thee is[23] i-thought[23] betwixt[26] world-crafts to-hold elderdom[29]?

C. Earth-tilth[30], forthat[8] the earthling[31] us all feeds.

The Smith sayeth:

Whence to-the earthling[31] sull-share[32] or coulter, that no gad hath but of craft mine? Whence fisher angle, or shoe-wright awl, or seamer needle? Nis[33] it of my (i-)work?

The I-thinking-*one* answereth:

Sooth, witterly[34], sayst thou; ac[35] to-all us liefer[36] is to-wick[37] mid[38] the earthling[31] than mid[38] thee; forthat[8] the earthling[31] selleth[39] us loaf and

---

[1] not. [2] furthermore (S.). [3] without (S.). [4] care for. [5] nor. [6] it. [7] needful (tharf=need, Ch.). [8] because. [9] roast (S.). [10] drive from you. [11] whether or no, notwithstanding. [12] truly (?). [13] comrades (S.). [14] very (H.). [15] ask about them=who are they? [16] copper-smith. [17] carpenter. [18] unlike, various (S.). [19] practisers (?). [20] counselor (?) [21] certainly (Ch.). [22] guided (Ch.). [23] seems. [24] foremost. [25] service (S.). [26] betwixt, amongst. [27] kingdom (bishop-*ric*, H.). [28] added (?). [29] supremacy. [30] farming (Wycl.). [31] farmer. [32] plow-share. [33] is not (Ch.). [34] certainly (P. P.). [35] but (S.). [36] pleasanter, better. [37] reside, have a *wick* or house. [38] with (P. P.). [39] giveth, supplieth.

eôpre grêne, and flǽsc-mettâs eôpre hreâpe, and ne furđon fæt brođ gê mâgon bûtan cræfte mînum habban.

Lp. Ƿê ne rêcađ be cræfte þînum, ne hê ûs neôdþearf is, forþam pê selfe mâgon seôđan þâ þing þe tô seôđenne sind, and brǽdan þâ þing þe tô brǽdenne sind.

C. Gif gê for þŷ mê fram-âdrîfađ, þæt gê þus dôn, þonne beô gê ealle þrǽlâs, and nân eôper ne biđ hlâford; and, þeâh-hpæđere bûtan cræfte mînum gê ne etađ.

13. Teacher and Scholar.

Lp. Eâlâ, þû munuc, þe mê tô spricst, efne ic hæbbe âfandôd þê habban gôde gefêran, and þearle neôdþearfe; and ic âhsie þâ.

Le. Ic hæbbe smiđâs, îsene-smiđâs, gold-smiđ, seolfor-smiđ, âr-smiđ, treôp-pyrhtan, and manige ôđre mislîcrâ cræftâ bîgengerâs.

Lp. Hæfst þû ǽnigne pîsne geþeahtan?

Le. Gepislîce ic hæbbe. Hû mæg ûre gegaderung bûtan geþeahtende beôn pîsôd?

14. Teacher, Counselor, Smith, and others.

Lp. Hpæt segst þû, Ƿîsa? Hpilc cræft þê is geþuht betpux þâs furđra pesan?

G. Ic secge þê, mê is geþuht Godes þeôpdôm betpeoh þâs cræftâs ealdorscipe healdan, spâ spâ hit is gerǽd on godspelle, Fyrmest sêceađ rîce Godes, and rihtpîsnesse his, and þâs þing ealle beôđ tôgeŷhte eôp.

Lp. And hpilc þê is geþuht betpux porold-cræftâs healdan ealdordôm?

G. Eorđ-tilđ, forþam se yrđling ûs ealle fêt.

Se Smiđ segeđ:

Hpanon þam yrđlinge sulh-scear ođđe culter, þe nâ gade hæfđ, bûton of cræfte mînum? Hpanon fiscere angel, ođđe sceô-pyrhtan ǽl, ođđe seâmere nǽdl? Nis hit of mînum gepeorce?

Se Geþeahtend andsperâđ:

Sôđ pitodlîce segst þû; ac eallum ûs leôfre is pîcian mid þam yrđlinge þænne mid þê; forþam se yrđling sylđ ûs hlâf and drenc: þû, hpæt sylst þû ûs on smiđđan þînre, bûtan îsene fŷr-spearcan, and spêgingâ beâtendrâ slecgeâ, and blâpendrâ byligâ?

Se Treôp-pyrhta segeđ:

Hpilc eôper ne notâđ cræftê mînê; þonne hûs, and mislîce fatu, and scipu eôp eallum ic pyrce?

Se Smiđ andpyrt:

Eâlâ treôp-pyrhta, for hpŷ spâ spricst þû, þonne ne furđon ân þyrl bûtan cræfte mînum þû ne miht dôn?

Se Geþeahtend segeđ:

Eâlâ geferan and gôde pyrhtan! Uton tôpeorpan hpætlîcôr þâs geflîtu, and sî sib and geþpærness betpeoh ûs, and fremige ânrâ gehpylc ôđrum on cræfte his, and geþpæriân symble mid þam yrđlinge, þær pê bigleofan ûs, and fôdor horsum ûrum habbađ; and þis geþeaht ic sylle eallum pyrhtum, þæt ânrâ gehpylc cræft his geornlîce begange; forþam se þe cræft his forlæt, hê byđ forlæten fram þam cræfte. Spâ hpæđer þû sî, spâ mæsse-preôst, spâ munuc, spâ ceorl, spâ cempa, begâ þê selfne on þisum: beô þæt þû eart, forþam micel hŷnđ and sceamu hit is men, nelle pesan þæt þe hê is, and þæt þe hê pesan sceal.

---

15. Teacher and Scholar.

Lp. Eâlâ cild, hû eôp lîcâđ þeôs spræc?

Le. Pel heô lîcâđ ûs, ac þearle deôplîce þû spricst, and ofer mæđe ûre þû forđtŷhđ þâ spræce; ac sprec ûs æfter ûrum andgite, þæt pê mægen understandan þâ þing þe þû spricst.

Lp. Ic âhsige eôp for hpŷ spâ geornlîce leornige gê?

Le. Forþam pê nellađ pesan spâ stunte nŷtenu, þâ nân þing pitađ bûtan gærs and pæter.

Lp. And hpæt pille gê?

Le. Pê pillađ pesan pîse.

Lp. In hpilcum pîsdôme? Pille gê pesan prætige, ođđe þûsendhipe, on leâsungum lytige, on spræcum gleâplîce, hindergeâpe, pel sprecende and yfele þencende, spæsum pordum underþeôdde, fâcen piđinnan tydrende, spâ spâ byrgels, mettum ofergepeorce, piđinnan ful stencê?

drink: thou, what sellest[1] thou us in smithy thine, but iron fire-sparks, and sweying[2] of-beating sledges, and of-blowing bellows?

The Tree-wright[3] sayeth:

Which of-you ne[4] noteth[5] craft mine; then[6] house, and mis-like[7] fats[8], and ships for-you all I work?

The Smith anwordeth[9]:

O lo, tree-wright[3], for why so speakest thou, then[6] ne[5] forthen[10] one thirl[11] but[12] craft mine thou ne[4] might do?

The I-thinking[13] sayeth:

O lo, i-feres[14] and good wrights! Wite-we[15] to-warp[16] whatliker[17] those i-flites[18], and *be* sib[19] and i-thwerness[20] betweohs[21] us, and frame[22] of-ones[23] i-which[23] to-other in craft his, and i-thwer[24] symble[25] mid[26] the earthling[27], there[28] we belive[29] for-us, and fodder for horses our have; and this i-thought I sell[1] to all wrights, that of-ones[30] i-which[30] craft his yernliche[31] be-go[32]; forthat that[33] that craft his for-letteth[34], he beeth for-let[34] from the craft. So whether[35] thou *be*, so[36] mass-priest, so monk, so churl, so kemp[37], be-go[32] thee self on this: be that thou art, forthat mickle hinth[38] and shame it is to-man, nill-he[39] *to-be* that that he is, and that that he be shall[40].

---

15. Teacher and Scholar.

T. O lo, child, how to-you liketh[41] this speech?

S. Well *she*[42] liketh[41] to-us, ac[43] thraly[44] deeply thou speakest, and over meeth[45] our thou forth-tuggest the speech; ac[43] speak to-us after our an-git[46], that we may understand the things that thou speakest.

T. I ask you for why so yernliche[31] learn ye?

S. Forthat we nill[47] *to-be* so-*as* stunt[48] neat[49], that none thing wit[50] but grass and water.

T. And what will ye?

S. We will *to-be* wise.

T. In which wisdom? Will ye be pretty[51], or thousand-hued, in leasings[52] litty[53], in speeches gleve[54], hinder-yeepe[55], well speaking and evil thinking, *to-sweet* words undertheed[56], faken[57] within tudring[58], so so[36] buryel[59], with meted[60] over-i-work, within full with-stench?

---

[1] give. [2] sounding (P. P.). [3] carpenter. [4] not. [5] useth (S.). [6] since. [7] unlike, various. [8] vessels, utensils. [9] answers (H.). [10] furthermore (S.). [11] hole; compare nos-*tril*. [12] without. [13] counselor (?). [14] comrades (S.). [15] go we=let us (S.). [16] throw away (S.). [17] very promptly (S.). [18] strifes (S.). [19] peace. [20] concord (?). [21] among (Ch.). [22] aid (H.). [23] each one the other. [24] agree (?). [25] always (?). [26] with (P. P.). [27] farmer. [28] with whom. [29] victuals (P. P.). [30] each one. [31] earnestly (S.). [32] practice (S.). [33] he. [34] let go, abandon (Ch.). [35] whatever. [36] as, for example. [37] champion. [38] loss (S.). [39] if he will not. [40] ought. [41] pleaseth (Ch.). [42] the speech. [43] but (S.). [44] very (H.). [45] age (S.). [46] understanding (?). [47] will not. [48] stupid. [49] cattle. [50] know. [51] crafty. [52] lies. [53] cunning, nimble (H.). [54] clever (S.). [55] sly (yeepe, cunning, P. P.). [56] addicted (?). [57] deceit (S.). [58] begetting (S.). [59] sepulchre (S.). [60] painted (S.).

S. We nill[1] so *to-be* wise, forthat he nis[2] wise that mid[3] dydring[4] him self biswiketh[5].

T. Ac[6] how will ye?

S. We will to-be bilewit[7], but[8] likening[9], and wise, that we bow from evil, and do good; yet though-whether[10] deeplier mid[3] us thou smeest[11] than eld[12] our anfon[13] may; ac[6] speak to-us after our i-wonts not so deeply.

T. I do all-so[14] ye bid. Thou, knave[15], what didst thou to day?

S. Many things I did. On this night, then-then[16] knell[17] I i-heard, I arose off my bed, and yode[18] to church, and sang uht-song[19] mid[3] i-brothers; after that we sang by all-hallows, and day-red-ly[20] love-songs[21], after these, prime, and seven psalms mid[3] litanies, and capital mass; sithen[22] undern-tide, and did mass by day; after these we sung midday, and ate, and drunk, and slept, and eft we arose, and sung nones, and now we are here afore thee, yare[23] to-i-hear what thou to us may say.

T. When will ye sing even, or night-song?

S. Then[16] it time be.

T. Wert thou to day (be-)swinged[24]?

S. I nas[25], forthat warily I me held.

T. And how thine i-feres[26]?

S. What me askest thou by that? I ne[27] dare ope to-thee digels[28] our. Of-ones[29] i-which[29] wots if he swinged[24] was or no.

T. What eatest thou a day?

S. Yet flesh-meats I brook[30], forthat child I am under yerde[31] *living*[32].

T. What more eatest thou?

S. Worts, and eggs, fish, and cheese, butter, and beans, and all clean things I eat mid mickle thanking.

T. Swithy[33] wax-yerne[34] art thou, then thou all things eatest that thee to-forn i-set *are*.

S. I ne[27] am so mickle swallower, that I all kinds of meats on one i-rerding[34] eat may.

T. Ac[6] how.

S. I brook[30] whilom these meats, and whilom others mid[3] soberness, so so is-deft for-a-monk, not with over-*eating*, forthat I am none glutton.

T. And what drinkest thou?

S. Ale, if I have, or water, if I have-not ale.

---

[1] will not. [2] is not (Ch.). [3] with (P. P.). [4] illusion, diddling (?). [5] deceiveth (P. P.). [6] but (S.). [7] gentle (S.). [8] without. [9] hypocrisy (?). [10] whether or no. [11] scrutinizest (?). [12] age. [13] receive (S.). [14] just as. [15] boy. [16] when. [17] bell. [18] went. [19] early morning (S.). [20] dawn (S.). [21] *lof*, praise, lauds (S.). [22] since. [23] ready. [24] whipped. [25] was not. [26] comrades (S.). [27] not. [28] secrets (S.). [29] each one. [30] use. [31] rod, yard. [32] perhaps akin to *drudging*. [33] very (Ch.). [34] greedy (?). [35] repast (?).

Le. Ƿê nellađ spâ pesan pîse, forþam hê nis pîs, þe mid dydrunge hine selfne bespîcđ.

Lp. Ac hû pille gê?

Le. Ƿê pillađ beôn bilepite, bûtan lîcetunge, and pîse, þæt pê bûgen fram yfele, and dôn gôd; git þeâh-hpæđere deôplîcôr mid ûs þû smeâgest þænne yld ûre anfôn mǣge; ac sprec ûs æfter ûrum gepunum næs spâ deôplîce.

Lp. Ic dô ealspâ gê biddađ. Þû, cnapa, hpæt dydest þû tô dæg?

Le. Manige þing ic dyde. On þisse nihte, þâþâ cnyl ic gehŷrde, ic ârâs of mînum bedde, and eôde tô cyricean, and sang uht-sang mid gebrôđrum; æfter þâ pê sungon be eallum hâlgum, and dægrêdlîce lofsángâs; æfter þissum, prîm, and seofon sealmâs mid letanium, and capitol-mæssan; siđđan underntîde, and dydon mæssan be dæge; æfter þissum pê sungon middæg, and ǣton, and druncon, and slêpon, and eft pê ârison, and sungon nôn, and nû pê sind hêr ætforan þê, gearpe gehŷran hpæt þû ûs secge.

Lp. Hpænne pille gê singan ǣfen, ođđe niht-sang?

Le. Þonne hit tîma biđ.

Lp. Ƿǣre þû tô dæg bespungen?

Le. Ic næs, forþam pærlîce ic mê heôld.

Lp. And hû þîne gefêran?

Le. Hpæt mê âhsâst þû be þam? Ic ne dear yppan þê dêglu ûre. Ânrâ gehpilc pât gif hê bespungen pæs ođđe nâ.

Lp. Hpæt itst þû on dæg?

Le. Git flǣsc-mettum ic brûce, forþam cild ic eom under gyrde drohtniende.

Lp. Hpæt mâre itst þû?

Le. Ƿyrtâ, and ægru, fisc, and cêse, buteran, and beânâ, and ealle clǣne þing ic ete mid micelre þancunge.

Lp. Spîđe paxgeorn eart þû, þonne þû ealle þing itst þe þê tôforan gesette sind.

Le. Ic ne eom spâ micel spelgere, þæt ic ealle cyn mettâ on ânre gereordunge etan mǣge.

Lp. Ac hû?

Le. Ic brûce hpîlum þissum mettum, and hpîlum ôđrum mid sŷfernesse, spâ spâ dafenâđ munuce, næs mid oferhropse, forþam ic eom nân glûto.

Lp. And hpæt drincst þû?

Le. Ealu, gif ic hæbbe, ođđe pæter, gif ic næbbe ealu.

Lp. Ne drincst þû ƿîn?

Le. Ic ne eom sƿâ spêdig þæt ic mǽge bycgan mê ƿîn; and ƿîn nis drenc cildâ, ne dysigrâ, ac ealdrâ and ƿîsrâ.

Lp. Hƿǽr slǽpst þû?

Le. On slǽp-erne mid gebrôðrum.

Lp. Hƿâ âƿecð þê tô uht-sange?

Le. Hƿîlum ic gehŷre cnyl, and ic ârîse; hƿîlum lâreôƿ mîn âƿecð mê stîðlîce mid gyrde.

Lp. Eâlâ gê gôde cildru, and ƿynsume leornerâs, eôƿ manâð eôƿer lâreôƿ þæt gê hŷrsumiân godcundum lârum, and þæt gê healdân eôƿ selfe ǽnlîce on ælcere stôƿe. Gâð þeâƿlîce, þonne gê gehŷrân cyricean bellan, and gâð intô cyricean, and âbûgað eâdmôdlîce tô hâlgum ƿefodum, and standað þeâƿlîce, and singað ânmôdlîce, and gebiddað for eôƿrum synnum, and gâð ût bûtan hygeleâste tô clûstre, oððe tô leornunge.

T. Ne[1] drinkest thou wine?

S. I ne[1] am so speedy[2] that I may buy me wine; and wine nis[3] drink of-children, ne[4] dizzy[5], ac[6] of-old and wise.

T. Where sleepest thou?

S. On sleep-erne[7] mid i-brothers.

T. Who awaketh thee to uht-song[8]?

S. Whilom I hear knell[9], and I arise; whilom lore*master* mine awakes me stithly[10] mid[11] yerde[12].

T. O lo, ye good childer[13], and winsome learners, you moneth[14] your lore*master* that ye hersumen[15] godcund[16] lores[17], and that ye hold you selves anlike[18] in each stow[19]. Go thewly[20], then[21] ye i-hear church's bells, and go into church, and (a-)bow edmodly[22] to holy *altars*, and stand thewly[20], and sing one-mood-ly[23], and i-bid[24] for your sins, and go out but[25] heedlessness to cloister or to learning[26].

---

[1] not. [2] rich. [3] is not (Ch.). [4] nor. [5] foolish. [6] but (S.). [7] *erne*, room. [8] early morning service (S.). [9] bell. [10] harshly (S.). [11] with (P. P.). [12] rod, yard. [13] (Ch.). [14] admonisheth (S.). [15] obey (S.). [16] divine (S.). [17] precepts. [18] elegantly (onliche, S.). [19] place (S.). [20] becomingly; see *thews*, customs. [21] when. [22] humbly (S.). [23] with one mind. [24] pray. [25] without. [26] gymnasium.

ANGLO-SAXON CHRONICLE.

Brytene îgland is ehta hund mîlâ lang, and tpâ hund mîlâ brâd; and hêr sind on þam îgland fîf geþeôdu, Englisc, Bryttisc, Scottisc, Pihtisc and Bôclæden. Ǽrest pǽron bûend þises landes Bryttâs; þâ cômon of Armorica, and gesǽton sûđanpearde Brytene ǽrest. Pâ gelamp hit þæt Pihtâs cômon sûđan of Sciđđian, mid langum scipum, nâ manegum; and þâ cômon ǽrest on norđ Ybernian up, and þâ cpǽdon þâ Scottâs, "Pê piton ôđer îgland hêr be eâstan, þǽr gê mâgon eardian, gif gê pillađ; and gif hpâ eôp piđstent, pê eôp fultumiađ." Pâ fêrdon þâ Pihtâs, and geſêrdon þis land norđanpeard.

Pâ gelamp hit ymbe geârâ ryne þæt Scottâ sum dǽl gepât of Ybernian on Brytene, and þæs landes sumne dǽl ge-côdon.

Sixtigum pintrum ǽr þam þe Crist pǽre âcenned, Gaius Iûlius se câsere ǽrest Rômânâ Brytenland gesôhte; and Bryttâs mid gefeohtê cnysede, and hî oferspîđde. Pâ flugon þâ Bryttâs tô þâm pudu-pêstenum, and se câsere ge-eôde pel manige heâh burh mid miclum gepinne, and eft gepât intô Galpalum.

A.D. 47. Hêr Claudius ôđer Rômânâ cyningâ Brytenland gesôhte, and þone mǽstan dǽl þæs îglandes on his gepeald onfêng. Pâ fêng Nero tô rîce æfter Claudie, se æt neâhstan forlêt Brytene îgland for his uncâfscipê.

A.D. 167. Hêr Eleutherius on Rôme onfêng bisceopdôme. Tô þam Lûcius Brytene cyning sende stafâs, and bæd fulpihtes; and hê him sôna sende; and þâ Bryttâs punôdon on rihtum geleâfan ôđ Dioclitiânes rîce.

A.D. 189. Sevêrus fêrde mid herê on Brytene, and mid gefeohtê geeôde þæs îglandes micelne dǽl; and þâ hê hine forgyrde mid dîcê and mid eorđpeallê fram sǽ tô sǽ. Hê rîcsôde seofontŷne geâr, and þâ geendôde on Eoferpîc.

A.D. 381. Hêr Gotan tôbrǽcon Rômeburh, and nǽfre siđđan Rômâne ne rîcsôdon on Brytene. Hî rîcsôdon on Brytene feôper hund pintrâ, and hund-seofontig pintrâ siđđan Gaius Iûlius þæt land ǽrest gesôhte.

A.D. 443. Hêr sendon Brytpalâs ofer sǽ tô Rôme, and heom fultumes bǽdon piđ Pihtâs; ac hî þǽr næfdon nânne, forþam þe Rômâne fyrdôdon piđ Ætlan Hunâ cyninge. And þâ sendon hî tô Anglum, and Angelcynnes æđelingâs þæs ilcan bǽdon.

A.D. 449. Hêr Hengest and Horsa fram Pyrtgeorne geladôde, Bryttâ cyninge, gesôhton Brytene Bryttum tô fultume. Hî cômon mid þrîm langum scipum. Se cyning geaf heom land on sûđan-eâstan þissum lande, piđ þam þe hî sceoldon feohtan piđ Pyhtâs. Hî þâ fuhton piđ Pyhtâs, and sige hæfdon spâ-hpǽr-spâ hî cômon. Hî þâ sendon to Angle, and hêton sendan heom mâre fultum; and þâ cômon þâ men of þrîm mǽgđum Germânie,—of Eald-Seaxum, of Anglum, of Iôtum.

Of Iôtum cômon Cantpare, and Pihtpare, and þæt cyn on Pest-Seaxum þe man nû git hêt Iôtenâ cyn. Of Eald-Seaxum cômon Eâst-Seaxe, Sûđ-Seaxe, and Pest-Seaxe. Of Angle, se â siđđan stôd pêste betpix Iôtum and Seaxum, cômon Eâst-Angle, Middel-Angle, Mearce, and ealle Norđhymbre.

Heorâ heretogan pǽron tpegen gebrôđru Hengest and Horsa, Pihtgilses sunâ; Pihtgils pæs Pitting, Pitta Pecting, Pecta Pôdening: fram þam Pôdne âpôc eal ûre cynecyn, and Sûđanhymbrâ eâc.

A.D. 455. Hêr Hengest and Horsa fuhton piđ Pyrtgeorne þam cyninge. Horsan man þǽr ofslôh; and æfter þam Hengest fêng tô rîce, and Æsc his sunu. Æfter þam Hengest and Æsc fuhton piđ Pealâs, and genâmon unârîmedlîcu herereâf; and þâ Pealâs flugon þâ Engle spâ fŷr.

A.D. 488. Hêr Æsc fêng tô rîce, and pæs feôper and tpêntig pintrâ Cantparâ cyning.

A.D. 495. Hêr cômon tpegen ealdormen on Brytene, Cerdîc and Cynrîc his sunu, mid fîf scipum, and on þam ilcan dæge fuhton piđ Pealâs.

A.D. 519. Hêr Cerdîc and Cynrîc Pest-Seaxenâ rîce onfêngon, and siđđan rîcsôdon Pest-Seaxenâ cynebearn of þam dæge. Æfter þam hî gefuhton piđ Bryttâs, and genâmon Pihte îgland.

A.D. 534. Hêr Cerdîc forđfêrde, and Cynrîc his sunu fêng tô rîce, and rîcsôde forđ six and tpêntig pintrâ.

A.D. 538. Hêr sunne âþŷstrôde feôpertŷne dagum ǽr calende Martii fram ǽrmorgene ôđ undern.

A.D. 540. Hêr sunne âþŷstrôde on tpelftan calendes Iûlii, and steorran hî æteôpdon fulneâh healfe tîd ofer undern.

A.D. 560. Hêr Ceâplîn rîce onfêng on Pest-Seaxum.

A.D. 565. Hêr Columba mæsse-preôst côm tô Pyhtum, and hî gecyrde tô Cristes geleâfan. Hî sind pærterâs be norđum môrum, and heorâ cyning him gesealde þæt îgland þe man Iî nemneđ. Pǽr se Columba getimbrôde mynster. Pâ stôpe habbađ nû git his yrfe-peardâs. Sûđ-Pyhtâs pǽron miclê ǽr gefullôde; heom bodôde fulpiht Ninna bisceop, se pæs on Rôme gelǽred, þæs cyrice is æt Hpîterne.

A.D. 596. Hêr Grêgorius pâpa sende tô Brytene Augustînum mid pel manegum munucum, þe Godes pord Englâ þeôde godspellôdon.

A.D. 601. Hêr sende Grêgorius pel manige godcunde lâreôpâs Augustîne tô fultume, and betpeônum þâm pæs Paulînus. Paulînus bisceop gehpyrfde tô Criste Eâdpine Norđhymbrâ cyning.

A.D. 604. Hêr Eâst-Seaxe onfêngon geleâfan and fulpihtes bæđ under Mellite bisceope, and Sǽbrihte cyninge, þone Æđelberht Cantparâ cyning gesette þǽr tô cyninge.

A.D. 606. Hêr forđfêrde Grêgorius pâpa, and hêr Æđelfriđ lǽdde his ferde tô Legaceastre, and þǽr ofslôh unrîm Palenâ; and spâ peard gefylled Augustînes pîtegung þe hê cpæđ, Gif Pealâs nellađ sibbe piđ ûs, hî sculon æt Seaxenâ handâ forpurđan. Pǽr man slôh eâc tpâ hund preôstâ, þâ cômon þider þæt hî sceoldon gebiddan for Palenâ here.

A.D. 611. Hêr Cynegils fêng tô rîce on Ƿest-Seaxum, and heôld ân and þrittig ƿintrâ, and hê ǣrest Ƿest-Seaxenâ cyningâ ƿæs gefullôd. Byrînus bodôde ǣrest Ƿest-Seaxum fulƿiht. Hê côm þider be Honôries ƿordum þæs pâpan, and hê þǣr ƿæs bisceop ôđ his lîfes ende.

A.D. 635. Hêr Cynegils ƿæs gefullôd from Byrîne in Dorceceastre.

A.D. 642. Hêr Cênƿealh, Cynegilses sunu, fêng tô Ƿest-Seaxenâ rîce, and heôld ân and þrittig ƿintrâ.

A.D. 645. Hêr Cênƿealh cyning ƿæs âdrifen of his rîce fram Pendan cyninge, forþam hê his sƿeostor forlêt; and hê ƿæs on Eâst-Anglum þreô geâr on ƿræce.

A.D. 646. Hêr Cênƿealh ƿæs gefullôd.

A.D. 658. Hêr Cênƿealh gefeaht ƿiđ Ƿealâs, and hî geflŷmde ôđ Pedridan.

A.D. 664. Hêr sunne âþŷstrôde on þam forman Þrîmilces, and côm micel mancƿealm on Brytene îgland, and on þam cƿealme forđfêrde Tuda bisceop; and Earcenbriht Cantƿarâ cyning forđfêrde, and Colman mid his gefêrum fôr tô his cŷđđe; and se arcebisceop Deusdedit forđfêrde.

A.D. 672. Hêr forđfêrde Cênƿealh, and Seaxburh his cƿên rîcsôde ân geâr æfter him.

A.D. 674. Hêr fêng Æscƿine tô rîce on Ƿest-Seaxum. Hê ƿæs Cênfûsing; Cênfûs Cênferđing; Cênferđ Cûđgilsing; Cûđgils Ceôlƿulfing; Ceôlƿulf Cynrîcing.

A.D. 676. Æscƿine forđfêrde and Centƿine fêng tô rîce, se ƿæs Cynegilsing. Hê geflŷmde Brytƿealâs ôđ sǣ and rîcsôde nigon geâr.

A.D. 678. Hêr ætŷƿde se steorra þe man clypâđ comêtan, and scân þrî mônđâs ælcê morgenê sƿilce sunnebeâm.

A.D. 685. Hêr Ceadpalla ongan æfter rîce pinnan. Se Ceadpalla pæs Cênbryhting; Cênbryht Ceadding; Ceadda Cûđing; Cûđa Ceâplîning; Ceâplîn Cynrîcing. Mûl pæs Ceadpallan brôđer. Pŷ ilcan geârê peard on Brytene blôdig rên, and meolc and butere purdon gepended tô blôde.

A.D. 686. Hêr Mûl and Ceadpalla Cent and Piht forhergôdon.

A.D. 687. Hêr Mûl peard on Cent forbærned, and þŷ geârê Ceadpalla eft forhergôde Cent.

A.D. 688. Hêr fôr Ceadpalla tô Rôme, and fulpiht onfêng æt Sergie þam pâpan, and se pâpa hine hêt Petrus, and hê siđđan ymbe seofon niht forđfêrde under Cristes clâđum, and þŷ ilcan geârû Ine fêng tô Pest-Seaxenâ rîce.

A.D. 693. Cantpare geþingôdon piđ Ine, and him gescaldon þrittig þûsend sceattâ tô cynebôte, forþam þe hî Mûl his brôđer forbærndon. Ine getimbrôde þæt mynster æt Glæstingabyrig, and hê rîcsôde seofon and þrittig pintrâ, and siđđan hê fêrde tô Rôme, and þǣr punôde ôđ his ende-dæg.

A.D. 726. Hêr Æđelheard fêng to Pest-Seaxenâ rîce, Ines mǣg; and heôld feôpertŷne geâr.

A.D. 729. Hêr comêta se steorra hine ætŷpde, and se hâlga Ecgbyrht forđfêrde.

A.D. 733. Hêr sunne aþŷstrôde, and peard eall þǣre sunnan trendel spilce speart scild; and Acca pæs âdrifen of bisceopdôm.

A.D. 734. Hêr pæs se môna spilce hê pǣre mid blôdê begoten, and forđfêrde Tâtpine arcebisceop, and eâc Bêda.

A.D. 740. Hêr forđfêrde Æđelheard cyning, and fêng Cûđrêd his mǣg tô Pest-Seaxenâ rîce, and heôld sixtŷne pintrâ, and heardlîce hê gepan piđ Æđelbald, Mearcenâ cyning, and piđ Pealâs.

A.D. 744. Hêr steorran fôron spîđe scotiende, and Pilfriđ se geonga, se pæs bisceop on Eoforpîc, forđfêrde.

A.D. 754. Cûđrêd forđfêrde, and Sigebriht his mǽg fêng tô Ƿest-Seaxenâ rîce, and heôld ân geâr; and Cyneƿulf and Ƿest-Seaxenâ ƿitan benâmon Sigebriht his mǽg his rîces for unrihtum dǽdum. And se Cyneƿulf oft mid miclum gefeohtum feaht ƿiđ Brytƿealâs.

And ymb ân and þrittig ƿintrâ þæs þe hê rîce hæfde, hê ƿolde âdrǽfan ût ânne æđeling, se ƿæs Cyneheard hâten, and ƿæs Sigebrihtes brôđer. Þâ geâhsôde hê þone cyning lytlê ƿerodê on ƿîf-cŷđđe on Merantûne, and hine þǽr berâd, and þone bûr ûtan beeôdon, ǽr hine þâ men onfundon, þe mid þam cyninge ƿǽron. Þâ ongeat se cyning þæt, and hê on þâ duru eôde, and þâ unheânlîce hine ƿerôde, ôđ hê on þone æđeling lôcôde; and þâ ûtrǽsde on hine, and hine miclum geƿundôde. And hî ealle on þone cyning feohtende ƿǽron ôđ þæt hî hine ofslægenne hæfdon.

Þâ on þæs ƿîfes gebǽrum onfundon þæs cyninges þegnâs þâ unstilnesse, and þider urnon, spâ-hƿilc-spâ þonne gearo ƿearđ hrađôst. And heorâ se æđeling ǽghƿilcum feorh and feoh beâd; and heorâ nǽnig þicgan nolde, ac hî simle feohtende ƿǽron, ôđ hî ealle lǽgon bûtan ânum Brytiscum gîsle, and hê sƿîđe geƿundôd ƿæs.

Þâ on morgene gehŷrdon þæt þæs cyninges þegnâs þe him beæftan ƿǽron, þæt se cyning ofslægen ƿæs, þâ ridon hî þider, and his ealdorman Osrîc and Ƿîgferđ his þegn; and þone æđeling on þǽre byrig mêtton. And beâd hê heom heorâ âgenne dôm feôs and landes, gif hî him þæs rîces ûđon; and heom cŷđde, þæt heorâ mǽgâs him mid ƿǽron, þâ þe him fram noldon. And þâ cƿǽdon hî, þæt heom nǽnig mǽg leôfra nǽre þonne heorâ hlâford, and hî nǽfre his banan folgian noldon.

And hî þâ ymb þâ geatu feohtende ƿǽron, ôđ þæt hî þǽr inne fulgon, and þone æđeling ofslôgon, and þâ men þe mid him ƿǽron, ealle bûtan ânum.

Se Cyneƿulf rîcsôde ân and þrittig ƿintrâ, and his lîc ligeđ on Ƿintanceastre, and þæs æđelinges on Axanminstre.

A.D. 757. Hêr Eâdberht Norđhymbrâ cyning fêng tô scære.

A.D. 761. Hêr ƿæs se micela ƿinter.

A.D. 773. Hêr ôđŷƿde reâd Cristes mǽl on heofenum æfter sunnan setlgange, and ƿundorlîce nædran ƿǽron gesepene on Sûđ-Seaxenâ lande.

A.D. 784. Hêr onfêng Beorhtrîc Pest-Seaxenâ rîce, and hê rîcsôde sixtŷne geâr: and on his dagum cômon ǽrest scipu Nordmannâ of Heredalande.

A.D. 785. Hêr pæs geflîtfullîc synod.

A.D. 793. Hêr pǽron rêde forebêcna cumene,—þæt pǽron ormete þodenâs and lîgræscâs, and fŷrene dracan pǽron gesepene on þam lyfte fleôgende. Pâm tâcnum sôna fyligde micel hunger, and earmlîce hǽdenrâ mannâ hergung âdiligôde Godes cyrican in Lindisfarena-eâ þurh reâflâc and manslilit.

A.D. 800. Hêr pæs se môna âþŷstrôd on þǽre ôdre tîde on nihte on þone seofonteôdan calendes Februâries; and Beorhtrîc cyning fordfêrde, and Ecgbryht fêng tô Pest-Seaxenâ rîce.

Hine hæfde ǽr Offa Mearcenâ cyning and Beorhtrîc Pest-Seaxenâ cyning ût âflŷmed þrî geâr of Angelcynnes lande on Francland, ǽr hê cyning pǽre; and for þŷ fultumôde Beorhtrîc Offan, þŷ þe hê hæfde his dôhtor him tô cpêne.

A.D. 823. Hêr Ecgbryht and Beornpulf Mearcenâ cyning fuhton on Ellendûne, and Ecgbriht sige nâm. Pâ sende hê Ædelpulf his sunu of þǽre fyrde and Ealhstân his bisceop and Pulfheard his ealdorman tô Cent miclê perodê, and hî Baldred þone cyning nord ofer Temese âdrifon; and Cantpare heom tô cyrdon, and Sûdrige, and Sûd-Seaxe, and Eâst-Seaxe; and þŷ ilcan geârê Eâst-Englâ cyning and seô þeôd gesôhton Ecgbriht cyning heom tô fride and tô mundboran for Mearcenâ ege.

A.D. 827. Hêr geeôde Ecgbriht cyning Mearcenâ rîce, and eal þæt be sûdan Humbre pæs; and hê pæs se eahtoda cyning þe Brytenpealda pæs. Ǽrest pæs Ælle þe þus micel rîce hæfde; se æftera pæs Ceâplîn, Pest-Seaxenâ cyning; se þridda pæs Ædelbriht, Cantparâ cyning; se feorda pæs Rǽdpald, Eâst-Englâ cyning; se fîfta pæs Eâdpine, Nordanhymbrâ cyning; sixta pæs Ospald, þe æfter him rîcsôde; seofoda pæs Ospio, Ospaldes brôder; eahtoda pæs Ecgbriht.

A.D. 837. Hêr Ecgbriht cyning fordfêrde, and fêng Ædelpulf Ecgbrihting tô Pest-Seaxenâ rîce. On his dagum cômon þâ Deniscan on Brytene. And se cyning and his ealdormen mid

Dorsǽtum and mid Somersǽtum gefuhton piđ hǽđenne here geond stôpâ; and þǽr peard manig man ofslægen on gehpæđere hand.

A.D. 853. Hêr sende Æđelpulf cyning Ælfrêd his sunu tô Rôme. Þâ pæs domne Leo pâpa on Rôme, and hê hine tô cyninge gehâlgôde, and hine him tô bisceop-sunâ genam.

A.D. 855. Hêr gebôcôde Æđelpulf cyning teôđan dǽl his landes ofer eal his rîce, Gode tô lofe and him selfum tô êcere hǽle; and þŷ ilcan geârê fêrde tô Rôme, and þǽr pæs tpelf-mônađ puniende; and þâ hê hâmpeard fôr: and him þâ Carl, Francenâ cyning, his dôhtor geaf him tô cpêne. Seô pæs gehâten Ieoþete. Æfter þam hê gesund hâm côm, and ymb tpâ geâr þæs þe hê of Francum côm, hê gefôr. Hê rîcsôde nigonteôđe healf geâr. Þâ fêng Æđelbald his sunu to Pest-Seaxenâ rîce, and rîcsôde fîf geâr.

A.D. 860. Hêr Æđelbald forđfêrde, and fêng Æđelbriht to eallum þam rîce, his brôđor; and hê hit heôld on gôdre geþpǽrnesse fîf geâr.

A.D. 866. Hêr fêng Æđerêd Æđelbrihtes brôđer to Pest-Seaxenâ rîce, and þŷ ilcan geârê côm micel hǽđen here on Angelcynnes land, and þæt land eal geeôdon, and fordidon ealle þâ mynstre þâ hî tô cômon. And gefeaht Æđerêd and Ælfrêd his brôđer piđ þone here geond stôpâ, and þǽr pæs micel pælsliht on gehpæđre hand.

A.D. 872. Hêr gefôr Æđerêd cyning. Þâ fêng Ælfrêd Æđelpulfing his brôđor to Pest-Seaxenâ rîce; and þæs ymb ânne mônađ gefeaht Ælfrêd cyning piđ ealne þone hǽđenne here lytlê perodê æt Piltûne, and hine lange on dæg geflŷmde; and þâ Deniscan âhton pælstôpe gepeald. And þæs geâres purdon nigon folc-gefeoht gefohten piđ þone here on þŷ cynerîce be sûđan Temese, bûtan þam þe heom Ælfrêd þæs cyninges brôđer, and ânlîpige ealdormen, and cyninges þegnâs oft râdâ onridon, þe man nâ ne rîmde.

A.D. 878. Hêr hine bestæl se here on midne pinter ofer tpelftan niht tô Cippanhâmme, and geridon Pest-Seaxenâ land, and þǽr gesǽton, and micel þæs folces ofer sǽ âdrǽfdon; and þæs ôðres þone mǽstan dǽl hî geridon and heom gecyrdon bûtan þam cyninge Ælfrêde. Hê lytlê perodê uneâðelîce æfter pudum fôr, and on môrfæstenum. And þæs ilcan pintres pæs se gûðfana genumen þe hî Hræfn hêton.

And þæs on Eâstran porhte Ælfrêd cyning lytlê perodê gepeorc æt Æðelingâ îge, and of þam gepeorce pæs pinnende pið þone here. Pâ on þǽre seofoðan pucan ofer Eâstran hê gerâd tô Ecgbrihtes stâne be eâstan Sealpudâ, and him cômon þǽr ongeân Sumorsǽte ealle and Ƿilsǽte and Hâmtûnscîr, se dǽl þe hire beheonan sǽ pæs; and his gefægene pǽron.

And hê fôr ymb âne niht of þâm pîcum to Igleâ, and þæs ymb âne niht to Eðandûne, and þǽr gefeaht pið ealne þone here, and hine geflŷmde, and him æfter râd ôð þæt gepeorc, and þǽr sæt feôpertŷne niht; and þâ sealde se here him gîslâs and micle âðâs, þæt hî of his cynerîce poldon; and him eâc gehêton þæt heorâ cyning fulpihte onfôn polde.

And hî þæt gelǽston; and þæs ymb þrî pucan côm se cyning Guðrum þrîtigâ sum þarâ mannâ þe on þam here peorðôste pǽron, æt Alre, þæt is pið Æðelingâ îge. And his Ælfrêd cyning onfêng þǽr æt fulpihte, and his crismlŷsing pæs æt Ƿedmôr; and hê pæs tpelf niht mid þam cyninge, and hê hine miclum and his gefêran mid feô peorðôde.

A.D. 885. Hêr forðfêrde se gôda pâpa Marînus, se gefreôde Angelcynnes scôle be Ælfrêdes bêne, Ƿest-Seaxenâ cyninges, and hê sende him micle gifâ, and þǽre rôde dǽl þe Crist on þrôpôde, and þŷ ilcan geârê se here bræc frið pið Ælfrêd cyning.

A.D. 897. Pâ hêt Ælfrêd cyning timbrian lange scipu ongeân þâs æscâs, þâ pǽron fulneâh tpâ spâ lange spâ þâ ôðre; sume hæfdon sixtig ârâ, sume mâ; þâ pǽron ǽgðer ge spiftran ge unpealtran, ge eâc heâhran þonne þâ ôðre. Nǽron hî nâðor nê on Frysisc gesceapene nê on Denisc, bûtan spâ him selfum þuhte þæt hî nytpeorðôste beôn mihton. Pŷ ilcan sumerâ forpearð nâ læs þonne tpêntig scipâ mid mannum mid eallê be þam sûðriman.

A.D. 901. Hêr gefôr Ælfrêd Æðulfing six nihtum ǽr ealrâ hâligrâ mæssan. Hê pæs cyning ofer eal Angelcyn bûtan þam dǽle þe under Denâ anpealde pæs. And þâ fêng Eâdpeard his sunu tô þam rîce. On his dagum bræc se here þone friđ, and forsâpon ælc riht þe Eâdpeard cyning and his pitan heom budon; and se cyning heom piđ feaht, and hî geflŷmde, and heorâ fela þûsendâ ofslôh; and hê geporhte, and getimbrôde, and genipôde fela burgâ þe hî hæfdon æ̂r tôbrocen.

A.D. 925. Hêr Eâdpeard cyning forđfêrde, and Ælfpeard his sunu spîđe hrađe. þæs, and heorâ lîc licgađ on Ƿintanceastre. And Æđelstân pæs of Mearcum gecoren tô cyninge, and hê fêng tô Norđanhymbrâ rîce, and ealle þâ cyningâs þe on þisum îglande pæ̂ron hê gepylde. Hê rîcsôde feôpertŷne geâr and tŷn pucan, and forđfêrde on Gleâpeceastre. Þâ Eâdmund his brôđer fêng tô rîce, and hê hæfde rîce seofođe healf geâr, and Liofa hine ofstang æt Puclancyrcan. Þâ æfter him fêng Eâdrêd æđeling his brôđer tô rîce. Eâdrêd rîcsôde teôđe healf geâr, and þâ fêng Eâdpîg to Ƿest-Seaxenâ rîce, Eâdmundes sunu cyninges.

A.D. 959. Hêr forđfêrde Eâdpîg cyning, and Eâdgâr his brôđer fêng tô rîce; and hê genam Ælfþryđe him tô cpêne. Heô pæs Ordgâres dôhtor ealdormannes.

A.D. 975. Hêr geendôde eorđan dreâmâs
Eâdgâr Englâ cyning,—ceâs him ôđer leôht.

And hêr Eâdpeard, Eâdgâres sunu, fêng tô rîce, and on hærfeste æteôpde comêta se steorra, and côm þâ ôn þam æftran geâre spîđe micel hunger. And þâ (A.D. 978) peard Eâdpeard cyning ofslægen on æ̂fentîde æt Corfes-geate. Ne peard Angelcynne nân pyrse dæ̂d gedôn þonne þeôs pæs. Æđelrêd æđeling Eâdpeardes brôđer fêng tô þam rîce.

A.D. 991. Hêr man geræ̂dde þæt man geald æ̂rest gafol Deniscum mannum for þam micelan brôgan þe hî porhton be þam sæ̂riman; þæt pæs æ̂rest tŷn þûsend pundâ. Þone ræ̂d geræ̂dde æ̂rest Sigerîc arcebisceop.

A.D. 994. Hêr côm Anlâf and Spegen mid feôper and hundnigontigum scipum; and hî porhton þæt mæ̂ste yfel þe æ̂fre æ̂nig here dôn mihte on bærnete and hergunge, and on manslihtum, æ̂gđer be þam sæ̂riman on Eâst-Seaxum, and on Centlande, and on Sûđ-Seaxum, and on Hâmtûnscîre. Þâ peard hit spâ micel ege fram þam here, þæt man ne mihte geþencan and ne âsmeâgan hû man hî of earde âdrîfan sceolde, ođđe þisne eard piđ hî gehealdan. Æt nŷhstan næs nân heâfodman þæt fyrde gaderian polde; ac ælc fleâh spâ hê mǽst mihte, nê furđon nân scîr nolde ôđre gelǽstan. Þonne nam man friđ and griđ piđ hî, and nâ þê læs for eallum þissum griđe and gafole, hî fêrdon ǽghpider flocmǽlum, and gehergôdon ûre earme folc, and hî rŷpton and slôgon. Ealle þâs ungesǽlđâ ûs gelumpon þurh unrǽdâs. Æđelrêd pende ofer þâ sǽ tô Rîcarde, his cpêne brêđer.

A.D. 1014. Hêr Spegen geendôde his dagâs, and se flota þâ eal gecuron Cnût tô cyninge. Þâ côm Æđelrêd cyning hâm tô his âgenre þeôde, and hê glædlîce from him eallum onfangen pæs. Þâ (A.D. 1016) gelamp hit þæt se cyning Æđelrêd forđfêrde, and ealle þâ pitan þe on Lundene pǽron, and seô burhparu gecuron Eâdmund Æđelrêding tô cyninge.

And Eâdmund and Cnût cômon tôgædre æt Olanîge, and heorâ freôndscipe þǽr gefæstnôdon and purdon pedbrôđru. And þâ fêng Eâdmund cyning tô Þestsexan and Cnût tô þam norđ-dǽle. Þâ forđfêrde Eâdmund cyning, and pæs byrged mid his ealdan fæder Eâdgâre on Glæstingabyrig; and Cnût fêng tô eal Angelcynnes rîce.

A.D. 1028. Hêr fôr Cnût cyning tô Norđpegum of Englâlande mid fîftigum scipum Engliscrâ þegenâ, and âdrâf Ôlâf cyning of þam lande, and geâhnôde him eal þæt land. And (A.D. 1031) Scottâ cyning him tô beâh, Mælcolm, and pearđ his man.

A.D. 1035. Hêr forđfêrde Cnût cyning æt Sceaftesbyrig, and hê is bebyrged on Þintanceastre. And Harold sǽde þæt hê Cnûtes sunu pǽre, and man ceâs Harold ofer eal tô cyninge. Hê forđfêrde on Oxnâforde, and man sende æfter Harđacnût, and hê pæs cyning ofer eal Englâland tpâ geâr bûtan tŷne nihtum, and ǽr þam þe hê bebyrged pǽre, eal folc geceâs þâ Eâdpeard Æđelrêding tô cyninge.

A.D. 1052. Hêr âlêde Eâdpeard cyning þæt heregyld þæt Æđelrêd cyning ǽr astealde; þæt pæs on þam nigon and þrittigôđan geare þæs þe hê hit ongunnen hæfde. Þæt gyld gedrehte ealle Englâ þeôde on spâ langum fyrste spâ hit bufan âpriten is. Þæt pæs ǽfre ætforan ôđrum gyldum þe man myslîce geald, and men mid manigfealdlîce drehte.

A.D. 1066. Hêr côm Ƿillelm eorl of Normandige intô Pefenasǣ, and Harold cyning gaderôde þâ micelne here, and côm him tôgeânes; and Ƿillelm him côm ongeân on unƿær ǣr his folc gefylced ƿǣre. Ac se cyning þeâh him sƿîðe heardlîce ƿið feaht mid þâm mannum þe him gelǣstan ƿoldon, and þǣr ƿearð micel ƿæl geslægen on ǣgðre healfe. Þǣr ƿearð ofslægen Harold cyning, and þâ Frenciscan âhton ƿælstôƿe geƿeald. Þâ Ƿillelm cyning âhte ǣgðer ge Englâland ge Normandige. Æfter þisum hæfde se cyning micel geþeaht and sƿîðe deôpe sprǣce ƿið his ƿitan ymbe þis land. Hê sende þâ ofer eal Englâland intô ælcere scîre his men, and lêt âgan ût hû fela hundredâ hîdâ ƿǣron innan þam lande, oððe hƿæt se cyning him sylfum hæfde landes and yrfes innan þam lande, oððe hƿilce hê âhte tô habbanne tô tƿelf mônðum of þǣre scîre; and hƿæt oððe hû micel ælce man hæfde þe landsittende ƿæs innan Englâlande on lande oððe on yrfe, and hû micel feôs hit ƿǣre ƿeorð: næs ân ǣlpig hîd nê ân gyrd landes, nê furðon (hit is sceamu tô tellanne, ac hit ne þuhte him nân sceamu tô dônne) ân oxa, nê ân cû, nê ân sƿîn næs belifen, þæt næs geset on his geƿrite.

A.D. 1087. Hêr Ƿillelm forðfêrde. Se þe ƿæs ǣr rîce cyning and maniges landes hlâford, hê næfde þâ ealles landes bûtan seofon fôtâ mǣl. Hê lǣfde æfter him þreô sunan. Rodbeard hêt se yldesta, se ƿæs eorl on Normandige æfter him. Se ôðer hêt Ƿillelm, þe bær æfter him on Englâland þone cynehelm. Se þridda hêt Heânrîc. Se cyning Ƿillelm ƿæs sƿîðe ƿîs man, and sƿîðe rîce, and ƿeorðful and strenge; man mihte faran ofer his rîce mid his bôsme fullum goldes, ungedered. Hê sette micel deôrfrið, and legde lagâ þǣrƿið þæt sƿâ-hƿâ-sƿâ slôge heort oððe hinde, þæt hine man sceolde blendian. Hê forbeâd þâ heortâs; sƿilce eâc þâ bârâs; sƿâ sƿîðe hê lufôde þâ heâhdeôr, sƿilce hê·ƿǣre heorâ fæder. Eâc hê sette be þâm haran þæt hî môston freô faran. His rîce men hit mǣndon, and þâ earme men hit beceorôdon. Ac hê ƿæs sƿâ stîð þæt hê ne rôhte heorâ ealrâ nîð.

CONVERSION OF THE ANGLO-SAXONS.

GREGORY.

1. Grêgorius se hâlga pâpa is rihtlîce Engliscre þeôde apostol. Pes eâdiga pâpa Grêgorius pæs of æðelborenre mǣgðe and ǣpfæstre âcenned; Rômânisce pitan pǣron his magâs; his fæder hâtte Gordiânus, and Fêlix, se ǣpfæsta pâpa, pæs his fîfta fæder. Grêgorius is Grêcisc nama, se spêigð on Ledenum gereorde "Vigilantius," þæt is on Englisc, "Ƿacolre." Hê pæs spîðe pacol on Godes bebodum, þâþâ hê sylf herigendlîce leofôde, and hê pacollîce ymbe manegrâ þeôdâ þearfe hogôde. Hê pæs fram cildhâde on bôclîcum lârum getŷd, and hê on þǣre lâre spâ gesǣliglîce þeâh, þæt on ealre Rômânâ-byrig næs nân his gelîca geþuht. Hê gecneordlǣhte æfter wîsrâ lâreôpâ gebisnungum, and næs forgytol, ac gefæstnôde his lâre on fæsthafelum gemynde. Hê hlôd þâ mid þurstigum breôste þâ flôpendan lâre, þe hê eft æfter fyrste mid hunig-spêtre þrotan þæslîce bealcette.

2. On geonglîcum gêarum, þâþâ his geôgoð æfter gecynde poruld-þing lufian sceolde, þâ ongan hê hine sylfne tô Gode geþeôdan, and tô êðele þæs uplîcan lîfes mid eallum gepilnungum orðian. Ƿitodlîce æfter his fæder forðsîðe seofon mynstru hê gelênde mid his âgenum. Pone ofer-eâcan his ǣhtâ hê âspende on Godes þearfum. Hê eôde ǣr his gecyrrednysse geond Rômânâburh mid pællenum gyrlum, and scînendum gymmum, and reâdum golde gefrætepôd; ac æfter his gecyrrednysse hê þênôde Godes þearfum, hê sylf þearfa, mid pâcum pǣfelse befangen. Hê lufôde forhæfednysse on mettum, and on drence, and pæccan on syndrigum gebedum; þǣr-tô-eâcan he þrôpôde singallîce untrumnyssâ.

3. Pâ gelamp hit æt sumum sǣle, spâ spâ gŷt for oft dêð, þæt Englisce cŷpmen brohton heorâ pare tô Rômânâ-byrig, and Grêgorius eôde be þǣre strǣt tô þâm Engliscum, heorâ þing sceâpigende. Pâ geseah hê betpux þâm parum cŷpecnihtâs gesette, þâ pǣron hpîtes lîchaman and fægeres andplitan men, and æðellîce gefexôde. Grêgorius þâ beheôld þǣrâ cnapenâ plite, and be-

fran of hpilcere þeôde hî gebrohte pǽron. Pâ sǽde him man þæt hî of Englâ-lande pǽron, and þæt þǽre þeôde mennisc spâ plitig pǽre. Eft þâ Grêgorius befran hpæđer þæs landes folc Cristen pǽre þe hǽđen. Him man sǽde þæt hî hǽđene pǽron. Grêgorius þâ of inpeardre heortan langsume siccetunge teâh, and cpæđ, "Pâlâpâ, þæt spâ fægeres hipes men sindon þam speartan deôfle underþeôdde." Eft hê âxôde, hû þǽre þeôde nama pǽre, þe hî of-cômon. Him pæs geandpyrd, þæt hî Angle genemnôde pǽron. Pâ cpæđ hê, "Rihtlîce hî sind Angle gehâtene, forþan þe hî englâ plite habbađ, and spilcum gedafenađ þæt hî on heofonum englâ gefêran beôn." Gyt þâ Grêgorius befran, hû þǽre scîre nama pǽre, þe þâ cnapan of-âlǽdde pǽron. Him man sæde, þæt þâ scîrmen pǽron Dêre gehâtene. Grêgorius andpyrde, "Pel hî sind Dêre gehâtene, forþan þe hî sind fram graman generôde, and tô Cristes mildheortnysse gecŷgede." Gyt þâ hê befran, "Hû is þǽre leôde cyning gehâten?" Him pæs geandsparôd þæt se cyning Ælle gehâten pǽre. Hpæt þâ Grêgorius gamenôde mid his pordum tô þam naman, and cpæđ, "Hit gedafenađ þæt Allelûia sŷ gesungen on þam lande tô lofe þæs Ælmihtigan Scyppendes."

4. Grêgorius þâ sôna eôde tô þam pâpan þæs apostolican setles, and hine bæd, þæt hê Angelcynne sume lâreôpâs âsende, þe hî tô Criste gebîgdon, and cpæđ, þæt hê sylf gearo pǽre þæt peorc tô gefremmenne mid Godes fultume, gif hit þam pâpan spâ gelîcôde. Pâ ne mihte se pâpa þæt geþafian, þeâh þe hê eal polde; forþan þe þâ Rômâniscan ceaster-geparan noldon geþafian þæt spâ getogen man, and spâ geþungen lâreôp þâ burh eallunge forlête, and spâ fyrlen præcsîđ genâme.

5. Æfter þisum gelamp þæt micel man-cpealm becom ofer þǽre Rômâniscan leôde, and ǽrest þone pâpan Pelagium gestôd, and bûton yldinge âdŷdde. Pitôdlîce æfter þæs pâpan geendunge, spâ micel cpealm peađ þæs folces, þæt gehpǽr stôdon âpêste hûs geond þâ burh, bûton bûgigendum. Pâ ne mihte spâþeâh seô Rômânâ-burh bûton pâpan punian, ac eal folc þone eâdigan Grêgorium tô þǽre geþincđe ânmôdlîce geceâs, þeâh þe hê mid eallum mægne piđerigende pǽre. Hpæt þâ Grêgorius, siđđan hê pâpanhâd underfêng, gemunde hpæt hê gefyrn Angelcynne gemynte, and þǽr-rihte þæt luftŷme peorc gefremôde. Hê nâ tô þæs hpon ne mihte þone Rômâniscan biscop-stôl eallunge forlǽtan, ac hê âsende ôđre bydelâs, geþungene Godes þeôpan, tô þisum îglande, and hê sylf miclum mid his bênum and tihtingum fylste, þæt þǽrâ bydelâ bodung forđgênge, and Gode pæstm-

bǣre purde. Pǣrâ bydelâ naman sind þus gecîgede, Augustînus, Mellitus, Laurentius, Petrus, Johannes, Justus. Augustînus þâ mid his gefêrum, þæt sind gerehte feôpertig perâ, fêrde be Grêgories hǣse, ôð þæt hî to þisum îglande gesundfullîce becômon.

6. On þâm dagum rîxôde Æðelbyrht cyning on Cantparebyrig rîclîce, and his rîce pæs âstreht fram þǣre miclan eâ Humbre ôð sûð sǣ. Augustînus hæfde genumen pealhstôdâs of Francenâ rîce, spâ spâ Grêgorius him gebeâd; and hê þurh þǣrâ pealhstôdâ mûð þam cyninge and his leôde Godes pord bodôde: hû se mildheorta Hǣlend mid his âgenre þrôpunge þisne scyldigan middaneard âlŷsde, and geleâffullum mannum heofonan rîces infǣr geopenôde. Pâ andpyrde se cyning Æðelbriht Augustîne, and cpæð, þæt hê fægere pord and behât him cŷdde; and cpæð, þæt hê ne mihte spâ hrædlîce þone ealdan gepunan þe hê mid Angel-cynne heôld forlǣtan; cpæð þæt hê môste freôlîce þâ heofonlîcan lâre his leôde bodian, and þæt hê him and his gefêran bîgleofan þênian polde, and forgeaf him þâ pununge on Cantparebyrig, seô pæs ealles his rîces heâfod-burh.

7. Ongan þâ Augustînus mid his munucum tô geefenlǣcenne þǣrâ apostolâ lîf, mid singalum gebedum, and pæccan, and fæstenum Gode þeôpigende, and lîfes pord þâm þe hî mihton bodigende, ealle middaneardlîce þing, spâ spâ ælfremede, forhogigende, þâ þing âna þe hî tô bîgleofan behôfedon underfônde, be þâm þe hî tǣhton selfe lybbende, and for þǣre sôðfæstnesse þe hî bodôdon, gearope pǣron êhtnesse tô þoligenne, and deâðê speltan, gif hî þorfton.

8. Hpæt þâ gelŷfdon forpel manige, and on Godes naman gefullôde purdon, pundrigende þǣre bilepitnesse heorâ unscæððigan lîfes, and spêtnesse heorâ heofonlîcan lâre. Pâ æt nextan, gelustfullôde þam cyninge Æðelbrihte heorâ clǣne lîf and heorâ pynsume behât, þâ sôðlîce purdon mid manegum tâcnum gesêðde; and hê þâ gelŷfende pearð gefullôd, and miclum þâ cristenan geârpurðôde, and spâ spâ heofonlîce ceastergeparan lufôde; nolde spâ-þeâh nǣnne tô cristendôme geneâdian; forþan þe hê ofâxôde æt þâm lâreôpum his hǣle þæt Cristes þeôpdôm ne sceal beôn geneâdôd, ac selfpilles. Ongunnon þâ dæghpamlîce forpel manige êfstan tô gehŷrenne þâ hâlgan bodunge, and forlêton heorâ hǣðenscipe and hî selfe geþeôddon Cristes gelaðunge, on hine gelŷfende.

9. Hpæt þâ Grêgorius miclum Gode þancôde mid blissigen-

dum môde, þæt Angel-cynne spâ gelumpen pæs, spâ spâ hê self geornlîce gepilnôde, and sende eft ongeân ǽrendracan tô þam geleâffullan cyninge Æđelbrihte, mid gepritum and manigfealdum lâcum, and ôđre gepritu tô Augustîne, mid andsparum ealrâ þǽrâ þingâ þe hê hine befran, and hine eâc þisum pordum mânôde: "Brôđer mîn se leôfôsta, ic pât þæt se Ælmihtiga God fela pundrâ þurh þê þǽre þeôde þe hê geceâs gesputelađ, þæs þû miht blissigan, and eâc þê ondrædan. Þû miht blissigan gepislîce þæt þǽre þeôde sâplâ þurh þâ yttran pundra beôđ getogene tô þǽre incundan gife. Ondrǽd þê spâ-þeâh þæt þîn môd ne beô âhafen mid dyrstignesse on þâm tâcnum þe God þurh þê gefremâđ, and þû þonon on îdelum puldre befealle piđinnan, þonon þe þû piđûtan on purđmynte âhafen bist."

10. Grêgorius âsende eâc Augustîne hâlige lâc on mæsse-reâfum, and on bôcum, and þǽrâ apostolâ and martyrâ *reliquias* samod; and bebeâd þæt his æftergengan symle þone *pallium* and þone ercehâd æt þam apostolican setle Rômâniscre gelađunge feccan sceoldon. Augustînus gesette æfter þisum biscopâs of his gefêrum gehpilcum burgum on Englâ þeôde, and hî on Godes geleâfan þeônde þurhpunôdon ôđ þisum dægđerlîcum dæge.

PAULINUS.

1. Þǽre tîde eâc spylce Norđanhymbrâ þeôd mid heorâ cyninge Eâdpine Cristes geleâfan onfêng, þe him Paulînus, se hâlga bisceop, bodôde and lǽrde. Þâ hæfde se cyning gesprǽce and geþeaht mid his pitum, and synderlîce pæs fram him eallum friggende, hpilc him þuhte and gesepen pǽre þeôs nipe lâr and þǽre godcundnesse bîgong, þe þǽr lǽred pæs? Him þâ andsparôde his ealdor-bisceop, Cêfî pæs hâten: "Geseoh þû, cyning, hpilc þeôs lâr sî, þe ûs nû bodôd is. Ic þê sôđlîce andette, þæt ic cûđlîce geleornôd hæbbe, þæt eallinga nâpiht mægenes nê nytnesse hafeđ seô ǽfæstnes, þe pê ôđ þis hæfdon and beeôdon, forþon nǽnig þînrâ þegnâ neôdlîcôr nê gelustfullîcôr hine selfne underþeôdde tô ûrâ godâ bîgange þonne ic; ac nôht þon læs manige sindon, þâ þe mâran gife and fremsumnesse æt þê onfêngon þonne ic, and on eallum þingum mâran gesynto hæfdon. Hpæt ic pât, gif ûre godâs ǽnige mihte hæfdon, þonne poldon hî mê mâ fultumian, forþon ic him geornlîcôr þeôdde and hŷrde. Forþon mê þynceđ

pîslîc, gif þû geseô þâ þing beteran and strengran, þe ûs nipan bodôde sindon, þæt pê þâm onfôn."

2. Pisum pordum ôđer þæs cyninges pita and ealdorman geþafunge sealde and tô þǣre sprǣce fêng and þus cpæđ: "Pyslîc mê is gesepen, cyning, þis andpearde lîf mannâ on eorđan tô piđmetenesse þǣre tîde, þe ûs uncûđ is, spâ gelîc spâ þû æt spǣsendum sitte mid þînum ealdormannum and þegnum on pintertîde, and sî fŷr onæled, and þîn heal gepyrmed, and hit rîne and snîpe and hægele and styrme ûte; cume þonne ân spearpa and hrædlîce þæt hûs þurhfleô, þurh ôđre duru in, þurh ôđre ût gepîte: hpæt hê on þâ tîd, þâ hê inne byđ, ne byđ rîned mid þŷ stormê þæs pintres! ac þæt byđ ân eâgan bryhtm and þæt læste fæc, and hê sôna of pintrâ in pinter eft cymeđ. Spâ þonne þis mannâ lîf tô medmiclum fæce ætŷpeđ; hpæt þǣr foregênge, ođđe hpæt þǣr æfterfylige, pê ne cunnon. Forþon gif þeôs nipe lâre âpiht cûđlîcre and gerisenlîcre bringe, heô þæs pyrđe is, þæt pê þǣre fyligeân."

3. Pisum pordum gelîcum ôđre ealdormen and þæs cyninges þeahterâs sprǣcon: þâ get tô geŷhte Cêfî and cpæđ, þæt hê polde Paulînus þone bisceop geornlîcôr gehŷran be þam gode sprecende, þe hê bodôde; þâ hêt se cyning spâ dôn. Pâ hê þâ his pord gehŷrde, þâ clypôde hê and þus cpæđ: "Geare ic þæt ongeat, þæt þæt nâpiht pæs, þæt pê beeôdon, forþon spâ miclê spâ ic geornlîcôr on þam bîgange þæt selfe sôđ sôhte, spâ ic hit læs mêtte. Nû þonne ic openlîce andette, þæt on þisse lâre þæt selfe sôđ scîneđ, þæt ûs mæg syllan þâ gife êcre eâdignesse and êces lîfes hǣlo. Forþon ic lǣre nû, cyning leôfôsta, þæt þæt tempel and þâ peofedu þâ þe pê bûtan pæstmum ǣnigre nytnesse hâlgôdon, þæt pê þâ hrađe forleôsân and on fŷre forbærnân."

4. Hpæt hê þâ se cyning openlîce andette þam bisceope and him eallum, þæt hê polde fæstlîce þâm deôfolgildum piđsacan and Cristes geleâfan onfôn! Mid þŷ hê þâ se cyning fram þam foresprecenan bisceope sôhte and âcsôde heorâ hâlignesse þe hî ǣr beeôdon, hpâ þâ pigbêd and þâ heargâs þârâ deôfolgildâ mid heorâ hegum þe hî ymbsette pǣron âîdlian sceolde and tôpeorpan; þâ andsparôde hê se bisceop: "Efne ic þâ godâs lange mid dysignesse beeôde ôđ þis; hpâ mæg hî gerisenlîcôr nû tôpeorpan tô bysne ôđrâ mannâ þonne ic selfa þurh þâ snyttro þe ic fram þam sôđan Gode onfêng?" And hê þâ sôna fram him âpearp þâ îdlan dysignesse þe hê ǣr beeôde, and þone cyning bæd, þæt hê him pǣpen sealde and gestêdhors, þæt hê mihte on

cuman and þæt deôfolgild tôpeorpan, forþon þam bisceope ne pæs âlŷfed, þæt hê môste pǽpen pegan, nê ælcôr bûtan on myran rîdan. Þâ sealde se cyning him speord, þæt hê hine mid be-gyrde, and nam him spere on hand, and hleôp on þæs cyninges stêdan, and tô þâm deôfolgildum râd.

5. Þâ þæt folc hine þâ geseah spâ gescyrpedne, þâ pêndon hî, þæt hê tela ne piste, ac þæt hê pêdde. Sôna þæs þe hê gelîhte tô þam hearge, þâ sceât hê mid his sperê, þæt hit sticôde fæste on þam hearge, and pæs spîđe gefeônde þǽre ongitenesse þæs sôđan Godes bîganges, and hê þâ hêt his gefêran tôpeorpan ealne hearh and þâ getimbro, and forbærnan. Is seô stôp git æteôped giû þârâ deôfolgildâ nâht feor eâst fram Eoforpîc-ceastre begeondan Deorpentan þǽre eâ, and git tô dæg is nemned Godmundingahâm, þǽr se bisceop þurh þæs sôđan Godes onbryrdnesse tôpearp and fordide þâ pigbed, þe hê self ǽr gehâlgôde.

Þâ onfêng Eâdpine cyning mid eallum þâm æđelingum his þeôde and mid miclê folcê Cristes geleâfan and fulluhtes bæđe.

6. Lǽrde Paulînus eâc spilce Godes pord on Lindesse. Seô mǽgđ is seô nŷhste on sûđ-healfe Humbre streâmes ligeđ ût on sǽ. Be þisse mǽgđe geleâfan cpæđ hê Bêda: "Mê sǽde sum ârpurđe mæsse-preôst and abbud of Peortanea þam hâm, se pæs Dêda hâten,—cpæđ þæt him sǽde sum eald pita, þæt hê pǽre gefullôd æt middum dæge fram Paulîne þam bisceope on Eâdpines andpeardnesse þæs cyninges, and micel menigo þæs folces on Trentan streâme be Teôlfinga-ceastre. Sǽde se ilca man hpilc pæs bisceopes hip pǽre sanctes Paulînes; cpæđ þæt hê pǽre lang on bodige and hpon forđheald; hê hæfde blæc feax and blâcne andplitan and hôcihte neôsu þynne, and hê pǽre ǽghpæđer ge ârpurđlîc ge ondrysenlîc on tô seônne."

7. Is þæt sǽd þæt on þâ tîd spâ micel sib pǽre on Brytene ǽghpider ymb spâ spâ Eâdpines rîce pǽre, þeâh þe ân pîf polde, mid hire nîcendum cilde heô mihte gegân bûtan ælcere sceađenesse fram sǽ tô sǽ ofer eal þis eâland. Spilce eâc se ilca cyning tô nytnesse fand his leôdum, þæt in manigum stôpum þǽr þe hlutre pyllan urnon be strǽtum þǽr mannâ færnes mǽst pæs, þæt hê þǽr hêt for pegfêrendrâ gecêlnesse stapulâs âsettan, and þǽr ǽrene ceâcâs onhôn: and þâ hpæđere nǽnig for his ege and for his lufan hî hrînan dorste ne nê polde bûtan tô his neôdþearflîcre þênunge.

ANGLO-SAXON LAWS.

ÆÐELBIRHTES DÔMÂS.

§ 4. Gif frigman cyninge stele, nigon-gylde forgelde.

9. Gif frigman frêum steld, þrî-gylde gebête and cyning âge þæt pîte and eal þâ æ̂htan.

21. Gif man mannan ofslæhđ, medume leôd-geld hund scillingâ gebête.

22. Gif man mannan ofslæhđ, æt openum græfe tpêntig scillingâ forgelde and in feôpertig nihtâ ealne leôd forgelde.

23. Gif bana of lande gepîteđ, þâ magâs healfne leôd forgelden.

25. Gif man ceorles hlâf-æ̣tan ofslæhđ, six scillingum gebête.

39. Gif ôđer eâre nâpiht gehêređ, fîf and tpêntigum scillingum gebête.

40. Gif eâre of peorđ âslagen, tpelf scillingum gebête.

41. Gif eâre þyrel peorđeđ, þrîm scillingum gebête.

42. Gif eâre sceard peorđeđ, six scillingum gebête.

43. Gif eâge of peorđ, fîftig scillingum gebête.

50. Se þe cin-bân forslæhđ, mid tpêntigum scillingum forgelde.

51. Æt þâm feôper tôđum fyrestum æt gehpilcum six scillingâs; se tôđ se þanne bîstandeđ, feôper scillingâs; se þe þonne bî þam standeđ, þrî scillingâs, and þonne siđđan gehpylc scilling.

52. Gif spræ̂c âpyrd peorđ, tpelf scillingâs; gif pido-bân gebroced peorđeđ, six scillingum gebête.

53. Se þe earm þurhstingđ, six scillingum gebête; gif earm forbrocen peorđ, six scillingum gebête.

54. Gif man þûman of âslæhđ, tpêntigum scillingum gebête; gif þûman nægl of peorđeđ, þrîm scillingum gebête; gif man scyte-finger of âslæhđ, eahta scillingum gebête; gif man middel-finger of âslæhđ, feôper scillingum gebête; gif man gold-finger of âslæhđ, six scillingum gebête; gif man þone lytlan finger of âslæhđ, endleofan scillingum gebête.

55. Æt þâm næglum gehpylcum scilling.

56. Æt þam lærestan plite-pamme, þrî scillingâs, and æt þam mâran six scillingâs.

57. Gif man ôðerne mid fŷste in nâso slæhð, þrî scillingâs.

58. Gif dynt sîe, scilling. Gif hê heâhre handâ dyntes onfêhð, scilling forgelde.

59. Gif dynt speart sîe bûton pǣdum, þrittig scættâ gebête.

60. Gif hit sîe binnan pǣdum, gehpylc XX. scættâ gebête.

HLÔÐHÆRE AND EÂDRÎC, CANTǷARÂ CYNINGÂS.

§ 11. Gif man mannan an ôðres flette mân-spara hâteð, oððe hine mid bîsmer-pordum scandlîce grête, scilling âgelde þam þe þæt flet âge, and six scillingâs þam þe hê þæt pord tô gecpǣde, and cyninge tpelf scillingâs forgelde.

12. Gif man ôðrum steâp âsette þǣr men drincen bûton scylde, an eald-riht scilling âgelde þam þe þæt flet âge, and six scillingâs þam þe man þone steâp âsette, and cyninge tpelf scillingâs.

13. Gif man pǣpn âbregde þǣr men drincen and þǣr man nân yfel ne dêð, scilling þam þe þæt flet âge, and cyninge tpelf scillingâs.

14. Gif þæt flet geblôdgâd pyrðe, forgelde þam men his mund-byrd, and cyninge fîftig scillingâs.

15. Gif man cuman feormeð þrî niht an his âgenum hâme, cêpeman oððe ôðerne, þe seô ofer mearce cumen, and hine þonne his metê fêde, and hê þonne ǣnigum men yfel gedô, se man þane ôðerne æt rihte gebrenge, oððe riht fore pyrce.

INES CYNINGES DOMÂS.

§ 6. Gif hpâ gefeohte on cyninges hûse, sîe hê scyldig ealles his yrfes, and sîe on cyninges dôme hpæðer hê lîf âge þe nâge.—Gif hpâ on mynstre gefeohte, hund-tpelftig scillingâs gebête.—Gif hpâ on ealdormannes hûse gefeohte, oððe on ôðres geþungenes pitan, sixtig scillingâs gebête hê, and ôðer sixtig scillingâs geselle tô pîte.—Gif hê þonne on gafol-geldan hûse oððe on gebûres gefeohte, þrîtig scillingâs tô pîte geselle, and þam gebûre six scillingâs.—And þeâh hit sîe on middum feldâ gefohten, þrîtig scillingâ tô pîte sîe âgifen.—Gif þonne on gebeôrscipe hîe gecîden, and ôðer heorâ mid geþylde hit forbere, geselle se ôðer þrîtig scillingâs tô pîte.

7. Gif hpâ stalie spâ his pîf nyte and his bearn, geselle sixtig scillingâs to pîte.—Gif hê þonne stalie on gepitnesse ealles his hîrêdes, gangen hîe ealle on þeôpot.—Tŷn-pintre cniht mæg beôn þŷfðe gepita.

20. Gif feorcund man oððe fremde bûtan pege geond pudu gange, and ne hrŷme nê horn blâpe, for þeôf hê bið tô prôfianne oððe tô sleânne oððe tô âlŷsanne.

43. Þonne man beâm on pudâ forbærne, and peorðe yppe on þone þe hit dyde, gylde hê ful pîte; geselle sixtig scillingâ forþam þe fŷr bið þeôf.—Gif man âfelle on pudâ pel manege treôpâ, and pyrðe eft undyrne, forgylde þreô treôpâ, ælc mid þrîtig scillingum. Ne.þearf hê heorâ mâ gyldan, pǣre heorâ spâ fela spâ heorâ pǣre, forþam seô æx bið melda, nalles þeôf.

ÆLFRÊDES DÔMÂS.

§ 1. Æt ǣrestan pê lǣrað, þæt mǣst þearf is, þæt ǣghpelc mon his âð and his ped pærlîce healde.—Gif hê þonne þæs peddie þe him riht sŷ tô gelǣstanne, and þæt âleôge, selle mid eâðmêdum his pǣpn and his ǣhtâ his freôndum tô gehealdanne, and beô feôpertig nihtâ on carcerne on cyninges tûne, þrôpige þǣr spâ bisceop him scrîfe, and his mǣgâs hine fêden, gif hê self mete næbbe.—Gif hê mǣgâs næbbe, oððe þone mete næbbe, fêde cyninges gerêfa hine.—Gif hine mon tôgenêdan scyle and hê elles nylle, gif hine mon gebinde, þolige his pǣpnâ and his yrfes.—Gif hine mon ofsleâ, licge hê orgylde.—Gif hê losige, sîe hê âflŷmed and sîe âmǣnsumôd of eallum Cristes ciricum.

5. Eâc pê settað ǣghpelcere cirican þe bisceop gehâlgôde, þis frið: gif hîe fâh-mon geyrne oððe geærne, þæt hine seofan nihtum nân mon ût ne teô.—Eâc cirican frið is: gif hpelc mon cirican gesêce for þârâ gyltâ hpylcum þârâ þe ǣr geypped nǣre, and hine þǣr on Godes naman geandette, sîe hit healf forgifen.—Se þe stalâð on Sunnan niht, oððe on Geôl, oððe on Eâstran, oððe on þone Hâlgan Þunres dæg, and on Gang-dagâs, þârâ gehpelc pê pillað sîe tpŷ-bôte, spâ on Lencten-fæsten.

6. Gif hpâ on cirican hpæt geþeôfige, forgylde þæt ângylde,

and þæt pîte spâ tô þam âńgylde belimpan pille, and sleâ mon þâ hand of þe hê hit mid gedyde.

23. Gif hund mon tôslîte oððe âbîte, æt forman misdǣde geselle six scillingâs gif hê him mete selle, æt æfteran cerre tpelf scillingâs, æt þriddan þrittig scillingâs.—Gif æt þissâ misdǣdâ hpelcere se hund losige, gâ þeôs bôt hpæðere forð.

32. Gif mon folc-leâsunge gepyrce, and heô on hine geresp peorðe, mid nânum leôhtran þinge gebête, þonne him mon âceorfe þâ tungan of.

35. Gif mon cyrliscne mon gebinde unsynnigne, gebête mid tŷn scillingum.—Gif hine mon bespinge, mid tpêntig scillingum gebête.—Gif hê hine on hengenne âlecge, mid þrittig scillingum gebête.—Gif hê hine on bîsmor tô homolan bescire, mid tŷn scillingum gebête.—Gif hê hine tô preôste bescire unbundenne, mid þrittig scillingum gebête.—Gif hê þone beard of âscire, mid tpêntig scillingum gebête.—Gif hê hine gebinde and þonne tô preôste bescire, mid sixtig scillingum gebête.

ECGBYRHT ARCEBISCEOP.

Confessionale, 32. Gif man medmycles hpæthpega deôflum onsǣgð, fæste ân geâr: gif hê mycles hpæt onsǣge, fæste tŷn pinter. Spâ hpylc man spâ corn bærne on þǣre stôpe þǣr man deâd pǣre, lifigendum mannum tô hǣle and on his hûse, fæste fîf pinter.

33. Ƿîf gif heô set hire dôhtor ofer hûs oððe on ofen forþam þe heô pille hîg fefer-âdle gehǣlan, fæste heô seofon pinter.

Poenitentiale, II., 23. Nis nâ sôðlîce âlŷfed nânum Cristenum men þæt hê îdele hpatungâ begâ spâ hǣðene men dôð, þæt is þæt hîg gelŷfon on sunnan and on mônan and on steorrenâ ryne, and sêcon tîdâ hpatungâ hyrâ þing tô begynnanne, nê pyrtâ gaderunge mid nânum galdre, bûtan mid pater-noster and mid crêdan oððe mid sumum gebede þe tô Gode belimpe.

IV., 16. Gif ǣnig man ôðerne mid picce-cræftê fordô, fæste seofon geâr, þreô on hlâfe and on pætere, and þâ feôper þrî dagâs on pucan on hlâfe and on pætere.

17. Gif hpâ drîfe stacan on ǣnigne man, fæste þreô geâr, ân geâr on hlâfe and on pætere, and þâ tpâ fæste on pucan þrî dagâs on hlâfe and on pætere. And gif se man for þǣre stacunge

deâd biđ, þonne fæste hê seofon geâr ealsƿâ hit hêr bufon âƿriten is.

18. Gif hƿâ ƿiccige ymbe ǣniges mannes lufe and him on ǣte sylle ođđe on drince ođđe on ǣniges cynnes gealdor-cræftum, þæt hyrâ lufu forþon þe mâre beôn scyle: gif hit lǣƿede man dô, fæste healf geâr Ƿôdnes dagum and Frîge dagum on hlâfe and on ƿætere, and þâ ôđre dagâs brûce hê his metes bûtan flǣsce ânum.

19. Gif hƿâ hlytâs ođđe hƿatungâ begâ, ođđe his ƿæccan æt ǣnigum ƿylle hæbbe, ođđe æt ǣnigre ôđre gesceafte bûton on Godes cyricean, fæste hê þreô geâr, þæt ân on hlâfe and on ƿætere, and þâ tƿâ Ƿôdnes dagum and Frîge dagum on hlâfe and on ƿætere and þâ ôđre dagâs brûce his metes bûton flǣsce ânum.

20. Ƿîfman beô þæs ylcan ƿyrđe, gif heô tilâđ hire cilde mid ǣnigum ƿicce-cræfte ođđe æt ƿegâ gelǣton þurh þâ eorđan tîhđ; eâlâ þæt is mycel hǣđenscipe.

CNUT CYNING.

II., 5. And ƿê forbeôdađ eornostlîce ælcne hǣđenscipe. Hǣđenscipe býđ þæt man deôfol-gyld ƿeorđige: þæt is þæt man ƿeorđige hǣđene godâs and sunnan ođđe mônan, fýr ođđe flôd, ƿæter-ƿyllâs ođđe stânâs ođđe ǣniges cynnes ƿudu-treôƿu, ođđe ƿicce-cræft lufige, ođđe morđ-ƿeorc gefremme on ǣnige ƿîsan, ođđe blôte ođđe fyrhte ođđe sƿylcrâ gedƿimerâ ǣnig þing dreôge.

73. And sitte ælc ƿuduƿe ƿerleâs tƿelf-mônađ, ceôse syđđan þæt heô sylf ƿille; and gif heô binnan geâres fæce ƿer geceôse, þonne þolige heô þǣre morgen-gyfe and ealrâ þǣrâ ǣhtâ þe heô þurh ǣrran ƿer hæfde, and fôn þâ nêhstan frýnd tô þam lande and tô þam ǣhtan þe heô ǣr hæfde.—And ne hâdige man ǣfre ƿuduƿan tô hrædlîce.

POETS.

ORPHEUS.

1. Gesǣlig byđ se man, þe mæg geseôn þone hlutran ǣpelm þæs hêhstan gôdes, and of him selfum âpeorpan mæg þâ þeôstro his môdes! Đê sculon get of ealdum leâsum spellum þê sum bî-spell reccan: Hit gelamp giô, þætte ân hearpere pæs on þǣre þeôde þe Prâcia hâtte, seô pæs on Crêcâ rîce. Se hearpere pæs spîđe ungefrǣglîce gôd, þæs nama pæs Orfeus. Hê hæfde ân spîđe ânlîc pîf, seô pæs hâten Eurydice. Pâ ongan man secgan be þam hearpere, þæt hê mihte hearpian þæt se pudu pagôde and þâ stânâs hî styredon for þŷ spêgê, and pildu deôr þǣr poldon tô irnan and stondan spilce hî tamu pǣron, spâ stille, þeâh hî men ođđe hundâs piđ eôdon, þæt hî hî nâ ne onscûnedon.

2. Pâ sǣdon hî, þæt þæs hearperes pîf sceolde âcpelan, and hire sâple man sceolde lǣdan tô helle. Pâ sceolde se hearpere peorđan spâ sârig, þæt hê ne mihte on-gemong ôđrum mannum beôn, ac teâh tô pudâ and sæt on þǣm muntum ǣgđer ge dæges ge nihtes, peôp and hearpôde, þæt þâ pudâs bifôdon and þâ eâ stôdon, and nân heort ne onscûnôde nǣnne leôn, nê nân hara nǣnne hund, nê nân neât nyste nǣnne andan nê nǣnne ege tô ôđrum for þǣre mergđe þæs sônes.

3. Pâ þæm hearpere þâ þuhte, þæt hine nânes þinges ne lyste on þisse porulde, þâ þohte hê, þæt hê polde gesêcan helle godu, and onginnan him ôleccan mid his hearpan, and biddan þæt hî him âgêfân eft his pîf. Pâ hê þâ þider com, þâ sceolde cuman þǣre helle hund ongeân hine, þæs nama pæs Ceruerus, se sceolde habban þreô heâfdu, and ongan fægenian mid his steortê, and plegian piđ hine for his hearpungâ. Pâ pæs þǣr eâc spîđe egeslîc geat-peard, þæs nama sceolde beôn Caron, se hæfde eâc þreô heafdu, and se pæs spîđe ôreald. Pâ ongan se hearpere hine biddan, þæt hê hine gemundbyrde þâ hpîle þe hê þǣr pǣre and hine gesundne eft þanon brohte; þâ gehêt hê him þæt, forþam hê pæs oflyst þæs seldcûđan sônes.

4. Pâ côde hê furđôr, ôđ hê mêtte þâ graman mettenâ, þe fclcisce men hâtađ Parcâs, þâ hî secgađ, þæt on nânum men nyton nâne âre, ac ælcum men precen be his gepyrhtum, þâ hî secgađ, þæt palden ælces mannes pyrde. Pâ ongan hê biddan heorâ blisse; þâ ongunnon hî pêpan mid him. Pâ eôde hê furđur, and him urnon ealle helparan ongeân, and lǽddon hine tô heorâ cyninge, and ongunnon ealle sprecan mid him and biddan þæs þe hê bæd. And þæt unstille hpeôl, þe Ixîon pæs tô gebunden Leuitâ cyning for his scylde, þæt ôđstôd for his hearpungâ; and Tantalus se cyning, þe on þisse porulde ungemetlîce gîfre pæs, and him þǽr þæt ilce yfel fylgde, þæs gîfernesse hê gestilde; and se ultor sceolde forlǽtan, þæt hê ne slât þâ lifre Tityes þæs cyninges, þe hine ǽr mid þŷ pîtnôde; and eal helparâ pîtu gestildon þâ hpîle, þe hê beforan þam cyninge hearpôde.

5. Pâ hê þâ lange and lange hearpôde, þâ cleopôde se helparenâ cyning, and cpæđ: "Duton âgifan þæm esne his pîf, forþæm hê hî hæfđ geearnâd mid his hearpungâ." Bebeâd him þâ, þæt hê geare pisse, þæt hê hine nǽfre underbæc ne besâpe siđđan hê þonan-peard pǽre, and sǽde, gif hê hine underbæc besâpe, þæt hê sceolde forlǽtan þæt pîf. Ac þâ lufe man mæg spîđe uneâđe ođđe nâ forbeôdan. Deilâ pei! hpæt Orfeus þâ lǽdde his pîf mid him, ôđ þe hê com on þæt gemǽre leôhtes and þeôstro; þâ eôde þæt pîf æfter him. Pâ hê furđum on þæt leôht com, þâ beseah hê hine underbæc piđ þæs pîfes: þâ losâde heô him sôna.

6. Pâs spel lǽrađ gehpilcne man þârâ þe pilnađ helle þeôstro tô fleônne, and tô þæs sôđan Godes leôhte tô cumanne, þæt hê hine ne beseô tô his ealdum yfelum, spâ þæt hê hî eft spâ fullîce fulfremme, spâ hê hî ǽr dide; forþæm spâ-hpâ-spâ mid fullê pillan his môd pent tô þâm yflum þe hê ǽr forlêt, and hî þonne fulfremeđ, and hî him þonne fullîce lîciađ, and hê hî nǽfre forlǽtan ne þencđ; þonne forlŷst hê eal his ǽrran gôd, bûton hê hit eft gebête.

CÆDMON.

1. On Hilde abbudissan mynstre pæs sum brôđor synderlîce mid godcundre gife gemǽred and gepeorđôd, forþon hê gepunôde gerisenlîce leôđ pyrcean, þâ þe tô ǽfæstnesse and tô ârfæstnesse belumpon, spâ þætte spâ-hpæt-spâ hê of godcundum stafum

þurh bôcerâs geleornôde, þæt hê æfter medmiclum fæce in sceôpgereorde mid þâ mǽstan spêtnesse and inbrydnesse geglencde and in Englisc gereorde pelgehpǽr forđ brohte; and for his leôđsongum manigrâ mannâ môd oft tô peorulde forhôhnesse and tô geþeôdnêsse þæs heofonlîcan lîfes onbærnde pǽron.

2. And eâc spilce manige ôđre æfter him on Angelþeôde ongunnon ǽfæste leôđ pyrcan, ac nǽnig hpæđre him þæt gelîce dôn meahte, forþon hê nalæs fram mannum nê þurh man gelǽred pæs, þæt hê þone leôđcræft geleornôde; ac hê pæs godcundlîce gefultumôd, and þurh Godes gife þone songcræft onfêng, and hê forþon nǽfre nôht leâsungâ nê îdeles leôđes pyrcan meahte, ac efne þâ ân þâ þe tô ǽfæstnesse belumpon and his þâ ǽfæstan tungan gedafenôde singan. Ƿæs hê se man in peoruldhâde geseted ôđ þâ tîde, þe hê pæs gelŷfedre yldo, and hê nǽfre nǽnig leôđ geleornôde, and hê forþon oft in gebeôrscipe, þonne þǽr pæs blisse intingan gedêmed, þæt hî ealle sceolden þurh endebyrdnesse be hearpan singan, þonne hê geseah þâ hearpan him neâlǽcan, þonne ârâs hê for sceame fram þam symble and hâm eôde tô his hûse.

3. Pâ hê þæt þâ sumre tîde dide, þæt hê forlêt þæt hûs þæs gebeôrscipes and ût pæs gangende tô neâtâ scypene, þârâ heord him pæs þǽre nihte beboden; þâ hê þâ þǽr in gelimplîcre tîde his limu on reste gesette, and onslǽpte, þâ stôd him sum man æt þurh spefn, and hine hâlette and grêtte, and hine be his naman nemde, "Cædmon, sing mê hpæthpegu." Pâ andsparôde hê and cpæđ: "Ne con ic nôht singan, and ic forþon of þisum gebeôrscipe ûteôde, and hider gepât, forþon ic nôht cûđe." Eft hê cpæđ, se þe mid him sprecende pæs, "Hpæđere þû meaht mê singan." Cpæđ hê, "Hpæt sceal ic singan?" Cpæđ hê, "Sing mê frumsceaft." Pâ hê þâs andsparc onfêng, þâ ongan hê sôna singan in herenesse Godes scyppendes þâ fers and þâ pord þe hê nǽfre ne gehŷrde; þârâ endebyrdnes þis is:

4. "Nû pê sceolon herian heofonrîces Ƿeard,
Metodes mihte and his môdgeþonc,
perâ Ƿuldorfæder, spâ hê pundrâ gehpæs,
êce Dryhten, ord onstealde.
He ǽrest gesceôp eorđan bearnum
heofon tô hrôfe, hâlig Scyppend;
þâ middangeard, moncynnes Ƿeard,
êce Dryhten, æfter teôde
firum foldan, Freâ ælmihtig."

5. Þâ ârâs hê fram þam slǣpe, and eal þâ þe hê slǣpende sang, fæste in gemynde hæfde, and þâm pordum sôna manig pord in þæt ilce gemet Godê pyrđes songes tôgeþeôdde. Þâ com hê on morne tô þam tûngerêfan, se þe his ealdorman pæs, and him sǣde hpilce gife hê onfêng, and hê hine sôna tô þǣre abbudissan gelǣdde, and hire þæt cŷđde and sægde. Þâ hêt heô gesamnian ealle þâ gelǣrdestan men, and þâ leornerâs, and him andpeardum hêt secgan þæt spefn and þæt leôđ singan, þætte ealrâ heorâ dômê gecoren pǣre, hpæt ođđe hponan þæt cumen pǣre. Þâ pæs him eallum gesepen spâ spâ hit pæs, þæt him pǣre fram Dryhtne selfum heofonlîc gifu forgifen. Þâ rehton hî him and sægdon sum hâlig spel and godcundre lâre pord, bebudon him þâ, gif hê mihte, þæt hê him sum sunge and in spinsunge leôđsanges þæt gehpyrfde. Þâ hê þâ hæfde þâ pîsan onfangene, þâ eôde hê hâm tô his hûse, and com eft on morgen, and þŷ betstan leôđê geglenged him âsang and âgeaf þæt him beboden pæs.

6. Þâ ongan seô abbudisse clyppan and lufian þâ Godes gife in þam men, and heô hine þâ monôde and lǣrde, þæt hê peoruldhâd forlête and munuchâde onfênge; and hê þæt pel þafôde; and heô hine in þæt mynster onfêng mid his gôdum, and hine geþeôdde tô gesamnunge þârâ Godes þeôpâ, and hêt hine lǣran þæt getæl þæs hâlgan stǣres and spelles, and hê eal þâ hê in gehêrnesse geleornian mihte mid hine gemyngôde, and spâ spâ clǣne nŷten eodorcende in þæt spêteste leôđ gehpyrfde, and his song and his leôđ pǣron spâ pynsum tô gehŷranne, þæt þâ selfan his lâreôpâs æt his mûđe priton and leornôdon.

7. Sang hê ǣrest be middangeardes gesceape and be fruman mancynnes and eal þæt stǣr Genesis, þæt is seô ǣreste Môyses bôc, and eft be ûtgange Israêlâ folces of Ægyptâ lande, and be ingange þæs gehâtlandes, and be ôđrum manigum spellum þæs hâlgan geprites canones bôcâ, and be Cristes menniscnesse, and be his þrôpunge, and be his upâstîgnesse on heofonâs, and bîg þæs Hâlgan Gâstes cyme, and þârâ Apostolâ lâre; and eft bî þam ege þæs tôpeardan dômes, and be fyrhto þæs tintreglîcan pîtes, and be spêtnesse þæs heofonlîcan rîces hê manig leôđ geporhte; and spilc eâc ôđer manig be þâm godcundum fremsumnessum and dômum hê geporhte. On eallum þâm hê geornlîce gŷmde, þæt hê men âtuge fram synnâ lufan and mândǣdâ, and tô lufan and tô geornfulnesse âpehte gôdrâ dǣdâ, forþon hê pæs se man spîđe ǣfest, and reogollîcum þeôdscipum eâdmôdlîce underþeôded; and pit þâm þâ þe on ôđre pîsan dôn poldon, hê pæs mid pylme mi-

celre ellenpôdnesse onbærned, and hê forþon fægrê endê his lîf betŷnde and geendôde.

8. Forþon þâ þǣre tîde neâlǣhte his gepitennesse and forðfôre, þâ pæs hê feôpertŷne dagum ǣr þæt hê pæs lîcumlîcre untrymnesse þrycced and hefigôd, hpæðere tôþon gemetlîce, þæt hê ealle þâ tîd mihte ge sprecan ge gangan. Pæs þǣr on neâpeste untrumrâ mannâ hûs, on þam hirâ þeâp pæs þæt hî þâ untruman and þâ þe æt forðfôre pǣron in lǣdan sceoldan, and him þǣr ætsomne þênian. Þâ bæd hê his þegn on ǣfenne þǣre nihte þe hê of peorulde gangende pæs, þæt hê on þam hûse him stôpe gegearpôde, þæt hê restan mihte. Þâ pundrôde se þegn forhpon hê þæs bǣde, forþon him þuhte þæt his forðfôre spâ neâh ne pǣre, dide hpæðere spâ spâ hê cpæð and bebeâd.

9. And mid þŷ hê þâ þǣr on reste eôde, and hê gefeôndê môdê sumu þing ætgædere mid him sprecende and gleôpiende pæs, þe þǣr ǣr inne pǣron, þâ pæs ofer middeniht þæt hê frægn, hpæðer hî ǣnig hûsel þǣr inne hæfdon. Þâ andsparôdon hî and cpǣdon, "Hpilc þearf is þê hûsles? Ne þînre forðfôre spâ neâh is, nû þû þus rôtlîce and þus glædlîce tô ûs sprecende eart." Cpæð hê eft, "Berað mê hpæðere hûsel tô." Þâ hê hit on handâ hæfde, þâ frægn hê, hpæðer hî ealle smylte môd, and bûtan eallum incan blîðe tô him hæfdon. Þâ andsparôdon hî ealle, and cpǣdon þæt hî nǣnigne incan tô him piston, ac hî him ealle spîðe blîðemôde pǣron, and hî prixendlîce hine bǣdon þæt hê him eallum blîðe pǣre. Þâ andsparôde hê, and cpæð, "Mîne brôðru þâ leôfan, ic eom spîðe blîðmôd tô eôp and tô eallum Godes mannum." And hê spâ pæs hine getrymmende mid þŷ heofonlîcan pegnestê, and him ôðres lîfes ingang gearpôde. Þâ git hê frægn, hû neâh þǣre tîde pǣre, þætte þâ brôðor ârîsan sceolden, and Godes lof rǣran and heorâ ûhtsang singan. Andsparôdon hî, "Nis hit feor tô þon." Cpæð hê, "Tela, utan pê pel þǣre tîde bîdan!" And þâ him gebæd, and hine gesênôde mid Cristes rôdetâcne, and his heâfod onhylde tô þam bolstre, and medmicel fæc onslǣpte, and spâ mid stilnesse his lîf geendôde.

10. And spâ pæs geporden, þætte spâ spâ hê hlutrê modê and bilepitê and smyltre pilsumnesse Drihtne þeôpde, þæt hê eâc spilce spâ smyltê deâðê middangeard pæs forlǣtende and tô his gesihðe becom, and seô tunge, þe spâ manig hâlpende pord on þæs Scyppendes lof gesette, heô þâ spilce eâc þâ ŷtemestan pord on his herenesse, hine selfne sêniende and his gâst in his handâ bebeôdende, betŷnde.

POETRY.

DESCRIPTIONS OF GLEE-MEN AND POETS.

(*Traveler*, 135–143.)

Spâ **SC**rîđende ge**SC**eapum hpeorfađ
Gleô-men **G**umenâ geond **G**rundâ fela,
Thearfe **s**ecgađ, **Th**onc-pord **s**precađ,
Simle **S**ûđ ođđe norđ **S**umne gemêtađ
Gyddâ **G**leâpne, **G**eofum unhneâpne,
se þe fore **D**ugTuđe pile **D**ôm ârǽran,
EOrlscipe **Æ**fnan, ôđ þæt **EA**l scaceđ
Leôht and **L**îf somod: **L**of se gepyrceđ,
Hafâđ under **H**eofonum **H**eâhfæstne dôm.

(*Beowulf*, 867–874.)

Hpîlum **C**yninges þegn,
Guma **G**ilp-hlæden, **G**iddâ gemyndig,
se þe **EA**l-fela **EA**ld-gesegenâ
VVorn gemunde, **VV**ord ôđer fand
Sôđe gebunden: **S**ecg eft ongan
Sîđ Beôpulfes **S**nyttrum styrian,
and on **SP**êd precan **SP**el gerâde,
VVordum **VV**rixlan.

(*Beowulf*, 89–98.)

—þǽr pæs **H**earpan spêg,
Sputol **S**ang scôpes. **S**ægde, se þe cûđe
Frumsceaft **F**irâ **F**eorran reccan,
cpæđ þæt se **Æ**lmihtiga **EO**rđan porhte
VVlite-beorhtne **VV**ang, spâ **VV**æter bebûgeđ,
ge**S**ette **S**ige-hrêđig **S**unnan and mônan
Leôman tô **L**eôhte **L**and-bûendum,
and ge**F**rætpâde **F**oldan sceâtâs
Leomum and **L**eâfum, **L**îf eâc gesceôp
Cynnâ ge**hvv**ylcum, þârâ þe **C**pice **hvv**yrfađ.

CÆDMON'S GENESIS.

(*The First Day*, 103–134.)

Ne pæs hêr þâ giet nymđe heolster-sceado
piht geporden, ac þes pîda grund
stôd deôp and dim, Drihtne fremde,
îdel and unnyt: on þone eâgum plât
stîđ-frihđ cyning, and þâ stôpe beheôld
dreâmâ leâse, geseah deorc gespeorc
semian sinnihte speart under roderum,
pon and pêste, ôđ þæt þeôs poruld-gesceaft
þurh pord gepeaŕđ puldor-cyninges.
Hêr ǽrest gesceôp êce Drihten
helm ealpihtâ heofon and eorđan,
rodor ârǽrde, and þis rûme land
gestađelôde strangum mihtum,
Freâ ælmihtig. Folde pæs þâ gyt
græs ungrêne: gârsecg þeahte
speart sinnihte sîde and pîde,
þonne pǽgâs. Þâ pæs puldor-torht
Heofon-peardes gâst ofer holm boren
miclum spêdum. Metod englâ hêht
lîfes Brytta leôht forđ cuman
ofer rûmne grund; rađe pæs gefylled
Heâh-cyninges hǽs: him pæs hâlig leôht
ofer pêstenne, spâ se Pyrhta bebeâd.
Þâ gesundrôde sigorâ Paldend
ofer lago-flôde leôht piđ þeôstrum,
sceade piđ scîman. Sceôp þâ bâm naman
lîfes Brytta; leôht pæs ǽrest
þurh Drihtnes pord dæg genemned,
plitebeorhte gesceaft. Pel lîcôde
Freân æt frymđe forđbǽro tîd:
dæg ǽresta geseah deorc sceado
speart spiđrian geond sîdne grund.

(*Satan's Speech*, 347–388.)

Satan mađelôde; sorgiende spræc
se þe helle forđ healdan sceolde,
gŷman þæs grundes: pæs ǽr Godes engel

CÆDMON'S GENESIS.

(*The First Day*, 103–104.)

Ne[1] was there then yet nymthe[2] holster[3]-shadow
wight[3] i-worthen[5], ac[6] this wide ground
stood deep and dim, to-Drihte[7] fremde[8],
idle and unnut[9]: on that with-eyes wlat[10]
stith[11]-frith[12] king, and the stows[13] beheld
of-dreams[14] less[14], i-saw dark i-swerk[15]
seme[16] sinnight[17] swart under roders[18],
wan and waste, oth[19] that this world-schaft[20]
through word i-worth[21] wulder[22]-king's.
Here erst[23] i-shaped eche[24] Drihte[7],
helm[25] of-all-wights[26], heaven and earth,
roder[18] a-reared, and this roomy land
i-statheled[27] with strong mights,
Frea[28] almighty. Folde[29] was then yet
as-to-grass ungreen: garsedge[30] thatched[31]
swart sinnight[17] side[32] and wide,
wan waves. Then was wulder[22]-tort[33]
Heaven-ward's[34] ghost[35] over holm[36] borne
with-mickle speeds. Metod[37] of-angels heht[38],
life's Brytta[39], light forth to-come
over roomy ground; rathe[40] was i-filled[41]
High-king's hest: to-him was holy light
over waste, so the Wright[42] (be-)bade.
Then i-sundered siyers'[43] Wielding[44]
over leye[45]-flood light with[46] thuster[47],
shade with[46] shimmer. Shope[48] then for-both names
life's Brytta[39]; light was erst[23]
through Drihte's[7] word day i-named,
wlite[49]-bright i-shaft[20]. Well liked[50]
Frea[28] at frumthe[51] forthbearing[52] tide[53]:
day erst[23] i-saw dark shadow
swart swither[54] yond[55] side[32] ground.

(*Satan's Speech*, 347–388.)

Satan matheled[56]; sorrowing spake
he that hell forth[57] hold should
to-yeme[58] the ground: was ere[59] God's angel

---

[1] not. [2] except (?). [3] cave, cavernous. [4] aught. [5] existent, created. [6] but (P. P.) [7] God (P. P.). [8] strange (Ch.). [9] useless (S.). [10] looked (S.). [11] strong. [12] mind (?). [13] places (S.). [14] joy-less. [15] murkiness (?). [16] remain (?). [17] in sem-piternal night (?). [18] heavens (?). [19] till (?). [20] creation (?). [21] came into being. [22] glory (S.). [23] first. [24] eternal (S.). [25] protector. [26] beings. [27] established (S.). [28] sovereign (?). [29] earth (S.). [30] ocean (?). [31] covered. [32] far, long (P. P.). [33] bright (H.). [34] warder, guardian. [35] spirit. [36] high sea. [37] creator (?). [38] ordered (P. P., Ch.). [39] allotter (?). [40] soon. [41] fulfilled. [42] maker. [43] victories' (?). [44] Ruler. [45] lake (H.). [46] from. [47] darkness (S.). [48] shaped, formed (Ch., P. P.). [49] beautiful (S.). [50] pleased (Ch., P. P.). [51] beginning (S.). [52] creation's. [53] time. [54] pass away (H.). [55] over, beyond. [56] spoke (S.). [57] thenceforth. [58] keep (P. P.). [59] once, before.

white in heaven, oth[1] him his huie[2] forspene[3]
and his overmet[4] of all swithest[5],
that he ne[6] would wereds'[7] Drihte's[8]
word worthy[9]. Welled to-him on in[10]
huie[2] ymb[11] his heart; hot was to-him out[12]
wrothly[13] wite[14]. He then with-word quoth:
Is this ange[15] stead[16] unlike swithe[17]
the other that we ere couth[18]
high on heaven-riche[19], that me mine herre[20] on-loaned[21],
though we hine[22] for the all-wielder owe[23] ne[6] must,
rome[24] our riche[19]. Nafth[25] he though right i-done
that he us hath i-felled in-fire to bottom
of-hell the hot, heaven-riche[19] be-numen[26],
hath it i-marked mid[27] mankind
to i-settle. That to-me is of-sorrows most
that Adam shall, that was of earth i-wrought,
mine strong stool[28] (be-)hold,
be to-him*self* in wynne[29], and we this wite[14] thole[30],
harm on this hell. Wo lo! owed[23] I my hands' i-wald[31],
and might one tide[32] out worth[33],
be one winter-stound[32], then I mid this wered[7]—!
Ac[34] lie me ymbe[11] iron bonds,
rideth[35] racket's[36] sole[37]: I am riche[19]-less!
have me so hard hell clomps
fast befangen[38]! Here is fire mickle
up and neath! I o[39] ne[6] i-saw
loather[40] landscipe! leye[41] ne[6] a-swome[42]
hot over hell. Me have rings' i-spang[43],
slith-hard[44] sole[37], from-sith[45] a-merred[46],
a-ferred[46] me from-my feeth[47], feet are i-bounden,
hands i-haft[48]; are these hell-doors'
ways forwrought[49]; so I mid[50] wight[50] ne[6] may
off these lith[51]-bonds. Lie me about
of-hard iron hot i-slain[52]
grindels[53] great; mid[27] that me God hath
i-hafted[48] by the halse[54]. So I wot, he my huie[2] cuth[18]
and that wist eke[55] wereds'[7] Drihte[8],
that should us, *me and* Adam, evil i-worth[56]
ymb[11] that heaven-riche[19], there[57] I owed[23] my hands' i-wald![31]

[1] till (?). [2] mind (S.). [3] seduced (?). [4] pride (S.). [5] mightiest (P. P., Ch.). [6] not. [7] hos[illegible] (S.). [8] Lord (P.P.). [9] honor, obey (S.). [10] within. [11] about (?). [12] without. [13] wrathful (S.). [14] punishment (Ch.). [15] narrow (S.). [16] place. [17] very (P.P., Ch.). [18] knew. [19] kingdom, -ric (S.). [20] lord (S.). [21] presented. [22] it (S.). [23] have, own. [24] use (?). [25] hath not (S.) [26] taken (Ch., P.P.). [27] with (P.P.). [28] seat. [29] joy (H.). [30] suffer. [31] power, control (S.). [32] hour. [33] be free. [34] but. [35] oppresseth. [36] bonds' (?). [37] rope (S.). [38] caught (S.). [39] ever (S.). [40] loathlier. [41] fire, low (P. P.). [42] smoulder (?). [43] fastening (H.). [44] terrible (?). [45] departure (P. P.). [46] prevented (S.). [47] path, departure (?). [48] held (?). [49] obstructed, closed (S.). [50] any way. [51] limbs. [52] forged (S.). [53] bars, clogs (S.). [54] neck. [55] also. [56] happen to. [57] if.

hpît on heofne, óð hine his hyge forspeôn
and his ofermetto ealrâ spîðôst,
þæt hê ne polde peredâ Drihtnes
pord purðian. Ðeôl him on innan
hyge ymb his heortan; hât pæs him ûtan
prâðlîc pîte. Hê þâ pordê cpæð:
"Is þes ænga stede ungelîc spîðe
þam ôðrum þe pê ǣr cûðon
heân on heofon-rîce, þe mê mîn hearra onlâg,
þeâh pê hine for þam alpealdan âgan ne môston,
rômigan ûres rîces. Næfð hê þeâh riht gedôn
þæt hê ûs hæfð befylled fŷre tô botme
helle þǣre hâtan, heofon-rîcê benumen,
hafâð hit gemearcôd mid mon-cynne
tô gesettanne. Þæt mê is sorgâ mǣst
þæt Adam sceal, þe pæs of eorðan geporht,
mînne stronglîcan stôl behealdan,
pesan him on pynne, and pê þis pîte þolien
hearm on þisse helle. Ðâ lâ! âhte ic mînrâ handâ gepeald
and môste âne tîd ûte peorðan,
pesan âne pinter-stunde, þonne ic mid þŷs perodê—!
Ac licgað mê ymbe îren-bendâs,
rîdeð racentan sâl: ic eom rîces leâs!
habbað mê spâ hearde helle clommâs
fæste befangen! Hêr is fŷr micel
ufan and neoðone! ic â ne geseah
lâðran landscipe! lîg ne âspâmâð
hât ofer helle. Mê habbað hringâ gespong,
slîð-hearda sâl sîðes âmyrred,
âfyrred mê mîn fêðe; fêt synt gebundene,
handâ gehæfte; synt þissâ hel-dorâ
pegâs forporhte: spâ ic mid pihte ne mæg
of þissum lioðo-bendum. Licgað mê ymbûtan
heardes îrenes hâte geslægene
grindlâs greâte; mid þŷ mê God hafâð
gehæfted be þam healse. Spâ ic pât, hê mînne hige cûðe
and þæt piste eâc perodâ Drihten,
þæt sceolde unc Adame yfele gepurðan
ymb þæt heofon-rîce, þǣr ic âhte mînrâ handâ gepeald!

CÆDMON'S EXODUS.

(*The Flight of the Israelites*, 68–85.)

Nearpe genŷddon   on norđ-pegâs,
piston him be sûđan   Sigelparâ land,
forbærned burh-hleođu,   brûne leôde
hâtum heofon-colum.   Pǣr hâlig God
piđ fǣr-bryne   folc gescylde,
bælcê oferbrǣdde   byrnendne heofon,
hâlgan nettê   hâtpendne lyft.
Hæfde peder-polcen   pîdum fæđmum
eorđan and uprodor   efne gedǣled,
lǣdde leôd-perod;   lîg-fŷr âdranc
hâte heofon-torht.   Hæleđ pâfedon,
drihtâ gedrŷmôst.   Dæg-scealdes hleô
pand ofer polcnum: hæfde pitig God
sunnan sîđ-fæt   seglê ofertolden,
spâ þâ mæst-râpâs   men ne cûđon,
nê þâ segl-rôde   geseôn meahton
eorđ-bûende   eallê cræftê,
hû âfæstnôd pæs   feld-hûsâ mǣst.

(106–134.)

Folc pæs on sâlum,
hlûd herges cyrm.   Heofon-beâcen âstâh
ǣfenâ gehpam,   ôđer pundor;
syllîc æfter sunnan   setl-râde beheôld
ofer leôd-perum   lîgê scînan
byrnende beâm.   Blâce stôdon
ofer sceôtendum   scîre leôman,
scinon scyld-hreôđan,   sceado spiđredon:
neôple niht-scûpan   neah ne mihton
heolstor âhŷdan.   Heofon-candel barn:
nipe niht-peard   nŷde sceolde
pîcian ofer peredum,   þŷ læs him pêsten-gryrê
hâr hǣđ   holmegum pedrum
ô fêrclammê   ferhđ getpǣfde.
Hæfde foregenga   fŷrene loccâs,
blâce beâmâs,   bǣl-egsan hpeôp
þam here-þreâte,   hâtan lîgê,

þæt hê on pêstenne perod forbærnde,
nymđe hîe môd-hpate Môyses hŷrde.
Sceân scîr perod, scyldâs lixton;
gesâpon rand-pîgan rihtre strǽte
segn ofer speotum, ôđ þæt sǽ-fæsten
landes æt ende leôd-mægne forstôd,
fûs on forđ-peg. Fyrd-pîc ârâs,
ꝑyrpton hîe pêrige; piste genǽgdon
môdige mete-þegnâs hyrâ mægen bêtan.
Brǽddon æfter beorgum, siđđan bŷme sang,
flotan feld-hûsum: þâ pæs feôrđe pîc,
rand-pîgenâ ræst be þam Reâdan sǽ.

(154–182.)

Þâ him eorlâ môd ortrŷpe pearđ,
siđđan hîe gesâpon of sûđ-pegum
fyrd Faraônes forđ ongangan,
ofer-holt pegan, eôred lixan,
þûfâs þunian, þeôd mearc tredan:
gârâs trymedon, gûđ hpearfôde,
blicon bord-hreôđan, bŷman sungon.
On hpæl hreôpon here-fugolâs
hilde grǽdige; hræfen gôl
deâpig-feđere ofer driht-nêum,
pon pæl-ceâsega. Đulfâs sungon
atol ǽfen-leôd ǽtes on pênan,
carleâsan deôr, cpyld-rôf beôdan
on lâđrâ lâst leôd-mægnes fyl,
hreôpon mearc-peardâs middum nihtum:
fleâh fǽge gâst, folc pæs gehǽged.
Hpîlum of þam perode plance þegnâs
mǽton mîl-pađâs mearâ bôgum.
Him þǽr sige-cyning piđ þone segn foran
mannâ þengel mearc-þreâtê râd;
gûđ-peard gumenâ grîm-helm gespeôn,
cyning cin-berge (cumbol lixton)
pîges on pênum, pæl-hlencan sceôc,
hêht his here-ciste healdan georne
fæst fyrd-getrum. Feônd onsêgon
lâđum eâgum land-mannâ cyme.
Ymb hine pǽgon pîgend unforhte;

hâre heoro-pulfâs   hilde grêtton
þurstige þræc-pîges,   þeôden-holde.

BEOWULF.

(*A Good King*, 1–11.)

Hpæt! pê Gâr-Denâ   in geâr-dagum
þeôd-cyningâ   þrym gefrunon,
hû þâ æđelingâs   ellen fremedon!
Oft Scyld Scêfing   sceađenâ þreâtum,
monegum mǣgđum   meodo-setlâ ofteâh;
egsôde eorl,   syđđan ǣrest pearđ
feâsceaft funden;   hê þæs frôfre gebâd,
peôx under polcnum,   peorđmyndum þâh,
ôđ þæt him ǣghpylc   þârâ ymb-sittendrâ
ofer hron-râde   hŷran scolde,
gomban gyldan: þæt pæs gôd cyning!

(*Obsequies of Scyld*, 26–52.)

Him þâ Scyld gepât   tô gescæp-hpîle
fela-hrôr fêran   on Freân pære.
Hî hyne þâ ætbǣron   tô brimes farôđe,
spǣse gesîđâs,   spâ hê selfa bæd,
þenden pordum peôld   pine Scyldingâ,
leôf land-fruma,   longe âhte.
Pǣr æt hŷđe stôd   hringed-stefna
îsig and ût-fûs,   æđelinges fær:
âlêdon þâ   leôfne þeôden,
beâgâ bryttan,   on bearm scipes,
mǣrne be mæste.   Pǣr pæs mâđmâ fela
of feor-pegum,   frætpâ, gelǣded:
ne hŷrde ic cymlîcor   ceôl gegyrpan
hilde-pǣpnum   and heađo-pǣdum,
billum and byrnum: him on bearme læg
mâđmâ mænigo,   þâ him mid scoldon
on flôdes ǣht   feor gepîtan.
Nalæs hî hine læssan   lâcum teôdan,
þeôd-gestreônum,   þonne þâ dydon,
þe hine æt frumsceafte   forđ onsendon

ǣnne ofer ŷđe umbor pesende:
þâ gyt hîe him âsetton segen gyldenne
heâh ofer heâfod, lêton holm beran,
geâfon on gâr-secg: him pæs geômor sefa,
murnende môd. Men ne cunnon
secgan tô sôđe, sele-rǣdende,
hæleđ under heofenum, hpâ þæm hlæste onfêng!

(*Hrothgar and Heorot*, 64–83.)

Þâ pæs HRÔÐGÂRE here-spêd gyfen,
pîges peorđmynd, þæt him his pine-magâs
georne hŷrdon, ôđ þæt seô geôgođ gepeôx,
mago-driht micel. Him on môd be-arn,
þæt hê heal-reced hâtan polde,
medo-ærn micel men gepyrcean,
þone yldo bearn ǣfre gefrunon,
and þǣr on-innan eal gedǣlan
geongum and ealdum, spylc him God sealde,
bûton folc-scare and feorum gumenâ.
Þâ ic pîde gefrægn peorc gebannan
manigre mǣgđe geond þisne middangeard,
folc-stede frætpan. Him on fyrste gelomp
ædre mid yldum, þæt hit pearđ eal gearo,
heal-ærnâ mǣst: scôp him HEORT naman,
se þe his pordes gepeald pîde hæfde.
Hê beôt ne âlêh, beâgâs dǣlde,
sinc æt symle. Sele hlifâde
heâh and horn-geâp.

(*Grendel*, 99–129.)

Spâ þâ driht-guman dreâmum lifdon
eâdiglîce, ôđ þæt ân ongan
fyrene fremman, feônd on helle:
pæs se grimma gǣst GRENDEL hâten,
mǣre mearc-stapa, se þe môrâs heôld,
fen and fæsten; fîfel-cynnes eard
ponsǣlig per peardôde hpîle,
siđđan him Scyppend forscrifen hæfde.
In Caines cynne þone cpealm gepræc
êce Drihten, þæs þe hê Abel slôg:
ne gefeah hê þǣre fǣhđe, ac hê hine feor forpræc,

Metod for þŷ mânê   man-cynne fram.
Þanon untydrâs   ealle onpôcon,
eotenâs and ylfe   and orcneâs,
spylce gigantâs,   þâ pið Gode punnon
lange þrage: hê him þæs leân forgeald!—
Gepât þâ neôsian,   syððan niht becom,
heân hûses,   hû hit Hring-Dene
æfter beôr-þege   gebûn hæfdon;
fand þâ þǣr inne   æðelingâ gedriht
spefan æfter symble: sorge ne cûðon,
ponsceaft perâ.   Ðiht unhǣlo
grim and grǣdig   gearo sôna pæs,
reôc and rêðe,   and on ræste genam
þrîtig þegnâ;   þanon eft gepât
hûðe hrêmig   tô hâm faran,
mid þǣre pæl-fylle   pîcâ neôsan.
Þâ pæs on uhtan   mid ǣr-dæge
GRENDLES gûð-cræft   gumum undyrne:
þâ pæs æfter piste   pôp up-âhafen,
micel morgen-spêg.

(144–152.)

Spâ rîxôde   and pið rihte pan
âna pið eallum,   ôð þæt îdel stôd
hûsâ sêlest.   Ðæs seô hpîl micel:
tpelf pintrâ tîd   torn geþolôde
pine Scyldingâ,   peânâ gehpelcne,
sîdrâ sorgâ;   forþam siððan pearð
yldâ bearnum   undyrne cûð,
gyddum geômore,   þætte GRENDEL pan
hpîle pið Hrôðgâr.

(*Beowulf sails for Heorot*, 194–228.)

Þæt fram hâm gefrægn   Higelâces þegn,
gôd mid Geâtum,   Grendles dǣdâ:
se pæs mon-cynnes   mægenes strengest
on þæm dæge   þysses lîfes,
æðele and eâcen.   Hêt him ŷð-lidan
gôdne gegyrpan;   cpæð hê gûð-cyning
ofer span-râde   sêcean polde,
mǣrne þeôden,   þâ him pæs mannâ þearf.

Hæfde se gôda   Geâtâ leôdâ
cempan gecorone,   þârâ þe hê cênôste
findan mihte: fîftênâ sum
sund-pudu sôhte;   secg pîsâde,
lagu-cræftig mon,   land-gemyrcu.
Fyrst forð gepât: flota pæs on ŷðum,
bât under beorge.   Beornâs gearpe
on stefn stigon;   streâmâs pundon
sund pið sande.   Secgâs bǽron
on bearm nacan   beorhte frætpe,
gûð-searo geatolîc: guman ût scufon,
perâs on pilsîð   pudu bundenne.
Gepât þâ ofer pǽg-holm   pindê gefŷsed
flota fâmig-heals   fugle gelîcôst,
ôð þæt ymb ân-tîd   ôðres dôgores
punden-stefna   gepaden hæfde,
þæt þâ lîðende   land gesâpon,
brim-clifu blîcan,   beorgâs steâpe,
sîde sǽ-næssâs: þâ pæs sund liden
eoletes æt ende.   Þanon up hraðe
Pederâ leôde   on pang stigon,
sǽ-pudu sǽldon: syrcan hrysedon,
gûð-gepǽdo;   Gode þancedon,
þæs þe him ŷð-lâde   eâðe purdon.

(*The Warden of the Shore*, 229+.)

Þâ of pealle geseah   peard Scyldingâ,
se þe holm-clifu   healdan scolde,
beran ofer bolcan   beorhte randâs,
fyrd-searu fûslîcu;   hine fyrpyt bræc
môd-gehygdum,   hpæt þâ men pǽron.
Gepât him þâ tô parôðe   picgê rîdan
þegn Hrôðgâres,   þrymmum cpehte
mægen-pudu mundum,   meðel-pordum frægn:
"Hpæt syndon gê   searo-hæbbendrâ
byrnum perede,   þe þus brontne ceôl
ofer lagu-strǽte   lǽdan cpômon,
hider ofer holmâs   Hrôðgâr sêcean?
Ic pæs ende-sǽta,   ǽg-pearde heôld,
þæt on land Denâ   lâðrâ nǽnig
mid scip-herge   sceððan ne meahte.

Nô hêr cûđlîcôr   cuman ongunnon
lind-hæbbende!   nê gê leâfnes-pord
gûđ-fremmendrâ   gearpe ne pisson,
magâ gemêdu!   Nǣfre ic mâran geseah
eorlâ ofer eorđan,   þonne is eôper sum,
secg on searpum;   nis þæt seld-guma
pǣpnum gepeorđâd,   næfne him his plite leôge,
ǣnlîc ansŷn.   Nû ic eôper sceal
frum-cyn pitan,   ǣr gê fyr heonan
leâse sceâperâs   on land Denâ
furđur fêran.   Nû gê feor-bûend
mere-lîđende,   mînne gehŷrađ
ânfealdne geþoht;   ôfost is sêlest
tô gecŷđanne,   hpanan eôpre cyme syndon."
Him se yldesta   andsparôde,
perodes pîsa   pord-hord onleâc:
"Pê synt gum-cynnes   Geâtâ leôde
and Higelâces   heorđ-geneâtâs.
Pæs mîn fæder   folcum gecŷđed,
æđele ord-fruma   Ecgþeôp hâten;
gebâd pintrâ porn,   ǣr hê on peg hpurfe
gamol of geardum;   hine gearpe geman
pitenâ pel-hpylc   pîde geond eorđan.
Pê þurh holdne hige   hlâford þînne
sunu Healfdenes   sêcean cpômon,
leôd-gebyrgean.   Pes þû ûs lârenâ gôd!"

286. Peard mađelôde,   þǣr on picge sæt
ombeht unforht: "Ǣghpæđres sceal
scearp scyld-pîga   gescâd pitan,
pordâ and porcâ,   se þe pel þenceđ.
Ic þæt gehŷre,   þæt þis is hold veorod
freân Scyldingâ: gepîtađ forđ beran
pǣpen and gepǣdu,   ic eôp pîsige."

301. Gepiton him þâ fêran.   Flota stille bâd,
seomôde on sôle   sîd-fæđmed scip,
on ancre fæst.   Eoforlîc scionon
ofer hleôr-beran   gehroden goldê
fâh and fyr-heard;   ferh pearde heôld.
Gûđ-môde grummon,   guman onetton,

sigon ætsomne, ôđ þæt hŷ sæl timbred
geatolîc and gold-fâh ongytan mihton;
þæt pæs fore-mǽrôst fold-bûendum
recedâ under roderum, on þæm se rîca bâd;
lixte se leôma ofer landâ-fela.
Him þâ hilde-deôr hof môdigrâ
torht getǽhte, þæt hŷ him tô mihton
gegnum gangan. Gûđ-beornâ sum
picg gepende, pord æfter cpæđ:
"Mǽl is mê tô fêran! Fæder alpalda
mid âr-stafum eôpic gehealde
sîđâ gesunde! ic tô sǽ pille
piđ prâđ perod pearde healdan."

A Feast of Welcome.—(*Wealhtheow, the Queen*, 612 +.)

Pǽr pæs hæleđâ hleahtor; hlyn spynsôde,
pord pǽron pynsume. Eôde ǷEALHÞEÔǷ forđ,
cpên Hrôđgâres cynnâ gemyndig,
grêtte gold-hroden guman on healle,
and þâ freôlîc pîf ful gesealde
ǽrest Eâst-Denâ êđel-pearde,
bæd hine blîđne æt þǽre beôr-þege,
leôdum leôfne; hê on lust geþeah
symbel and sele-ful, sige-rôf cyning.
Ymb-eôde þâ ides Helmingâ
duguđe and geôgođe dǽl ǽghpylcne;
sinc-fato sealde, ôđ þæt sǽl âlamp,
þæt hiô Beôpulfe, beâg-hroden cpên
môdê geþungen, medo-ful ætbær;
grêtte Geâtâ leôd, Gode þancôde
pîs-fæst pordum, þæs þe hire se pilla gelamp,
þæt heô on ǽnigne eorl gelŷfde
fyrenâ frôfre. Hê þæt ful geþeah,
pæl-reôp pîga, æt ǷEALHÞEÔN,
and þâ gyddôde gûđe gefŷsed;
Beôpulf mađelôde, bearn Ecgþeôpes:
"Ic þæt hogôde, þâ ic on holm gestâh,
sǽ-bât gesæt mid minrâ secgâ gedriht,
þæt ic ânunga eôprâ leôdâ
pillan geporhte, ođđe on pæl crunge,
feônd-grâpum fæst. Ic gefremman sceal

eorlîc ellen, ođđe ende-dæg
on þisse meodu-healle mînne gebîdan."
Þam pîfe þâ pord pel lîcôdon,
gilp-cpide Geâtes; eôde gold-hroden
freôlîcu folc-cpên tô hire freân sittan.
Þâ pæs eft spâ ǽr inne on healle
þryđ-pord sprecen, þeôd on sǽlum,
sige-folcâ speg, ôđ þæt semninga
sunu Healfdenes sêcean polde
ǽfen-ræste.

(*Good-Night.*)

651. Ƿerod eal ârâs.
Grêtte þâ guma ôđerne,
HRÔÐGÂR BEÔƿULF, and him hǽl âbeâd.

1789. Niht-helm gespearc
deorc ofer dryht-gumum. Duguđ eal ârâs;
polde blonden-feax beddes neôsan,
gamela Scylding. Geât ungemetes pel
rôfne rand-pîgan restan lyste:
sôna him sele-þegn sîđes pêrgum,
feorran-cundum forđ pîsâde,
se for andrysnum ealle bepeotede
þegnes þearfe, spylce þŷ dôgorê
heâđo-lîđende habban scoldon.
Reste hine þâ rûm-heort; reced hlifâde
geâp and gold-fâh, gæst inne spæf,
ôđ þæt hrefn blaca heofenes pynne
blîđ-heort bodôde, côman beorhte leôman
ofer scadu scacan.

(*Hrunting, the Good Sword,* 1455 +.)

Næs þæt þonne mǽtôst mægen-fultumâ,
þæt him on þearfe lâh þyle Hrôđgâres;
pæs þæm hæft-mêce HRUNTING nama,
þæt pæs ân foran eald-gestreônâ;
ecg pæs îren, âter-tânum fâh,
âhyrded heađo-spâtê; nǽfre hit æt hilde ne spâc
mannâ ǽngum þârâ þe hit mid mundum bepand,
se þe gryre-sîđâs gegân dorste,

folc-stede fârâ; næs þæt forma sîđ,
þæt hit ellen-peorc æfnan scolde.

(*It fails at Need*, 1512 +.)

Þâ se eorl ongeat,
þæt hê in niđ-sele nât-hpylcum pæs,
þæ̂r him næ̂nig pæter pihtê ne sceđede,
nê him for hrôf-sele hrînan ne mehte
fæ̂r-gripe flôdes: fŷr-leôht geseah,
blâcne leôman beorhte scînan.
Ongeat þâ se gôda grund-pyrgenne,
mere-pîf mihtig; mægen-ræ̂s forgeaf
hilde-billê, hond spenge ne ofteâh,
þæt hire on hafelan hring-mæ̂l âgôl
græ̂dig gûđ-leôđ; þâ se gist onfand,
þæt se beado-leôma bîtan nolde,
aldre sceđđan, ac seô ecg gespâc
þeôdne æt þearfe: þolôde æ̂r fela
hond-gemôtâ, helm oft gescær,
fæ̂ges fyrd-hrægl: þâ pæs forma sîđ
deôrum mâđme, þæt his dôm âlæg.
Eft pæs ân-ræ̂d, nalas elnes læt,
mæ̂rđâ gemyndig mæ̂g Hygelâces;
pearp þâ punden-mæ̂l prættum gebunden
yrre oretta, þæt hit on eorđan læg,
stîđ and stŷl-ecg; strenge getrûpôde,
mund-gripe mægenes. Spâ sceal man dôn
þonne hê æt gûđe gegân þenceđ
longsumne lof, nâ ymb his lîf cearâđ.

(*The Right Weapon*, 1557 +.)

Geseah þâ on searpum sige-eâdig bil,
eald speord eotenisc ecgum þyhtig,
pîgenâ peorđ-mynd: þæt pæs pæ̂pnâ cyst,
bûton hit pæs mâre þonne æ̂nig mon ôđer
tô beadu-lâce ætberan meahte,
gôd and geatolîc gigantâ gepeorc.
Hê gefêng þâ fetel-hilt, freca Scyldingâ,
hreôh and heoro-grim hring-mæ̂l gebrægd.

1687. Hrôđgâr mađelôde, hilt sceâpôde,

ealde lâfe, on þæm ƿæs ôr ƿriten
fyrn-geƿinnes: syđđan flôd ofslôh,
gifen geôtende, gigantâ cyn,
frêcne gefêrdon: þæt ƿæs fremde þeôd
êcean Dryhtne, him þæs ende-leân
þurh ƿæteres ƿylm ƿaldend sealde.
Sƿâ ƿæs on þæm scennum scîran goldes
þurh rûn-stafâs rihte gemearcôd,
geseted and gesǣd, hƿâm þæt sƿeord geƿorht,
îrenâ cyst, ǣrest ƿǣre,
ƿreođen-hilt and ƿyrm-fâh.

ALFRED'S METERS OF BOETHIUS.

Þus Ælfrêd ûs eald-spel reahte
cyning Ƿest-Sexnâ, cræft meldôde,
leôđ-ƿyrhtâ list: him ƿæs lust micel,
þæt hê þiossum leôdum leôđ spellôde,
monnum myrgen, mislîce cƿidâs.

Meter VI.

Þâ se Ƿîsdôm eft ƿord-hord onleâc,
sang sôđ-cƿidâs, and þus selfa cƿæđ:
Þonne siô sunne sƿeotolôst scîneđ
hâdrôst of hefone, hræđe biôđ âþîstrôd
ealle ofer eorđan ôđre steorran;
forþæm hiorâ birhtu ne biđ âuht
tô gesettanne ƿiđ þǣre sunnan leôht.
Þonne smolte blǣƿđ sûđan and ƿestan
ƿind under ƿolcnum, þonne ƿeaxađ hrađe
feldes blôstman fægen þæt hî môton:
ac se stearca storm, þonne hê strong cymđ
norđan and eâstan, hê genimeđ hrađe
þǣre rôsan ƿlite, and eâc þâ rûman sǣ
norđerne ŷst nêde gebǣdeđ,
þæt hiô strange geondstyred on stađu beâteđ.
Eâ lâ! þæt on eorđan âuht fæstlîces
ƿeorces on ƿorulde ne ƿunâđ ǣfre!

Meter X.

83. Hpæ̂r sind nû þæs pîsan   Ƿêlandes bân,
þæs gold-smiđes,   þe pæs geô mæ̂rôst?
Forþŷ ic cpæđ þæs pîsan   Ƿêlandes bân,
forþŷ æ̂ngum ne mæg   eorđ-bûendrâ
se cræft losian,   þe him Crist onlæ̂nđ.
Ne mæg mon æ̂fre þŷ êđ   æ̂nne præccan
his cræftes beniman,   þe mon oncerran mæg
sunnan on-spîfan   and þisne spiftan rodor
of his riht-ryne   rincâ æ̂nig.
Hpâ pât nû þæs pîsan   Ƿêlandes bân,
on hpelcum hî hlæ̂pâ   hrusan þeccen?
Hpæ̂r is nû se rîca   Rômânâ pita
and se ârôda,   þe pê ymb sprecađ,
hiorâ heretoga,   se gehâten pæs
mid þæ̂m burhparum   Brûtus nemned?
Hpæ̂r is eâc se pîsa   and se peorđgeorna
and se fæst-ræ̂da   folces hyrde,
se pæs ûđpita   ælces þinges
cêne and cræftig,   þæm pæs Catôn nama?
Hî pæ̂ron gefyrn   forđ gepitene:
nât næ̂nig mon,   hpæ̂r hî nû sindon!
Hpæt is hiorâ here   bûton se hlîsa ân?
se is eâc tô lytel   spelcrâ lâriôpâ,
forþæm þâ mago-rincâs   mâran pyrđe
pæ̂ron on porulde.   Ac hit is pyrse nû,
þæt geond þâs eorđan   æ̂ghpæ̂r sindon
hiorâ gelîcan   hpôn ymbspræ̂ce,
sume openlîce   ealle forgitene,
þæt hî se hlîsa   hîp-cûđe ne mæg
fore-mæ̂re perâs   forđ gebrengan!
Peâh gê nû pênen   and pilnigen,
þæt gê lange tîd   libban môten,
hpæt iôp æ̂fre þŷ bet   biô ođđe þince,
forþæm þe nâne forlêt,   þeâh hit lang þince,
deâđ æfter dôgorrîme,   þonne hê hæfđ Drihtnes leâfe?
Hpæt þonne hæbbe   hæleđâ æ̂nig,
guma æt þæm gilpe,   gif hine gegrîpan môt
se êca deâđ   æfter þissum porulde?

SAWS.

Forst sceal freôsan, fŷr pudu meltan,
eorđe grôpan, îs brycgian,
pæter-helm pegan, pundrum lûcan
eorđan cîđâs: ân sceal inbindan
forstes fetre, fela-meahtig God;
pinter sceal gepeorpan, peder eft cuman,
sumor spegle hât, sund unstille:
deôp deâda pǣg dyrne biđ lengest.
Holen sceal inæled, yrfe gedǣled
deâdes monnes: dôm biđ sêlâst.
Cyning sceal mid ceâpê cpêne gebicgan,
bunum and beâgum: bu sceolon ǣrest
geofum gôd pesan. Gûđ sceal in eorle
pîg gepeaxan, and pîf geþeôn
leôf mid hyre leôdum, leoht-môd pesan,
rûne healdan, rûm-heort beôn
mearum and mâđmum, meodo-rǣdenne
for gesîđ-mægen; simle ǣghpǣr
eodor æđelingâ ǣrest gegrêtan,
forman fullê tô freân hond
ricene gerǣcan and him rǣd pitan,
bold-âgendum bǣm ætsomne.
Scip sceal genægled, scyld gebunden,
leôht linden bord; leôf pilcuma
frysan pîfe, þonne flota stondeđ;
biđ his ceôl cumen and hyre ceorl tô hâm,
âgen ǣtgeofa, and heô hine in lađâđ,
pæsceđ his pârig hrægl
  and him syleđ pǣde nipe;
liđ him on londe þæs his lufu bǣdeđ.
Pîf sceal piđ per pǣre gehealdan;
fela biđ fæst-hydigrâ,
  fela biđ fyrpet-geornrâ,
freôđ hŷ fremde monnan,
  þonne se ôđer feor gepîteđ.
Lida biđ longe on sîđe;
  â mon sceal seþeâh leôfes pênan,
gebîdan þæs hê gebǣdan ne mæg,
  hponne him eft gebyre peorđe;

hâm cymeđ, gif hê hâl leofâđ,
nefne him holm gestŷređ;
mere hafâđ mundum, mægđ egsan pyn.
Ceâp-eâdig mon cyning pîc þonne
leôdon cŷpeđ, þonne lîđan cymeđ:
pudâ and pætres nyttâđ
þonne him biđ pîc âlŷfed;
mete bygeđ, gif hê mâran þearf,
ǣrþon hê tô mêđe peorđe.
Seôc se biđ þe tô seldan ieteđ;
þeâh hine mon on sunnan lǣde,
ne mæg hê be þŷ pedrê pesan,
þeâh hit sŷ pearm on sumerâ;
ofercumen biđ hê, ǣr hê âcpele,
gif hê nât hpâ hine cpicne fêde.
Mægen mon sceal mid mete fêdan,
morđor under eorđan befeolan,
hinder under hrusan, þe hit forhelan þenceđ;
ne biđ þæt gedêfe deâđ, þonne hit gedyrned peorđeđ.
Heân sceal gehnîgan, âdl gesîgan,
ryht rogian. Rǣd biđ nyttôst,
yfel unnyttôst, þæt unlǣd nimeđ;
gôd biđ genge and piđ God lenge.
Hyge sceal gehealden, hond gepealden;
seô sceal in eâgan, snyttro in breôstum,
þǣr biđ þæs monnes môd-geþoncâs.
Mûđâ gehpylc mete þearf, mæl sceolon tîdum gongan.
Gold gerîseđ on guman speorde,
sellîc sige-sceorp, sinc on cpêne,
gôd scôp gumum, gâr nîđ-perum
pîg tô-piđre, pîc-freođâ healdan.
Scyld sceal cempan, sceaft reâfere;
sceal brŷde beâg, bêc leornere,
hûsl hâlgum men, hǣđnum synne.
Pôden porhte peôs, puldor Alpalda,
rûme roderâs; þæt is rîce God,
sylf sôđ cyning, sâplâ nergend,
se ûs eal forgeaf, þǣr pê on lifgađ,
and eft æt þâm ende eallum pealdeđ
monnâ cynne; þæt is meotud sylfa.

THRENES.

Ƿindê bipâune peallâs stondađ
hrîmê bihrorene, hrŷđge þâ ederâs.
Ƿôriađ þâ pîn-salo, paldend licgađ
dreâmê bidrorene; dugruđ eal gecrong
plonc bî pealle: sume pîg fornom,
ferede in forđpege; sumne fugel ôđbær
ofer heâhne holm; sumne se hâra pulf
deâđe gedǣlde; sumne dreôrig-hleôr
in eorđ-scræfe eorl gehŷdde:
ŷđde spâ þisne eard-geard ældâ Scyppend,
ôđþæt burgparâ breahtmâ leâse
eald entâ gepeorc îdlu stôdon.
Se þonne þisne peal-steal pîsê geþohtê
and þis deorce lîf deôpe geondþenceđ,
frôd in ferđe, feor oft gemon
pæl-sleahtâ porn and þâs pord âcpiđ: [đum-gyfa?
"Hpǣr cpom mearg, hpǣr cpom mago? hpǣr cpom mâđ-
hpǣr cpom symblâ gesetu? hpǣr sindon sele-dreâmâs?
Eâlâ beorht bune, eâlâ byrn-pîga,
eâlâ þeôdnes þrym! hû seô þrag gepât,
genâp under niht-helm, spâ heô nô pǣre!
Stondeđ nû on lâste leôfre duguđe
peal pundrum heâh pyrmlîcum fâh:
eorlâs fornôman ascâ þryđe,
pǣpen pæl-gîfru, Ƿyrd seô mǣre,
and þâs stân-hleođu stormâs cnyssađ;
hrîđ hreôsende hruse bindeđ
pintres pôma: þonne pon cymeđ,
nîpeđ niht-scûa, norđan onsendeđ
hreô hægl-fare hæleđum on andan.
Eal is earfôđlîc eorđan rîce:
onpendeđ pyrdâ gesceaft peoruld under heofenum.
Hêr biđ feoh lǣne, hêr biđ freônd lǣne,
hêr biđ mon lǣne, hêr biđ mǣg lǣne:
eal þis eorđan gesteal îdel peorđeđ."
Spâ cpæđ snottor on môde,
gesæt him sundor æt rûne.
Til biđ seþe his treôpe gehealdeđ:
ne sceal nǣfre his torn tô rycene

beorn of his breôstum âcŷđan,
nemđe hê ǣr þâ bôte cunne,
eorl mid elnê gefremman:
pel biđ þam þe him âre sêceđ,
frôfre tô Fæder on heofonum,
þǣr ûs eal seô fæstnung stondeđ.

Pêland him be purman præces cunnâde,
ânhydig eorl, earfôđâ dreâg;
hæfde him tô gesîđđe sorge and longâđ,
pinter-cealde præce: peân oft onfond,
siđđan hine Nîđhâd on nêde legde
sponcre seono-benne, on sŷllan mon.
Pæs ofereôde, þisses spâ mæg!
Beadohilde ne pæs hyre brôđrâ deâđ
on sefan spâ sâr, spâ hyre sylfre þing,
* * * * *
* * * ǣfre ne meahte
þrîste geþencan, hû ymb þæt sceolde.
Pæs ofereôde, þisses spâ mæg!
Pê geâscôdan Eormanrîces
pylfenne geþoht: âhte pîde folc
Gotenâ rîces; þæt pæs grim cyning.
Sæt secg monig sorgum gebunden,
peân on pênan, pŷscte geneahhe,
þæt þæs cyne-rîces ofercumen pǣre.
Pæs ofereôde, þisses spâ mæg!
Ic hpîle pæs Heodeningâ scôp
dryhtne dŷre: mê pæs Deôr noma;
âhte ic fela pintrâ folgâđ tilne,
holdne hlâford, ôđ þæt Heorrenda nû
leôđ-cræftig mon lond-ryht geþah,
þæt mê eorlâ hleô ǣr gesealde.
Pæs ofereôde, þisses spâ mæg!

RHYMES.

Þer-cyn gepîteđ,   pæl-gâr slîteđ,
flâh mâh flîteđ,   flân mân hpîteđ,
borg-sorg bîteđ,   bald ald þpîteđ,
præc-fæc prîteđ,   prâđ âđ smîteđ,
syn-gryn sîdeđ,   searo-fearo glîdeđ.
Grorn torn græfeđ,   græft ræft hæfeđ,
searo hpît sôlâđ,   sumur-hât côlâđ,
fold-pela fealleđ,   feôndscipe pealleđ,
eorđ-mægen ealdâđ,   ellen cealdâđ.
Mê þæt pyrd gepæf   and gepyrht forgeaf,
þæt ic grôfe græf;   and þæt grimme geræf
fleôn flǣscê ne mæg,   þonne flân-hred dæg
nŷd-grâpum nimeđ,   þonne seô neaht becymeđ,
seô mê êđles ofon   and mê hêr eardes oncon.
Þonne lîchoma ligeđ: limu pyrm þigeđ
and him pynne gepigeđ   and þâ pist geþigeđ,
ôđ þæt beôđ þâ bân   gebrosnâd on ân
and æt nŷhstan nân   nefne se nêdâ tân
balapum hêr gehloten.   Ne biđ se hlîsa âþroten.
Ǣr þæt eâdig geþenceđ;
  hê hine þê oftôr spenceđ,
byrgeđ him þâ bitran synne,
  hycgâđ tô þǣre betran pynne,
gemon meorđâ lisse,
  þǣr sindon miltsâ blisse
hyhtlîce in heofenâ rîce.
  Uton nû hâlgum gelîce
scyldum biscerede   scyndan generede
pommum biperede,   puldrê gehêrede,
þǣr mon-cyn môt   for meotude rôt
sôđne God geseôn   and â in sibbe gefeôn!

NOTES.

PAGE 1. THE GOSPELS were read in Anglo-Saxon as part of the Church service. Several manuscripts written before the Norman Conquest are preserved. An edition was printed by Parker in 1571, by Marshall in 1665, by Thorpe in 1842. Bouterwek published the Northumbrian version of the Lindisfarne Codex (Durham Book) in 1857, and both the Lindisfarne and Rushworth for the three first Gospels have been printed for the Surtees Society, 1854–1863. Kemble at his death in 1857 was at work on an edition, of which Matthew has since been printed for the Syndics of the University Press at Cambridge. It has the Latin Vetus Italica and four Anglo-Saxon texts printed together, with the various readings of three others. Two of these are the Lindisfarne and Rushworth, the others are copies of the received version of the West-Saxon Church: the best was written about 1000. A critical edition of the Gospels is still wanting. We have a careful edition of the Psalms by Grein. Ælfric's translation of the Heptateuch was published by Thwaites, 1698.

PAGE 2. THE LORD'S PRAYER. The end of Matthew, vi., 13, *For thine is the kingdom*, etc., is not in the Latin, and so not in the Anglo-Saxon. It is wanting in many Greek manuscripts.

PAGE 9. ULFILAS (Gothic VULFILA) was born in 311, and died in 381. He was a Goth, and for forty years bishop of the Goths in Dacia. Fragments of his translation of the Bible have been found in eight manuscripts. The extract here given is from the so-called Codex Argenteus, written on parchment in silver and gold letters, in Italy, in the fifth century, and, after various fortunes, now in the library of the University of Upsala. It had originally 330 leaves, and contained the four Gospels; of these 177 remain. The other fragments are mainly from Paul's epistles, enough to make about 145 more such pages. See further for Gothic, §§ 7–9, and the Index.

PAGE 12. THE LORD'S PRAYER. *Father* our thou in *heavens, Hallowed-be* name thine. Come *kingdom* thine. Worth will thine, so in *heaven and* on earth. Loaf our the *daily* give us *this* day. *And* off-let us that *in which we debtors are*, so so *also* we off-let them debtors ours. And not bring us in *temptation, but* loose us of the evil; *since* thine is *kingdom and* might *and glory* in ever. Amen.

Atta, v. 45; *unsar*, A.-S. *ûser*, *ûre* > our, Ger. *unser*, § 132; *þu*, v. 39, § 130, for its use as a relative, § 381; *in himinam*, v. 45; *veihnâi* < *veihnan*, § 170, akin to *veihs*, holy, A.-S. *pîh*, Ger. *weih-*, akin to *witch; namô*, declens., § 95, A.-S. *nama* > name, Ger. *name*, Lat. *nomen* > noun, Gr. *ὄνομα*, Sansk. *nâman*, √*gna*, know; *þein*, v. 39; *kvimâi*, v. 47; *þiudi-*

nassus, declens., § 93, from *þiuda*, v. 46; *vairþâi*, v. 45; *vilja*, declens., § 95, v. 40; *spê*, v. 48; *jah*, v. 38; *ąna*, v. 45; *airþ-a*, dat. *-âi*, declens., § 88, A.-S. *eorðe*, Ger. *erde*, √*ar*, plough, till? *Hlâifs*, § 70, A.-S. *hlâf* > loaf, Ger. *laib*; *þana*, § 104; *sinteins*, declens., § 107, akin to A.-S. *sin-*, O. H. G. *sin-*, Lat. *sem-*, Gr. ἕνο-ς, Sansk. *sa-nâ'*, § 254; *gif*, v. 42; *uns*, *himma*, A.-S. *him*, § 130; *dags*, § 70, A.-S. *dæg*, Ger. *tag*; *aflêt'*, v. 40; *þatei*, v. 38; *skula*, declens., § 95, verb *skulan*, A.-S. *sculan*>shall, Ger. *sollen*, § 212; *sijâima*, v. 48; *veis*, § 130; *pê*, Ger. *wir*; *briggâis*, A.-S. *bringan* > bring, Ger. *bringen*; *frâistubn-i*, dat. *-jâi* <*frâisan*, A.-S. *frâsian* > O. Engl. *fraise*, to tempt, question, O. H. G. *freısa*; *ak*, v. 39; *lâusei*, A.-S. *leôsan* > loose, Ger. *liesen*, Lat. *luo*, *so˙-lu-tus*, Gr. λύω, Sansk. *lû*; *ubilin*, *untê*, v. 45; *þiudan-gardi*, king-court, see *þiudinassus* above, *-gards*, A.-S. *geard* > yard, garden, Ger. *garten*, Lat. *hortus*, Gr. χόρτος, a place *girt*, enclosed; *mahts*, § 89, A.-S. *meahte*>might, Ger. *macht*<verb *mag*, may; *vulþus*, A.-S. *puldor*, glory, declens., § 93; *âivs*, time, declens., § 89, A.-S. *âpa*>aye, Ger. *je*; *Amên*, true, Hebrew.

PAGE 13. DIALOGUES OF CALLINGS. This was one of the standard text-books for the study of Latin in the Anglo-Saxon schools. It was prepared with interlinear Latin and Anglo-Saxon by Ælfric, the grammarian, after the Homilies (see p. 75), and enlarged by Ælfric Bata, his pupil. Manuscripts are in the British Museum and the Oxford library. It was printed by Thorpe in 1834, and has been often reprinted. It is good school-master's Anglo-Saxon, and gives a lively picture of the manners and customs of the time. It is nearly all brought in, in one place or another, in Sharon Turner's History.

1. TEACHER AND SCHOLAR.—*tæce*, teach, subj., §§ 423, 425.—*pille* < *pillað*, *rêce*<*recað*, § 165.—*sprecân*=*sprecen*, subj., § 170.—*bûtan* . . ., if only it be correct speech.—*pille gê*, Do you wish.—*hpæt spricst þû?* what will you talk about? pres. for future, § 413, 4.—*hpæt peorces*, what kind of work, § 312, *a*.—*ælcê dæg*, each day, instrumental of *dæg* without *-ê*, like the dative, § 71, *b*.—*eâc spylce*, also likewise, also.

2. TEACHER AND PLOUGHMAN.—These dialogues are a continuation of the first.—*nis hit*, it is never, *nis* = *ne is*, § 213.—*gefæstnôdum sceare and cultrê*, share and colter having been fastened, dative absolute, § 304, *d*.

PAGE 14. TEACHER AND OXHERD.—*betæce*, *tæcan*, teach, show, Lat. *adsigno*, assign, hand over; distinguish *betæce*, take, p. 15.

PAGE 15.—*rân*, from *râ*, *n*, m., roebucks, *rægan*, f., roe.

PAGE 16.—*spâ fela* . . . *spâ fela spâ*, so many . . . as.—*for hpŷ*, for what reason, instrumental of *hpæt*, § 135.—*mê is*, dative of possessor, § 298, *b*.—*fela spilces*, many (of) such, partitive, § 312.—*þænne þe* . . ., than one which is able to sink or kill not only me, but also my comrades: *one* understood, *þe hê*, which, § 381, *nâ þæt ân*, not only, *ac eâc spylce*, but also. EXTRACT 7.—*fela pîsenâ*, many (of) ways, § 312.—*sceoldon*, what should they be to me, i. e., of what use? infinitive omitted, § 435, *d*, so after *can*, I know (how to tame them)

PAGE 17.—*pintrâ, pudâ, sumerâ,* § 93.—*ôđ þæt ân,* to that alone, so much.—*nâ þæt,* not only. EXTRACT 8.—*eal spâ,* all so, for the same price as.—*þanon,* whence, from which.

PAGE 18.—*nytpyrđnesse,* partitive genitive after *hpæt,* § 312, *a.* EXTRACT 10.—*gereordunge,* luncheon, *metê,* dinner.—*Hpilc mannâ . . .* Which of men enjoys (sweet meats) savory dishes? *pered,* adj., sweet, dative after *purh-brŷcđ,* § 300.—*bûton ic . . .* unless I as a guard am with you, who do not even eat your vegetables without me. EXTRACT 11.—*hpæđer,* interrogative sign, need not be translated, § 397.—*tô pel,* well to that degree, so well. EXTRACT 12.—*on ǽnigum,* in any way.

PAGE 19.—EXTRACT 13.—*ic âhsie þâ,* I ask about those=who are those? EXTRACT 14.—*is geþuht,* seems, Lat. *videtur,* § 408, *c.*

PAGE 20.—*slecgeâ,* gen. plur., § 85, *a.*—*cræftê mînê,* instrumental, § 300; the text has *mînum,* dative; the schoolmaster's license has been taken to introduce the instrumental for drill.—*ne furđon,* not even.—*hpætlîcôr,* very quickly.—*ânrâ gehpylc,* each of ones, each one, § 386, *b,* 7.—*nelle, ne pille,* subj. pres., if he wish not to be, perhaps really a mistake for infinitive *nellan,* in analogy with Lat. *nolle.*—*pitađ* rare for *piton.*

PAGE 21.—*be eallum hâlgum,* of all saints, all-hallows.—*be þam,* about that, dative of theme, § 334.

PAGE 23.—THE ANGLO-SAXON CHRONICLE. A Chronicle is known to have been kept at the monasteries as early as the time of Alfred. It has been supposed that he had it compiled, and copies made for the libraries. How the later records were kept is not known; they come down to 1154, Henry II. The Chronicle has been often printed and translated. Thorpe's edition, 1861, contains seven fully printed parallel texts, a translation, and indexes. It has been used in preparing these extracts. They are, however, much condensed and freely handled, so that the students will find it easier to read them by the aid of the vocabulary than to look up the passages in Bohn. As far as Beda's history extends, the Chronicle is, for the most part, abridged from it or drawn from a common source.

bûend, inhabitants, nom. plur., § 87.—*Armorica,* Lat., undeclined, the Chr. have *Armenia,* but see Beda, 1, 1.—*ǽr þam þe,* before this that, before.—*ge-eôde pel manige . . .,* subdued very many (a) great town, § 395, 2. A.D. 47.—*æt neâhstan* generally means *at last,* here Beda has *pene,* almost, declension of proper names, § 101. A.D. 167—*onfêng* may take a dative, accusative, or genitive object, § 299.—*bæd* with genitive, § 315, *a.* A.D. 381.—*feôþer hund,* 400, the numerals in the Chronicle are generally denoted by the Roman letters, oftenest followed by a partitive genitive, § 393.—*hund-,* § 139. A.D. 443.—*heom,* for themselves, §§ 366, 8, 315, *a.* A.D. 449.—*Hengest* and *Horsa* are both *horses,* some suppose them mythic.—*pîđ þam þe,* in exchange for this, that=for which, §§ 359, 380, 3.—*Angel, es,* m., Angeln is now the name of a tract in Schleswig, between the Schley and Flensburg.—*nû gît,* now yet.—*se â siđđan . . .,* which ever since has stood waste: they are Beda's statements, 1, 15.—Woden, the god from whom

Wednesday is named, Scandinavian Odin, who is the supreme deity. A.D. 538.—*ǣr calende: calend*, like Lat. *calendæ* in the poets, is used for *month.* It is sometimes singular, sometimes plural. A.D. 540.—*steorran hi*, stars they appeared; repeated subject, § 288, *b*. A.D. 565.—*se Columba*, the Columba (above mentioned), § 368, *a*. A.D. 603.—*tô cyninge*, whom Æthelbert, king of the men of Kent, established there *as king:* compare English *took to wife*, § 352, factitive.—*æt handâ*, at (by) the hand. A.D. 611.—*côm, cpam > cpom > cuom > côm > com*, Orm. *comm*, is very often marked long in the Chronicle, though the discrimination from plur. *cômon* favors *com*. A.D. 664.—*forman*, first, Beda and the Chr. have the *5th of the nones of May*, incorrectly. Colman was from Scotland, and had been made bishop in Northumbria. He would not use the Roman mode of tonsure, but shaved the front hair from ear to ear in the form of a crescent; he kept Easter at the wrong time, and had great controversies with the Romanists on these matters, getting the worst of it. A.D. 687.—*eft*, again. A.D. 688.—*Petrus*, nominative of enunciation, § 288, *e*.—*under Christes clâdum*, in his baptismal clothes. A.D. 693.—*cynebôte*, besides the wergild paid to the heirs of a murdered king, a *bôt*, or compensation was made to the state, generally equal to the other. The amount here paid is variously estimated, probably £120. A.D. 754.—*pitan*, the original of Parliament.—*þæs þe*, from this that, after.—*þâ on þæs pifes gebærum*, then by the woman's gestures.—*heorâ ǣghpilcum*, to each of them.—*lǣgon*, lay dead.—*þâ on morgene . . .*, when in the morning the king's thanes, who had been left behind him, heard that, that the king had been slain, then rode they.—*ealdorman*, Lat. *dux*, was the governor of a shire. The king's *thanes* were dignitaries like king's ministers now: they were of many kinds—*horse-thane*, marshal; *bower-thane*, chamberlain, etc.—*þâ þe*, who, *him fram noldon*, would not (go) from him, §§ 380, 3, 440.—*nǣnig mǣg nǣre*, no kinsman could be; emphatic negation. A.D. 784.—*Heredaland*, Norway. A.D. 800.—*for þŷ . . . þŷ þe*, for this reason . . . because (that).—*tô cpêne*, as queen, § 352. A.D. 823.—*heom tô fride*, for themselves for peace, and as protector. A.D. 855.—*And him þâ*, and to him then Charles, king of the Franks, his daughter gave as a queen for him—Charles the Bald.—*þæs þe*, from the time that, after.—*nigonteóde healf*, 18½, § 147. A.D. 872.—*and þâ Deniscan*, and (=but) the Danes held possession of the slaughter-place (battle-field).—*bûtan þam þe heom*, besides which, against them—rode. A.D. 878.—*hine bestæl*, stole (itself), § 290, *d*.—*heom gecyrdon*, brought into allegiance to themselves.—*æfter wudum*, among the forests, § 331.—The Danes Ingvar and Hâlfdân bore the Raven, 840 Danes died around it. —*him ongeân*, to meet him.—*hire*, § 312.—*his*, § 315.—*him æfter*, after it, pursued it to its intrenchment.—*poldon*, would (go), § 440.—*þritigâ sum*, one of thirty, with twenty-nine companions, § 388.—*crismlŷsing*, compare *Cristes clâdum*, A.D. 688. A.D. 897.—*ongeân þâs æscâs*, against the *æscs*, Danish long ships, like ashen spears.—*mid eallê*, and every thing. A.D. 901.—*ealrâ hâligrâ mæssan*, All-hallowmass (Oct. 26).—*forsâpon*, despised every compact that King Edward and his Parliament offered them. A.D. 925.—*seofođe healf*, 6½, § 147. A.D. 975–978.—*Corfe* was the royal residence of Elfrida, the mother-in-law of Edward. The king while hunting was allured thither alone. She received him at the gate and kissed him. The cup was offered, and as he drank, one of her attendants stabbed him in the back. He spurred away, but soon died, and the frightened horse dragged the corpse of "Edward the Martyr." Æthelred, "the Unready," was her son. A.D. 994.—*þâ peard hit*, then there was, § 397.—*friđ and griđ*, rhyming and alliterating emphatic tautology is a characteristic of legal and other forms in the Teutonic languages. The lawyers distinguish *friđ* as general peace, *griđ* a special security of particular property.—*ǽghpider*, every whither.—*flocmǽlum*, adv., in flocks or troops, § 144.—Richard II., count of Normandy. The queen's name was Emma Ælfgife, afterward wife of Cnût. A.D. 1014.—*seô burhparu*, the city, a collective singular for the body of citizens. A.D. 1028.—*peard his man*, was his man=paid him *hom*-age. A.D. 1052.—*â-lêde*, abolished, § 209.—*þæs þe*, after.—*mid*, adv., also, it tormented men also manifoldly. A.D. 1066.—*Normandige*, Lat. *Normannia* (*nn* > *nd*, *î* > *ig*, dissimilation, §§ 27, 5; 175, *b*) usually is of feminine strong declension, but genitive in *-es* occurs, A.D. 1101. The *hide* is about thirty acres, the *gird* (>yard) one fourth of a hide. A.D. 1087.—*mǽl*, portion.—*þæt . . . þæt*, repeated, as in A.D. 754, and often.—*mǽndon*, bemoaned.—*níđ*, *es*, m., opposition.

Conversion of the Anglo-Saxons.

Page 35.—Gregory. This is taken from a homily of Ælfric, the grammarian, Hom. ii., 116. It is in Thorpe's Analecta, and elsewhere. It is here abridged. These homilies are eighty in number, and were compiled and translated from Latin works, about A.D. 990, for the unlearned, whose books, except Alfred's translations, he says were full of errors. They are, therefore, written in simple English (Anglo-Saxon), without obscure words. A careful edition, with a translation, was prepared by Thorpe for the Ælfric Society, 1844–1846.

Page 36, line 35.—*hpæt*, an interjection of emphasis, § 377, *b*; compare *What, Lucius! ho!* (Shakespeare, J. C., ii., 1), *What, warder! ho!* (Scott, Marmion); so Beowulf, p. 56.

Page 37, line 3.—*þæt*, relative, used without agreement in gender or number like English *that*, § 374, 2. 26.—*pǽron*, they were ready, *hî* understood.

Page 38, line 8.—*þê*, reflexive dative, § 298, *c*. 14.—*mæsse-reâfum*, robes in which to celebrate mass. 15.—*reliquias*, Latin, accusative plural of *reliquiæ*, relics. 16.—*pallium*, Latin, accusative sing. of *pallium*, pall, a consecrated scarf, embroidered with purple crosses.

Page 38.—Paulinus. From Beda's Ecclesiastical History of the Angles and Saxons, book ii., chap. 13, with an introduction from chap. 9, and conclusion from chap. 16. Beda, "The Venerable Bede," was born near Wearmouth and Yarrow, A.D. 673. He went to the abbey when seven years old, and studied there till he died, May 26, 735. He was made deacon at 19, priest at 30; declined to be abbot, as bringing distraction of mind, which hinders the pursuit of learning. He was making a translation of the Gospel of John when he died. A list of 44 of his works is given by Wright. Among them are Commentaries on the Bible, Biographies, History, Treatises on Natural Science, Grammar, Versification. He was fond of his native language and poetry, and composed verses both in Anglo-Saxon and Latin. This extract may be compared with Cædmon, page 47. The liveliest parts of Gregory and the Chronicle are also in Beda. He is one of the great authors of the world. An acute observer and profound thinker, with what our critics call a poet's heart and eye, he sets forth the gentle and beautiful traits of character in the saintly heroes of his time with unmistakable relish, and in a style graceful, picturesque, at times dramatic. Some of his best scenes have often been rendered in English verse. That from Paulinus may be read in Wordsworth's Ecclesiastical Sonnets, xv.–xvii. Beda's Works have been repeatedly published both on the Continent and in England. The Ecclesiastical History was translated from the Latin by Alfred. Wheloc's edition has Latin and Anglo-Saxon in parallel columns. Folio, Cambridge, 1644. Smith's has various readings. Folio, Cambridge, 1722. A new edition is much needed.

Page 38, line 21.—*þǽre tîde*, A.D. 625–627. 25.—*hpilc*, of what kind to them seemed and appeared; Beda's Latin *videtur* is tautologically rendered by *þuhte and gesepen pǽre*. 27.—(who) was called Cefi, § 385. 33.—*þâ þe*, who, § 380, 3. 34.—*I know what*, introductory exclamation still in colloquial use: there is no Latin for it in Beda.

Page 39, line 4.—*tô fêng*, took up the discussion. 5.—One text has *cyning leófósta*. 11.—*hpæt*, lo; *rined*, wet, looks like a mistake for *hrinen*, touched, Beda's *tangitur*. 13.—*pintrâ*, § 93, *i*. 30.—Lo, he then, the king; repeated subject, § 288, *b*. 32.—*Mid þý*, When he then, the king, from the aforesaid bishop of their religion which they practised before, sought and asked who should desecrate and overthrow the idols, etc., . . . then answered.

Page 40, line 19.—*liged*, which extends out to the sea; relative omitted, § 385. 20.—*hê Bêda*, so says Alfred. 24.—*and* connects *hê* and *menigo*. 28.—*hôcihte neôsu þynne*, Bêd. *nâso adunco pertenui*, his prominent feature like an eagle's beak (Wordsworth, l. c.); the texts read for *hôcihte*, *medmicle*, small, which destroys the feature; *nôsu*, f., is the more common form. 31.—*ǽghpider ymb spâ spâ*, whithersoever.—*þeâh þe*, even if. 33.—*spilce*, so much also the same king attended to utility for his people. 34–36.—*þæt* . . . *þæt*, repeated. 37.—*þâ hpædere*, then yet, however.

Anglo-Saxon Laws.

A considerable body of Anglo-Saxon laws remains. Their most striking general feature is the payment of money for all sorts of offenses. Confinement was not easy or safe. The kind of offenses specified, and their comparative estimate, are fruitful in suggestions concerning the life and the character of our ancestors. The laws have been often printed. The best editions are those of Thorpe (2 vols., pp. 631, 551) and Schmid (Leipzig, 1858). The latter is in one volume, and has a critical text and translations in Latin and German in parallel columns, notes, and a glossary. The sections here selected are numbered as in Schmid.

Page 41.—Æthelbirht (-briht, i > y) was king of Kent at its conversion. See page 37. The laws were written 597–614. One manuscript copy only remains, written for Ernulf, bishop of Rochester, 1115–1125. The language used indicates that it was copied from older text, but how near the original it comes we know not.

Line 1.—*forgelde*, let him pay, subj. for imperative, § 421, 3. 2.—*gebête*, *pîte*; besides the *bôt* paid to the injured party, a penalty, *pîte*, was generally paid to the crown. Compare Tacitus, Germania, c. 12. 4.—*leôd-geld*=*per-geld*, wergild, compensation for a man to his kin or representatives, to be distinguished from the *bôt* to the lord of the slain and the *pîte* to the king; *medume*, small, half; the *bôt* is to be 100 shillings, half the wergild; *man* is freeman. 9.—*ceorl* is a freeman of low rank; *hlâf-æta*, compare *hlâf-ord*. 10.—§§ 39 and 40 are perhaps transposed. *ôđer*, either. 16.—*cin-bân*, jawbone. Compare Goth. *kinnu*, page 10, verse 39. 17–20.—*æt* . . . *æt*, repeated: For the four front teeth, for each = for each of the four front teeth (pay) six shillings; the tooth which then stands by, —(pay for it) four shillings, anacoluthon, § 288, *a*. 22.—*gebroced* is common for *gebrocen* in the laws.

Page 42, line 5.—*forgelde*, let (the striker) pay; *heâh hand*, right hand, the common Scandinavian idiom. Compare *spŷđre*, page 10, verse 39.

Hlôthhere succeeded his brother Ecgberht as king of Kent in July, 673, and reigned 11 years and 7 months. He died of wounds received in battle with his nephew *Eâdric*, who then reigned one year and a half (Bêd., iv., 5, 26). These laws are in the same manuscript with those of *Æthelbirht*.

Line 19.—*mund-byrd*, the fine for violating protection guaranteed by any one: a ceorl gave six shillings' worth of protection, an earl twelve, a king fifty, in Æthelbirht's time.

Ine, king of Wessex at the resignation of Ceadwalla, A.D. 688, abdicated and went to Rome in 725 (Bêd., v., 7; and see Chronicle). His laws are found in the same manuscripts as those of Alfred, written like a continuation of Alfred's Code.

Line 27.—*geþungenes*, full grown, eminent, a member of Parliament.

Page 43, line 8.—Out of the highway through the forest, § 340. 9.—He is to be regarded as a thief, § 451, 337, II. 11.—And it is detected in the one that did it. 14.—*þrîtig*, undeclined, for *þrîtigum*. 15.—*pǽre*, subj., §§ 421, 427, let there be of them so many as there may be of them.

Alfred's Laws.—Alfred was born in 848, the youngest child of Æthelwulf and Osburga; but he outlived his brothers, and became king of Wessex A.D. 871. He died A.D. 901. Students using this book will have read some outlines of his public life in the Chronicles; but the whole story of his brilliant youth, and his suffering and struggling manhood, with all its romantic adventures, should be made familiar. He is often called Alfred the Great; the traditions of the Saxons call him The Wise, The Truthteller, England's Shepherd, England's Darling. He was a good king, master of the arts of war and peace; a strong fighter, and an inventor of battle-ships; a statesman, a giver and codifier of laws; an educator and founder of schools; a philosopher, historian, and bard. Well he loved God's men and God's Word. He loved men of learning, and brought them about him from far countries. He loved his people, their land, and speech, and old ballads, and Bible songs; and he was the preserver of the literature and language, as well as the liberties and laws of the Anglo-Saxons.

The book of his laws begins with a history of law, gives an outline of the laws of Moses, and states the relation of them to Christ, the apostles, and Christian nations. He concludes: "I, then, Alfred, king, gathered these together, and commanded many of those to be written which our forefathers held, those which to me seemed good; and many of those which to me seemed not good, I rejected them by the counsel of my *witan*, and in other wise commanded them to be holden, for I durst not venture to set in writing much of my own, for it was unknown to me what of it would suit those who should be after us. But those which I met, either of Ine's day, my kinsman, or Æthelbirht's, who first received baptism among the English race, which seemed to me rihtest, I have here gathered, and rejected the others. I, then, Alfred, king of the West-Saxons, shewed these to all my *witan*, and they then said that it seemed good to them all to keep them." The introduction in Schmid takes up pp. 58–68, the following laws pp. 68–105. For Alfred's other works, see notes on pages 23, 38, 46, 64.

PAGE 43, line 18.—*mon*=*man*, §§ 23, 35, 2, *a*. 29.—*frið*, a privilege of granting protection.—*fâhmon*, one exposed to *fæhð*, the deadly feud allowed by the laws, a right of the kinsmen to whom the wergild was due to kill a murderer, adulterer, and certain other offenders, and such of their kindred as were responsible for the wergild.—*ge-ærne* and *ge-yrne* are variations of the same word; one was probably originally a gloss. 31.—For any of those offenses which was not before disclosed: *þârâ þe* together is used like a nominative singular, a common idiom, the *þârâ* being a repeated partitive. 33.—*Sunnan niht*, Sunday, Lat. *dies Solis;* compare fort-night, seven-night, and see note on line 34.—*Geôl* (sun-wheel), Yule, was a great pagan festival at the beginning of the year, the winter solstice, afterward confounded with Christmas.—*Eâstre* was a heathen goddess. April was named *Eâster-mônað*, because feasts were then celebrated in honor of her (Bêd., De Temp., 13). The name is akin to *east*, Lat. *aurora*, the dawn. The festival commemorating the resurrection of Christ has in Anglo-Saxon and German received this name, but other kindred nations use *pascha*. 34.—*þunres dæg* is a translation of Latin *dies Jovis*. The astrological week was allotted to the planets by hours in the received order of their orbits; the first hour to "the widest orbit and the highest power," Saturn, the second to Jupiter, the third to Mars, the fourth to the Sun, the fifth to Venus, the sixth to Mercury, the seventh to the Moon, the eighth to Saturn again, and so on through the week. Each day was named from the planet of its first hour. Hence the order of the Latin names—*dies Saturni, dies Solis, Lunæ, Martis, Mercurii, Jovis, Veneris* (Dion Cassius, xxxvii., 18). The first use of any of these names by Roman writers is in the time of Julius Cæsar, *dies Saturni* for the Jewish Sabbath (Tibul., i., 3, 18), probably from associations with the Saturnalia as a time of rest. This first became common; the names of the other days gradually came in: all were in use at the end of the second century, and the week was finally established, in place of the old nine-day period, by Constantine. It spread from Rome over the North in advance of Christianity. The greatest of the gods of the North, the father and ruler of gods and men, is *Wôden*, Norse *Odin*, and we should have expected him to take Jupiter's day; but the early Romans did not recognize their Jupiter in any of the Germanic gods, and identified Woden with Mercury, whom indeed he does resemble in his tricks, his care of traders, and some other traits and offices (Tacitus, Germ., 9; Annal., 13, 57; compare Cæsar, 6, 17). So *dies Mercurii* was called *Wôdenes dæg*, Wednesday; and Jupiter's day was given to *þuner*, Norse *Thôr*. He is the son of Odin and the Earth, the strongest of the gods, the enemy of the giants, the friend of man. He has three treasures—his hammer, his belt of power, which doubles his strength, and his iron gloves. His eyes flame, his hair is red as the lightning; when he drives by with his two he-goats, the mountains tremble. He is a very fair Jupiter as thus described in Norse. The Anglo-Saxons have left no mythological matter. Holy Thursday is the day on which Christ's ascension is commemorated, ten days before Whitsuntide, which is the seventh Sunday after Easter. Three days before were procession days, *Gang-dagâs*. 35.—*Lencten* is spring, when the days *lengthen*. It began with the great festival of Odin. It has given name to the Church *Lent*.

PAGE 44, line 3.—*geselle*, let (the master) pay. 7.—*folc-leâsung* Thorpe explains as a false report leading to breach of the peace, Schmid as a false accusation of crime, an offense which is visited with this penalty in Henry I., 34, 7. The tongue could be compounded for in this case as in others by a third of the wergild. 11.—*tpêntig*, undeclined, for *tpêntigum*; so *þrittig*, *sixtig*, afterwards. 13—*homola*, see vocabulary.

ECGBYRHT was archbishop of York, 735–766. He was one of Beda's friends. He wrote much, and formed a library at York. His Confessionale and Pœnitentiale are translations from similar Latin works, in great part from the Pœnitentiale of Theodore, archbishop of Canterbury, 668–690, give rules relating to confession and penance, and were standard guides in the Church. No known manuscript has them in their original Northumbrian. They are in Thorpe's Laws, pp. 128–239. The extracts here made are in Rieger's Lesebuch.

PAGE 44, line 18.—*medmycles hpæt-hpega*, somewhat of small value, *in minimis*, Theodore. 19.—*geâr* =*pinter*. 21.—*lifigendum mannum to hæle and on his hûse*, for health to living men and (health) in his house, *pro sanitate viventium et domus*, Theodore. 23.—*þîf . . . heô*, repeated subject, § 288, *b*. This fever-cure is several times mentioned in the old laws. Sometimes the child was put in the oven, sometimes over a furnace, or on the roof in the sun. The burning away of dross and disease is a natural thought, and gives rise to superstitions all over the world. So Thetis buried the infant Achilles nightly in the fire, and Demeter the child of Demophoon. Its repute for *fever* suggests homœopathy. 28.—*nê . . .*, nor (is it permitted that he practise) the gathering of herbs. 34.—*staca*, n., commonly *stake*, is here for Latin *acus*, needle. The making of an image of a person with magic spells, and affecting the person by treating the image, drowning, hanging, melting, piercing it with a needle, etc., is an ancient and wide-spread form of magic art:

> Sagave Punicea defixit nomina cera,
> Et medium tennes in jecur egit acus?

(Ovid, Amor., iii., 7, 29. Compare Horace, Epod., 17, 76). For northern examples of needle-piercing, see Thorpe's Northern Mythology, 3, 24, 240; Grimm, Myth., 1045.

Page 45, line 4.—*sylle*, give (any thing) to him. 6.—*Woden's day*, *Frîge's day*, see note on page 43, line 34. *Frîge dæg*, Friday, is intended to be a translation of Latin *dies Veneris*, the day of the goddess of love. There are, however, two northern goddesses, who seem to have been confounded. Norse *Frigg* < *fria*, O. H. G. *Frija*, A.-S. *frig*, *frî* > free; and Norse *Freyja*, akin to Goth. *frauja*, O. H. G. *frô*, A.-S. *freâ* > frau, mistress. The former is Woden's wife, and the goddess of marriage; the latter is the wife of a man, the goddess of beauty and love, Venus, but the name of the day phonetically agrees best with *Frigg*. 10.—*gescæfte*, at any other object, *ubicunque*, Theodore. 13.—*bûton*, except. 15.—*þæs ylcan*, of the same penance. 16.—The meeting of roads is a well-known place for raising the devil: there idlers congregate. Drawing through the earth, through a hole, or along in a trench scooped for the purpose, is condemned as devil's craft in Edgar's Canons, XVI. Drawing through hollow stones, trees, and bramble bushes was practised with the same thought of scraping away magical bad influences, or sometimes apparently of magnetizing with good influences (Grimm, Myth., 1118).

Page 45. Cnut, king of Denmark, was crowned king of England A.D. 1017. See the Chronicle, 1014–1035. He made vigorous and wise efforts to unite the Danes and Anglo-Saxons under a common government. He called assemblies of their representatives, and with their advice reissued a large body of laws, both civil and ecclesiastical. In Schmid they occupy pp. 250–321. He died A.D. 1035.

Line 27.—*morgen-gyfe*, a gift from the husband to the wife on the morning after marriage. It was hers after his death. 29.—*hâdige*, consecrate as a member of a religious order.

PAGE 46.—ORPHEUS. This is an extract from Boethius, De Consolatione Philosophiæ, chap. 35, § 6, of Alfred's translation. The life of Boethius may be read in the Classical Dictionaries. The Latin of this work is printed in Valpy's Delphin edition of the Latin Classics. It opens with the complaints of Boethius; Philosophy appears, and converses with him. She persuades him that blessedness is not in riches, power, honors, glory, or fame, but that adversity often leads to it. The Supreme Good is to be found in the Deity alone. She illustrates these views, and answers objections at length. Meter and prose alternate. This work was far more read and cherished in the Middle Ages than the classic authors of pagan times. It came home to their experiences, while Homer and Virgil, with their lying myths and barbaric tales, were as remote and unreal as the Veda and Sacu'ntala are to us. Alfred recast it, and introduced much new matter, especially Christian precepts and allusions, which are wholly absent from the original. The extract here given is written on the suggestion of Book III., Metrum 12. The story is much enlarged, and has little verbal resemblance to the Latin. Two manuscripts have been used in preparing editions, one of them thought by Wanley to be of Alfred's age. We have editions by Rawlinson, 1698; Cardale, 1829; Fox, in Bohn's library, 1864. The extract here given is in Thorpe's Analecta, Ettmüller's Sceôpas and Bôceras, and elsewhere.

PAGE 46, line 1.—"The clear well-spring of the highest good" is God: this is the language of Philosophia to Boethius in Latin verse. 20.—When to the harper then it seemed, that it pleased him of nothing (=he was pleased with nothing) in this world, then thought he, *þâ þâ . . . þâ*, correlative, so line 23, page 47, 16, § 472, 3; *þuhte*, § 297; *lyste hine þinges*, §§ 290, *c*; 315, *c*. 23.—*sceold*, should (according to the story). 25.—*ongan*, he began; change of mode in lively narrative. 30.—*brohte*, subj., would bring, §§ 423, 425, *c*. 31.—*oflyst*, much pleased with; compare *lyste*, line 21, § 315, 1.

PAGE 47, line 2.—*þâ*, *who*, they say, (that *they*) know no respect for any man, but punish each man according to his works,—*who*, they say, (that *they*) control each other's fate: a repeated subject implied, § 288, *b*. 11.—*þæs* (*þære?*), takes the gender of *yfel?* 22.—*hpæt*, interj. 24.—*beseah he hine*, he looked around him backwards after the woman, § 359, III. 33.—*gebête*, make *bót*, do penance for it again. Compare *gebête* in the Laws, page 41, 2, and after.

CÆDMON.—From Alfred's translation of Beda's Ecclesiastical History of the Angles and Saxons, Book IV., 24. See notes on Paulinus, page 38, and to Cædmon, page 52.

PAGE 47, line 34.—St. Hild was abbess of Whitby, and died A.D. 680. Beda was born in 673 in the same region, and must have known about Cædmon, may have seen him. 35.—*mid . . .*, by divine grace singularly magnified and dignified, since he was wont to make appropriate poems, which conduced to religion and piety.

PAGE 48.—*geglencde* agrees with *sceôpgercorde*.—*imbrydnesse* renders *compunctione*, stimulation to pious feeling, feeling; so Cuthbert speaks of Beda's repeating verses, *multum compunctus*, much touched, with deep feeling. 11.—*ac efne*, but even. 12.—*þâ ân*, those alone, *þâ þe*, which.—*his þâ* . . ., *which* it became his (the) pious tongue to sing, § 489, *gedafenôde* governs a dative generally in West Saxon, § 299, but *mec gedæfned*, North., Luc., iv. 43. 15.—*gebeôrscipe*, by etymology, a social beer-drinking, is applied to any convivial, like Gr. *συμπόσιον*, *sym-posium*. Here the Latin is *convivium; symble*, line 18, is *cœna*. For German beer-drinking, see Tacitus, Germ., 22, 23.—*þonne þǽr pæs gedêmed*, when it was decided for pleasure, § 397. 20–23.—*þâ þâ* . . . *þâ*, when . . . then.—*þæt* . . . *þæt*, § 468.—33. Only the substance of the verses in Latin is given in Beda. It has been questioned whether Alfred rendered the Latin back or supplied the original verses. The latter is most probable. An older copy has been found added in a Latin Beda supposed to be of the 8th or 9th century. The forms resemble the earliest Anglo-Saxon Northumbrian which we have:

Nu scylun **h***ergan* **h***efaenricaes uard,*
m*etudæs* **m***aecti* *end his* **m***odgidanc,*
u*erc* **u***uldurfadur;* *sue he* **u***undra gihuaes,*
e*ci dryctin,* **o***r astelidæ.*
He **ae***rist scop* **ae***lda barnum*
h*eben til* **h***rofe,* **h***aleg scepen:*
þa **m***iddungeard* **m***oncynnæs uard,*
e*ci dryctin,* **æ***fter tiadæ,*
firum **f***old~,* **f***rea allmectig.*

Now we-shall (should) laud heaven-realm's Ward (guardian),
the-Creator's might and his thought,
the-wôrks of-the-glorious-Father: how he, of wonders all,
eternal Lord, the beginning established.
He first shaped for men's children
heaven as a roof, holy Shaper (creator),
then mid-earth mankind's Ward,
eternal Lord, afterward created,
for men a world, Master almighty.

This text is from Smith's Beda, p. 597; that on page 48 is from Thorpe, Analecta, p. 105, adopted on the supposition that he has corrected from some manuscript the readings given by Wheloc and Smith. 35.—*perâ* is a change from *peorc*, the reading of more manuscripts, *facta patris gloriæ*, Beda.—*pundrâ*, partitive after *gehpæs*.—*gehpæs*, governed by *ord*. 36.—*Dryhtin*, appositive with *hê*. 38–41.—*Scyppend*, appositive with *hê*.—*Dryhten, Freâ*, appositive with *peard*. The Northumbrian variations are mostly orthographic, §§ 26, 31. The vowel quantities are like those marked in the other text.

PAGE 49, line 3.—*Godê pyrdes songes*, words of song worthy of God, *Deo digni, pyrde* usually takes a genitive, here an instrumental in analogy with the Latin ablative of price so-called, §§ 320, 302, *c*. 4.—*ealdorman*, governor (law term)=*qui sibi pre-erat.* 9.—*gecoren pǽre*, it might be decided. 10.—*pæs gesepen*, it appeared, *videtur, visum est.* 13.—That he would sing something for them, and would convert that, etc.—*sum sunge and* is not in some texts; Beda reads *hunc in modulationem carminis transferre.* 14.—*þâ pisan*, undertaken the matter. 15.—*geglenged* describes *þæt him beboden pæs.* 27.—*be*, of, with dative of theme, § 334.

PAGE 50, line 2.—*betŷnde and geendôde*, emphatic tautology for *conclusit;* so in the next line Beda has only *discessus* for *gepitnesse and fordfôre;* and so elsewhere, repetition for emphasis and perspicuity is Anglo-Saxon. 3.—*neâlǽhte*, impersonal. 4.—*ǽr*, before (his death), *þæt*, (in this condition, namely) that, etc., conjunction: then he was fourteen days before, that he was oppressed = then there were fourteen days, etc. 25.—*mîne þâ leôfan*, § 289, *a.* 31.—*þon* = *þam*, § 133. 32.—*him gebæd*, prayed for himself, § 298, *c:* a frequent idiom=he offered his prayers. Alfred has added these two words. 35, 36.—*þætte . . . þæt*, repeated *that.*—*eâc spilce*, also. 39.—*heô þâ*, it then, repeated subject, § 288, *b.* 40.—*sêniende*, he signing himself, nominative absolute, § 295; really an imitation of the Latin gerund *signando sese*, rather than a native idiom.

ANGLO-SAXON PROSE.

Specimens of Anglo-Saxon prose have now been given, arranged for ease of reading. We have remaining—

(1.) THEOLOGICAL writings.—Translations of the Bible (see pages 1–12, and notes); Homilies, page 35, and notes.

(2.) PHILOSOPHY.—Boethius, page 46, and notes.

(3.) HISTORY.—The Chronicle, page 23, and notes. Beda's Ecclesiastical History: see Paulinus, page 38, and Cædmon, page 47. Orosius, a general history of the ancient world, translated by Alfred, with additions of considerable geographical and ethnological value; repeatedly printed. Thorpe's edition, with translation and glossary, 1857, is in Bohn's Library. Many brief BIOGRAPHIES are contained in Beda and the Homilies, of which Cædmon, page 47, and Gregory, page 35, are examples. Some separate lives have been found; that of St. Guthlâc has been several times printed. Goodwin, 1848.

(4.) LAW.—Pages 41–45, and notes.

(5.) NATURAL SCIENCE and MEDICINE.—Popular Treatises of Science, pp. 19, are Anglo-Saxon, Thorpe, 1841. Leechdoms, 3 vols., O. Cockayne, 1864–66.

(6.) GRAMMAR.—Ælfric, in Somner's Dictionary, 1659. Colloquy, 12–22, and notes. A few Glossaries, Wright, 1857.

ANGLO-SAXON POETRY.

[For the Anglo-Saxon versification, see §§ 496–515.]

We learn from the story of Cædmon how universal the knowledge of popular poetry was among the Anglo-Saxons. It was such a disgrace not to be able to chant in turn at feasts that Cædmon left in shame as his turn approached. Most of the poetry has perished. The early Anglo-Saxon Christians condemned whatever was mixed with idolatry, and the Normans despised or neglected all Saxon literature. But enough remains to enable us to judge pretty well of the nature of their poetry. We have—

(1.) THE BALLAD EPIC. Here, as in Greek and most other tongues, the heroic ballads of the race were brought together, exalted and beautified, and fused into long poems. Beowulf (3184 lines), and a few fragments, are left from this great world of poetry, to be compared with the Homeric poems.

(2.) THE BIBLE EPIC is a treatment of the Bible narrative, similar in exaltation and other epic traits to the ballad epic. The origin and something of the history of this style of composition has been read in this book in Cædmon, pages 47–50. We have remaining under the name of Cædmon four poems, called by Grein Genesis (2935 lines), Exodus (589 lines), Daniel (765 lines), Christ and Satan (733 lines). We have also a fragment of Judith (350 lines), Cynewulf's Christ (1694 lines), The Harrowing of Hell (137 lines), and some fragments. These poems are to be compared with the Paradise Lost and Paradise Regained of Milton, and the Christ in Hades of Lord.

(3.) ECCLESIASTICAL NARRATIVES. The lives of Saints, versified Chronicles. Of these we have Andreas (1724 lines), Juliana (731 lines), Guthlac (1353 lines), Elene (1321 lines).

(4.) PSALMS AND HYMNS. Translations of a large part of the Hebrew Psalms, and a few Christian hymns and prayers.

(5.) SECULAR LYRICS. A few from the Chronicle celebrating the heroes, and others mostly elegiac, of which those on pages 68–69 are a specimen.

(6.) ALLEGORIES, GNOMES, AND RIDDLES. The Phœnix, a translation from Lactantius, expanded (677 lines); The Panther (74 lines); The Whale (89 lines); Gnomic verses, some in dialogue between Solomon and Saturn (Grein, ii., pages 339–368); Riddles (Grein, ii., pages 369–407). Pages 66–67 are specimens.

(7.) DIDACTIC ETHICAL. Alfred's Meters of Boethius (Grein, ii., pages 295–339). Pages 64–65 are specimens. Some of the Allegories, and other pieces classed under the sixth head, have a didactic purpose in natural science.

PAGE 51. THE TRAVELER is one of the most ancient Anglo-Saxon poems. A poet tells through what countries he has traveled and whom he has seen. It is little more than a sounding roll of names, with epithets and the briefest incidents, like the catalogues in Homer and Milton. Names enough are identified to give it reality. The lines here quoted are the last.

A single copy remains in the Codex Exoniensis. This was presented by Leofric, bishop of Exeter (A.D. 1046), to the library of his cathedral. It was edited by Thorpe for the Society of Antiquaries of London (1842), with an English translation, notes, and indexes. The text and translation make 500 pages.

Line 1. So roving in their destinies wander
gleemen of men through many lands,
their need tell, thank-words speak,
always south or north some one *they* meet
in songs clever, in gifts unsparing,
who before man wishes honor to rear,
(nobleness) earlship to gain, till that all departs,
light and life together : praise whoever winneth,
has under heavens high-fast (immutable) honor.

BEOWULF, see page 56.

Line 9. The hero Beowulf has slain a monster. This is part of the celebration.

At times *a* king's thane,
a man glory-laden, of songs mindfull,
who full-many of old sagas,
very-many remembered, other words found
rightly connected. *This* hero again began
the feat of Beowulf with craft to recite,
and artfully to utter sentences cunning,
with words to exchange (thoughts).

10.—*gilp-hlæden*, defiance laden, having passed through many battles. 12.—*porn* adds emphasis to *eal-fela*. 13.—*sôđe*, according to the laws of verse. 15.—*gerâde*, exact in meter. 16.—To narrate. 16.—*þǽr*, in the great hall Heorot, see page 57. 18.—*sægde*, (he) said, *se þe*, who.—*cpæđ*, repetition of *sægde*. 21.—*spâ*, which.

PAGE 52. CÆDMON'S GENESIS. For Cædmon, see page 47–51, and the notes. Only one copy of these poems has survived in old manuscript. It was apparently written in the tenth century, the last seventeen pages in a different hand from the rest (212). All that is known of it is that it belonged to Archbishop Usher, who gave it to Junius, who printed it at Amsterdam in 1655, and who bequeathed it to the Bodleian Library. It is illuminated. A careful edition, with a translation, notes, and verbal index, was edited by Thorpe for the Society of Antiquaries of London, 1832. The illuminations were published in 1833. It has since been much studied in Germany, and many valuable articles upon it have been published. Grein's critical edition and translation, Bouterwek's copious Essays in his edition (1849–1854), and Dietrich's criticisms in Haupt's Zeitschrift, deserve special attention.

There is nothing but internal evidence to show that these poems are really those described as Cædmon's by Beda, and scholars have differed about it. It seems likely that they are from his original, but changed by free rewriting in a different dialect after the lapse of three or four centuries.

Those who do not know what liberties were taken by the early copyists and bards, may compare with the four first lines of Cædmon in Beda, page 48 and note, the following opening in the manuscript of Junius.

Ûs is riht micel þæt þê roderâ peard
peredâ pûldorcining pordum herigen,
môdum lufien: hê is mægnâ spêd,
heâfod ealrâ heâhgesceaftâ,
freâ ælmihtig. Næs him fruma æfre
ôr geporden, ne nu ende cymđ
êcean drihtnes.

For us it is a great duty that we heavens' Ward,
men's Glory-king with words laud,
with minds love: he is of might the fullness,
head of all high creations,
Lord almighty. There has not to him beginning ever,
origin been, nor will now end come
of the eternal Lord.

Cædmon has been called the Anglo-Saxon Milton. The extracts here given will indicate on what ground.

PAGE 52. GENESIS. The opening of this book has been given above. It goes on with the story of man's first disobedience and his fall, beginning with the fallen angels. The description of Satan, *gelîc þâm leohtum steorrum*, like the bright stars; his first speech as here given; some striking expressions in the description of his fall, of hell, heaven, of Adam and Eve, strongly suggest that Milton borrowed from Cædmon; but it is most likely that these resemblances arise from their drawing from the same sources—from the Bible most; in demonology and the lore of angels from Gregory the Great. A large part of Cædmon's Genesis is occupied with the story of Abraham.

Line 1.—*pæs geporden*, had been.—*þâ giet*, as yet: there had not here as yet, except gloom-of-shadow, aught been. 6.—*geseah*, (he) saw dark obscurity brood in perpetual night swart under heavens, wan and waste, till that this world-creation through the word existed of the king of glory. 11.—*helm*, (helmet) protector of all things, appositive with *Drihten*. 14.—*Freâ*, repeated subject, or appositive like *helm*. 15.—*græs*, instrumental accus., § 295, *b*. 17.—*þonne pægâs*, appositive with *gârsecg*. 20.—*lîfes Brytta*, appositive with *metod*. 29.—*gesceaft*, appositive with *leôht*. 31–32.—The coming on of the first night. 34.—*forđ*, henceforth. 35.—*gŷman*, (who should) govern the abyss.—*pæs*, (he) was.

PAGE 53, line 6. Compare Paradise Lost, 1, 75. 10.—*þeâh* . . ., though we it for the All-powerful must not own, (must not) possess our realms. 11.—*næfd=ne hæfd*, he has not. 13.—*benumen*, p. p. (in that he hath) deprived (us) of heaven-realm, § 301. 18.—*him*, expletive reflexive: shall be to himself in pleasure, § 298, *c*. 19.—*âhte*, subj., expressing a wish, § 421, 4. 20.—and might I one hour out be be one winter hour. 21.—broken sentence. 28.—*habbađ âmyrred* governs accusative *mê* and genitive *sîdes*, § 317, *a*.—*sâl* appositive with *gespong*. 32.—*mid pihte*, in any way, *mæg of*, may (escape) from, § 436. 37.—and (I know) that the Lord of hosts also knew that (there) should to us, (me and) Adam, evils occur in that heaven-realm, if I had the use of my hands; *unc Adame* § 287, *g*, . . . *þær*, if, § 475.

PAGE 54. EXODUS has been pronounced by some a lyric in honor of Moses. It has not the rapid narrative movement of an epic, but dilates imaginatively on a few scenes. It has the usual formal opening:

Hpæt! pê feor and neâh gefrigen habbađ
ofer middangeard **Moyses** *dômâs.*

What! we far and near have heard
over middle-earth Moses' laws.

It has been generally considered one of the grandest and most characteristic poems of early Teutonic literature. It is characteristic of a certain class of writing; but it should not be forgotten that if we have an Anglo-Saxon Milton we also have an Anglo-Saxon Homer.

PAGE 54, line 1.—*Nearpe* . . ., Straitly *they* (the Israelites marching from Egypt) struggled-forward on the northways, they knew to them on the south the Sunfolks' (Ethiopian) land. 2.—*piston land*, knew the land; knew that the land lay. 4.—*heofon-colum*, instrumental after *brûne*. 5.—*fær-bryne*, fearful burning (of the sun). 5.—*bælcê*, Ger. *gebälk*, canopy, the so-called "pillar of cloud." 7.—*nettê*, repetition of *bælce*. 8.—*pederpolcen*, Ger. *wetterwolke* (weather-welkin), storm-cloud, is the "pillar of cloud." 10.—*lîg-fŷr*, *hâte heofontorht*, describes the sun; *hâte*, definite form, epic epithet, § 362, 1; others read it as an instrumental of *hât*, heat. 12.—*drihtâ gedrŷmôst*, gladdest of throngs, appositive with *Hæleđ*. 13.—*Dæg-scealdes*, trope for *sun*, *hleô dæg-scealdes*, the "pillar of cloud." 15.—*spâ*, although. 18.—*mæst*, the greatest of tents. 19.—*on sâlum*, in safe places, in safety. 20.—*Heofon-beâcen*, the "pillar of fire." 22.—*syllic* agrees with beam; Strange after sun's set took care over the people with flame to shine a burning pillar. 27.—*neôple* . . ., deepest night-shadows not enough might lurking-places hide; *i. e.*, Midnight was not dark enough to hide them, the pillar was so bright. 30.—*þŷ læs* . . ., lest to them by the horrors-of-the-waste the hoar heath with raging storms ever with sudden peril their minds might distract. 35.—*hâtan*, weak instrumental, epic epithet, § 362, 1.

PAGE 55, line 2.—*hŷrde*, subj. imperf. for *hŷrden*, § 170. 5.—*segn*, the pillar of fire. 10–11.—*flotan bræddon*, the sailors spread (with) tents over the mountains. 13.—Then to them (=the warriors) the warriors' mind became despondent. 20.—*on hpæl*, in circuit, round them; Grein suggests another *hpæl*, akin to *hpelan*, to clang, Dan. *hvael*, a shriek; *on hpæl*, with clangor. 25.—*deôr*, appositive with *pulfâs*; *cpyldrôf* . . ., ravenous to demand on enemies' track the host's slaughter. 27.—*marc-peardâs* are the wolves. 32.—*þengel*, appositive with *sige-cyning*, the king of Egypt. 38.—*land-mannâ*, the Egyptians.

BEOWULF has been found in only one manuscript, thought to be of the tenth century. Its existence is mentioned first in Wanley's Catalogue, 1705;

but little notice of it was taken till 1786, when two copies were made for Thorkelin, a Dane, by whom an edition was published in 1815. The manuscript had been badly injured by fire in 1731, and has had hard usage since. Since the revival of Anglo-Saxon scholarship under the impulse of Grimm, the interest in Beowulf has risen to a great heighth, and many editions, translations, and essays of elucidation and interpretation have appeared in England, Germany, and Denmark. Among others, Kemble, 1833–1837; Ettmüller, translation, 1840; Thorpe, 1855; Grein, two editions, 1857, 1867; Gruntvig, 1861; Heyne, two editions, 1863, 1868. The poem celebrates the exploits of Beowulf. We learn from it that he was the son of a sister of Hygelâc, king of the Geâts (Goths), and Ecgtheôw, one of the royal family of the Danes, and that after the death of Hygelâc and his son he succeeded to the throne of the Goths. The exploits here celebrated are combats with monsters, after the manner of Hercules. The tendency at first was to regard Beowulf as one of the gods, and the whole poem as mythology; but it now seems clear that Beowulf was a real prince, and that a body of fact lies under the fables. The time is the beginning of the sixth century. See the note on Hygelâc, page 58, line 30. The place is the island of Seeland (Zealand, the seat of Copenhagen) and the opposite Gothland. An attempt has, however, been made to locate it in England by Haigh, and very remarkable coincidences of names and distances are pointed out in favor of that theory.

Page 56, line 3.—*Gâr-Denâ*, the *Dene* (Danes) appear in Beowulf as the subjects of Scyld and his descendants, as living "*in Scedelandum*," "*on Scedenigge*," "by two seas," as we suppose, in Denmark. Their epithets are *Gâr-Dene*, Spear-Danes, *Hring-Dene*, Mailed-Danes, *Beorht-Dene*, Bright-Danes. They are divided into East, West, North, and South Danes. 6.—*Scyld*, the son of *Scêf*, was drifted to Denmark, an infant alone in a boat; he there established a royal family; at his death was again committed to the sea in a boat, and departed, as he came, into the unknown. Such was the founding of the royal line of *Hrothgar*. *Scêf* is referred to in Anglo-Saxon poetry only in line 4 of Beowulf. He is identified by Grein with *Sceâfa*, mentioned in the *Traveler* (see note on page 51) as king of the Longo-bards. He is probably also the *Sceâf* in the pedigree of Æthelwulf, Alfred's father, inaccurately described as the son of Noah, born in the ark, Chr., 855. 7.—*mægdum*, appositive, *ofteâh*, elsewhere, as here, sometimes governs the dative of the person and genitive of the object of separation, §§ 298, 317. 8.—The earl inspired terror, after he first had been found deserted. Kings are called earls as being of the same noble stock. 9.—He experienced solace for *that*, *i. e.* his desertion, § 315. 14.—*Him*, reflexive expletive, § 298, *c.*—*gepât fêran*, § 448, 4. 18.—*pordum peôld*, ruled with words; perhaps should read *pord-onpeald âhte*, had word-sway.—*Scyldingâ*, the descendants of Scyld; (2) the people ruled by them. 26.—*gegyrpan*, infinitive, to equip a ship, *i. e.* of equipping, § 449, *a.* 31.—*læss-an* = *-um*.

Page 57, line 6.—*sele-rædende*, hall possessors, appositive with *men;* so *hæleð*. 7.—*onfêng*, with dative, § 299. 8.—*Hrôthgâr*, son of *Healfdene*, is the king of the Danes for whose relief occurred the exploits of Beowulf here sung. His wife is *Wealhtheow*. See *Scyld*, page 56, line 6. 11.—*mago-driht*, appositive with *geôgod*, the band of youth, the squires. 13.—*medo-ærn*, repetition of *heal-reced*; *men*, accusative, subject of *gepyrcean*. 14.—*þone* for *þonne*, (greater) than the children of the age (men) ever heard of. 15.—(*polde*) *gedǽlan*. 17.—All, except the public lands and the lives of the people. 20.—*gelomp*, it happened. 22.—*Heort*, *Heorot*, *i. e.* hart, is found by Grein in the Danish *Hjort-holm*, a town in Zealand, about two miles from the sea. Near by is *Siæl* lake, answering to Grendel's lake. At the right distance on the opposite coast of the main-land for Beowulf's grave, he finds the ruined castle of *Bô-hûs*. See note on Hygelâc, page 58, line 30. 24.—*beôt ne âlêh*, did not belie his promise, *âlêh*<*âleôgan*. Here follows the passage quoted on page 51. 30.—*Grendel* was a monster of the moors, of the race of Cain. He broke into Heorot every night and carried off thirty warriors. This lasted twelve years. Then came Beowulf, fought him, wrenched his arm off. He escaped to his lair, and died. Beowulf pursued his mother to the place, killed her; found his body, cut off his head, and bore it to Hrothgar.

PAGE 58, line 1.—*Metod*, repeated subject of *forpræc*. 5.—*him*, plur. dat., indirect object. § 297; *þæs*, genitive of crime, § 320, *d*. 6.—*neosian hûses*, examine the house, § 315, III. 7.—How the Mailed-Danes had inhabited it (the house)=how they had disposed themselves to sleep. 21.—So (Grendel) ruled. 26.—*forþam* . . ., therefore afterward was it to the children of men plainly known, by songs sadly (known), that Grendel warred long against Hrothgar. 30.—*þæt*, it, Grendel's deeds, *dǽdâ* appositive with *þǽt*, § 374, 2. Higelac's thane is Beowulf. Higelac (*Hygelâc*) appears in Beowulf as reigning king of the Geâten (Goths). The seat of his kingdom was in the Swedish Gothland, near the River Gotha, and nearly opposite the Danish *Hjort-holm*. Several of his kindred, and two successive wives, are mentioned in Beowulf, and that he fell in an expedition against the Franks, Friesians, and *Húgen*. This seems to identify him with a Gothic king, Chocilagus, mentioned by Gregory of Tours, and the Gesta Regum Francorum, as having so adventured and died, A.D. 511; and in a tenth century tradition of the same event described as *Huiclaucus*, king of the *Geti*. 33.—In the day of this life=at that time, then.

PAGE 59, line 1.—*se gôda*, used substantively. 3.=*fîftênâ sum*, one of fifteen, with a party of fifteen, § 388. 12.—*pudu bundenne*, perhaps originally a raft, a ship. 17.—*þæt*, so far that. 20.—*eoletes* (bay<*eolh?* sea?) has not been clearly made out, *eâ-lâda*, watery way, Thorpe; *eâ-let*, water-stay, time on the voyage, Leo, Heyne; *eolet*, hastening, rapid voyage, Ett., Grein. Compare the puzzling *sioleða*, found once only (Beowulf, 2367), meaning *bay*, *cove*, or *sea*. 25.—*geseah beran*, saw (persons) bear, § 449, *a*. 29.—*hpæt*, § 377. 30.—*gepât rîdan*, § 448, 4; *gepât him*, § 298, *c*. 35.—*lǽdan cpômon*, § 448, 4. 36.—The second section of the line is gone in the manuscript: *helmâs bǽron*, Ett., Heyne; *hýðe sêcean*, Grein. Compare the answer to this question, page 60, line 25, We *through kind feeling* come to seek thy lord.

PAGE 60, line 1.—*cûdlîcôr*, more openly, with franker courtesy. 2.—Nor have ye words-of-permission of warriors completely known, the assent of men=but yet ye do not know surely whether ye can obtain permission from us warriors. 26.—*lârenâ gôd*, good in respect of instructions, *i. e.* kindly direct us.

PAGE 61, line 4.—*se rîca*, Hrothgar. 16.—*cynnâ*, fitting things, manners, courtesies. 17.—*gold-hroden*, Wealhtheow. 20.—*bæd hine blîdne* bade him blithe; ellipsis of *pesan*, to be, making a factitive like *wish him well*. Compare *bade him hail*, page 62, line 13. 21.—*leôfne*, appositive with *hine*. 23.—*Helmingâs*, the race of Helm. He is mentioned in the Traveler as ruling the Wulfings. Wealh-theow was of this race. 28.—*þancôde*, with dative *Gode* and genitive *þæs*, § 297, *d*.

PAGE 62, line 17.—*gamela*, weak form, epic epithet, § 362, 1. 18.—*rand-pîgan*, appositive with *Geât*, Beowulf. 27.—*côman . . . scacan:* for this text of Grein's first edition his last has *þâ com beorht leôma scacan ofer scadu*.—The manuscript is illegible : *þâ com beorht scacan*, is one of the early copies ; then came the bright light to beam over the shadows. 30.—*þyle Hrôdgâres*, the court officer who directed the conversation, the orator. His name was *Hûnferd*. He had boasted much over the wine, but did not venture to meet Grendel. He lent Beowulf his famous sword *Hrunting* for the conflict with Grendel's mother.

PAGE 63, line 3.—*se eorl*, Beowulf. He has followed the mother of Grendel deep into the water, and comes up in a cave, her hall. Then the earl found that he in hostile hall, he knew not what, was. 36.—The blood of the monster melts the blade, Beowulf presents the hilt to *Hrôdgâr*.

PAGE 64, line 5.—*him*, to them the lord paid ; *þæs*, therefore.

ALFRED'S METERS are versifications of parts of Boethius. They were found in one manuscript, transcribed by Junius, but since lost. Editions are by Rawlinson, 1698 ; Fox, 1835 ; Grein, 1858. See farther in the notes to Orpheus, page 46.

Line 12.—This introduction is not by Alfred. Thus Alfred to us old-lore rehearsed king of the West Saxons, skill displayed, the poets' art.

Line 17.—Meter VI. is from Book II., Metrum III., of Boethius, which is given for comparison. The two first lines are Alfred's introduction.

Cum polo Phœbus roseis quadrigis
Lucem spargere cœperit,
Pallet albentes hebetata vultus
Flammis stella prementibus.
Cum nemus flatu Zephyri tepentis
Vernis irrubuit rosis,
Spiret insanum nebulosus Auster,
Jam spinis abeat decus.

Sæpe tranquillo radiat sereno
  Immotis mare fluctibus:
Sæpe ferventes Aquilo procellas
  Verso concitat æquore.
Rara si constat sua forma mundo
  Si tantas variat vices,
Crede fortunis hominum caducis,
  Bonis crede fugacibus.
Constat, æterna positumque lege est,
  Ut constet genitum nihil.

PAGE 65. METER X. is founded on the 7th meter of Book II. The first 25 lines are expanded from two:

Ubi nunc fidelis ossa Fabricii jacent?
  Quid Brutus, aut rigidus Cato?

Line 1.—*Wêland* is the hero-smith of the North. Stories of him were among the most popular of the Middle Ages. They are mostly such as the Greeks told of Hephaistos, Erichthonios, and Daidalos. He made rings, and set them with precious stones. Nîđhâd, a king in Sweden, had him bound in his sleep with heavy chains, and took from him a famous sword, and a ring which he gave to his daughter Beadohild. He afterward had him hamstringed, and confined to work for him. Wêland killed the sons of Nîđhâd. Beadohild, who had come to him to get her ring mended, he first stupefied with beer, and then ravished. He made himself wings and flew away, boasting of his revenge. He made Beowulf's famous coat of mail. The story of shooting the apple from his son's head, and the arrow "to kill thee, tyrant, had I slain my boy," familiar in connection with William Tell and William of Cloudesle, is a Wêland story, told of his brother Egil. Scott's Wayland Smith, in Kenilworth, has his name, though little else, from this source. Alfred substitutes *Wêland* for *Fabricius*, as though *Fabricius* were from *faber*, artificer.

Line 4.—*ǣngum* . . ., to any one may not the skill escape=no one may attain the skill. 6.—*þŷ ēđ* . . . *þe*, easier than; *beniman præccan cræftes*, deprive a wretch (even) of his skill, § 317;—than one may turn the sun to swerve, and this swift heaven (to swerve) from his orbit, any of heroes; *ǣnig*, appositive with *mon*. 30.—*perâs*, accusative, appositive with *hî*; bring them forth well known=make them familiar. 37.—*guma*, repeated subject; What then may have any of heroes, a man, from fame . . .?

PAGE 66. SAWS. These are often called Gnomic verses. They are from pages 338+ of the Codex Exoniensis, already described in a note on the Traveler, page 51.

Line 3.—*pundrum*, wondrously. The ice, the water-helmet, locks up the plants. 14.—*pig*, repetition of *gûđ*. 22.—*bold-âgendum*, appositive with *him*, the wife should know wise counsels for them (herself and husband), the house holders both together. 25.—*frisan*, frizzled, ringleted, with a wealth of tresses, Ett., Grein; other editors "Frisian." 30.—Waiteth for him on the land that his love demandeth. 31.—*pǽre* . . ., keep faith.

Page 67, line 3.—*mǽgđ egsan þyn,* the chief of terrors, *i. e.* the sea, (holdeth) a family (many sailors). Thorpe reads *mægđ eâgnâ þyn,* a maid is the delight of the eyes. 4.—A rich man, a king, a settlement then for his people buys, when he comes to sail, *i. e.* sailing, § 448, 4. 32.—*sceal,* ought to belong to, becomes; infinitive omitted, § 435, *d.*—*Alþalda,* The All-ruling, *i. e.* the true God, (made) the glorious (world).

Page 68. Threnes. This extract is from a poem in the Codex Exoniensis, pages 286+, called by Thorpe The Wanderer. The ruined castle strikes the imagination powerfully in all ages, and in the decline of the Roman Empire men thought of themselves as living in a decaying world. The Anglo-Saxon poets seem to have been especially affected by this mode of thought.

Line 6.—*sumne* . . ., one a bird bore away over the high sea: *bird* trope for *ship,* Thorpe. Grein refers it to the bird *Greif,* O. H. G. *Grif, Grifo,* which figures in Germanic story, a counterpart to Gr. *Gryps,* griffon. 11.—*burgþarâ* . . ., till free from sounds of citizens old works of giants empty stood. Cities, stone figures, roads, stone swords, caves of dragons, are spoken of in Anglo-Saxon poems as *entâ geþeorc,* and that is the only way in which *ent* occurs in them. 17.—Where has come horse = what has become of horse? 21.—*genâp,* has vanished, *spâ,* as if. 22.—*on lâste,* in the place of, forsaken by. 39.—*tô rycene,* too quickly.

Page 69, line 2.—*eorl,* appositive with *hê,* unless he first the remedy know how, the earl, with might to obtain. 4.—*him,* for himself.

The Second Threne is from page 377 of the Codex Exoniensis, printed as "Deor the Scald's Complaint." See note on The Traveler, page 41.

Line 7.—*Wêland,* see page 65, 1, and note. Wêland for himself among dragons exile experienced. No dragon story is known of Wêland. Grein proposes *þimman,* by means of woman. Rieger reads *be þornum,* manifoldly. 11.—*Nidhâd,* see note on page 65. 12.—*sŷllan=sêllan<sêl,* weak form, as epic epithet, § 362, 1. 13.—*ofereôde,* impersonal; there was a surviving of that, so there may be of this. 16.—The omitted line and a half reads:

þæt heô gearolice ongieten hæfde
þæt heô eâcen pæs:

See for Beadohild's misfortune the note on page 65, line 1. 20.—*Eormanric.* The Gothic king *Emanaricus,* the Alexander of the North, is mentioned in the Traveler's Song and in Beowulf. He was king of the Ostro-Goths, A.D. 375. The stories told of him are full of anachronisms and inconsistencies. 25.—*cyne-rîces,* genitive of separation, § 317. 27.—*Heodening,* Heoden, is Hetele in Gudrun, Hedin in Snorri's Edda, Hithinus in Saxo. 30.—*Heorrenda* is celebrated in the German heroic poetry as *Horant,* in Snorri as *Hiarrandi.*

Page 70.—These rhymes are part of a poem of 87 verses in the Codex

Exoniensis. It is plainly a task poem to exhibit riming skill. The spelling obscures the sense, which needs all the light to be had. I have, therefore, used Grein's reformed orthography, and I add a Latin version by Ettmüller. Thorpe had pronounced it unintelligible. For the meter, see § 511.

Hominum genus perit, pugnæ hasta lacerat,
versutia procax pugnat, sagittam fraus præparat,
fidejussionem cura mordet, audaciam senectus exscindit.
Exilii tempus succrescit, iracundia jusjurandum cudit,
criminum funes expanduntur, machinationes instructæ labuntur.
Mœsta ira fodit, fovea retinaculum habet;
ornatus albus polluitur, æstas calida frigescit.
Populi prosperitas ruit, amicitia volvitur [evanescit],
terræ vires inveterascunt, fervor frigescit.
Mihi id Parca texuit et opus imposuit,
ut foderem sepulcrum; neque hanc diram constitutionem
evitare carne possum, quo ex tempore dies celer fugerit,
arreptione necessaria me arripit [mors], ex quo nox venerit,
quæ mihi patriam negat, et me hîc habitatione privat.
Si cadaver jacet, membra vermis comedit,
verrucam non curat et cibum sumit,
donec ossa tantum ex viro supersint,
et ultimo nullum [os], nisi necessitatis virgula
malum omen hic præbuerit, non erit fama tædio affecta.
Priusquam felix hoc cogitat, sæpissime se ipsum fatigat;
gustat amarum crimen, non curat meliorem voluptatem,
non recordatur hilaritatum gratias, hîc sunt misericordiæ gaudia
speranda in cœlorum regno. Eamus nunc sanctis similes
criminibus liberati, a dedecoribus redempti,
maculis puri, splendore cincti,
ubi humanum genus debet coram creatore lætum
verum Deum aspicere et in pace semper gaudere.

Note the use of adjectives as substantives: *flâh mâh flited*, subtle hostile fighteth = hostile one, fiend; *bald ald þpited*, bold old severeth = old age cuts off the bold.

A BRIEF GRAMMAR

OF THE

ANGLO-SAXON LANGUAGE.

The sections are numbered like the corresponding sections in the Author's Comparative Grammar of the Anglo-Saxon Language, so that the references in the notes of the Reader may answer for both when the topic is treated in both. The Comparative Grammar illustrates the forms of the Anglo-Saxon by those of the Sanskrit, Greek, Latin, Gothic, Old Saxon, Old Friesic, Old Norse, and Old High German.

INTRODUCTION.

1. During the fifth and sixth centuries, England was conquered and peopled by pagans (Saxons, Angles, Jutes, etc.) from the shores of the North Sea; the center of emigration was near the mouth of the Elbe. The conquerors spoke many dialects, but most of them were Low German. Missionaries were sent from Rome (A.D. 597) to convert them to Christianity. The Roman alphabetic writing was thus introduced, and, under the influence of learned native ecclesiastics, a single tongue gradually came into use as a literary language through the whole nation. The chief seat of learning down to the middle of the eighth century was among the Angles of Northumberland. The language was long called Englisc (English), but is now called Anglo-Saxon. Its Augustan age was the reign of Alfred the Great, king of the West Saxons (A.D. 871–901). It continued to be written till the colloquial dialects, through the influence of the Anglo-Norman, had diverged so far from it as to make it unintelligible to the people; then, under the cultivation of the Wycliffite translators of the Bible, and of Chaucer and his fellows, there grew out of these dialects a new classic language—the English.

2. The spelling in the manuscripts is irregular, but the Northumbrian is the only well-marked dialect of the Anglo-Saxon, as old as its classic period (10th century), which has yet been explored. The Gospels and some other works have been printed in it. The common Anglo-Saxon is sometimes called West-Saxon.

3. After the period of pure Anglo-Saxon, there was written an irregular dialect called Semi-Saxon. It has few strange words, but the inflections and syntax are broken up (12th century).

4. The former inhabitants of Britain were Celts, so unlike the invaders in race and speech, and so despised and hated, that they did not mix. There are in the Anglo-Saxon a handful of Celtic common names, and a good many geographical names: the relation of the Celtic language to the Anglo-Saxon is like that of the languages of the aborigines of America to our present English.

5. The Anglo-Saxon was shaped to literary use by men who wrote and spoke Latin, and thought it an ideal language; and a large part of the literature is translated or imitated from Latin authors. It is not to be doubted, therefore, that the Latin exercised a great influence on the Anglo-Saxon: if it did not lead to the introduction of wholly new forms, either of etymology or syntax, it led to the extended and uniform use of those forms which are like the Latin, and to the disuse of others, so as to draw the grammars near each other. There are a considerable number of words from the Latin, mostly connected with the Church; three or four through the Celts from the elder Romans.

6. There are many words in Anglo-Saxon more like the words of the same sense in Scandinavian than like any words which we find in the Germanic languages; but the remains of the early dialects are so scant that it is hard to tell how far such words were borrowed from or modified by the Scandinavians. Before A.D. 900 many Danes had settled in England. Danish kings afterward ruled it (A.D. 1013–1042). Their laws, however, are in Anglo-Saxon. The Danes were illiterate, and learned the Anglo-Saxon. Of course their pronunciation was peculiar, and they quickened and modified phonetic decay. It is probable that they affected the spoken dialects which have come up as English more than the written literary language which we call Anglo-Saxon.

7. The other languages sprung from the dialects of Low German tribes are Friesic, Old Saxon, and, later, Dutch (and Flemish), and Platt Deutsch. The talk in the harbors of Antwerp, Bremen, and Hamburg is said to be often mistaken by English sailors for corrupt English. These Low German languages are akin to the High German on one side, and to the Scandinavian on the other. These all, with the Mœso-Gothic, constitute the Teutonic class of languages. This stands parallel with the Lithuanic, the Slavonic, and the Celtic, and with the Italic, the Hellenic, the Iranic, and the Indic, all of which belong to the Indo-European family of languages. The parent speech of this family is lost, and has left no literary monuments. Its seat has been supposed to have been on the heights of Central Asia. The Sanskrit, an ancient language of India, takes its place at the head of the family. Theoretical roots and forms of inflection are given by grammarians as those of the Parent Speech, on the ground that they are such as might have produced the surviving roots and forms by known laws of change.

8. The following stem shows the order in which these classes branched, and their relative age and remoteness from each other. At the right is given the approximate date of the oldest literary remains. The languages earlier than these remains are made out like the Parent Speech; that is, roots and forms are taken for the language at each period, which will give the roots and forms of all the languages which branch from it, but not those peculiar to the other languages.

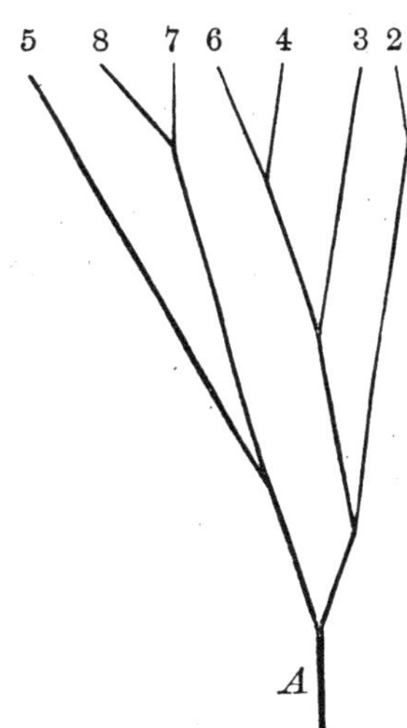

A. Indo-European. Parent Speech.
1. Indic. B.C. 1500. Sanskrit Vedas.
2. Iranic. B.C. 1000. Bactrian Avesta.
3. Hellenic. Before B.C. 800. Greek.
4. Italic. B.C. 200. Latin.
5. Teutonic. 4th Century. Mœso-Gothic Bible.
6. Celtic. 8th Century.
7. Slavonic. 9th Century. Bulgarian Bible.
8. Lithuanic. 16th Century.

9. The following stem shows the manner in which the languages of the Teutonic class branch after separating from the Slavonic. The Gothic (Mœso-Gothic) died without issue; the Low German is nearer akin to it than the High German is. The branches of the Scandinavian (Swedish, Danish, Norwegian) are not represented.

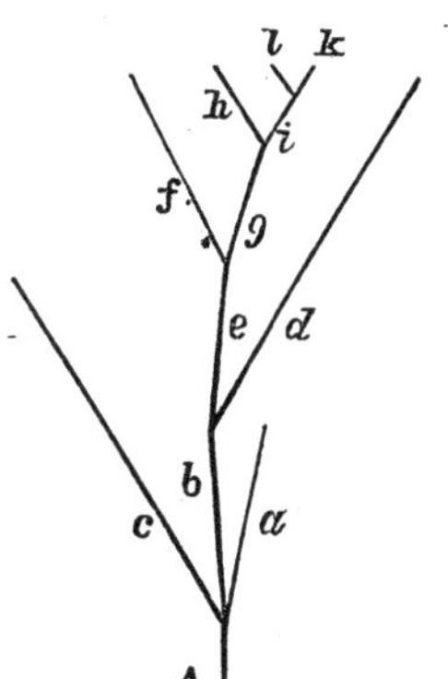

A. Teutonic. Theoretic.
a. Gothic. 4th Century.
b. Germanic. Theoretic.
c. Scandinavian. 13th Century.
d. High German. 8th Century.
e. Low German. Theoretic.
f. Friesic. 14th Century.
g. Saxon. Theoretic.
h. Anglo-Saxon. 8th Century.
i. Old Saxon. 9th Century.
k. Platt Deutsch. 14th Century.
l. Dutch. 13th Century.

PART I.

PHONOLOGY.

10. **Alphabet.**—The Anglo-Saxon alphabet has twenty-four letters. All but three are Roman characters: the variations from the common form are cacographic fancies. Þ þ (thorn), and Ƿ ƿ (wên), are runes. Ð đ (edh) is a crossed d, used for the older þ, oftenest in the middle and at the end of words.

Old Forms.		Simple Forms.		Roman.		Names.
A	a	A	a	A	a	ah
Æ	æ	Æ	æ	Æ	æ	ă
B	b	B	b	B	b	bay
C	c	C	c	C	c	cay
D	ð	D	d	D	d	day
Ð	ð	Ð	đ	DH	dh	edh
E	e	E	e	E	e	ay
F	ꝼ	F	f	F	f	ef
G	ᵹ	G	g	G	g	gay
Ƕ ƕ	h	H	h	H	h	hah
I	ı	I	i	I	i	ee
L	l	L	l	L	l	el
M	m	M	m	M	m	em
N	n	N	n	N	n	en
O	o	O	o	O	o	o
P	p	P	p	P	p	pay
R	ꞃ	R	r	R	r	er
S	ꞅ	S	s	S	s	es
T	ꞇ	T	t	T	t	tay
Þ	þ þ	Þ	þ	TH	th	thorn
U	u	U	u	U	u	oo
Ƿ	ƿ	Ƿ	ƿ	{ VV (W)	vv (w) }	wên
X	x	X	x	X	x	ex
Y	ẏ	Y	y	Y	y	ypsilon

Some of the German editors use ä for æ, æ for ǣ, ë for e derived from i, ö for œ, œ for œ̂, j for i when a semi-vowel, and v for ƿ. Now and then k, q, v, z get into the manuscripts, mostly in foreign words, and uu or u for ƿ. The Semi-Saxon has a peculiar character for j (ȝ).

11. **Abbreviations.**—The most common are ⁊ = and, ꝥ = þæt (*that*), ꝉ = oððe (*or*), and ¯ for an omitted m or n; as, þā = þam.

12. An **Accent** (´) is found in Anglo-Saxon manuscripts, but in none so regularly used as to make it an objective part of an Anglo-Saxon text. It is found oftenest over a long vowel; sometimes over a vowel of peculiar sound, not long; seldom, except over syllables having stress of voice. Sometimes it seems to mark nothing but stress. Most of the English editors represent it by an acute accent; the Germans generally print Anglo-Saxon with a circumflex over all single long vowels in the stem of words, and an acute over the diphthongs, as brôðer, freónd. In this book, to guide the studies of beginners, a circumflex is used over all long vowels and diphthongs, and the acute accent (′) over vowels only to denote stress.

13. **Punctuation.**—The Anglo-Saxons used one dot (.) at the end of each clause, or each hemistich of a poem, and sometimes three dots (:·) at the end of a sentence. Modern pointing is generally used in printed text.

14. **Sounds of Letters.**—*Vowels:*

a like *a* in *far*.
â " *a* " *fall*.
æ " *a* " *glad*.
ǣ " *a* " *dare* in New England.
e " *e* " *let*.
e in the breakings (not diphthongs) ea, eo, eâ, eô, very light.
ê like *e* in *they*.

i like *i* in *dim*.
î " *ee* " *deem*.
o " *o* " *wholly*.
ô " *o* " *holy*.
u " *u* " *full*.
û " *oo* " *fool*.
y " *i* " *dim*, but with the lips thrust out and rounded. (French u.)
ŷ same sound prolonged.

Unaccented vowels are like accented in kind, but obscure.

The *consonants* have their common English sounds; but note

c like *k*, always.
ch " *kh* in *work-house*.
cƿ " *qu*.
ð, like Engl. *th* in a similar word; *óðer*, other, *dôð*, doth.
g like *g* in *go*, always.
h very distinct.
hƿ like *wh* in New England.

i (=j) before a vowel, like *y*.
s like *s* in *so*.
t " *t* " *to*.
þ " *th* " *thin*.
ƿ " *w*.
ƿl, ƿr, and final ƿ nearly close the lips. (German w.)
x like *ks*.

15. **Accent.**—Rule 1. The primary accent is on the first syllable of every word: *brōđ'-er*, brother; *un'-cūđ*, uncouth.

Exception 1. Proper prefixes in verbs and particles take no primary accent: such are *â*, *an*, *and*, *æt*, *be*, *bi*, *ed*, *for*, *ful*, *ge*, *geond*, *in*, *mis*, *ôđ*, *of*, *ofer*, *on*, *or*, *tô*, *þurh*, *un*, *under*, *wiđ*, *wiđer*, *ymb*, *ymbe*: *an-gin'nan*, begin; *æt-gad'ere*, together; *on-geân'*, again. The syllable after the prefix takes the accent.

(*a*.) But derivatives from nouns, pronouns, or adjectives retain their accent: *and'-sparian* < *and'sparu*, answer; *in'-peardlîce* < *in'-peard*, adj., *inward*; *ed'-nipian* < *ed'nipe*, renewed. Such are all verbs in *and-*, *ed-*, *or-*, found in Anglo-Saxon poetry; many adverbs in *un-*, etc.

(*b*.) Many editors print as compounds adverbs+verbs, both of which retain their accent. Such are those with *æfter*, *bî*, *bîg*, *efen*, *eft*, *fore*, *forđ*, *from*, *fram*, *hider*, *mid*, *niđer*, *gegn*, *geân*, *gên*, *tô*, *up*, *ût*, *wel*.

Exception 2. The inseparable prefixes *â-*, *be-* (*bi-*), *for-*, *ge-*, are unaccented: *â-lŷs'-ing*, redemption; *be-gang'*, course.

Rule 2. A secondary accent may fall on the tone syllable of the lighter part of a compound or on a suffix: *o`fer-cum'an*, overcome; *heof'on-steor`-ra*, star of heaven; *hŷr'end`e*, hearing.

EUPHONIC CHANGES.

27. **Gemination** is the doubling of a letter: when final or next to a consonant it is simplified or dissimilated, *mm* to *mb*, *nn* to *nd*, *ss* to *st*, *ii* to *ig*, *uu* to *up*: *dippan*, dip, makes *dip*, *dipte*; *timbr* for *timmr*, timber; *spindl* for *spinnl*, spindle; *lufast*, lovest, for *lufass*, *lufige* for *lufiie*, love; *bearupes* for *bearuues*, grove. Double *g* is written *cg*, double *f*, *bb*.

32. **Umlaut** is the assimilation of a vowel by the vowel of the following syllable.

	a-umlaut.	i-umlaut.	u-umlaut.
It changes	i, u,	a, u, ea, eo, â, ô, û, eâ, eô,	a, i,
to	e(eo), o.	e, y, y, y, ǣ, ê, ŷ, ŷ, ŷ.	(o)ea, eo.

a-umlaut: *helpan*, from root *hilp*, help; *leofađ*, root *lif*, live; *boga*, from root *bug*, bow. The **i** which produces *i*-umlaut is often changed to **e** or dropped; *man*, plur. *men*, from *meni*; *fôt*, plur. *fêt*, feet, from *fêti*. **u**-umlaut: *hliđ*, plur. *hleodu*, slopes.

33. **Breaking** is the change of one vowel to two by a consonant. **g**, **c**, and **sc** may break a following *a* to *ea*, *o* to *eo*, *i* to *ie*, *â* to *eâ*, *ô* to *eô*. **l**, **r**, and **h** may break a preceding *a* to *ea*, *i* to *eo* (*io*), *ie*: *geaf*, gave; *ceaster*, Latin *castrum*, camp; *sceô*, shoe; *sealm*, psalm; *earm*, arm; *hleahtor*, laughter; *meolc*, milk.

41. **Shifting** is a weakening of a letter not produced by other letters: *a* to *æ*, *ǣ* to *ē*, *eâ eô* to *ē*, etc.: *dæg* from *dag*, day.

PART II.

ETYMOLOGY.

NOUNS.

65. There are two classes of Declensions of Anglo-Saxon nouns:

(1.) **Strong**: those which have sprung from vowel stems.

(2.) **Weak**: that which has sprung from stems in **an.**

There are four declensions distinguished by the endings of the Genitive Singular:

Declension 1.	Declension 2.	Declension 3.	Declension 4.
es	**e**	**a**	**an**

66. SUMMARY OF CASE-ENDINGS.

	Strong.							Weak.		
	Decl. I.				Decl. II.		Decl. III.	Decl. IV.		
	Masc.	Neut.	Masc.	Neut.	Feminine.		Masc. Fem.	Masc.	Fem.	Neut.
Stem.........	a	a	ia	ia	â	i	u	an	an	an
Singular.—										
N. & V.......	–	–	e	e	u	–	u	a	e	e
Gen.	es	es	es	es	e	e	â	an	an	an
Dat.	e	e	e	e	e	e	â	an	an	an
Acc.	–	–	e	e	u, e	e, –	u	an	an	e
Inst...........	ê	ê	ê	ê	e	e	â	an	an	an
Plural.—										
N., A., & V.	âs	u	âs	u	â, e	e, â	u, o, â	an		
Gen.	â	â	â	â	â, enâ		â, enâ	enâ		
D. & Inst.....	um	um	um	um	um		um	um		

A few masculines of Decl. 1st have some forms from **i**-stems or **u**-stems, §§ 86, 93.

67. **Gender.** General rules. For particulars, see §§ 268–270.

1. **Strong nouns.** All masculines are of the first or third declension; all feminines of the second or third; all neuters of the first.

2. *Abstract Nouns* have their gender governed by the terminations. In derivatives the feminine gender prevails.

3. *Compound Nouns* follow the gender of the last part.

4. Masculine are names of males; of the moon; of many weeds, flowers, winds; *man, guma*, man; *ƿêland; môna*, moon; *mear*, horse; *þorn*, thorn; *blôstma*, blossom; *ƿind*, wind.

5. Feminine are names of females; of the sun; of many trees, rivers, soft and low musical instruments: *cƿên*, queen; *cû*, cow; *Ælf-þryđe; sunnu, sunne*, sun; *âc*, oak; *Danubie*, Danube; *hƿistle*, whistle; *hearpe*, harp.

6. Neuter are names of wife, child; diminutives; many general names; and words made an object of thought: *pîf*, wife; *bearn*, *cild*, child; *mægden*, maiden; *græs*, grass; *ofet*, fruit; *corn*, corn; *gold*, gold.

7. *Epicene Nouns* have one grammatical gender, but are used for both sexes. Such names of mammalia are masculine, except of a few little timid ones: *mûs*, mouse (feminine); large and fierce birds are masculine; others feminine, especially singing birds: *nihtegale*, nightingale; large fishes are masculine, small feminine; insects are feminine.

68. **Cases alike.**—(1.) The nominative and vocative are always alike.

(2.) The nominative, accusative, and vocative are alike in all plurals, and in the singular of all neuters and strong masculines.

(3.) The genitive plural ends always in **â** or **enâ.**

(4). The dative and instrumental plural end always in **um** (*on*).

DECLENSION I.

Stem in **a.** Genitive singular in **es.**

70.—I. Case-endings from stem **a**+relational suffixes. Nominative in —.

	Masculine.		Neuter.
Stem.......	pulfa, *wolf.*		scipa, *ship.*
Theme	pulf.		scip.
Singular.—			
Nominative ..	pulf,	*a wolf.*	scip.
Genitive......	pulf*es*,	*of a wolf, wolf's.*	scip*es.*
Dative	pulf*e*,	*to* or *for a wolf.*	scip*e.*
Accusative....	pulf,	*a wolf.*	scip.
Vocative......	pulf,	*O, wolf.*	scip.
Instrumental..	pulf*ĕ*,	*by* or *with a wolf.*	scip*ĕ.*
Plural.—			
Nominative ..	pulf*âs*,	*wolves.*	scip*u.*
Genitive......	pulf*â*,	*of wolves.*	scip*â.*
Dative	pulf*um*,	*to* or *for wolves.*	scip*um.*
Accusative ...	pulf*âs*,	*wolves.*	scip*u.*
Vocative......	pulf*âs*,	*O, wolves.*	scip*u.*
Instrumental..	pulf*um*,	*by* or *with wolves.*	scip*um.*

73. 2.—Long syllables drop plur. *-u*. 3.—*a* does not shift to *æ* in plur. of monosyllables in a single consonant. 4.—Umlaut of *i* to *eo* is rare. 5.—Gemination, see § 27. 6.—An unaccented short vowel before a single consonant is often dropped. 7, 8.—*g* and *h* interchange and drop. 9.—See § 27. 10.—Like *æg* decline *cealf*, *cild*, *lamb*.

	2. Long monosyllables.	3. Shifting.		4. U-umlaut.	5. Gemination.	
Stem	*porda*, n. word.	*daga*, m. day.	*fata*, n. vat.	*hliða*, n. slope.	*torra*, m. tower.	*spella*, n. speech.
Theme...	*pord*	*dæg*	*fæt*	*hlið*	*tor*	*spel*
SINGULAR.—						
N., A., & V.	*pord*	*dæg*	*fæt*	*hlið*	*tor*	*spel*
Gen.	*pord*es	*dæg*es	*fæt*es	*hlið*es	*torr*es	*spell*es
Dat.	*pord*e	*dæg*e	*fæt*e	*hlið*e	*torr*e	*spell*e
Inst.	*pord*ê	*dæg*ê	*fæt*ê	*hlið*ê	*torr*ê	*spell*ê
PLURAL.—						
N., A., & V.	*pord*	*dag*âs	*fat*u	*hleoð*u (-i-)	*torr*âs	*spel*
Gen.	*pord*â	*dag*â	*fat*â	*hleoð*â (-i-)	*torr*â	*spell*â
D. & Inst....	*pord*um	*dag*um	*fat*um	*hleoð*um (-i-)	*torr*um	*spell*um

	6. Syncope.		7. Stem in -ga.	8. Stem in -ha.	
Stem....	*tungola*, m. star.	*tungola*, n. star.	*beâga*, m. ring.	*mearha*, m. horse.	*hôha*, m. hough.
Theme...	*tungol*	*tungol*	*beâg*	*mearh*	*hôh*
SINGULAR.—					
N., A., & V.	*tung-ol, -ul, -el, -l*		*beâ(g), h*	*mear(h), g*, -	*hôh, hô*
Gen.	*tung-ol*es, *-ul*es, *-el*es, *-l*es		*beâg*es	*mear*es	*hô*s
Dat.	*tung-ole, -ule, -ele, -le*		*beâg*e	*mear*e	*hô*
Inst.	*tung-ol*ê, *-ul*ê, *-el*ê, *-l*ê		*beâg*ê	*mear*ê	*hô*
PLURAL.—					
N., A., & V.	m. *tung-ol*âs, *-ul*âs, *-el*âs, *-l*âs	n. *tung-ol*u, *-ol, -ul, -el, -l*	*beâg*âs	*mear*âs	*hô*s
Gen.	*tung-ol*â, *-ul*â, *-el*â, *-l*â		*beâg*â	*mear*â	*hô*â
D. & I.	*tung-ol*um, *-ul*um, *-el*um, *-l*um		*beâg*um	*mear*um	*hô*um

	9. Stem in -pa.		10. Stem + er.
Stem	*bearpa*, m., grove.	*cneôpa*, n., knee.	*æga*, egg.
Theme...	*bearu*	*cneôp*	*æg*, plur. *æger*
SINGULAR.—			
N., A., & V.	*bear-u, -o*	*cneôp, cneô*	*æg*
Gen.	*bear-p*es, *-up*es, *-op*es, *-ep*es	*cneô-p*es, -s	*æg*es
Dat.	*bear-pe, -upe, -ope, -epe*	*cneô-pe*, –	*æg*e
Inst.	*bear-p*ê, *-up*ê, *-op*ê, *-ep*ê	*cneô-p*ê, –	*æg*ê
PLURAL.—			
N., A., & V.	*bear-p*âs, *-up*âs, *-op*âs, *-ep*âs	*cneô-p*u, *-p*, –	*æg*-er-u, -ru
Gen.	*bear-p*â, *-up*â, *-op*â, *-ep*â	*cneô-p*â, *cneâ*	*æg*-er-â, -râ
D. & I.	*bear-p*um, *-up*um, *-op*um, *-ep*um	*cneô-p*um, -um, -m	*æg*-er-um, -rum

83.—II. Case-endings from stem **-ia**+relational suffixes.			84.—III. Case-endings from stem **-i**+relational suffixes.		
Stem .	hirdia, m., *shepherd.*	rîcia, n., *realm.*	byri, m., *son.*	fôti, m., *foot.*	mani, m., *man.*
Theme	hird.	rîc.	byr	fôt	man
SINGULAR.—					
Nom.	hird*e*	rîc*e*	byr*e*	fôt	man
Gen...	hird*es*	rîc*es*	byr*es*	fôt*es*	mann*es*
Dat...	hird*e*	rîc*e*	byr*e*	fêt, fôt*e*	men
Acc...	hird*e*	rîc*e*	byr*e*	fôt	man
Voc...	hird*e*	rîc*e*	byr*e*	fôt	man
Inst...	hird*ĕ*	ric*ĕ*	byr*ĕ*	fêt, fôt*ĕ*	men.
PLURAL.—					
Nom.	hird*âs*	rîc*u*	byr*e*, *-âs*	fêt, fôt*âs*	men
Gen...	hird*â*	rîc*â*	byr*â*	fôt*â*	mann*â*
Dat...	hird*um*	rîc*um*	byr*um*	fôt*um*	mann*um*
Acc...	hird*âs*	rîc*u*	byr*e*, *-âs*	fêt, fôt*âs*	men
Voc...	hird*âs*	rîc*u*	byr*e*, *-âs*	fêt, fôt*âs*	men
Inst...	hird*um*	rîc*um*	byr*um*	fôt*um*	mann*um*

86. *Stem in* **i**. The plur. *-e* is found in names of peoples : *Dene*, Danes ; *Rômâne*, Romans ; *leôde*, men ; and in *pine*, friend ; *mere*, sea ; and a few others. Umlaut, as in *fôt*, is found in *tôđ*, tooth ; so also in the feminines *bôc*, book ; *brôc*, breeches ; *gôs*, goose ; *mûs*, mouse ; *lûs*, louse ; *cû*, cow, plur. gen. *cûnâ ; burh*, gen. dat. *byrig*, borough ; *turf*, turf. See § 90.

87. A few anomalous consonant stems which sometimes have genitive *-es* may be placed here.

Stems in **-nd** *and* **-r**.

	nd-stem.	**r**-stem.
SINGULAR.—		
Nom., A., & V...........	feônd.	brôđor (ur, er).
Gen.........................	feôndes.	brôđor.
Dat. & Inst.	feônde.	brêđer.
PLURAL.—		
Nom., A., & V...........	feônd, -âs, fŷnd.	brôđor, brôđru (a).
Gen.........................	feôndâ,	brôđrâ.
Dat. & Inst.............	feôndum.	brôđrum.

Participial nouns in *-nd*, plur. *-nd*, *-ndâs*, are common. Like *brôđor* are fem. *môdor*, mother ; *dôhtor*, daughter ; *speostor*, sister. *Fæder* has undeclined forms, and also gen. *-es*, plur. *-âs*, *-â*, *-um*. *Neaht*, f., night, gen. *nihte*, *nihtes*, plur. *niht*. *Feld*, field ; *ford*, ford ; *sumor*, summer ; *pinter*, winter, etc., have dat. *-â*.

Stem in **â** or **i.** Genitive singular in **e.**

88.—I. Case-endings from stem **â**+relational suffixes.		II.—Case-endings from stem **i**+relational suffixes.
Stem....	gifâ, *gift.*	dæ̂di, *deed.*
Theme...	gif.	dæ̂d.
SINGULAR.—		
Nominative..	gif*u*.	dæ̂d.
Genitive.....	gif*e*.	dæ̂d*e*.
Dative.......	gif*e*.	dæ̂d*e*.
Accusative...	gif*u*, gif*e*.	dæ̂d, dæ̂d*e*.
Vocative.....	gif*u*.	dæ̂d.
Instrumental..	gif*e*.	dæ̂d*e*.
PLURAL.—		
Nominative..	gif*á*, gif*e*.	dæ̂d*e*, dæ̂d*á*.
Genitive..	gif*á*, gif*ená*.	dæ̂d*á*.
Dative....	gif*um*.	dæ̂d*um*.
Accusative...	gif*á*, gif*e*.	dæ̂d*e*, dæ̂d*á*.
Vocative.....	gif*á*, gif*e*.	dæ̂d*e*, dæ̂d*á*.
Instrumental..	gif*um*.	dæ̂d*um*.

90. Stem..	4. bôci, *book.*	5. mûsi, *mouse.*	6. ceasteri, *city.*
Theme	bôc.	mûs.	ceaster, ceastr.
SINGULAR.—			
Nom...	bôc.	mûs.	ceaster.
Gen....	bêc.	mŷs.	ceastr*e*.
Dat....	bêc.	mŷs.	ceastr*e*.
Acc....	bôc	mûs.	{ ceaster. ceastr*e*.
Voc....	bôc.	mûs.	ceaster.
Inst....	bêc.	mŷs.	ceastr*e*.
PLURAL.—			
Nom...	bêc.	mŷs.	ceastr*e* (*á*).
Gen....	bôc*á*.	mûs*á*.	ceastr*á*.
Dat....	bôc*um*.	mûs*um*.	ceastr*um*.
Acc....	bêc.	mŷs.	ceastr*e* (*á*).
Voc....	bêc.	mŷs.	ceastr*e* (*á*).
Inst....	bôc*um*.	mûs*um*.	ceastr*um*.

Feminines in *-ung* and a few others sometimes have dative *-á*.

92. *Head-cases in a Vowel.*—Genitive in **a.**

	1. sunu, *son.*	2. handu, *hand.*
Stem......		
Theme....	sun.	hand.
SINGULAR.—		
Nominative..	sun*u*.	hand.
Genitive.....	sun*á*.	hand*á*.
Dative.......	sun*á*, sun*u*.	hand*á*, hand.
Accusative...	sun*u*.	hand.
Vocative.....	sun*u*.	hand.
Instrumental.	sun*á*.	hand*á*, hand.
PLURAL.—		
Nominative..	sun*u* (*o*), sun*á*.	hand*á*.
Genitive.....	sun*á*, sun*end*.	hand*á*.
Dative.......	sun*um*.	hand*um*.
Accusative...	sun*u* (*o*), sun*á*.	hand*á*.
Vocative.....	sun*u* (*o*), sun*á*.	hand*á*.
Instrumental.	sun*um*.	hand*um*.

95. WEAK NOUNS.

Case-endings < stem **an** + relational suffixes.—Genitive in **an.**

(DECLENSION IV.)

	1. MASCULINES.	2. FEMININES.	3. NEUTERS.	CONTRACTS.
Stem..	hanan, *cock.*	tungan, *tongue.*	eâgan, *eye.*	tâan, *toe.*
Theme	han.	tung.	eâg.	tâ.
SINGULAR.—				
Nom. ..	han*a*.	tung*e*.	eâg*e*.	tâ*e*, tâ.
Gen. ...	han*an*.	tung*an*.	eâg*an*.	tâ*an*, tân.
Dat. ...	han*an*.	tung*an*.	eâg*an*.	tâ*an*, tân.
Acc. ...	han*an*.	tung*an*.	eâg*e*.	tâ*an*, tân.
Voc. ...	han*a*.	tung*e*.	eâg*e*.	tâ*e*, tâ.
Inst. ...	han*an*.	tung*an*.	eâg*an*.	tâ*an*, tân.
PLURAL.—				
Nom. ..	han*an*.	tung*an*.	eâg*an*.	tâ*an*, tân.
Gen. ...	han*end*.	tung*end*.	eâg*end*.	tâ*end*, tânâ.
Dat. ...	han*um*.	tung*um*.	eâg*um*.	tâ*um*.
Acc. ...	han*an*.	tung*an*.	eâg*an*.	tâ*an*, tân.
Voc. ...	han*an*.	tung*an*.	eâg*an*.	tâ*an*, tân.
Inst. ...	han*um*.	tung*um*.	eâg*um*.	tâ*um*.

101. PROPER NAMES.

(1.) PERSONS.—*Names of women in* -u *or a consonant are strong, those in* -e *or* -a *are weak. Declension II., â-stem:* Begu, Freâparu; *i-stem:* Beadohild, Hygd, *and most others. Declension IV.:* Elene, Eve, Ada, Maria, *etc., from foreign names;* Ꝥealhþeô(p), *dat.* Ꝥealhþeôn (§ 99).

Names of men in -u, -e, *or a consonant are strong, those in* -a *are weak. Declension III., u-stem:* Leôfsunu? *Declension I., a-stem:* Ælfrêd, Beôpulf, Eâdmund, Sigemund (*gen. also* Sigemunde<mund, *f. Rask*)? Ꝥêland, *and most other strong names; syncopated:* Ecgþeô(p), *gen.* Ecgþeôpes, Ecgþeôes, *etc.;* Ongenþeô(p); Grendel, *gen.* Grendeles, Grendles, *etc.;* Hrêđel; *ia-stem:* Ine, Hedde, Gîslhere, Ꝥulfhere, Eâdpine, Godpine, *and others from* -here *and* -pine; *umlaut not found:* Hereman, *dat.* Heremanne. *Declension IV.:* Ætla, Becca, *and many others.*

(*a.*) *Foreign names sometimes retain foreign declension, or are undeclined, but are generally declined as above; those in* -as, -es, -us *do not often increase in the genitive. Those from Latin* -us, *Greek* -ος, *of the second declension, sometimes drop their endings and take those of the Anglo-Saxon first:* Crist (<Christus), Cristes, Criste, *etc. In less familiar words* -us *oftenest stands in the nom. and gen., but Latin and Anglo-Saxon forms may mix throughout:* Petrus, *gen.* Petrus, Petruses, Petres, Petri, *dat.* Petro, Petre, *acc.* Petrus, Petrum; *so* -as *and* -es: Andreâs, *gen.* Andreâs, *dat.* Andreâ, *acc.* Andreâs, Andream; Hêrôdês, Hêrôdes, Hêrôde, Hêrôd-em, -ês, *or* -e.

(*b.*) *In Gothic these Latin and Greek names of the second declension are regularly given in the u-declension:* Paitrus, *gen.* Paitraus, *dat.* Paitrau, *acc.* Paitru (§ 93, *a*). *The Anglo-Saxon genitive* Petrus *may be a relic of the u-declension.*

(2.) PEOPLES.—*Plurals in* -âs *and* -e *are strong, in* -an *weak. Declension I., a-stem:* Brittâs, Scottâs, *etc.; ia-stem and i-stem:* Dene, *gen.* Den-â, -iâ, -igâ, -geâ (§ 85, *a*); Românê, *etc. Declension IV.:* Gotan, Seaxan, *etc.*

The singular is oftenest an adjective in -isc *regularly declined:* Egyptisc man, *Egyptian man;* Egyptisc ides, *Egyptian woman;* þâ Egyptiscan, *the Egyptians, etc. Sometimes* ân Brit, *a Briton.*

Often is found a collective with a genitive, or with an adjective, or compounded: Seaxnâ þeôd; Filisteâ folc; Caldêâ cyn; Ebrêâ perâs; Sodomisc cyn; Rôm-pare (§ 86); Norđ-men (§ 84, 3), *etc. Foreign names are treated as are names of persons.*

(3.) COUNTRIES.—*A few feminine names are found:* Engel, *England;* Bryten, *Britannia. Oftenest is found the people's name in the genitive with* land, rîce, êđel, *etc., or in an oblique case with a preposition:* Englâ land; Sodomâ rîce; on Eâst-Englum; of Seaxum; on Egyptum. *Foreign names are treated as are names of persons.*

(4.) Cities.—*Names found alone are regularly declined according to gender and endings:* Rôm, *f.* Rôme; Babylon, *n.* Babylones; Sodoma, *m.* Sodoman. *Oftenest they are prefixed undeclined to* burg, ceaster, pîc, dûn, hâm, *etc.:* Lunden-pîc, Rôma-burg, *etc.; or the folk's name in the genitive followed by* burg, ceaster, *etc., is used:* Caldêâ burg. *Foreign names treated as names of persons.*

IV. ADJECTIVES.

INDEFINITE AND DEFINITE DECLENSIONS.

103. An adjective in Anglo-Saxon has one set of strong and one of weak endings for each gender. The latter are used when the adjective is preceded by the definite article or some word like it. Hence there are two declensions, the indefinite and the definite.

104.—I. *The Indefinite Declension.*

Case-endings < stem **a**, **â**, or **i** + relational suffixes.

	Masculine.	Feminine.	Neuter.
Stem...	blinda, *blind.*	blindâ, blindi, *blind.*	blinda, *blind.*
Theme .	blind.	blind.	blind.
Singular.—			
Nom.	blind	blind(*u*) (*o*) (*e*)	blind
Gen.	blind*es*	blind*re*	blind*es*
Dat.	blind*um*	blind*re*	blind*um*
Acc.	blind*ne*	blind*e*	blind
Voc.	blind	blind(*u*)	blind
Inst.	blind*ĕ*	blind*re*	blind*ĕ*
Plural.—			
Nom.	blind*e*	blind*e*	blind(*u*) (*o*) (*e*)
Gen.	blind*râ*	blind*râ*	blind*râ*
Dat.	blind*um*	blind*um*	blind*um*
Acc.	blind*e*	blind*e*	blind*u*
Voc.	blind*e*	blind*e*	blind*u*
Inst.	blind*um*	blind*um*	blind*um*

105.—II. *The Definite Declension.*

Case-endings < stem **an** + relational suffixes.

	MASCULINE.	FEMININE.	NEUTER.
Stem..	blindan, *blind.*	blindan,	blindan,
Theme	blind.	blind.	blind.
SINGULAR.—			
Nom.....	se blind*a*.	seô blind*e*.	þæt blind*e*.
Gen......	þæs blind*an*.	þǽre blind*an*.	þæs blind*an*.
Dat......	þam blind*an*.	þǽre blind*an*.	þam blind*an*.
Acc......	þone blind*an*.	þâ blind*an*.	þæt blind*e*.
Voc......	se blind*a*.	seô blind*e*.	þæt blind*e*.
Inst......	þŷ blind*an*.	þǽre blind*an*.	þŷ blind*an*.
PLURAL.—			
Nom.....		þâ blind*an*.	
Gen......		þârâ blind*enă*.	
Dat......		þâm blind*um*.	
Acc......		þâ blind*an*.	
Voc......		þâ blind*an*.	
Inst......		þâm blind*um*.	

106.—*Theme ending Short* (*Root Shifting*).

Stem..	glada, *glad.*	gladâ, gladi.	glada.
Theme	glad > glæd.	glad > glæd.	glad > glæd.
SINGULAR.—			
Nom.....	glæd.	glad*u*.	glæd.
Gen......	glad*es*.	glæd*re*.	glad*es*.
Dat......	glad*um*.	glæd*re*.	glad*um*.
Acc......	glæd*ne*.	glad*e*.	glæd.
Voc......	glæd.	glad*u*.	glæd.
Inst......	glad*ĕ*.	glæd*re*.	glad*ĕ*.
PLURAL.—			
Nom.....	glad*e*.	glad*e*.	glad*u*.
Gen......	glæd*ră*.	glæd*ră*.	glæd*ră*.
Dat......	glad*um*.	glad*um*.	glad*um*.
Acc......	glad*e*.	glad*e*.	glad*u*.
Voc......	glad*e*.	glad*e*.	glad*u*.
Inst......	glad*um*.	glad*um*.	glad*um*.

In the Definite Declension it has √*glad* throughout, and agrees wholly with *blind.* The ending -*u* may change to -*o*, -*e*, —.

122. Comparison.

Comparison is a variation to denote degrees of quantity or quality. It belongs to adjectives and adverbs.

(*a.*) In Anglo-Saxon it is a variation of stem, and is a matter rather of derivation than inflection; but the common mode of treatment is convenient.

(*b.*) The suffixes of comparison were once less definite in meaning than now, and were used to form many numerals, pronouns, adverbs > prepositions, and substantives, in which compared correlative terms are implied: *either*, *other*, *over*, *under*, *first*, etc.

(*c.*) Anglo-Saxon adverbs are in brackets: (*spîđe*).

123. Adjectives are regularly compared by suffixing to the theme of the positive *-ir* > *-er* or *-ôr* for the theme of the comparative, and *-ist* > *-est* or *-ôst* for the theme of the superlative.

The *Comparative* has always weak endings and syncopated stem.

The *Superlative* has both weak and strong endings.

Adverbs are compared like adjectives: the positive uses the ending *-e*, the comparative and superlative have none; *-ir* drops.

Strong,	spîđ, *strenuous;*	spîđra;	spîđôst.
Weak,	se spîđa;	se spîđra;	se spîđôsta.
Adverb,	(spîđe);	(spîđôr);	(spîđôst).

124. i-umlaut may change a, â, ea, eâ, eo, ô, u, û,
to e, ǣ, y, e, ŷ, y, ê, y, ŷ.

lang, long; *lengra* (*leng*); *lengest.*
eald, *ald*, old; *yldra*, *eldra;* *yldest*, *eldest.*

128. Heteroclitic forms abound from themes in *-ir* and *-ôr*, *-ist*, *-ôst:* *sēl*, good; *-ra*, *-la*, (*sēl*);—*est*, *-ôst;* *rîce*, rich; *rîcest*, *rîcôst;* *glæd*, glad; *glædra*, *gledra*, etc. (§ 125). Some have themes with and without double comparison: *læt*, late; *lætra;* *latôst*, *latemest;* *sîđ*, late; *sîđra* (*sîđ*, *sîđôr*); *sîđ-âst*, *-est*, *-mest.*

129. Defective are the following. Words in capitals are not found.

(1.) *Mixed Roots:*

	Positive.	Comparative.	Superlative.
good,	gôd / BAT (pel)	betera, betra, § 124 / bættra, § 125 (bet)	betst, betôst, -âst / (betst)
bad,	yfel / peor / sâm- (yfele)	pyrsa, (pyrs), § 123, *b* / sǣmra, § 124	pyrst, pyrresta, (pyrst), (pyrrest) / sǣmest

	POSITIVE.	COMPARATIVE.	SUPERLATIVE.
great, much,	micel (micle), fela (fela), MÂ	mâra, (mâ)	mǣst, § 124; 123, *a*
little,	lytel, LÆS (Goth. *lasivs*)	(lyt), læssa (læs), § 35, *B*	læs-ûst, -est, -t

(2.) *From Adverbs of time and place* (compare §§ 126, 127):

ever, ere, erst,	â-, ǣ-	(ǣr)>ǣrra, (ǣr-ôr, -ur)	ǣr-est
after-ward,	af-, æf-=of, æfterpeard	(æf-ter)> æftera	æf-tem-est, æfter-mest, § 127
else,	(elles)	(ellôr), elra	———
fore,	forepeard, (fore)	fyrra	for-ma > (fyrmest), fyrst, fruma, § 51
far,	feor, (fyr)	fyrre, (fyr)	fyrrest (eo>y)
forth,	forđpeard, (forđ)	(furđ-ôr, -ur)	(furđ-um), forđ-m-est
behind,	hinde(r)peard, (hindan)	(hinder)	hinduma, hinde-ma, § 126, *b*
inner,	innepeard, (in)	innera	inne-ma, (-m-est)
mid,	middepeard, (mid)	———	med-ema (-uma?), mid-m-est
north,	norđepeard, (norđ)	(norđ-ôr)	norđ-m-est
nether,	niđepeard, (niđe)	niđ-ra, (niđ-ôr, -er (i>eo)	niđema, § 126, niđe-m-est (i>eo)
upper,	ûfepeard, (up)	ufera, (ufôr)	yf(e)-m-est, § 124
outer,	ûtepeard, (ût)	ûtra, (uttôr, ûtôr)	ûtema, ûtmest, ŷt(e-)m-est, § 124

So *sûđemest, eâstemest, pestemest,* south-, east-, west-most.

DECAY OF ENDINGS. —(1), Declension: Layamon, strong, sing. masc. —, *-es, -en, -ne;* fem. —, *-re, -re, -e;* neut. —, *-es, -en,* —; plur. *-e, -re, -en, -e;* but *n, s, r* may drop. Weak, *-e, -en,* as in § 102.—Ormulum, strong, sing. —, plur. *-e.* Weak, *-e.*—Chaucer, monosyllables as in Orm.; others undeclined.—Shakespeare, no declension.

(2), Comparison: Layamon, Ormulum, *-re, -est.*—Chaucer (=Modern English), *-er, -est.*

V. PRONOUNS (*Relational Names*, § 56).

130. Personal Pronouns (*Relational Substantives*).

Sing.—	1. *I.*	2. *thou.*	3. *he,*	*she,*	*it.*
N.	ic	þû	hê	heô	hit
G.	mîn	þîn	his	hire	his
D.	mê	þê	him	hire	him
A.	mec, mê	þec, þê	hine	hîe, hî, heô	hit
V.	——	þû	——	——	——
I.	mê	þê	him	hire	him
Plural.—					
N.	pê	gê	hîe, hî, heô	hîe, hî, heô	heô, hîe, hî
G.	ûser, ûre	eôper	heorâ, hyrâ	heorâ, hyrâ	heorâ, hyrâ
D.	ûs	eôp	him	him	him
A.	ûsic, ûs	eôpic, eôp	hîe, hî, heô	hîe, hî, heô	heô, hîe, hî
V.	——	gê	——	——	——
I.	ûs	eôp	him	him	him
Dual.—					
N.	pit	git			
G.	uncer	incer			
D.	unc	inc			
A.	uncit, unc	incit, inc			
V.	——	git			
I.	unc	inc			

	Sing. Nom.	Genitive.	Plur. Nom.
P. Sp. ..	i-s, i-ja, i-t	i-sja	aj-as
Latin ...	i-s, ea, i-d	ejus	ii, eæ, ea
Gothic ..	i-s, si, i-ta	is, izôs, is	eis, ijôs, ija
O. Sax. ..	hi, siu, i-t	is, ira, is	siâ, siâ, siu
O. H. G.	i-r, siu, i-z	sîn, irâ, is	sîê, siô, siu
O. Norse	hann, hon, —	hans, hen-nar, —	——

131. Reflexives are supplied by the personal pronouns with *self* (self), or without it. *Self* has strong adjective endings like *blind* (§ 103); in the nominative singular also weak *selfa*.

132. Possessives are *mîn*, *þîn*, *sîn*, *ûser*, *ûre*, *eôper*, *uncer*, *incer*. They have strong adjective endings (§ 103). Those in *-er* are usually syncopated (§ 79). *Ûser* has assimilation of *r* > *s* (§ 35, *B*).

Sing.—	Masculine.	Feminine.	Neuter.	Plur.— Masc. & Fem.	Neut.
N.	ûser	ûser	ûser	(ûsere) ûsse (a)	ûser
G.	(ûseres) ûsses	(ûserre) ûsse	(ûseres) ûsses	(ûserrâ) ûssâ	
D.	(ûserum) ûssum	(ûserre) ûsse	(ûserum) ûssum	(ûserum) ûssum	
A.	ûserne	(ûsere) usse	ûser	(ûsere) ûsse	ûser
V.	ûser	ûser	ûser	(ûsere) ûsse	ûser
I.	(ûserê) ûssê	(ûserre) ûsse	(ûserê) ûssê	(ûserum) ûssum	

133. Demonstratives.

Definite Article.

	1. *that* and *the.*			2. *this.*		
Nom.	se	seô	þæ̂t	þes	þeôs	þis
Gen.	þæs	þǣre	þæs	þisses	þisse	þisses
Dat.	þam, þæm	þǣre	þam, þæm	þissum	þisse	þissum
Acc.	þone (a, æ)	þâ	þæt	þisne	þâs	þis
Voc.	se	seô	þæt	——	——	——
Inst.	þŷ	þǣre	þŷ, þê	þŷs	þisse	þŷs
Nom.	þâ			þâs		
Gen.	þârâ, þǣrâ			þissâ		
Dat.	þâm, þǣm			þissum		
Acc.	þâ			þâs		
Voc.	þâ			——		
Inst.	þâm, þǣm			þissum		

134. Relatives. — (1.) *se, seó, þæt,* who, which, that, is declined as when a demonstrative (§ 133). (2.) *þe* used in all the cases, both alone and in combination with *se, seó, þæt,* or a personal pronoun, is indeclinable. (3.) *sƿâ,* so, used like English *as* and Old German *so* in place of a relative, is indeclinable.

135. Interrogatives are *hƿâ,* who; *hƿæder,* which of two; *hƿylc, hûlîc,* of what kind. They have strong adjective endings: *hƿæder* is syncopated (§ 84.)

Sing.—	Masc.	Fem.	Neut.	
Nom.	hƿâ	——	hƿæt	
Gen.	hƿæs	——	hƿæs	
Dat.	hƿam	——	hƿam	Plural wanting.
Acc.	hƿone	——	hƿæt	
Voc.	——	——	——	
Inst.	hƿam	——	hƿŷ	

136. Indefinites.

(1.) *The Indefinite Article* Ân < *ân,* one.

Sing.—	Masc.	Fem.	Neut.	Plur.— M., F., N.
Nom. . .	ân	ân	ân	ân*e*
Gen. . . .	ân*es*	ân*re*	ân*es*	ân*râ*
Dat. . . .	ân*um*	ân*re*	ân*um*	ân*um*
Acc. . . .	ân*ne*, ǣn*ne*	ân*e*	ân	ân*e*
Voc. . . .	ân	ân	ân	ân*e*
Inst. . . .	ân*ê*	ân*re*	ân*ê*	ân*um*

138. NUMERALS.

Cardinals.	Ormulum.	Ordinals.	Symbols.
1. ân	ân	forma (fruma, æresta) / fyrsta, § 129	I.
2. tpegen, tpâ, tu <tpa	twâ	ôđer	II.
3. þrî, þreô	þreo, þrê	þridda	III.
4. feôper	fowwerr	feôperđa (feôrđa)	IV.
5. fîf	fîf	fîfta	V.
6. six	sexe	sixta	VI.
7. seofon (syfone)	se(o)fenn, (-ffne)	seofođa (-eđa)	VII.
8. eahta	ehhte	eahtođa (-eđa)	VIII.
9. nigon (-en)	niȝhenn	nigođa (-eđa)	IX.
10. tŷn, tên	têne, (tenn)	teôđa	X.
11. endleofan (ellefne)		endleofta (eo>u, y, e)	XI.
12. tpelf	twellf	tpelfta	XII.
13. þreôtŷne	þrittêne	þreôteôđa	XIII.
14. feôpertŷne		feôperteôđa	XIV.
15. fîftŷne		fîfteôđa	XV.
16. sixtŷne	sextêne	sixteôđa	XVI.
17. seofontŷne		seofonteôđa	XVII.
18. eahtatŷne		eahtateôđa	XVIII.
19. nigontŷne		nigonteôđa	XIX.
20. tpêntig	twenntiȝ	tpêntigôđa	XX.
21. ân and tpêntig		ân and tpêntigôđa / tpêntigôđa and forma	XXI.
30. þrîtig, þrittig	þrittiȝ	þrîtigôđa	XXX.
40. feôpertig	fowwerrtiȝ	feôpertigôđa	XL.
50. fîftig	fifftiȝ	fîftigôđa	L.
60. sixtig	sextiȝ	sixtigôđa	LX.
70. hundseofontig	seofenntiȝ	hundseofontigôđa	LXX.
80. hundeahtatig		hundeahtatigôđa	LXXX.
90. hundnigontig		hundnigontigôđa	XC.
100. hundteôntig / hund	hunndredd	hundteôntigôđa	C.
101. hund and ân		ân and hundteôntigôđa / hundteôntigôđa and forma	CI.

	Cardinals.	ORMULUM.	Ordinals.	Symbols.
110.	hundendleofantig		hundendleofantigôđa	CX.
120.	hundtpelftig		hundtpelftigôđa	CXX.
130.	hund and þrittig		hund and þrîtigôđa	CXXX.
200.	tpa hund		tpa hundteôntigôđa	CC.
1000.	þûsend	þûsennde	(*not found.*)	M.

(*a.*) The order of combined numbers is indicated by the examples. The substantive defined is oftenest placed next the largest of the numbers.

(*b.*) Combined numbers are sometimes connected by *eâc* (added to) or *and* governing a dative: *þridda eâc tpêntigum* = 23d; sometimes by the next greater ten and *pana, læs*, or *bûtan: ânes pana þrittig*, thirty less one; *tpâ læs XXX*, two less than thirty; *XX bûtan ân*, § 393.

(*c.*) For *hund-* from 70 to 120, see § 139, *e;* indefinites, § 136, 2.

(*d.*) The unaccented syllables often suffer precession, sometimes syncope, often cacography.

DECLENSION.

141. CARDINALS.—1, *ân*, is declined, § 136.

N., A., V.	2, tpegen tpâ tu<tpa	3, þrî (-ŷ, -ie)	þreô þreô (-iâ, -iô)
Gen.	tpegrâ, tpegâ		þreôrâ
D., Inst. .	tpâm>tpǣm		þrîm (-ŷm)

Like *tpegen* decline *begen, bâ, bu*, both.

4–19.—Cardinals from *feóper* to *tpelf*, and from *þreó-tŷne* to *nigon-tŷne*, are used as indeclinable, but are also declined like *i*-stem nouns of the First Declension (*byre*, § 84), oftenest when used as substantives: nom. acc. voc. *feópere*, gen. *feóperâ*, dat. inst. *feóperum*. Such forms of *eahta* are not found. *Tŷne*<*teón*, umlaut, § 32, 2.

(*a.*) Those in *-tŷne* have also sometimes a neut. nom. and acc. in *-u*>*-o*, or *-a: fiftŷn-u, -o, -a* (fifteen); *þreóteno* (=thirteen). (*ŷ*>*î*>*e.*)

(*b.*) They are quasi-adjectives like *Dene*, § 86.

20–120.—Forms in *-tig* are declined as singular neuter nouns: *þrîtig* (thirty), gen. *þrîtiges;* or, as adjectives, have plural gen. *-râ*, dat. *-um: þrîtigrâ, þrîtigum.*

100–1000.—*Hund*, n., is declined like *pord*, § 73; *hundred* and *þûsend*, like *scip*, § 70; pl. *þûsend-u, -o, -e, -a* (Psa. lxvii, 17), § 393.

142. Ordinals have always the regular weak forms of the adjective, except *ôđer* (second), always strong. Indefinites, § 136, 2.

143. Multiplicatives are found in *-feald* (fold): *ânfeald*, simple: *tpî-feald*, two-fold; *þûsend-mǣlum*, thousandfoldly.

144. Distributives may be expressed by repeating cardinals, or by a dative: *seofon and seofon*, seven by seven; *bi tpâm*, by twos.

145. In answer to *how often*, numeral adverbs are used, or an ordinal or cardinal with *sîđ* (time): *ǣne*, once; *tpîpa* (*tpîga*), twice; *þrîpa* (*þrîga*), thrice; *þriddan siđe*, the third time; *feôþer sîđum*, four times.

146. For adverbs of division the cardinals are used, or ordinals with *dǣl*: *on þreô*, in three (parts); *seofeđan dǣl*, seventh part.

147. An ordinal before *healf* (half) numbers the whole of which the half is counted: *hê pæs þâ tpâ geâr and þridde healf*, he was there two years and (the) third (year) half=2½ years. The whole numbers are usually understood: *hê rîcsôde nigonteôđe healf geâr*, he reigned half the nineteenth year=18½ years. A similar idiom is used in German and Scandinavian.

148. *Sum*, agreeing with a numeral, is indefinite, as in English: *sume tên geâr*, some ten years, more or less; limited by the genitive of a cardinal it is a partitive of eminence: *eôde eahta sum*, he went one of eight=with seven attendants or companions.

VERB.

149. The notion signified by a verb root may be predicated of a subject or uttered as an interjection of command, or (2) it may be spoken of as a substantive fact or as descriptive of some person or thing. In the first case proper verb stems are formed, or auxiliaries used, to denote time, mode, and voice; and suffixes (personal endings) are used to indicate the person and number of the subject: thus is made up the verb proper or finite verb. In the second case a noun stem is formed, and declined in cases as a substantive or adjective.

150. Two Voices.—The *active* represents the subject as acting, the *passive* as affected by the action. The *active* has inflection endings for many forms, the *passive* only for a participle. Other passive forms help this participle with the auxiliary verbs *eom* (am), *beôn*, *pesan*, *peorđan*.

(*n.*) The *middle* voice represents the subject as affected by its own action. It is expressed in Anglo-Saxon by adding pronouns, and needs no paradigms.

151. Six Modes.—The *indicative* states or asks about a fact, the *subjunctive* a possibility; the *imperative* commands or in-

treats; the *infinitives* (and gerunds) are substantives, the *participles* adjectives. Certain forms of possibility are expressed by auxiliary modal verbs with the infinitive. They need separate discussion, and are conveniently called a *potential* mode.

152. Five Tenses.—*Present, imper'fect, future, perfect, pluper'fect.* The present and imper'fect have tense stems; the future is expressed by the present, or by aid of *sceal* (shall) or *pille* (will); the perfect by aid of the present of *habban* (have) or, with some intransitives, *beôn* (be), *pesan* or *peorðan* (be); the pluper'fect by aid of the imper'fect of *habban, beôn, pesan,* or *peorðan.*

157. Conjugation.—Verbs are classified for conjugation by the stems of the imperfect tense.

Strong Verbs express tense by varying the root vowel; *weak verbs,* by composition. Strong verbs in the imperfect indicative singular first person have the root vowel *unchanged,* or changed by accent (*progression*), or *contraction* with old reduplication.

No change.	*Progression.*	*Contraction.*	*Composition.*
Conjugation I.	II., III., IV.	V.	VI.
a > (æ, ea)	**â, eâ, ô**	**eô > ê**	**+ de > te**

158. Further subdivision gives the following classes. The Roman numerals give Grimm's numbers. We arrange in alphabetical order of the stem vowels of the imperfect. For the vowels in ( ), see §§ 32, 33, 41.

Strong.

Class.	Root Vowel.	Present.	Imperfect Sing.	Plur.	Passive Participle.
1, X., XI.	a	i (>e, eo)	a (>æ, ea)	â (>æ̂, ê)	e, u>o
2, XII.	a	i (>e, eo)	a (>æ, ea)	u	u>o
3, VIII.	i	î	â	i	i
4, IX.	u	eô, û	eâ	u	o
5, VII.	â	a (>ėa)	ô	ô	a
6, I.-VI.	a>ea, â, eâ, æ̂, ê, ô		eô>ê	eô>ê	a>ea, â, eâ, æ̂, ê, ô

Weak (§§ 160, 165, *d*).

Class.		Present.	Imperfect Sing.	Plur.	Passive Participle.
7,	affix -ia>-ie>-e>—		+ede>de>te		+ed>d>t
8,	affix -ô>-â; -ia>-ige, -ie		+ôde		+ôd

The present has the same radical vowel throughout all the modes, except in the *indic. sing. 2d* and *3d persons* of Conj. 1, 3, 4, 5. These, especially if syncopated, retain *i, y* in Conj. 1; and have by i-umlaut *ŷ* in Conj. 3, *e* in Conj. 4, *y, æ̂, ŷ,* or *ê* in Conj. 5.

The imperfect has one radical vowel throughout, except in the indic. sing. 1st and 3d persons of Conj. 1, 2, 3.

The passive participle retains the root vowel, or, in Conj. 1, 3, has it assimilated, *a* changing to *e, u,* or *o,* and *u* to *o.*

	INDICATIVE PRESENT. 1st. 2d. 3d.	IMPERFECT. SING. PLUR.	PART. PAST.	
I.	*ete, it(e)st, it(eđ)*;	*æt, ǣton;*	*eten,*	eat.
	sitte, sit(e)st, sit;	*sæt, sǣton;*	*ge-seten,*	sit.
	nime, nim(e)st, nim(e)đ;	*nam, nâmon;*	*numen,*	take.
	stele, stilst, stilđ;	*stæl, stǣlon;*	*stolen,*	steal.
	spimme, spimst, spimđ;	*spam, spummon;*	*spummen,*	swim.
	peorđe, pyrst, pyrđ(eđ);	*peard, purdon;*	*porden,*	become.
II.	*rîse, rîsest (rîst), rîseđ (rîst)*;	*râs, rison;*	*risen,*	rise.
	stîge, stîhst, stîhđ;	*stâh, stigon;*	*stigen,*	ascend.
III.	*sûpe, sýpst, sýpþ;*	*seâp, supon;*	*sopen,*	sup.
	leôfe, lýfst, lýfđ;	*leâf, lufon;*	*lofen,*	love.
	ceôse, ceôsest (cýst), ceôseđ (cýst);	*ceâs, curon;*	*coren,*	choose.
IV.	*gale, gæl(e)st, gæl(e)đ;*	*gôl, gôlon;*	*galen,*	sing.
	stande, standest, standeđ (stent);	*stôd, stôdon;*	*standen,*	stand.
	sperie, sperest, speređ;	*spôr, spôron;*	*sporen,*	swear.
	hebbe (<hafie), hef(e)st, hêf(e)đ;	*hôf, hôfon;*	*hafen,*	heave.
V.	*fealle, feal(le)st (fylst), feal(le)đ (fylđ, felđ)*;	*feôl, feôllon;*	*feallen,*	fall.
	sâpe, sâpest (sǣpst), sâpeđ (sǣpđ);	*seôp, seôpon;*	*sâpen,*	sow.
	beâte, beâtest (býtst), beâteđ (být);	*beôt, beôton;*	*beâten,*	beat.
	grǣte, grǣt(e)st, grǣt(eđ);	*grêt, grêton;*	*grǣten,*	greet.
	pêpe, pêp(e)st, pêp(e)đ;	*peôp, peôpon;*	*pêpen,*	weep.
	rôpe, rôpest (rêpst), rôpeđ (rêpđ);	*reôp, reôpon;*	*rôpen,*	row.
VI.	*nerie, nerest, neređ;*	*ner(e)de, ner(e)don;*	*nered,*	save.
	lufige, lufâst, lufâđ;	*lufô-de, -don;*	*ge-lufôd,*	love.
	telle, telest, teleđ;	*teal-de, -don;*	*teald,*	tell.
	sêce, sêcest, sêceđ;	*sôh-te, -ton;*	*sôht,*	seek.

164. First Conjugation.

Active Voice.

niman, to take.

Pres. Infinitive.	Imperfect Sing.,	Plur.	Passive Participle.
niman;	nam,	nâmon;	numen.

Indicative Mode.

Present (and Future) Tense.

Singular.	Plural.
ic nim*e*, *I take.*	pê nim*ađ*, *we take.*
þû nim*est*, *thou takest.*	gê nim*ađ*, *ye take.*
hê nim*eđ*, *he taketh.*	hî nim*ađ*, *they take.*

Plur. *-ađ*, and other plurals, change to *-e* before a subject pronoun.

Imperfect.

SINGULAR.	PLURAL.
ic nam, *I took.*	pê nâm*on*, *we took.*
þû nâm*e*, *thou tookest.*	gê nâm*on*, *ye took.*
hê nam, *he took.*	hî nâm*on*, *they took.*

Future.

I shall or *will take.*

ic sceal (pill*e*) nim*an*.	pê scul*on* (pill*að*) nim*an*.
þû sceal*t* (pil*t*) nim*an*.	gê scul*on* (pill*að*) nim*an*.
hê sceal (pill*e*) nim*an*.	hî scul*on* (pill*að*) nim*an*.

Perfect.

TRANSITIVE FORM.	INTRANSITIVE FORM.
SING. *I have taken.*	*I have (am) come.*
ic hæbbe num*en*.	ic eo*m* cum*en*.
þû hæf*st* (haf*ast*) num*en*.	þû ear*t* cum*en*.
hê hæf*ð* (haf*að*) num*en*.	hê is cum*en*.
PLUR.	
pê habb*að* num*en*.	pê *sind* (sindon) cum*ene*.
gê habb*að* num*en*.	gê *sind* (sindon) cum*ene*.
hî habb*að* num*en*.	hî *sind* (sindon) cum*ene*.

Pluper'fect.

SING. *I had taken.*	*I had (was) come.*
ic hæf*de* num*en*.	ic pæs cum*en*.
þû hæf*dest* num*en*.	þû pǣre cum*en*.
hê hæf*de* num*en*.	hê pæs cum*en*.
PLUR.	
pê hæf*don* num*en*.	pê pǣr*on* cum*ene*.
gê hæf*don* num*en*.	gê pǣr*on* cum*ene*.
hî hæf*don* num*en*.	hî pǣr*on* cum*ene*.

OTHER FORMS: *nam, nom; nâmon, -an* (*â* > *ô*); *sceal, scel; scul-on, -un, -an; sceol-on, -un, -an; pille, pile, pilt* (*i* > *y*); *hæbbe, hebbe, habbe, haf-a, -u, -o; hafest; hæfeð; hæbbað; eom, eam; is, ys; sind, sint, sindan* (*i* > *y, ie, eo*), *ear-on, -un.* For *eom* may be used *peorðe* or *beôm;* for *pæs, pearð* (§ 178). Imp. plur. *-an, -um, -un, -en, -e,* occur.

169. Subjunctive Mode.

Present Tense.

Singular.	Plural
ic nime, (*if*) *I take.*	ƿê nim*en*, (*if*) *we take.*
þû nime, (*if*) *thou take.*	gê nim*en*, (*if*) *ye take.*
hê nime, (*if*) *he take.*	hî nim*en*, (*if*) *they take.*

Imperfect.

ic nâme, (*if*) *I took.*	ƿê nâm*en*, (*if*) *we took.*
þû nâme, (*if*) *thou took.*	gê nâm*en*, (*if*) *ye took.*
hê nâme, (*if*) *he took.*	hî nâm*en*, (*if*) *they took.*

Future.

(*If*) *I shall* (*will*) *take.*

ic scyl*e* (pill*e*) nim*an*.	ƿê scyl*en* (pill*en*) nim*an*.
þû scyl*e* (pill*e*) nim*an*.	gê scyl*en* (pill*en*) nim*an*.
hê scyl*e* (pill*e*) nim*an*.	hî scyl*en* (pill*en*) nim*an*.

Perfect

Transitive Form.	Intransitive Form.
Sing. (*If*) *I have taken.*	(*If*) *I have* (*be*) *come.*
ic hæbb*e* num*en*.	ic *sî* cum*en*.
þû hæbb*e* num*en*.	þû *sî* cum*en*.
hê hæbb*e* num*en*.	hê *sî* cum*en*.
Plur.	
ƿê hæbb*en* num*en*.	ƿê *sîn* cum*ene*.
gê hæbb*en* num*en*.	gê *sîn* cum*ene*.
hî hæbb*en* num*en*.	hî *sîn* cum*ene*.

Pluperfect.

Sing. (*If*) *I had taken.*	(*If*) *I had* (*were*) *come.*
ic hæf*de* num*en*.	ic *ƿæ̂re* cum*en*.
þû hæf*de* num*en*.	þû *ƿæ̂re* cum*en*.
hê hæf*de* num*en*.	hê *ƿæ̂re* cum*en*.
Plur.	
ƿê hæf*den* num*en*.	ƿê *ƿæ̂ren* cum*ene*.
gê hæf*den* num*en*.	gê *ƿæ̂ren* cum*ene*.
hî hæf*den* num*en*.	hî *ƿæ̂ren* cum*ene*.

Other Forms: *scyle, scyl-en, -on, -an, -e* (*y*>*i, u, eo*); *hæbben, habban, habbon*; *sî, sîn* (*î*>*ŷ, îe, eô, ig*); *ƿæ̂r-en, -an, -on* (*æ̂*>*ê*). For *sî* may be *beô, ƿese, ƿeorðe*; for *ƿæ̂re, ƿurde*. Plur. *-ân, -an, -on, -e*, occur.

172. Imperative Mode.

Sing.	Plur.
2. nim, *take.*	nim*ad*, *take.*

173. Infinitive.	Gerund.
nim*an*, *to take.*	tô nim*anne*, *to take.*
Present Participle.	**Past Participle.**
nim*endè*, *taking.*	num*en*, *taken.*

174. Imperative Stem *nama*.

	Sanskrit.	Greek.		Gothic.	O. Saxon.	O. Norse.	O. H. G.
Sing. —	náma	*νέμε,*	*Latin* eme	nim	nim	nem	nim
Plur. —	náma-ta	*νέμε-τε,*	*Latin* emi-te	nimi-*þ*	nima-*d*	nemi-*đ*	nema-*t*

Plural **-tata** > *ta* > *t* (§ 38) > *đ* (shifting, § 41, *a*). O. F. = A. Sax.

175. Noun Forms.

1. Infinitive *nam + ana;* 2. Gerund. *nam + ana + ja.*

1. *Dative* ...	nám-anâj-a (§ 79, *a*)	*νέμ-ειν<-εναι* (§ 70, *a*)	nim-*an*	nim-*an*	nem-*a*	nem-*an*
2. (§ 120),	nám-anîja, *Latin* em-endo, *O. Saxon* nim-annia > -anna.					nem-*enne*
3. *Pr. Part.*	náma-nt	*νέμο-ντ-ος* *Lat.* eme-nt-is	nima-*nd*(*a*)-*s*	nima-*nd*	nema-*nd-i*	nema-*nt-i*
4. *P. Part.* (*Strong.*)	bhug-ná (*bent*)	*τέκ-νο-ν* (*born*) do-nu-m (*gift*)	numa-*n-s*	numa-*n*	numi-*nn*	ga-nom-*an-êr*
5. *P. Part.* (*Weak.*)	na(m)-tá	*νεμ-η-τό-ς* em(p)-tu-s	nasi-*þ*(*a*)*s*	(gi-)neri-*d*	tal-d-*r*	ga-neri-*t*

(*a.*) The dative case ending is gone in Teutonic infinitives. § 38.

(*b.*) Gerund *-enne>-ende* (§ 445, 2, *nn>nd*, § 27, 5), so in O. N.; M. H. Ger.; Friesic, O. Sax., and O. H. Ger. have a genitive *nim-annias*, *-an-nas* (*-es*); *nem-ennes;* and M. H. German has gen. *nem-endes.*

(*c.*) To these stems of the participles are added suffixes contained in the case endings. §§ 104–106.

(*d.*) The Greek verbals in *-τός* are not counted participles (Hadley, 261, *c*). Only weak verbs have *-đa*, *-da*, in Teutonic. Few verbs have the participle in *-na* in Sanskrit; only relics are found in Greek and Latin, but all the strong verbs use it in Teutonic.

(*e.*) Weak stems in *-ia* and *-ô* have *i*, *e*, *ig* or *ige*, before *-an*, *-anne*, *-end.* § 165, *d.*

176. Periphrastic Conditional Forms.

Potential Mode.

Modal verbs	*magan*,	*cunnan*,	*môtan*,	*durran*,	*pillan*,	*sculan*,	*pîtan>utan*,
	may,	can,	must,	dare,	will,	shall,	let us.

Present Tense.

	Indicative Forms.		Subjunctive Forms.	
SING.	*mæg, can, môt, dear*	niman.	*mǽge, cunne, môte, durre*	niman.
	meaht, canst, môst, dearst		*mǽge, cunne, môte, durre*	
	mæg, can, môt, dear		*mǽge, cunne, môte, durre*	
PLUR.	*mâgon, cunnon, môton, durron*		*mǽgen, cunnen, môten, durren, utan*	

Imperfect Tense, Indicative Forms.

SING.
meahte, cúđe, móste, dorste, polde, sc(e)olde
meahtest, cúđest, móstest, dorstest, poldest, sc(e)oldest
meahte, cúđe, móste, dorste, polde, sc(e)olde
PLUR.
meahton, cúđon, móston, dorston, poldon, sc(e)oldon
} *niman.*

Imperfect Tense, Subjunctive Forms.

SING. *meahte, cúđe, môste, dorste, polde, sc(e)olde*
PLUR. *meahten, cúđen, môsten, dorsten, polden, sc(e)olden* } *niman.*

GERUNDIAL FORM.

I am to take = I must *or* ought to take *or* be taken.

SING.		PLUR.	
ic eom	*tô nimanne.*	*pê sind*	*tô nimanne.*
þû eart		*gê sind*	
hê is		*hî sind*	

177. OTHER PERIPHRASTIC FORMS.

1. *eom* (am) + present participle.

Present .... *eom, eart, is; sind nimende.*
Imperfect............. *pæs, pǽre, pæs; pǽron nimende.*
Future .... *beóm, bist, biđ; beóđ nimende.*
sceal pesan nímende.
Infinitive Future... *beôn nimende.*

2. *dôn* (do) + infinitive, § 406, *a.*

OTHER FORMS: *meaht, meahte,* etc. (*ea*>*i*); *mâg-on, -um, -un, -an* (*â*>*ǽ*); *meahtes; meaht-on, -um, -an, -en, -e* (§§ 166, 170); *can, con; const; cunn-on, -un, -an; cuđes; cuđ-on, -an, -en; môt-on, -um, -un, -an, -en; môt-en, -an, -e; môst-es; môst-um, -on, -an; durre* (*u*>*y*); *durr-on, -an; dorst-on, -en; poldes; pold-on, -um, -un, -an, -e; sc(e)oldes; sc(e)old-on, -un, -an, -en, -e.* Forms of *eom, peorđe,* and *beóm* interchange (§ 178).

178. Passive Voice.

Indicative Mode.

Present and Perfect, *I am taken* or *have been taken.*

Singular.	Plural.
ic eo*m** (peorđ*e*) numen.	pê *sind*(*on*) (peorđ*ađ*) num*ene*.
þû ear*t* (peorđ*est*) num*en*.	gê *sind*(*on*) (peorđ*ađ*) num*ene*.
hê is (peorđ*eđ*) num*en*.	hî *sind*(*on*) (peorđ*ađ*) num*ene*.

Past and Pluperfect, *I was taken* or *had been taken.*

ic pǣs (pearđ) num*en*.	pê pǣr*on* (purd*on*) num*ene*.
þû pǣr*e* (purd*e*) num*en*.	gê pǣr*on* (purd*on*) num*ene*.
hê pǣs (pearđ) num*en*.	hî pǣr*on* (purd*on*) num*ene*.

Future.

1. *I shall be taken.*

ic beô(*m*)* num*en*.	pê beô*đ* num*ene*.
þû bi*st* num*en*.	gê beô*đ* num*ene*.
hê bi*đ* num*en*.	hî beô*đ* num*ene*.

2. *I shall* or *will be taken.*

ic sceal (pill*e*) beô*n* num*en*.	pê scul*on* (pill*ađ*) beô*n* num*ene*.
þû sceal*t* (pil*t*) beô*n* num*en*.	gê scul*on* (pill*ađ*) beô*n* num*ene*.
hê sceal (pill*e*) beô*n* num*en*.	hî scul*on* (pill*ađ*) beô*n* num*ene*.

Perfect, *I have been taken.*

ic eom geporden numen.	*pê sind(on) gepordene numene.*
þû eart geporden numen.	*gê sind(on) gepordene numene.*
hê is geporden numen.	*hî sind(on) gepordene numene.*

Pluperfect, *I had been taken.*

ic pæs geporden numen.	*pê pǣron gepordene numene.*
þû pǣre geporden numen.	*gê pǣron gepordene numene.*
hê pæs geporden numen.	*hî pǣron gepordene numene.*

179. Subjunctive Mode.

Present.

(If) I be taken.

Sing.	Plur.
ic (þû, hê) beô num*en*.	pê (gê, hî) beô*n* num*ene*.

* The forms of *peorde*, *eom*, and *beôm* interchange.

Past.

(If) I were taken.

SING.	PLUR.
ic (þû, hê) pǽre num*en*.	pê (gê, hî) pǽr*en* num*ene*.

180. IMPERATIVE MODE.

SING. *Be thou taken.*	PLUR. *Be ye taken.*
pes þû num*en*.	pes*að* gê num*ene*.

181. INFINITIVE.	PARTICIPLE.
beô*n* num*en*, *to be taken.*	num*en*, *taken.*

---

182. PERIPHRASTIC CONDITIONAL (§ 176).

POTENTIAL MODE.

Present Tense.

SING. Indicative Forms.		Subjunctive Forms.	
mæg (&c.)	*beón numen*(*e*).	*mǽge* (&c.)	*beón numen*(*e*).
meaht (&c.)		*mǽge* (&c.)	
mæg (&c.)		*mǽge* (&c.)	
PLUR.			
mâgon (&c.)		*mǽgen* (&c.)	

Imperfect.

SING.			
meahte (&c.)	*beón numen*(*e*).	*meahte* (&c.)	*beón numen*(*e*).
meahtest (&c.)		*meahte* (&c.)	
meahte (&c.)		*meahte* (&c.)	
PLUR.			
meahton (&c.)		*meahten* (&c.)	

For *beón* (infinitive) is found *pesan* or *peorðan*. The forms interchange of *beô*, *sî*, *pese*, *peorðe;* of *pǽre*, *purde;* of *pes*, *beô*, *peorð*. *Bist*, *bið* (*i*>*y*); *beô*, *beôð* (*eô*<*iô*). Ælfric's grammar has indic. pres. *eom*, imperf. *pæs*, fut. *beô*, perf. *pæs fulfremedlîce* (completely), pluperf. *pæs gefyrn* (formerly); subjunctive for a wish, pres. *beô gyt* (yet), imperf. *pǽre*, pluperf. *pǽre fulfremedlîce;* for a condition, pres. *eom nu* (now), imperf. *pæs*, fut. *beô gyt* (yet); imperative *sî;* infinitive *beón*.

183. WEAK VERBS.—(Conjugation VI.)

Active Voice.

Pres. Infinitive.	Imperf. Indicative.	Passive Participle.
ner*ian*, *save;*	ner*ede;*	ner*ed.*
hŷr*an*, *hear;*	hŷr*de;*	hŷr*ed.*
luf*ian*, *love;*	luf*ôde;*	(*ge-*)luf*ôd.*

Indicative Mode.

Present (and Future) Tense (§ 165, *d*).

I save, hear, love.

Singular.	Plural.
ic ner*ie*, hŷr*e*, luf*ige.*	ƿê ner*iað*, hŷr*að*, luf*iað.*
þû ner*est*, hŷr*est*, luf*âst.*	gê ner*iað*, hŷr*að*, luf*iað.*
hê ner*eð*, hŷr*eð*, luf*âð.*	hî ner*iað*, hŷr*að*, luf*iað.*

Imperfect (§§ 160, 166, 168).

I saved, heard, loved.

ic ner*ede*, hŷr*de*, luf*ôde.*	ƿê ner*edon*, hŷr*don*, luf*ôdon.*
þû ner*edest*, hŷr*dest*, luf*ôdest.*	gê ner*edon*, hŷr*don*, luf*ôdon.*
hê ner*ede*, hŷr*de*, luf*ôde.*	hî ner*edon*, hŷr*don*, luf*ôdon.*

Future (§ 167).

I shall (will) save, hear, love.

ic sceal (ƿill*e*)	ner*ian*, hŷr*an*, luf*ian.*	ƿê scul*on* (ƿill*að*)	ner*ian*,
þû sceal*t* (ƿil*t*)		gê scul*on* (ƿill*að*)	hŷr*an*,
hê sceal (ƿill*e*)		hî scul*on* (ƿill*að*)	luf*ian.*

Perfect (§ 168).

Transitive.		Intransitive.	
I have saved, heard, loved.		*I have (am) returned.*	
Sing.			
ic hæbb*e*	ner*ed*, hŷr*ed*, luf*ôd.*	ic eo*m*	gecyrr*ed.*
þû hæf*st*, haf*âst*		þû ear*t*	
hê hæf*ð*, haf*âð*		hê is	
Plur.			
ƿê habb*að*	ner*ed*, hŷr*ed*, luf*ôd.*	ƿê s*ind* (sindon)	gecyrr*ede.*
gê habb*að*		gê s*ind* (sindon)	
hî habb*að*		hî s*ind* (sindon)	

Ia, iga, igea, ga interchange, and *ie, ige, ge: ô* to *â, a, u, e.* For variations of auxiliaries and endings, see corresponding tenses of strong verbs.

Pluper′fect (§ 168).

TRANSITIVE.		INTRANSITIVE.	
I had saved, heard, loved.		*I had (was) returned.*	
SING.			
ic hæf*de* þû hæf*dest* hê hæf*de*	nere*d*, hŷre*d*, lufô*d*.	ic ƿæs þû ƿǽre hê ƿæs	gecyrre*d*.
PLUR.			
ƿê hæf*don* gê hæf*don* hî hæf*don*	nere*d*, hŷre*d*, lufô*d*.	ƿê ƿǽr*on* gê ƿǽr*on* hî ƿǽr*on*	gecyrre*de*.

184. SUBJUNCTIVE MODE.

Present (§ 170).

(If) I save, hear, love.

SINGULAR.		PLURAL.	
ic þû hê	ner*ie*, hŷre, luf*ige*.	ƿê gê hî	ner*ien*, hŷr*en*, luf*igen*.

Imperfect (§ 171).

(If) I saved, heard, loved.

ic þû hê	nere*de*, hŷr*de*, lufô*de*.	ƿê gê hî	nere*den*, hŷr*den*, lufô*den*.

Future (§ 167).

(If) I shall (will) save, hear, love.

ic scyl*e* (ƿill*e*) þû scyl*e* (ƿill*e*) hê scyl*e* (ƿill*e*)	ner*ian*, hŷr*an*, luf*ian*.	ƿê scyl*en* (ƿill*en*) gê scyl*en* (ƿill*en*) hî scyl*en* (ƿill*en*)	ner*ian*, hŷr*an*, luf*ian*.

Perfect (§ 168).

TRANSITIVE.		INTRANSITIVE.	
(If I) have saved, &c.		*(If I) have (be) returned.*	
SING. hæbbe PLUR. hæbb*en*	nere*d*, hŷre*d*, lufô*d*.	s*î* s*în*	gecyrre*d*(*e*).

Pluper′fect (§ 168).

(If I) had saved, &c.		*(If I) had (were) returned.*	
SING. hæfde PLUR. hæfd*en*	nere*d*, hŷre*d*, lufô*d*.	ƿǽre ƿǽr*en*	gecyrre*d*(*e*).

185. Imperative Mode (§ 174).

Save, hear, love.

Sing.	Plur.
2. ner*e*, hŷr, luf*a*.	ner*iaď*, hŷr*aď*, luf*iaď*.

186. Infinitive Mode (§ 175).

To save, hear, love.

Present. ner*ian*>ner*igan*, ner*igean*, ner*gan*; hŷr*an*; luf*ian*> luf*igan*, luf*igean*.

Gerund. tô ner*ianne*, hŷr*anne*, luf*ianne*.

Participles.

Saving, hearing, loving.

Present.	ner*iende*,	hŷr*ende*,	luf*igende*.
	saved.	*heard.*	*loved.*
Past....	ner*ed*,	hŷr*ed*,	(*ge-*)luf*ôd*.

187. The special periphrastic forms and the whole passive voice of weak verbs are conjugated with the same auxiliaries as those of strong verbs (§§ 176–182).

---

188. PRESENTS (*Weak*).

(*a.*) Like *nerian* inflect stems in *-ia* from short roots: *derian*, hurt; *helian*, cover; *hegian*, hedge; *scerian*, apportion; *spyrian*, speer; *sylian*, soil; *þunian*, thunder, etc.

(*b.*) But many stems in *-ia* from short roots have compensative gemination of their last consonant where it preceded *i*—(throughout the present, except in the indicative singular second and third, and the imperative singular); *ci* > *cc*, *di* > *dd*, *fi* > *bb*, *gi* > *cg*, *li* > *ll*, etc.; indicative *lecge* (< *legic*), lay, *legest*, *legeď*; *lecgaď* (< *legiaď*); subjunctive *lecge*, *lecgen*; imperative *lege*, *lecgaď*; infinitive *lecgan*; part. pres. *lecgende*; part. past *leged*. So *reccan*, reach; *hreddan*, rescue; *habban*, have; *sellan*, give; *tellan*, tell; *fremman*, frame; *clynnan*, clang; *dippan*, dip; *cnyssan*, knock; *settan*, set, etc.

(*c.*) Like *hŷran* inflect stems in *-ia* > *-e* > — from long roots: *dǣlan*, deal; *dēman*, deem; *belǣpan*, leave; *mǣnan*, mean; *sprengan*, spring; *styrman*, storm; *cennan*, bring forth; *cyssan*, kiss, etc. Infinitives in *-ean* occur: *sēc-ean*, § 175, *e*.

(*d.*) Like *lufian* inflect stems showing *-ó* in the imperfect: *árian*, honor; *beorhtian*, shine; *cleopian*, call; *hopian*, hope. Past participles have *ó*, *ă*, *e*; *gegearp-ód*, *-ăd*, *-ed*, prepared.

189. SYNCOPATED IMPERFECTS (*Weak*).

(*a.*) Stem *-e* < *-ia* is syncopated after long roots: *cíg-an*, call, *cíg-de*; *dǽl-on*, deal, *dǽl-de*; *dēm-an*, deem, *dēm-de*; *drēf-an*, trouble, *drēf-de*; *fēd-an*, feed; *hēd-an*, heed; *hýr-an*, hear; *lǽd-an*, lead; *be-lǽp-an*, leave; *mǽn-an*, mean; *nýd-an*, urge; *rēd-an*, read; *spēd-an*, speed; *spreng-an*, spring, *spreng-de*; *bærn-an*, burn, *bærn-de*; *styrm-an*, storm; so *sep-de* and *sep-te*, showed.

(*b.*) Assimilation.—After a surd, *-d* becomes surd (*-t*). (Surds *p*, *t*, *c* (*x*), *ss*, *h*, not *f* or *s* alone, §§ 17, 30): *rǽp-an*, bind, *rǽp-te*; *bēt-an*, better, *bēt-te*; *grēt-an*, greet, *grēt-te*; *mēt-an*, meet, *mēt-te*; *drenc-an*, drench, *drenc-te*; *lýx-an*, shine, *lýx-te*; but *lýs-an*, release, *lýs-de*; *fýs-an*, haste, *fýs-de*; *rǽs-an*, rush, *rǽs-de*.

(*c.*) Dissimilation.—The mute *c* becomes continuous (*h*) before *-t*: *tǽc-an*, teach, *tǽh-te*; *ēc-an*, eke, *ēh-te* and *ēc-te*, 36, 3.

(*d.*) Umlaut lost.—Themes in *ecg*; *ecc*, *ell*; *enc*, *eng*; *ēc*; *ycg*, *ync*, i-umlaut for *acg*; *acc*, *all*; *anc*, *ang*; *óc*; *ucg*, *unc*, may retain *a* (> *æ*; *ea*; *o*); *ó*; *u* > *o* in syncopated imperfects (§§ 209–211): *lecgan*, lay, *lægde*; *reccan*, rule, *reahte*; *cpellan*, kill, *cpealde*; *þencan*, think, *þohte*; *brengan*, bring, *brohte*; *rēcan*, reck, *róhte*; *bycgan*, buy, *bohte*; *þyncan*, seem, *þohte*.

(*e.*) Gemination is simplified, and *mn*>*m* (Rule 13, page 10): *cenn-an*, beget, *cen-de*; *clypp-an*, clip, *clip-te*; *cyss-an*, kiss, *cys-te*; *dypp-an*, dip, *dyp-te*; *ēht-an*, pursue, *ēhte*; *fyll-an*, fill, *fyl-de*; *gyrd-an*, gird, *gyrde*; *hredd-an*, rescue, *hredde*; *hyrd-an*, harden, *hyrde*; *hyrt-an*, hearten, *hyrte*; *hæft-an*, bind, *hæfte*; *lecg-an*, lay, *leg-de*; *merr-an*, mar, *mer-de*; *mynt-an*, purpose, *mynte*; *nemn-an*, name, *nem-de*; *rest-an*, rest, *reste*; *riht-an*, right, *rihte*; *scild-an*, guard, *scilde*; *send-an*, send, *sende*; *spill-an*, spill, *spil-de*; *sett-an*, set, *sette*; *still-an*, spring, *stil-de*; *stylt-an*, stand astonished, *stylte*; *pemm-an*, spoil, *pem-de*.

(*f.*) Ecthlipsis occurs (*g*): *cēgan*, call, *cēgde*, *cēde*. See § 209.

190. Past Participles are syncopated like imperfects in verbs having lost umlaut, often in other verbs having a surd root (§ 189, *b*), less often in other verbs: *sellan*, give, *sealde*, *seald*; *ge-sēc-an*, seek, *ge-sóh-te*, *gesóht*; *sett-an*, set, *sette*, *seted* and *set*; *send-an*, send, *sende*, *sended* and *send*; *heán*, raise, *heád*, raised.

191. Presents.—*Illustrations of Umlaut.*

Conjugation……	(I.)	(I.)	(I.)	(III.)	(III.)
	drep*an*,	cum*an*,	beorg*an*,	scûf*an*,	creôp*an*,
	strike.	*come.*	*guard.*	*shove.*	*creep.*
Sing.— 1.	drep*e*	cum*e*	beorg*e*	scûf*e*	creôp*e*
2.	drip(*e*)*st*	cym(*e*)*st*	byrh*st*	scŷf(*e*)*st*	crŷp(*e*)*st*
	drep*est*	cum*est*	beorg*est*(*y*)	scûf*est*	creôp*est*
3.	drip(*e*)*ð*	cym(*e*)*ð*	byrh*ð*	scŷf(*e*)*ð* (*t*)	crŷp(*e*)*ð*
	drep*eð*	cum*eð*	beorg*eð*(*y*)	scûf*eð*	creôp*eð*
Plur.—	drep*að*	cum*að*	beorg*að*	scûf*að*	creôp*að*

Conjugation…	(IV.)	(IV.)	(V.)	(V.)	(V.)
	far*an*,	bac*an*,	feall*an*,	lâc*an*,	grôp*an*,
	fare.	*bake.*	*fall.*	*leap.*	*grow.*
Sing.— 1.	far*e*	bac*e*	feall*e*	lâc*e*	grôp*e*
2.	fær(*e*)*st*	bec*st*	fel*st*	lǽc*st*	grêp*st*
	far*est*	bac*est*	feall*est*	lâc*est*	grôp*est*
3.	fær(*e*)*ð*	bec*ð*	fel*ð*	lǽc(*e*)*ð*	grêp*ð*
	far*eð*	bac*eð*	feall*eð*	lâc*eð*	grôp*eð*
Plur.—	far*að*	bac*að*	feall*að*	lâc*að*	grôp*að*

192. *Illustrations of Assimilation.*

Conjugation….	(I.)	(I.)	(I.)	(I.)	(I.)
	et*an*,	tred*an*,	bind*an*,	cpeð*an*,	les*an*,
	eat.	*tread.*	*bind.*	*quoth.*	*collect.*
Sing.— 1.	et*e*	tred*e*	bind*e*	cpeð*e*	les*e*
2.	it(*e*)*st*	tri(de)*st*	bin(t)*st*	cpi*st*	li*st*
	et*est*	tred*est*	bind*est*	cpeð*est*	les*est*
3.	it*eð*, it	trit	bint	cpið	li*st*
	et*eð*	tred*eð*(*i*)	bind*eð*	cpeð*eð*	les*eð*
Plur.—	et*að*	tred*að*	bind*að*	cpeð*að*	les*að*

Conjugation……	(I.)	(III.)	(IV.) sleân<	(III.) fleôn<	(I.)
	berst*an*,	leôg*an*,	sleah*an*,	fleoh*an*,	licg*an*,
	burst.	*lie.*	*slay.*	*flee.*	*lie.*
Sing.— 1.	berst*e*	leôg*e*	sleâ	fleô	licg*e*
2.	birst	lŷh*st*	sleh*st* (*y*)	flŷh*st*	lig*st*
	berst*est*	leôg*est*	slea*gest*		licg*est*
3.	birst(*eð*)	lŷh*ð*	sleh*ð* (*y*)	flŷh*ð*	li(g)*ð*
	berst*eð*	leôg*eð*	slea*geð*		li(c)g*eð*
Plur.—	berst*að*	leog*að*	sleâ*ð*	fleô*ð*	licg*að*

	cpeđan, quoth.	*sleahan*> *sleân,* slay.	*seahan*> *seôn,* see.	*ceôsan,* choose.
SING.—	*cpæđ*	*slôh* (*g*)	*seah*	*ceâs*
	cpǣde	*slôge*	*sǣge, sâpe*	*cure*
	cpæđ	*slôh* (*g*)	*seah*	*ceâs*
PLUR.—	*cpǣdon*	*slôgon*	*sǣgon, sâpon*	*curon*
PART.—	*cpeden*	*slægen*	*sepen*	*coren.*

212. PRETERITIVE PRESENTS.—FIRST CONJUGATION.—√a.

	Indicative Sing. 1st & 3d. 2d.	Plur.	Subjunctive.	Imperat.	Infin.	Part.
Pres. .... (§§ 199, 200).	*mæg, meah-t* (*i*);	*mâgon* (*ǣ*) (*u*);	*mǣg-e, -en;*	——;	*mag-an* (*u*);	——;
Imperf.	*meah-te* (*i*), *meah-ton* (*i*);		*-te, -ten;*	am strong, (may), <have grown.		
Pres. (§ 199).	*be-neah,* ——;	*be-nugon;*	*benug-e, -en;*	——;	*benugan?;*	——;
Imperf.	*be-noh-te, -ton* (§ 211);		*-te, -ten;*	hold and use<have come to.		
Pres. (§ 201).	*an*(*o*), ——;	*unnon;*	*unne, -en;*	——;	*unn-an;*	(*ge*)*unn-en;*
Imperf.	*û-đe, -đon* (Goth. *þ* irregular), § 37;		*-đe, -đen;*	favor<have given.		
Pres. (§ 201).	*can* (*o*), *canst* (*o*);	*cunnon;*	*cunne, -en;*	——;	*cunn-an;*	——;
Imperf.	*cû-đe, -đon* (Goth. *kunþa*), § 37;		*-đe, -den;*	know<have got.		*cûđe.*
Pres. (§ 201).	*ge-man* (*o*), *-manst;*	*-munon;*	*-e, -en;*	*gemun, -ađ;*	*gemun-an;*	——;
Imperf.	*ge-munde, -don;*		*-de, -den;*	remember<have called to mind.		
Pres. (§ 203).	*sc*(*e*)*al* (*scel*), *sc*(*e*)*alt;*	*scul-on* (*eo*);	*scul-e, en* (*eo, y, i*);	——;	*sculan;*	——;
Imperf.	*sc*(*e*)*ol-de* (*io*), *-don;*		*-de, -den;*	shall<ought<have got in debt.		
Pres. (§ 204).	*d*(*e*)*ar, d*(*e*)*arst;*	*durr-on;*	*-e, -en* (*y*);	——;	*durran;*	——;
Imperf.	*dors-te, -ton* (Goth. *daursta*);		*-te, -ten;*	dare<have fought.		
Pres. (§ 204).	*þ*(*e*)*arf, þ*(*e*)*arf-t;*	*þurf-on;*	*þurf-e, -en*(*y*);	——;	*þurf-an;*	——;
Imperf.	*þorf-te, -ton;*		*-te, -ten;*	need<have worked (opus est).		

SECOND CONJUGATION (§ 205).—√ i; *îgan,* not found, *pitan,* § 205.

Pres. ...	*âh, âhst;*	*âgon;*	*âg-e, -en;*	——;	*âgan, -ne;*	*âgende;*
Imperf..	*âh-te, -ton;*		*-te, -ten;*	own<have earned or taken.		

nâh = (*ne* + *âh*), &c., not own.

Pres. ...	*pât, pâst* (*ǣ*);	*piton;*	*pit-e, -en;*	*pit-e, -ađ;*	*pitan*(*y*)*-ne;*	*piten, -de;*
Imperf..	*pis-te* (*y*), *-ton;*	*pis-se, -son,* §§ 36,3; 35, *B, pestan;*	*-te, -se, -ten, -sen;*	know<have seen.		
Pres. ...	*nât* (=*ne*+*pât*),	*nyton* (*e*);	*nyt-e, -en;*	——;	*nitan* (*y*);	*nyten, -de;*
Imperf..	*nyste, nysse;*	*nyston* (&c.);		not know.		

THIRD CONJUGATION (§ 206).—√ u; *dûgan* not found.

Pres. ...	*deâh* (*g*), ——;	*dugon;*	*dug-e, -en;*	——;	*dugan;*	*dugende;*
Imperf..	*doh-te, -ton* (§ 211);		*-te, -ten;*	is fit<has grown.		

FOURTH CONJUGATION (§ 207).—√ â; *matan* not found.

	Indicative Sing. 1st & 3d. 2d.	Plur.	Subj.	Imp.	Infin.	Part.
Pres. ...	*môt, môst;*	*môton;*	*môt-e, -en;*	——;	*môtan;*	——;
Imperf..	*môs-te, -ton* (§ 36, 3);		*-te, -ten;*	is meet<has met.		

Grimm takes *beô*, be, for a præteritive present from a *bûan*, to dwell, of the Fifth Conjugation.

From an imperfect subjunctive of the Second Conjugation (Goth. *viljau*< √ *vil*, inflected like *nemjau*, § 171) arise

Pres. ...	*pille, pilt;*	*pillađ*(*y*);	*pill-e, -en;*	*-e, -ađ;*	*pill-an;*	*-ende,*
Imperf..	*pol-de, -don* (Goth. *vilda*);		*-de, -den;*	will<have wished.		
Pres. ...	*nelle, nelt;*	*nellađ*(*y, i*);	*-e, -en;*	*-e, -ad;*	*-an;*	*-ende;*
Imperf..	*nol-de, -don,* &c.			*ne*+*pille*, will not.		

pi>*po*, assimilation (§ 35, 2, *a*); *i*>*e*, a-umlaut; *pi*>*y*, §§ 32, 23; *'ll*>*l*.

213.—II. VERBS WITHOUT CONNECTING VOWEL (Relics of Sanskrit 2d Class, § 158):

(1.) The common forms of the substantive verb are from three roots: √ *as*, √ *bhu*, √ *vas*.

(*a*.)—

	Sanskrit.	Greek.	Latin.	Gothic.	O. Saxon.	Anglo-Saxon.		O. Norse.
Stem,	as, s	εσ	es, s	is, s	is, s	is, ir, s;	ar	er
SING.—1.	ás-mi	εἰ-μί>ἐσ-μι	*s-u-m	i-m<is-m	——	eo-m	ea-m	e-m<er-m
2.	ás-(s)i	ἐσ-σί, εἶ	es-	is-	——	——	ear-t	er-t
3.	ás-ti	ἐσ-τί	es-t	is-t	is-t	is-	——	er-
PLUR.—1.	*s-más	ἐσ-μέν	*s-u-mus	——	*s-ind	*s-ind(on)	ear-on	er-u-m
2.	*s-thá	ἐσ-τέ	es-tis	——	*s-ind	*s-ind(on)	ear-on	er-u-đ
3.	*s-ánti	ἔ-ᾱσι, ε-ἰσί	*s-unt	*s-ind	*s-ind(un)	*s-ind(on)	ear-on	er-u

As>*s*, compensation, gravitation (§§ 37, 38); *as*>*is*, precession (§ 38); *ys*<*is*, bad spelling; *s*>*r*, shifting (§ 41, 3, *b*); *irm*>(*eorm*)>*eom*, *arm*>(*earm*) *eam*, breaking (§ 33); second person *-s* and *-t* (§ 165); *nt*>*nd*, shifting (§ 19), *nt* is often found. *Seond-on, -un* (*ie, y*), u-umlaut? (§ 32); *-on* in *earon* (O. Norse *er-u-m*) (§ 166, *a*); in *sind-on*, a double plural through conformation (§ 40); *aron, earon*, are rare in West Saxon.

The subjunctive (Sansk. *s-*jâ-m*, Greek ε*-ἴη-ν, Lat. *s-*iê-m*>*sîm*, Goth. *s-*ija-u*, O. H. Ger., O. Sax., Ang.-Sax. *s-*î*, O. Norse *s-*ê*) is inflected like the imperfect given in § 171. Anglo-Saxon has also *sî*>*sig* (dissimilated gemination, § 27)>*sîe*, *seô* (a peculiar progression, § 25)>*sŷ* (bad spelling); so plur. *sîn, sîen, seôn, sŷn*. The subjunctive often has the force of an imperative, and is given as the imperative in Ælfric's grammar.

(*b*.) √ *bhu*, be. Sansk. *bhav-âmi*, Greek φύ-ω, Lat. *fu-i*, correspond in form to Goth. *báu-an*, Ang.-Sax. *bû-an*, dwell. From the same root are found forms without a connecting vowel in Ang.-Sax., O. Sax., O. H. Ger. In O. Sax. are only *biu-m, bi-st;* in O. H. Ger. *pi-m, pi-s*, —, plur. *pi-rumes, pi-rut, pi-run* (*r*<*s*<√*as*). Ang.-Sax. has *beô-*(*m*) (*iô*), *bi-st* (*y*), *bi-đ* (*y*), plur. *beôđ* (*iô*), and a present subjunctive, imperative, and infinitive, with the common endings; *eô*>*ŷ*>*y*>*i*, umlaut, precession, and shifting (§§ 32, 38, 41).

(*c*.) √ *vas*>*vis* (ablaut) is inflected in the First Conjugation, §§ 199, 197, but the present indicative forms are so rare that they are not given in the grammars.

PARADIGMS FOR PRACTICAL USE.

PRESENT:

SING.—	Indicative.	Subjunctive.	Imperative.	Infinitive.	Participle.
ic	*eom, beô(m)*;	*sî, beô, pese*;			
þû	*eart, bist*;	*sî, beô, pese*;	*beô, pes*;		
hê	*is, bið*;	*sî, beô, pese*;		*beôn,*	
PLUR.—				or	*pesende.*
pê	*sind(on), beôð*;	*sîn, beôn, pesen*;		*pesan*;	
gê	*sind(on), beôð*;	*sîn, beôn, pesen*;	*beôð, pesað*;		
hî	*sind(on), beôð*;	*sîn, beôn, pesen*;			

IMPERFECT:

SING.—		
ic pæs;	*pǽre*;	
þû pǽre;	*pǽre*;	
hê pæs;	*pǽre*;	*ge-pesen.*
PLUR.—		
pê, gê, hî pǽron;	*pǽren*;	

The negative *ne* often unites with forms beginning with a vowel or *p*: *neom* = *ne* + *eom*; *nis*; *næs* = *ne* + *pæs*, p. p. *nærende* < *ne pærende*, etc.

(2.) √ *dha*, place: Sansk. *da-dhâ-mi*, Greek τί-θη-μι, Goth. —, O. Sax. *dô-n*, O. H. Ger. *tuo-n*, do. Anglo-Saxon imperfect from reduplicated theme *dad*; *a*>*æ* (ablaut, § 199) >*y*>*i*, irregular weakening. § 168.

	Indicative Sing.	Plur.	Subj.	Imperat.	Infin.	Participle.
Pres. ..	*dô, dê-st, dê-ð*;	*dô-ð*;	*dô, -n*;	*dô, -ð*;	*dô-n*;	*do-nde.*
Imperf.	*did-e* (*y*), *-est, -e*;	*-on* (*æ*);	*-e* (*æ*), *n*;			*dô-n, dê-n.*

(3.) √ *ga*, go: Sansk. *g'i-gâ-mi*, Greek βί-βη-μι, Goth. *gaggan*, O. Sax. *gâ-n*, O. H. Ger. *gê-n*. Imperfect from √ *i* (Sansk. *ê'-mi*, Greek εἶ-μι, Lat. *î-re*, go, § 158, *a*)>Goth. *i-ddja*, weak form strengthened.

Pres. ..	*gâ, gǽ-st, gǽ-ð*;	*gâð*;	*gâ, -n*;	*gâ, -d*;	*gâ-n*;	
Imperf.	*eô-de, -dest, -de*;	*-don* (§ 37);				*ge-gâ-n.*

From the same root are the nasalized forms *gangan*, imperf. *geông, gêng, giêng* (§ 208, *b*); *geongan* (§ 201); and *gengan*, imperf. *gengde*.

214. REDUPLICATE PRESENTS (Relics of Sanskrit 3d Class, § 158): *gangan*<√*ga*>*ga-gâ-mi*, go (§ 213); so *hangan*, *standan*, § 216).

215. STEMS IN *-ia* of strong verbs (Relics of Sanskrit 4th Class, § 158): *fricge*, inquire, etc. (§ 199); *sperie*, swear, etc. (§ 207, *d*).

PART III.

SYNTAX.

271. **Syntax** is the doctrine of grammatical *combinations of words.* It treats of the use of the etymological forms in discourse—their agreement, government, and arrangement.

SIMPLE COMBINATIONS.

272. There are four simple combinations: the *predic'ative, attrib'utive, objective,* and *adverbial.*

273.—I. **Predicative**

=*nominative substantive + agreeing verb;*
=*nominative substantive + agreeing predicate noun;*
=*nominative substantive + predicate adverb.*

gold glisnâd, gold glistens; *gold is beorht*, gold is bright;
Ælfrêd pæs cyning, Alfred was king; *ic eom hêr*, I am here.

(*a.*) This is a combination between a
subject, of which something is said (=*gold, Ælfrêd, ic*), and a
predicate, which is said of the subject (=*glisnâd, beorht, cyning, hêr*).

(*b.*) **Copula.**—The sign of predication is the stem-ending of a notional verb (=*â* in *glisnâd*), or is a relational verb (*is, pæs, eom*). The substantive verb, when so used, is called the *copula*—a good name for any sign of predication. **Copulative** verbs take a predicate noun.

(*c.*) *Quasi-predicative* is the relation between the implied subject and predicate in a *quasi-clause.* § 278, *d.*

274.—II. **Attributive**=*agreeing noun + substantive;*
=*genitive substantive + substantive.*

gôd cyning, good king; *Ælfrêd ædeling*, Alfred the prince;
Englâ land, land of the Angles.

(*a.*) This combination expresses the relation of **subject + attribute** as taken for granted. The leading substantive is called the
subject, that to which the attribute belongs (*cyning, Ælfrêd, land*);
an **attributive** is the agreeing adjective (*gôd*), or genit. substantive (*Englâ*);
an **appositive** is the agreeing substantive (*ædeling*).

(*b.*) The sign of this relation is the agreeing case-endings, or the attributive genitive ending, or a preposition (§ 277, 2).

275.—III. **Objective** = *verb* + *governed noun.*
= *adjective* + *governed noun.*

ic huntige heortâs, I hunt harts; *hê sylđ him hors*, he sells him a horse; *gilpes þû gyrnest*, thou wishest fame; *þǣre fǣhđe hê gefeah*, he rejoiced at the vengeance; *hî macađ hine* (*tô*) *cyninge*, they make him king; *hpî segst þû mê gôdne*, why callest thou me good? *beôđ gemindige Lođes pîfes*, remember Lot's wife.

(*a.*) This combination expresses the relation of an *act* or *quality* to its *completing notional object.*

Objective verbs or adjectives are those which need such object (*huntige*, etc.).
Subjective need no such object (*ic slǣpe*, I sleep).
Transitive verbs have a suffering object (*huntige*, *sylđ*, *macađ*, etc.).
Intransitive have no suffering object (*gyrnest*, *gefeah*).

The completing object may be
suffering (=*direct*), an accusative merely affected (*heortâs*, *hors*, *hine*, *mê*);
dative (=*indirect*=*personal*), a receiver to or for whom is the act (*him*);
genitive, suggesting or exciting the act (*gilpes*, *fǣhđe*, *pîfes*);
factitive, a product or result in fact or thought (*cyninge*, *gôdne*).

(*b.*) The sign of relation is the case-ending or a preposition.

(*c.*) Many Anglo-Saxon verbs require an object, when the English by which we translate them do not. Many objects conceived as *exciting* in Anglo-Saxon are conceived as *suffering* in English; many as merely adverbial.

(*d.*) The factitive object often has a quasi-predicative relation to the suffering object, agreeing with it like a predicate noun (*mê*+*gôdne*). Such clauses are nearly equivalent to two (why sayest thou that I am good?).

276.—IV. **Adverbial**=*verb*+*adverb* or *adverbial phrase.*
=*adjective*+*adverb* or *adverbial phrase.*
=*adverb*+*adverb* or *adverbial phrase.*

ic gâ ût, I go out; *ic singe ælcê dæg*, I sing each day; *pê sprecađ gepemmodlîce*, we speak corruptly; *hê com mid þâ fǣmman*, he came with the woman; *mid sorgum libban*, to live having cares; *hpî fandige gê mîn*, why tempt ye me? *miclê mâ man is sceâpe betera*, man is much (more) better than a sheep.

(*a.*) This combination is between an *act* or *quality* and its *unessential relations.* The most common relations are **place** (*ût*), **time** (*ælcê dæg*), **manner** (*gepemmodlîce*), **co-existence** (*mid fǣmman*, *mid sorgum*), **cause** (*hpî*), **intensity** (*miclê*, *mâ*, *sceâpe*).

(*b.*) The sign is an adverbial ending, case-ending, or preposition.

(*c.*) The *adverbial* combination is given by Becker as a subdivision of the *objective*, but the linguistic sense of the Indo-European races uniformly recognizes the adverb as a separate part of speech.

277. **Equivalents of the Noun and Adverb** in the combinations:

(1.) For a SUBSTANTIVE may be used a *substantive noun* or *pronoun*, an *adjective* or any of its equivalents, an *infinitive*, a *clause*, any *word* or *phrase* viewed merely as a thing.

(2.) For an ADJECTIVE may be used an *adjective noun* or *pronoun*, an *article* (attributively), a *participle*, a *genitive substantive*, an *adverb*, a *preposition with its case*, a *relative clause.*

(3.) For an ADVERB may be used an *oblique case* of a noun with or without a preposition, a *phrase*, a *clause.*

SENTENCES.

278. A **Sentence** is a thought in words. It may be **declarative**, an assertion, *indicative*, *subjunctive*, or *potential;* **interrogative**, a question, *indicative*, *subjunctive*, or *potential;* **imperative**, a command, exhortation, entreaty; a species of **exclamatory**, an expanded interjection. §§ 149–151.

(*a.*) A **clause** is *one finite verb* with its subject, objects, and all their attributives and adjuncts. Its *essential part* is its predicative combination. The (*grammatical*) subject of the predicative combination, its attributives and adjuncts, make up the *logical* subject of the clause; the *grammatical* predicate and its objects with their attributives and adjuncts make up the *logical* predicate.

(*b.*) A **subordinate** clause enters into grammatical combination with some *word* in another (**principal**) clause; **co-ordinate** clauses are coupled as wholes.

(*c.*) The sign of relation between clauses is a relative or conjunction.

(*d.*) **Quasi-clauses.** — (1) *Infinitives*, *participles*, and *factitive* objects mark quasi-predicative combinations, and each has its quasi-clause. (2) *Interjections* and *vocatives* are exclamatory quasi-clauses.

279. A **Sentence** is *simple*, *complex*, or *compound.*

280. A **simple** sentence is *one independent* clause.

I. A predicative combination.

Verb for predicate: *fisceràs fisciad*, fishers *fish.*
Adjective: *God is gôd*, God is *good.*
Genitive: *tôl Cǽsares is*, tribute is *Cæsar's.*
Substantive: *Cædmon pæs leôđpyrhta*, Cædmon was a *poet.*
Adverb: *pê sind hêr*, we are *here.*
Adverbial: *God is in heofenum*, God is *in heaven.*
Subject indefinite: (*hit*) *snîpđ*, it snows; *mê þyrst*, me it thirsteth.

II. Clause with attributive combination.

Adjective attribute: *gôd gold glisnâð, good* gold glistens.
Genitive: *folces stemn is Godes stemn, folk's* voice is *God's* voice.
Appositive: *pê cildra sind ungelǣrede*, we *children* are untaught.

III. Clause with objective combination.

Direct object: *Cædmon porhte leôðsangâs*, Cædmon made *poems.*
Dative: *lǣn mê þrî hlâfâs*, give *me* three loaves.
Genitive: *þæt pîf âhlôh drihtnes*, the woman laughed at *the lord.*
Factitive: *Simônem hê nemde Petrum*, Simon he named *Peter.*

IV. Clause with adverbial combination.

Place: *ic gâ ût*, I go *out.*
Time: *ic gâ ût on dægrêd*, I go out *at dawn.*
Manner: *se cyning scrŷt mê pel*, the king clothes me *well.*
Co-existence: *mid sorgum ic libbe*, I live *with cares.*
Cause: *hê hâs is for cylde*, he is hoarse *from cold; se cnapa þŷpâð oxan mid gadîsenê*, the boy drives oxen *with an iron goad.*

281.—V. Abridged complex sentence. Clause containing a quasi-clause. § 278, *d.*

Infinitive: *tǣc ûs sprecan*, teach us *to speak.*
Factitive: *hpî segst þû mê gôdne*, why callest thou *me* (to be) *good?*
Participle (adjectival): *ic hæbbe sumne cnapan, þŷpendne oxan*, I have a boy, (*driving*) *who drives oxen;* (adverbial, gerund), *Boetius gebæd singende*, Boethius prayed *singing;* (absolute), *þînre durâ belocenre, bide þînne fæder, thy door having been locked*, pray thy father.

282.—VI. Abridged compound sentence (§ 284). Verbs>verb.

Compound subject: *hê and seô singað, he and she* sing.
Compound predicate: *hê is gôd and pîs*, he is *good and wise; seô lufâð hine and mê*, she loves *him and me.*

283. A **complex** sentence is one *principal* clause with its *subordinate* clause or clauses. § 278, *b.* The subordinate may be a

Substantive: (subject), *is sægd þæt hê com, that he came* is said; (object), *ic pât þæt hê com*, I wot *that he came;* (appositive), *ic com tô þam, þæt hê pǣre gefulpôd*, I came for this, *that he might be baptized.*
Adjective: *stæf-cræft is seô cǣg, þe þǣrâ bôcâ andgit unlŷcð*, grammar is the key, *that unlocks the sense of the books.*
Adverb: (place), *hpider þû gǣst, ic gâ*, I go *whither thou goest;* (time), *ic gâ hpænne þû gǣst*, I go *when thou goest;* (manner), *þû sprǣce spâ spâ ân stunt pîf*, thou spakest *as a stupid woman speaks;* (intensity),

beóð gleápe spâ nædran, be wise *as serpents; leófre is hlehhan þonne grǣtan*, it is better to laugh *than cry;* (cause = efficient, motive, means, argument, condition [**protasis** to an **apodosis**], concession, purpose): *hit þunrâð forþam God pilt*, it thunders *because God wills; paciað, forþam þe gê nytonþone dæg*, watch, *because ye know not the day; Onsend Higelâce, gif mec hild nime*, (protasis) *if me battle take*, (apodosis) send to Higelac, etc. Co-existence is usually in an abridged participial clause (§ 281).

284. A **compound** sentence is a number of *co-ordinate* clauses. § 278, *b*.

Copulative: *ic gâ ût and ic geocie oxan*, I go out *and* I yoke oxen.

Adversative: *fŷr is gôd þegn, ac is frêcne freâ*, fire is a good servant, *but* is a bad master; *ne nom hê mâ, þeâh hê monige geseah*, he took no more, *though* he saw many.

Disjunctive: *ic singe oððe ic rǣde*, I sing *or* I read.

Causal: *forþŷ gê ne gehŷrað, forþam þe gê ne synd of Gode, therefore* ye do not hear, (*for this that*) *because* ye are not of God.

---

482. PRINCIPAL RULES OF SYNTAX.

SUBSTANTIVES.

Agreement.

I. A **predicate** noun denoting the same person or thing as its **subject**, agrees with it in *case*, § 286.

II. An **appositive** agrees in *case* with its **subject**, § 287.

NOMINATIVE CASE.

III. The **subject** of a *finite* verb is put in the **nominative**, § 288.

VOCATIVE CASE.

IV. A **compellative** is put in the **vocative**, § 289.

ACCUSATIVE CASE.

Objective Combinations.

V. The **direct object** of a *verb* is put in the **accusative**, § 290.

VI. **Impersonals** of *appetite* or *passion* govern an **accusative** of the person suffering, § 290, *c*.

VII. Some verbs of **asking** and **teaching** may have **two accusatives**, one of a *person*, and the other of a *thing*, § 292.

Quasi-predicative Combinations.

VIII. The **subject** of an *infinitive* is put in the **accusative**, § 293.

IX. Some verbs of **making**, **naming**, and **regarding** may have **two accusatives** of the *same person* or thing, § 294.

Adverbial Combinations.

X. The **accusative** is used to express **extent** of time and space after verbs, § 295.

XI. The **accusative** is used with **prepositions**, § 295, *c*.

Dative and Instrumental Cases.

Objective Combinations.

XII. An object of **influence** or **interest** is put in the **dative**, § 297.

XIII. Verbs of **granting**, **refusing**, and **thanking** may take a **dative** and **genitive**, § 297, *d*.

XIV. Words of **nearness** and **likeness** govern the **dative**, § 299.

XV. The **instrumental** or **dative** may denote an object of **mastery**, § 300.

XVI. Some words of **separation** may take an object **from which** in the **dative** or **instrumental**, § 301.

Adverbial Combinations.

XVII. The **instrumental** or **dative** may denote **instrument**, **means**, **manner**, or **cause**, § 302.

XVII. The **instrumental** or **dative** may denote **price**, § 302, *c*.

XVIII. The **instrumental** or **dative** may denote **measure of difference**, § 302, *d*.

XIX. The **instrumental** or **dative** may denote an **object sworn** by, § 302, *e*.

XX. The **comparative** degree may govern a **dative**, § 303.

XXI. The **dative** may denote **time when** or **place where**, § 304.

XXII. A **substantive** and **participle** in the **dative** may make an adverbial clause of **time**, **cause**, or **co-existence**, § 304, *d*.

XXIII. The dative with a preposition may denote an object of influence or interest, association, mastery, or separation; or an instrumental, ablative, or locative adverbial relation, § 305. **Instrumental**, §§ 306–308.

The dative, with or without *of*, is sometimes used for the genitive.

Genitive.

Attributive Combinations.

XXIV. An **attributive genitive** may denote the **possessor** or **author** of its *subject*, § 310.

XXV. An **attributive genitive** may denote the **subject** or **object** of a *verbal*, § 311.

XXVI. An **attributive genitive** may denote the **whole** of which its subject is **part**, § 312.

XXVII. An **attributive genitive** may denote a **characteristic** of its *subject*, § 313.

Predicative Combinations.

XXVIII. A **predicate** substantive may be put in the **genitive** to denote a **possessor** or **characteristic** of the subject, or the **whole** of which it is part, § 314.

Objective Combinations.

XXIX. The **genitive** may denote an **exciting** object, § 315.

XXX. Verbs of **asking, accusing, reminding,** may take an **accusative** and **genitive,** § 315, *a.*

XXXI. Verbs of **granting, refusing,** and **thanking** may take a **dative** and **genitive,** § 315, *b.*

XXXII. The **genitive** may denote an object affected **in part,** § 316.

XXXIII. The **genitive** may denote an **object of separation,** § 317.

XXXIV. The **genitive** may denote an **object of supremacy** or use, § 318.

XXXV. The **genitive** or **instrumental** may denote the **material** of which any thing is made or full, § 319.

XXXVI. The **genitive** in combination with *adjectives* may denote **measure,** § 320.

XXXVII. The **genitive** in combination with *adjectives* may denote the **part** or **relation** in which the quality is conceived, § 321.

Adverbial Combinations.

XXXVIII. The **genitive** may denote **by what way,** § 322.

XXXIX. The **genitive** may denote **time when,** § 323.

XL. The **genitive** may denote **means, cause,** or **manner,** §§ 324, 325.

XLI. The genitive with a preposition is sometimes used to denote instrumental, ablative, or locative adverbial relations, § 326.

Prepositions.

XLII. A **preposition** governs a **substantive**, and shows its **relation** to some other word in the clause, § 327.

Adjectives.

XLIII. An **adjective** agrees with its **substantive** in *gender*, *number*, and *case*, § 361.

XLIV. The **weak forms** are used after the **definite article, demonstratives**, and **possessives**; and often in attributive *vocatives*, *instrumentals*, and *genitives*. **Comparative** forms are all weak, § 362.

Pronouns.

XLV. A **substantive pronoun** agrees with its **antecedent** in *gender*, *number*, and *person*, § 365.

Adverbs.

XLVI. **Adverbs** modify *verbs*, *adjectives*, and other *adverbs*, § 395.

Verbs.

Agreement.

XLVII. A **finite verb** agrees with its **subject** in *number* and *person*, § 401.

Voices.

XLVIII. The **active** voice is used to make the *agent* the *subject* of predication, § 408.

XLIX. The **passive** voice is used to make the direct *object* of the action the *subject* of predication, § 409.

Tenses.

L. **Principal** tenses depend on **principal** tenses, **historical** on **historical**, § 419.

Modes.

LI. The **indicative** is used in *assertions*, *questions*, and *assumptions* to express **simple predication**, § 420.

LII. The **subjunctive** is used to express **mere possibility, doubt**, or **wish**, § 421.

LIII. The **subjunctive** may be used by **attraction** in clauses **subordinate** to a subjunctive, § 422.

LIV. The **subjunctive** may be used in a **substantive** clause expressing something *said*, *asked*, *thought*, *wished*, or *done*, § 423.

LV. The **subjunctive** may be used in **indefinite adjective** clauses, § 427.

LVI. The **subjunctive** may be used in **indefinite** adverbial clauses of **place,** § 428.

LVII. The **subjunctive** may be used in adverbial clauses of **future** or *indefinite time*, § 429.

LVIII. The **subjunctive** may be used in clauses of **comparison** expressing that which is *imagined* or *indefinite*, or descriptive of a *force.*

LIX. The **subjunctive** is used in a **protasis** when proposed as **possible,** the *imperfect* when assumed as *unreal*, § 431.

LX. The **subjunctive** may be used in a **concessive** clause, § 432.

LXI. The **subjunctive** is used in clauses expressing **purpose,** § 433.

LXII. The **subjunctive** may express a **result,** § 434.

LXIII. The **potential** expresses **power,** liberty, permission, necessity, or duty, § 435.

LXIV. The **imperative** is used in **commands,** § 444.

XLV. The **infinitive** is construed as a **neuter noun,** § 446.

XLVI. The **gerund** after the **copula** expresses what *must*, *may*, or *should* be done, § 451.

LXVII. The **gerund** is sometimes used to describe or define a **noun,** § 452.

LXVIII. The **gerund** may be used as a **final object** to express an act **on** the first object, § 453.

LXIX. The **gerund** is used to denote the **purpose** of motion, § 454.

LXX. The **gerund** with an **adjective** may express an act for which any thing is *ready*, or in respect to which any thing is *pleasant*, *unpleasant*, *easy*, *worthy*, § 454.

LXXI. A **participle** agrees with its **substantive** in *gender*, *number*, and *case*, § 456.

LXXII. A **participle** may **govern the case** of its verb, § 456.

INTERJECTIONS.

LXXIII. The **interjection** has the syntax of a **clause,** § 461.

CONJUNCTIONS.

LXXIV. **Co-ordinate** conjunctions connect **sentences** or **like parts** of a sentence, § 462.

LXXV. A **subordinate conjunction** connects a **subordinate clause** and the **word** with which it combines, § 467.

PART IV.

PROSODY.

496. **Prosody** treats of the *rhythm* of Poetry.

497. **Rhythm** is an orderly succession of beats of sound.

This beat is called an *ictus* or **arsis**, and the syllable on which it falls is also called the *arsis*. The alternate remission of voice, and the syllables so uttered, are called the **thesis.**

498. **Feet** are the elementary combinations of syllables in verse.

(*a.*) Feet are named from the order and make of their arsis and thesis. A monosyllabic *arsis*+a monosyllabic *thesis* is a *trochee;* +a dissyllabic *thesis* is a *dactyle*, etc.

Stress. In Anglo-Saxon these depend on the *accented* syllables, which are determined by the stress they would, if the passage were prose, receive to distinguish them from other syllables of the same word, or from other words in the sentence.

Accent is therefore verbal, syntactical, or rhetorical. An unemphatic dissyllable may count as two unaccented syllables, like the second part of a compound. Secondary accents may take the arsis.

1. A **tonic** is a single accented syllable+a pause.
2. A **trochee** is an accented+an unaccented syllable.
3. A **dactyle** is an accented+two unaccented syllables.
4. A **pæon** is an accented+three unaccented syllables.
5. A **pyrrhic** is two unaccented syllables; a **spondee** is two accented; an **iambus** is an unaccented+an accented; an **anapæst** is two unaccented+an accented; a **tribrach** is three unaccented; a single unaccented syllable is called an **atonic**; and unaccented syllables preliminary to the normal feet of a line are called an **anacrusis** (striking up) or *base*.

(*b.*) **Time.** The time from each ictus to the next is the same in any section. It is not always filled up with sound. More time is given to an accented than an unaccented syllable.

(*c.*) **Pitch.** The English and most other Indo-Europeans raise the pitch with the verbal accent; the Scots lower it. With the rhetorical accent the pitch varies every way.

(*d.*) **Expression.** Feet of two syllables are most conversational; those of three are more ornate; those of one syllable are emphatic, like a *thud* or the blows of a hammer. The trochee, dactyle, and pæon, in which the accented syllable precedes, have more ease, grace, and vivacity. Those feet in which the accented syllable comes last have more decision, emphasis, and strength (Crosby, § 695). The Anglo-Saxon meters are trochaic and dactylic; the English oftener iambic and anapæstic.

499. A **verse** is an elementary division of a poem.

It has a twofold nature; it is a series of feet, and also a series of words.

(*a.*) As a series of feet, it is a sing-song of regular ups and downs, such as children sometimes give in repeating rhymes.

As a series of words, each word and pause would be the same as if it were prose, as persons who do not catch the meter often read poetry.

The cantilation never is the same as the prose utterance; lines in which it should be would be prosaic.

The art of versification consists in so arranging the prose speech in the ideal framework of the line that the reader may adjust one to the other without obscuring either, and with continual happy variety.

(*b.*) The manner of adapting the *arsis* and *thesis* to the prose pronunciation is different in different languages. In Sanskrit, and classical Greek and Latin, the *arsis* was laid on syllables having a *long sound*, and variety was found in the play of the prose accent. In other languages, including modern Greek and Latin, the *arsis* is made to fall on *accented* syllables, and free play is given to long and short vowel sounds, and combinations of consonants. The Sanskrit and Greek varied farther from prose speech in the recitation of poetry than modern habits and ears allow. The Hindoos still repeat Sanskrit poetry in recitative.

500. Verses are named from the prevailing foot *trochaic*, *dactylic*, *iambic*, and *anapæstic*, etc.

Verses are named from the number of feet. A **monometer** is a verse of one foot; a **dimeter** of two; a **trimeter** of three; a **tetrameter** of four; a **pentameter** of five; a **hexameter** of six; a **heptameter** of seven; an **octometer** of eight.

(*a.*) A verse is *catalectic* when it wants a syllable, *acatalectic* when complete, *hypercatalectic* when redundant.

501. **Cæsura.**—Anglo-Saxon verses are made in two *sections* or **hemistichs.** The pause between these sections is called the **cæsura.** A *foot cæsura* is made by the cutting of a *foot* by the end of a *word.*

(*a.*) **Expression.** The character of versification depends much on the management of the cæsuras. When the weight of a verse precedes the cæsura, the movement has more vivacity; when it follows, more gravity.

502. **Rime.**—Rime is the rhythmical repetition of letters.

Nations who unite arsis and prose accent need to mark off their verses plainly. They do it by rime. Other nations shun rime.

1. When the riming letters begin their words, it is called **alliteration.**
2. When the accented vowels and following letters are alike, it is called **perfect rime** (=rhyme).
3. When only the consonants are alike, it is called **half rime.**
4. When the accented syllable is final, the rime is *single;* when one unaccented syllable follows, the rime is double; when two, it is *triple.*

(*a.*) **Line-rime** is between two words in the same section. **Final-rime** between the last words of two sections or verses.

503. **Alliteration** is the recurrence of the same initial sound in the first accented syllables of words.

1. **Consonants.**—The first initial consonant of alliterating syllables must be the same, the other consonants of a combination need not be;

Beôpulf: *breme*:: *blæd* (B., 18); *Caines* : *cynne*:: *cpealm* (107); *Cristenrâ*:: *Cyriacus* (El., 1069); *cûde*:: *cniht* (B., 372); *funden*:: *frôfre* (7); *frætpum* : *flet* (2054); *geong* : *geardum*:: *God* (13); *geôgode*:: *gleâpôst* (C., 221, 1); *grimma* : *gæst* (B., 102); *heofenum* : *hlæste* (52); *hæledâ* : *hryre*:: *hpate* (2052); *hnîtan*:: *hringum* (Rid., 87, 4): *sôdlice*:: *speotolan* (B., 141); *scearp* : *scyld*:: *scâd* (288); *scridende*:: *sceapum* (Trav., 135); *Scottâ*:: *scip*. (Chr., 938); *þeôd*:: *þrym* (B., 2); *pên* : *plenco*:: *præc* (338).

2. **Vowels.**—A perfect vowel alliteration demands different vowels: *isig* : *ûtfûs*:: *ædelinges* (B., 33);—sometimes the same vowels repeat: *eorlâ* : *eordan*:: *eôper* (B., 248).

(*a.*) **sc, sp,** or **st** seldom alliterate without repeating the whole combination; but: *scyppend*:: *scrifen* (B., 106); *spere* : *sprengde*:: *sprang* (By., 137); *strælâ* : *storm*:: *strengum* (B., 3117).

(*b.*) Words in **ia**-, **iŏ**-, **iu**-, **Hie**-, alliterate with those in **g**-. They are mostly foreign proper names. See §§ 28, 34.

Iacobes:: *gôde* (Psa., lxxxvi, 1, and often); *Iafed* : *gumrincum* (C., 1552); *Iordane*:: *grêne* (C., 1921); *Iôbes*:: *God* (Met., 26, 47); *gôda* : *geâsne* :: *Iudas* (El., 924); *Iudêâ*:: *God* (El., 209); *gleâp* : *Gode*:: *Iuliana* (Jul., 131, and often); *gomen* : *geardum*:: *iu* (B., 2459), so frequently *iu*=*geô*, *giô* (formerly) and its compounds; *Hierusolme*:: *God* (Ps. C., 50, 134); *gongad* : *gegnunga*:: *Hierusalem* (Gûth., 785); written *gold* : *Gerusalem*:: *Iudêâ* (C., 260, 11).

(*c.*) It is said that *þ* may alliterate with *s* by Dietrich (Haupt Zeit., x, 323, 362). No sure examples found. C., 287, 23, is a defective line.

504. A perfect Anglo-Saxon verse has three alliterating syllables, two in the first section, the other in the second.

F*rum*'|*sceaft*\` | **F***ir*'|*â*\` ‖ **F***eor*'|*ran*\` | *rec*'|*can*\` (B., 91).
the origin of men from far relate.

(*a.*) The repeated letter is called the *rime-letter;* the one in the second couplet the *chief-letter*, the others the *sub-letters*. The **F** of *feorran* in the line above is the *chief-letter*; the **F** in *frumsceaft* and *firâ* the *sub-letters*.

(*b.*) One of the *sub-letters* is often wanting.

(*c.*) Four or more rime-letters are sometimes found.

L*eânes* . . **L***eôhte* . . ‖ . . **L***ête* . . **L***ange* (C., 258).

In pairs: *þæt*' *he* | *God'e* | *pol'd*|*e*\` ‖ *geong'*|*ra*\` | *peord*'|*an*\`,
that he to God would a vassal be (C., 277), where *g* and *p* both rime, and so often.

505. The Anglo-Saxons used line-rime and final-rime as an occasional grace of verse. See § 511.

506. Verse in which alliteration is essential, and other rime ornamental, is the prevailing form in Anglo-Saxon, Icelandic, Old Saxon. Specimens are found in Old High

German. Alliteration in these languages even ran into prose, and is one of the causes of the thoroughness with which the shifting of the initial consonants has affected the whole speech, § 41, B.

507. Verse with final rime, and with alliteration as an occasional grace, is the common form in English and the modern Germanic and Romanic languages. It is common in the Low-Latin verses of the Anglo-Saxon poets, and it is by many supposed to have spread from the Celtic.

COMMON NARRATIVE VERSE.

508. Beda says of rhythm: "It is a modulated composition of words, not according to the laws of meter, but adapted in the number of its syllables to the judgment of the ear, as are the verses of our vulgar poets. * * * Yet, for the most part, you may find, by a sort of chance, some rule in rhythm; but this is not from an artificial government of the syllables. It arises because the sound and the modulation lead to it. The vulgar poets effect this rustically, the skillful attain it by their skill."—Bêd., 1, 57. These remarks on the native poets are doubtless applicable to their Anglo-Saxon verses as well as their Latin; and whatever general rules we may find running through these poems, we may expect to find many exceptional lines, which belong in their places only because they can be recited with a cadence somewhat like the verses around them.

509. The common narrative verse has four feet in each section.

A. 1. **An arsis** *falls* on every prose accent, § 15, and the last syllable of every section. But note contractions below, 7.

2. At least one arsis on a primary accent, or two on other syllables follow the chief alliterating letter, § 504.

3. An arsis *should* fall on the former of two unaccented syllables after an accented-long (the vowel long or followed by two consonants), and on the latter after an accented short.

scyld'|um' bi|scer'e|de', ‖ *scynd'|an' ge|ner'e|de'* (Rime Song, 84).

4. An arsis *should not* fall on an unaccented proper prefix (*â-*, *be-*, *ge-*, etc., § 15), or proclitic monosyllables (*be*, *se*, *þe*, etc.), or short endings of dissyllabic particles (*nefne*, *odde*, *þonne*, etc.), or short tense-endings between two accented shorts in the same section.

5. An arsis *may* fall on a long, on a short between two accents (after a long frequent, after a short, less so), on the former of two unaccented shorts.

grorn' | *torn'* | *græf'|ed'*, ‖ *græft'* | *ræft' hæf'|ed'* (Rime Song, 66).
spylc'e | *gi'* | *gant'* | *âs'* ‖ *þâ' pid* | *God'e* | *punn'* | *on'* (B., 113).
nıp'|e' | *niht'-|peard'* ‖ *nyd'|e'* | *sceol'|de'* (C., 185, 1).
pord' purd'|i' | *an'*, ‖ *Veôl'* | *him' on* | *inn'* | *an'* (C., 353).
burh' | *tim'|bre'* | *de'* (C., 2840). Rare with short penult of trisyllable.

B. 6. **The thesis** is mute or monosyllabic; but syncope, elision, synizesis, or synalœpha is often needed to reduce two syllables.

7. **An anacrusis** may introduce any section. It is of one syllable, rarely two, sometimes apparently three, with the same contractions as the thesis.

Lêt'on | *þ(â) of'er* | *fif'el* | *pæ̂g'* ‖ *fâm'|i'ge* | *scrid'|an'* (El., 237).
puld'or|-cyn'ing|es' | *pord'* ‖ *ge)peot'an* | *þâ' þâ* | *pît'(ı)gan* | *þrŷ'* (An., 802).
spic'ôd|(e) ymb' þâ | *sâp'|le'* ‖ *þe) hir'e* | *æ̂r' þâ* | *sien'(e) on|lâh'* (C., 607).

Synizesis of *-anne*, *-lîc*, *-scipe*, *þenden*, and the like. *Synalœpha* of *ge-*, *þe*, and the like.

sorh' is | mê' tô | secg'|anne' ‖ *on' | sef'an | mîn'|um'* (B., 473).
prætlîc'ne | pund'or|-madd'|um' ‖ (B., 2174).
fyrd'|-sear'o | fûs' | lîcu' ‖ (B., 232).
eaht'|ô'don | eorl'|-scipe' ‖ (B., 3174).
pes'an | þend'en ic | peald'|e' ‖ (B., 1859).
þegn'âs | synd'on ge|-þpær'|e' ‖ (B., 1230).
þâr'â þe | pid' spâ | mic'|lum' ‖ (C., 2095).
þæt næfre)Grend'|el' spâ | fel'|a' ‖ *gry'|râ' ge|frem'e | de'* (B., 591).

So we find *hpædere* (B., 573), dissyllabic; *hine* (B., 688), *ofer* (B., 1273), monosyllabic; and many anomalous slurs in the thesis or anacrusis.

8. The order of the feet is free, varying with the sense. In later poetry, as more particles are used, the fuller thesis grows more common.

9. The Anglo-Saxons like to end a sentence at the cæsura. So Chaucer and his French masters stop at the end of the first line of a rhyming couplet. So Milton says that "true musical delight" is to be found in having the sense "variously drawn out from one verse into another."

10. The two alliterating feet in the first section, and the corresponding pair in the second section, are chief feet. Some read all the rest as thesis.

510. Irregular sections are found with three feet, or two.

1. Sections with contracted words where the full form would complete the four feet.

heân hûses=heâ'|han' | hû'|ses' (B., 116).
deâdpic seôn=deâd'|pic' | seo'|han' (B., 1275).

2. Sections with three feet and a thesis:

prym' | (ge)|-frun'|on' (B., 2).
lif' | eâc' | (ge)|sceôp' (B., 97).

Heyne finds in Beowulf feet of this kind with *â-*, *æt-*, *be-*, *for-*, *ge-*, *of-*, *on-*, *to-*, *þurh-*. Similar sections with proclitic particles are found: *men' | (ne)|cunn'|on'* (B., 50); *(be)|ŷd'|lâf'|e'* (B., 566); *Lêt' | (se)|heard'|a'* (B., 2977); *(þe)|him' | þæt' | pîf'* (C., 707).

3. Sections with Proper Names. Foreign Names are irregular:

Sem' | and' | Cham' | (C., 1551), and so often.

4. Sections with two feet and a thesis:

man' | (ge)|þeôn' (B., 25). *Loth' | (on)|fôn'* (C., 1938).

511. Rhyme is found occasionally in most Anglo-Saxon poems. A few contain rhyming passages of some length. One has been found which is plainly a Task Poem to display riming skill. All sorts of rimes are crowded together in it. It has eighty-seven verses.

LINE-RIME.

Half-rime: **sâr'** | *and'* | **sor'**|*ge'*; ‖ *sûsl'* | *þrôp'*|*ed'*|*on'*,
pain and sorrow; sulphur suffered they (C., 75).

Perfect-rime:

Single: *flâh'* | *mâh'* | *flît'*|*ed'*, || *flân'* | *mân'* | *hpît'*|*ed'*,
foul fiend fighteth, darts the devil whetteth (Rime-song, [62]).
gâst'|*â'* | *peard'*|*um'*. || *Hæfd'*|*on'* | *gleâm'* *and* | *dreâm'*,
They had light and joy (C.,

Double: *frôd'*|**ne'** *and* | *gôd'*|**ne'** || *fæd'er* | *Un'*|*pên'*|*es'*, [12).
wise and good father of Unwen (Trav., 114).

Triple: *fer'*|**ed**|**e'** *and* | *ner'e*|**de'**. || *Fîf'*|*tên'*|*a'* | *stôd'*—,
(God) led and saved (C., 1397).

FINAL-RIME.

Half-rime: *spâ'* | *lîf'* | *spâ'* | *deâd'*, || *spâ' him* | *leôf'*|*re'* | *bid'*.
either life or death, as to him liefer be (Ex., 37, 20; Crist., 596, and a riming passage).

Perfect-rime:

Single: *nê'* | *forst'*|*es'* | *fnæst'*, || *nê'* | *fŷr'*|*es'* *blæst'*,
no frost's rage, nor fire's blast,

Double: *ne) hægl'*|*es'* | *hryr'*|*e'*, || *ne) hrîm'*|*es'* | *dryr'*|*e'*,
nor hail's fall, nor rime's descent (Phœnix, 15, 16; Ex., 198, 25, where see more).

Triple: *hlûd'*|*e'* | *hlyn'e*|*de'*; || *hleôd'*|*or'* | *dyn'e*|*de'*,
(The harp) loud sounded; the sound dinned (Rime-song, 28).

Long Narrative Verse.

512. The common narrative verse is varied by occasional passages in longer verses. The alliteration and general structure of the long verse is the same as of the common; but the length of the section is six feet. Feet are oftenest added between the two alliterating syllables of the first section, and before the alliterating syllable of the second section.

S*pâ'* | *cpæd'* | **s***nott'*|*or on* | *môd'*|*e'*, ||
ge) **s***æt'* | *hîm'* | **s***und'*|*or'* *æt* | *rûn'*|*e'*. ||
T*il' bid* | *se'þe his* | **t***reôp'*|*e'* *ge*|*heald'*|*ed'*: ||
ne) sceal' | *næf're his* | **t***orn' tô* | *ryc'ê*|*ne'*
b*eorn'* | *of' his* | **b***reôst'*|*um'* *â*|*cŷd'*|*an'*,
nemd'e hê | *ær' þâ* | **b***ôt'*|*e'* | *cunn'*|*e'*,
e*orl'* | *mid'* | **e***ln'*|*ê'* *ge*|*fremm'*|*an'*:
pel' bid | *þam' þe him* | **â***r'*|*e'* | *sêc'*|*ed'*,
f*rôf'*|*re' tô* | **F***æd'*|*er'* *on* | *heof'on*|*um'*,
þær' | *ûs'* | *eal' seô* | **f***æst'nung* | *stond'*|*ed'* (Wanderer, 111+).

(*a.*) Sometimes a section of four feet is coupled with one of six:
ge) pinn'|*es'* | *pid'* | *heor'â* | *pald'*|*end'* || *pît'*|*e'* | *þol'*|*iad'* (C., 323).

(*b.*) Four or more alliterative letters are found oftener than in common verse. Three seldom fail. A secondary weak alliteration is sometimes found in one of the sections.

(*c*.) This verse is rather a variety of the Common Narrative than another kind.

513. The Common Narrative is the regular Old Germanic verse. Rules 1, 2, 3, 4, 6, 7, of § 509, are rules of that vèrse. In the 5th the Anglo-Saxon uses greater freedom. It also corresponds with the Old Norse *fornyrðalag*. In it Old English alliterating poems are written.

In' a | som'er | ses'|on' ‖ whan) soft' | was' the | sonn'|e'
I) shop'e | me' in | shroud'|es' ‖ as) I' a | shep'e | wer'|e'
In) hab'ite | as' an | her'e|mite' ‖ un)hol'|y' of | work'|es'
Went' | wyd'e | in' þis | world' ‖ wond'|res' tô | her'|e'.
Ac) on' a | May' | morn'yng|e' ‖ on) Mal'|uern'e | hull'|es'
Me' by|fel' a | fer|ly' ‖ of) fair'|y' me | thouȝt'|e'.

Piers the Plowman, 1–6.

(*a*.) The *anacrusis* has a tendency to unite with the following accented syllable, and start an *iambic* or *anapæstic* movement. The change of inflection endings for prepositions and auxiliaries has also favored the same movement. In Old English it often runs through the verses. See Final perfect-rime, § 511.

Alliterative Prose.

514. Some of the Anglo-Saxon prose has a striking rhythm, and frequent alliteration, though not divided by it into verses. Some of the Homilies of Ælfric are so written (St. Cuðbert). Parts of the Chronicle have mixed line-rime and alliteration.

515. Verses with the same general form as the Anglo-Saxon continued to be written in English to the middle of the fifteenth century. Alliteration is still found as an ornament of our poetry, and the old dactylic cadence runs through all racy Anglo-Saxon English style.

So they went | up to the | Mountains ‖ to be|hold the | gardens and | orchards,
The | vineyards and | fountains of | water; ‖ where | also they | drank and | washed themselves,
And did | freely | eat of the | vineyards. ‖ Now there | were on the | tops of those | Mountains,
Shepherds feeding their flocks; and they stood by the highway side.
The pilgrims therefore went to them, and leaning upon their staffs,
As is common with weary pilgrims, when they stand to talk with any by the way,
They asked, Whose Delectable Mountains are these?
And whose be the sheep, that feed upon them?—Bunyan, *Pilgrim's Progress.*

VOCABULARY.

The letters have the following order: *a, æ, b, c, d, đ, e, f, g, h, i, l, m, n, o, p, r, s, t, þ, u, p, x, y.* A figure after a verb denotes its conjugation as given in the author's Grammar: (1) meaning a verb having ablaut from a root in *-a-;* (2) one in *-i-;* (3) one in *-u-;* (4) one in *-a*>*ô;* (5) having a contracted imperfect in *-ê-, -eô-;* (6) having a compound imperfect in *-de*>*-te.* < or > is placed between two expressions, one of which is derived from the other, the angle pointing to the derived one; § denotes a section in the Grammar.

â, adv., aye, always, ever.
abbud, es, m., abbot.
abbudiss-e, an, f., abbess.
Abel, es, m., Abel.
âbeôdan (3), bid.
âbîtan (2), bite.
âbregdan (1), brandish.
âbûgan (3), bow.
ac, conj., but.
Acca, n, m., Acca.
âcennan (6), bear, produce.
âceorfan (1), carve, cut.
âcsian (6), ask.
âcpeđan (1), speak.
âcpelan (1), die.
âcýđan (6), show.
Adam, es, m., Adam.
âdiligian (6), destroy.
âdl, e, f., sickness.
âdræ̂fan (6), drive.
âdreôgan (3), support.
âdrîfan (2), drive.
âdýdan (6), kill.
âđ, es, m., oath.
âfandian (6), find.
âfæstnian (6), fasten.
âfêdan (6), feed.
âfellan (6, § 209), fell.
âflýman (6), drive.
âfyrran (6), remove.
âgalan (4), sing.
âgan (§ 212), own, have; *âgan ût*, to make out.
âgeldan (1), pay.
âgen, adj., own.
âgifan (1, § 199), give.
âhebban (4), elevate.
âhsian (6), ask.
âhte<âgan.
âhýdan (6), hide.
âhyrdan (6), harden.
âîdlian (6), profane.
ald, adj., old.
aldor, es, n., life.
âlecgan (6), lay, put.
âleôgan (3), belie.
Aler, es, m., Aller.
âlicgan (1), fail.
Alleluia, n, m., Hallelujah.
alpalda, adj., almighty.
alpealda, n, m., almighty.
âlýfan (6), permit.
âlýsan (6), ransom.
âmæ̂nsumian (6), excommunicate.
âmyrran (6), obstruct.
an, prep., on.
ân, num., art., one, an, a, alone.
ancor, es, m., anchor.
and, conj., and.
anda, n, m., rage, spite.
andettan (6), confess.
andgit, es, n., understanding.
andrysno (§ 88, g.), f., ceremony.
andsparian (6), answer.
andspar-u, -e, f., answer.
andsperian (6), answer.
andpeard, adj., present.
andpeardnes, se, f., presence.
andplita, n, m., countenance.
andpyrdan (6), answer.
ânfeald, adj., simple.
anfôn (5, § 224), comprehend.
angel, es, m., hook.
Angelcyn, nes, n., race of Angles.
Angelþeôd, e, f., nation of Angles.
Angle, plur. m. (§ 86), Angles.
ângyld, es, n., restitution.
ânhydig, adj., constant.
Anlâf, es, m., Anlaf.
ânlîc, adj., peerless.
ânlîpig, adj., individual.
ânmôdlîce, adv., with one accord.
ânræ̂d, adj., constant.
ansyn, e, f., face.
ântîd, e, f., same time.
ânungâ, adv., wholly.
anpeald, es, m., power.
apostol, es, m., apostle.
apostolîc, adj., apostolic.
âr, e, f., honor, favor.
âr, e, f., oar.
âræ̂ran (6), rear.
arcebisceop, es, m., archbishop.
ârfæstnes, se, f., piety.
ârian (6), honor.
ârîsan (2), arise.
Armorica, n, m.
ârsmiđ, es, m., coppersmith.
ârstæf, es, m., blessing.
ârpurđe, adj., venerable.
ârpurđlîc, adj., venerable.
âscâ<æsc.
âsceran (1), shear.
âsendan (6), send.
âsettan (6), fasten up, throw down.
âsingan (1), sing.
âsleân (4, § 207), strike.
âsmeâgan (6), contrive.
âspendan, (6), expend.
âstellan (6), establish.
âstîgan (2), go up, go upon.
âstreccan (6), stretch.
âspâmian (6), smoulder.
âteôn (3), draw away.
âter-tân, es, m., poison twig.
atol, adj., direful.
âþreôtan (3), become irksome.
âþýstrian (*ý*>*î*), (6), be darkened.
Augustîn-us, es (§ 101), Augustine.
âuht, es, n., aught.
âpacan (4), spring.
âpeccan (6), awake.
âpeorpan (1), throw.
âpêste, adj., deserted.
âpiht, es, n., aught.
âprîtan (2), write.
âpyrdan (6), injure.
âxian (6), ask.

æcer, es, m., acre.
ædre, adv., quickly.
Ædelbald, es, m.
Ædelberht (*er=ir=ri*), *es*, m.
ædelboren, adj., noble born.
ædele, adj., noble.
ædeling, es, m., noble, prince.
Ædelingâ ige, Athelney.
Ædelfrid, es, m.
Ædelheard, es, m.
ædellîce, adv., nobly.
Ædelrêd, es, m.
Ædelrêding, es, m., son of Æthelred.
Ædelstân, es, m.
Ædelpulf, es, m.
Ædelpulfing, es, m., son of Æthelwulf.
Æderêd, es, m.
Ædulfing=Ædelpulfing.
æ̂fæst, adj., orthodox.
æ̂fæstnes, se, f., religion.
æ̂fen, nes, n., evening.
æ̂fen-leôđ, es, n., evening song.
æ̂fen-ræst, e, f., evening rest.
æ̂fen-tîd, e, f., eventide.
æ̂fest=æ̂fæst.
æfnan (6), accomplish.
æ̂fre, adv., ever, always.
æfter, prep., after.
æftera, adj., second, next.
æfterfyligan (6), follow.
æg, es, plur. *-eru*, n., egg.
æ̂gđer ... and, æ̂gđer ge ... ge, both ... and.
æ̂gđer, pron., either, each.
æ̂ghpæ̂đer, pron., either, each.
æ̂ghpæ̂r, adv., every where.
æ̂ghpelc (*e=i=y*), pron., every.
æ̂ghpider, adv., in every direction.
æ̂gpeard, e, f., wardenship of the sea.

æht, e, f., possession, power.
æht-e, an, f.=*æht.*
æl, es, m., eel.
ælc, pron., each, all.
ælcôr, adv., otherwise.
ælde (§ 86), plur. m., men.
ælepûta, n, m., eel pout.
Ælfrêd, es, m.
ælfremede, adj., foreign.
Ælfþryd, e, f., Ælfthryth.
Ælfpeard, es, m., Ælfweard.
Ælle, es, m.
ælmihtig, adj., all mighty.
ælpig=ânlipig.
æmtig, adj., empty.
ænge, adj., narrow.
ænig, pron., any.
ænlîc, adj., peerless.
ænlîce, adv., elegantly.
ænne<ân.
ær, prep. adv., before, early.
ærdæg, es, m., dawn.
æren, adj., brazen.
ærend-raca, n, m., messenger.
ærest, adj., adv., first, erst.
ærmergen (e=o), es, m., dawn.
ærra, adj. comp., former.
ærþon, conj., before.
æsc, es, m., ash, spear, ship.
Æsc, es, m.
Æscpine, s, m., Æscwine.
æt, prep., at, to.
æt, es, e, m. and f., food, eating.
æt, æton<etan.
ætberan (1), bear to.
ætberstan (1), escape.
æteôpan (6), show.
ætforan, prep., before.
ætgædere, adv., together.
ætgeofa, n, m., food giver.
Ætla, n, m., Attila.
ætsomne, adv., together.
ætpesan (1), assist.
ætpindan (1), fly out.
ætŷpan=æteôpan.
æpelm, es, m., fountain.
æpfæst, adj.=*æfæst.*
æx, e, f., ax.

bâd<bîdan.
balapum<bealu.
bald, adj., stout.
bâm<begen.
bân, es, n., bone.
bana, n, m., murderer.
bâr, es, m., boar.
barn<beornan.
bât, es, m., boat.
bæcere, s, m., baker.
bæd<biddan.
bædan (6), demand.
bæd, es, n., bath.
bælc, es, m., canopy.
bæl-egsa, n, m., prodigy of fire.
bæm<begen.
bær<beran.
bærnan (6), burn.
bærnet, es, n., burning.
be, prep., by.
Beadohild, e, f.
beado-leôma, n, m., slaughter-flame, sword.
beadu-lâc, es, n., slaughter-play, battle.
beág, beâh, es, m., ring, bracelet, diadem.
beâg-hroden, adj., adorned with a diadem.
bealcettan (6), utter.
beal-u, -apes, n., evil.
beâm, -es, m., beam, pillar.
beân, e, f., bean.
beard, es, m., beard.
bearm, es, m., bosom, lap.
bearn, es, n., child, son.
be-arn<be-irnan.
beâtan (5), beat.
beæftan, prep., behind.
bebeôdan (3), order.
bebod, es, n., command.
bebûgan (3), circle, extend.
bebyrgan (6), bury.
bêc<bôc.
beceorian (6), murmur at.
becuman (1), come.
Bêda, n, m.
bed, des, n., bed.
bedrîfan (2), drive.
be-eôde<begân.
befeallan (5), fall.
be-fôn, -fêng, -fangen (5), hold.
beforan, prep., before.
befrinan (1), ask.
befyllan (6), fell, throw down.
be-gân, -eôde, -gân (5), exercise.
begangan (5), practise.
begeondan, prep., beyond.
begeôtan (3), pour over.
begen, bâ, bu (§ 141), both.
beginnan (i=y), (1), begin.
begitan (1), get.
begrinian (6), snare.
begyrdan (6), gird.
behât, es, n., promise.
behealdan (5), hold, behold.
behêfe, adj., becoming.
behôfian (6), need.
be-irnan (1), occur.
belîfan (2), leave.
belimpan (1), pertain, belong, conduce.
bell-e, an, f., bell.
bên, e, f., prayers.
beniman (1), deprive.
beôd, es, m., table.
beôn (§ 213), be.
beôdan (3), offer, bode.
beorg, es, m., mountain.
beorht, adj., bright.
beorhte, adv., brightly.
Beorhtrîc, es, m.
beorn, es, m., hero.
beornan (1), burn.
Beornpulf, es, m., Beornwulf.
beôr-þegu, e, f., beer-drinking, convivial.
Beôpulf, es, m., Beowulf.
beran (1), bear.
berîdan (2), beset.
besciran (2), shear.
besencan (6), sink.
beseôn (1, § 197), look.
bestelan (1), steal.
bespîcan (2), trick, catch.
bespingan (1), whip.
bet, adv., better.
betacan (a>æ) (4), take.
betra, betst (§ 129), adj., better, best.
betpeoh, prep., among.
betpeônan, adverb, between times.
betpeônum, prep., among.
betpux, prep., among.
betŷnan (6), close.
beþurfan (1, § 212), need.
bepeotian (6), care for.
bepindan (1), grasp.
bî, prep., by.
bîdan (2), bide.
biddan (1), ask.
bedroren<bedreôsan (3), bereft.
bifian (6), tremble.
big=bî.
bîgang (a>o), es, m., course, worship.
bîgengere, es, m., cultivator.
bîgleofa, n, m., food.
bihreôsan (3), ruin.
bil, les, n., bil, sword.
bilepit, adj., gentle.
bilepitnes, se, f., gentleness.
bindan (1), bind.
binnan, prep., within.
biô=beô, biôd=beôd.
birhtu, e, f., brightness.
bisceop, es, m., bishop.
bisceopdôm, es, m., bishopric.
bisceopstôl, es, m., bishop's seat.
bisceopsunu, a, m., bishop's son.
bismor, es, n., contempt.
bismerpord, es, n., abusive word.
bistandan (4), stand by.
bispel, les, n., fable.
bîtan (2), bite.
biter, adj., bitter.
bipaune<bipâpan (5), blow.
blâpan (5), blow.
blæc, adj., black.
blendian (6), blind.
blîcan (2), shine.
blîde, adj., blithe.
blîd-heort, adj., blithe-hearted.
blîd-môd, adj., blithe-minded.
blis, se, f., bliss.
blissigan (6), rejoice.
blôd, es, n., blood.
blonden-feax, es, n., gray head.
blôstma, n, m., flower.
bôc, bêc, f., book.
bôcere, s, m., book-man, scholar.
Bôclæden, adj., Roman.
bôclîc, adj., scholarly.
bodian (6), preach.
bodung, e, f., preaching.
bôg, es, m., leg.
bolca, n, m., gangway.
bold-agend, adj., householder.
bolster, es, m., bolster.
bord, es, n., shield.
bord-hreôda, n, m., shield.
borg-sorg, e, f., borrow-sorrow.
bôsm, es, m., bosom.
bôt, e, f., expiation.
botm, es, m., bottom.
brâd, adj., broad.
brædan (6), spread.
brædan (6), roast.
breahtm, es, m., noise.
brecan (1), break.
bredan (1), braid.
brengan, brohte (6), bring.
breôst, es, n., breast.
brid, des, m., young bird.
bridel-þpang, es, m., bridle-thong.

brim, es, n., tide, sea.
brim-clif, es, n., sea-cliff.
brod, es, n., broth.
brôdor, brêder (§ 87), brother.
brôga, n, m., terror.
bront, adj., high.
brûcan (3), use, feel, have.
brûn, adj., brown.
Brutus (§ 101), m.
brycgian (6), bridge.
brŷd, e, f., bride.
bryhtm, es, m., glance.
Brytene, f., Britannia.
Brytenland, es, n., Britain.
Brytenpealda, n, m., sovereign of Britain.
brytta, n, m., distributor.
Bryttâs, plur. m., Britons.
Bryttisc, adj., British.
Brytpealâs, plur. n., British.
bu<begen.
budon<beôdan.
bufon, adv., above.
bûan (3), inhabit.
bûgan (3), turn.
bûgian (6), inhabit.
bun-e, -a, f., goblet.
bûr, es, n., chamber, bower.
burg, burh, e, f., city.
burgpare, plur. m., citizens.
burh-hlid, es, n., slope from a citadel.
bûtan (*on*), prep., without.
bûtan (*on*), conj., unless.
butere, an, f., butter.
butergeþpeor, es, n., butter-churning.
buteric, es, m., bottle.
bycgan (6), buy.
bydel, es, m., preacher.
byligu, plur. f., bellows.
bŷm-e, -an, f., trumpet.
byrgan (6), taste.
byrgan (6), bury.
byrgels, es, m., sepulcher.
byrig<burg.
Byrin-us, es, m.
byrnan (6), burn.
byrn-e, -e, f., coat of mail.
byrn-piga, n, m., mailed warrior.
bysen, e, f., example.
bysgian (6), occupy, busy.

Cain, es, m.
calend, es, m., month.
can<cunnan.
Cantpare, plur. m. (§ 86), people of Kent.
Cantparebyrig, e, f., Canterbury.
capitol-mæss-e, an, f., first mass.
carcern, es, n., prison.
Carl, es, m., Charles.
carleâs, adj., careless.
Caron, es, m., Charon.
câsere, s, m., cæsar, emperor.
Caton, es, m., Cato.
Cædmon, es, m.
ceâc, es, m., cup.
Ceadda, n, m.; *Ceadding, es,* m., son of Ceadda.
Ceadpalla, n, m.
cealdian (6), grow cold.
ceâp, es, m., price, goods.
ceâp-eâdig, adj., rich.

ceâs<ceôsan.
ceaster, e, f., city.
ceaster-gepar-e, an, f., citizen.
ceasterpare, plur. m. (§ 86), citizen.
Ceâplin, es, m. *Ceâplining, es,* m., son of Ceawlin.
Cêfi, ind. m.
cempa, n, m., soldier.
Cênbryht, es, m.; *Cênbryhting, es,* m., son of Cenbryht.
cêne, adj., bold.
Cênferd, es, m.; *Cênferding, es,* m., son of Cenferth.
Cênfûs, es, m.; *Cênfûsing,* son of Cenfus.
Cent, ind. f., Kent.
Centland, es, n., Kent.
Centpine, s, m.
Cênpealh, es, m.
ceôl, es, m., keel, ship.
Ceôlpulf, es, m.; *Ceôlpulfing, es,* m., son of Ceolwolf.
ceorl, es, m., man, husband, layman, farmer, freeman.
ceôsan (3), choose.
cêpeman, nes, m., merchant.
Cerber-us, -es (§ 101), m., Cerberus.
Cerdic, es, m.
cer, res, m., turn, time.
cêse, s, m., cheese.
cîd, es, m., growth, shoot.
cild, es, plur. *cild* and *cildru* (§ 82), n., child.
cildhâd, es, m., childhood.
cinbân, es, n., chin-bone.
cinberg, e, f., chin-cover.
Cippanhâm, mes, m.
ciric-e, an, f., church.
clâd, es, m., cloth, clothes.
Claudi-us, -es (§ 101), m., Claudius.
clǣne, adj., clean, pure.
cleôfa, n, m., cellar.
clom, mes, me, m., f., chain, clamp.
clûstor, es, n., cloister.
clypian (6), call, cry.
clyppan (6), embrace, accept.
cnapa, n, m., boy, youth.
cniht, es, m., boy, youth.
Cnût, es, m.
cnyl, les, m., bell-stroke.
cnyssan (6), knock, beat.
coc, es, m., cook.
côlian (6), cool.
Colman, nes, m.
Columba, n, m.
com, côm<cuman.
comêta, n, m., comet.
con=can<cunnan.
Corfes-geat, es, n., Corfgate.
corn, es, n., corn, grain.
crabba, n, m., crab.
cræft, es, m., craft, trade, skill.
cræftig, adj., crafty, skillful.
Crêcâs, plur. m., Greeks.
crêda, n, m., creed.
cringan (1), cringe, fall.
crismlŷsing, e, f., loosing of the fillet bound round the head at baptism, crism-loosing.
Crist, es, m., Christ.
Cristen, adj., Christian.
crystendôm, es, m., christendom.

cûd, adj., known.
Cûda, n, m.
cûthe<cunnan.
Cûdgils, es, m.; *Cûdgilsing, es,* m., son of Cuthgils.
Cûding, es, m., son of Cutha.
cûdlic, adj., certain.
cûdlice, adv., clearly, openly, courteously.
Cûdred, es, m.
culter, es, n., coulter.
cuman (1, § 200), come.
cumbol, es, n., signal.
cunnan, pres. *can,* imp. *cûde* (§ 212), know, am able.
cunnian (6), experience.
cpealm, es, m., death.
cpeccan (6), shake.
cpedan (1), say.
cpên, e, f., woman, wife, queen.
cpic, adj., alive.
cpide, s, m., sentence, saying.
cpiman>cuman (1), come.
cpyld-rôf, adj., ravenous.
cŷdde<cŷdde<cŷdan.
cŷd, de, f., home.
cŷdan (6), announce.
cŷle, s, m., cold.
cyme, s, m., coming.
cymlice, adv., comely.
cyn, nes, n., kin, kind.
cyne-bearn, es, n., prince.
cyne-bôt, e, f., king's blood-money.
cyne-cyn, es, n., royal race.
Cynegils, es, m.; *Cynegilsing, es,* m., son of Cynegils.
Cyneheard, es, m.
cyne-helm, es, m., crown.
cyne-rice, s, n., kingdom.
Cynepulf, es, m., Cynewolf.
cyning, es, m., king.
Cynric, es, m.; *Cynricing, es,* m., son of Cynric.
cŷpan (6), sell.
cŷpecniht, es, m., youth for sale.
cŷpman, nes, m., merchant.
cyric-e, -an and *-ean,* church.
cyrlisc, adj., *cyrlisc man=ceorl.*
cyrran (6), turn.
cŷs-gerun, es, n., curd.
cyst, es, m., choice, best.

dafenian (6), become.
dǣd, e, f., deed.
dæg, es, m., day.
dægderlic, adj., present.
dæghpamlice, adv., daily.
dægrêd, es, n., dawn.
dægrêdlic, adj., matin.
dægsceald, es, m., day-shield.
dǣl, es, m., share, part.
dǣlan (6), deal, divide.
deâd, adj., dead.
deâd, es, m., death.
dear<durran.
deâpig-federe, adj., dewy-feathered.
Dêda, n, m.
dêd<dôn.
dêgol, es, n., secret.
Dene, plur. m., Danes.
Denisc, adj., Danish.
deôfol, es, m., n., devil.
deôfolgild (*i=y*), *es,* n., idol, idolatry.

deôp, adj., deep.
deôpe, adv., deeply.
deôplîce, adv., deeply.
deôr, *es*, n., beast.
Deôr, *es*, m.
deorc, adj., dark.
deôre, adj., precious, dear.
deorfan (1), work.
Deorƿent-e, *-n*, f., Derwent.
deôrƿyrðe, adj., precious.
Dêre, plur. m., inhabitants of Deira. Latin *de ira* means *from wrath.*
dêst<*dôn.*
dîc, *es*, m., ditch, dike.
Dioclitian-us, *-es* (§ 101), m., Diocletian.
dôgor, *es*, m. n., day.
dôgor-rîm, *es*, n., number of days.
dôhtor (§ 87, 100), f., daughter.
dôm, *es*, m., doom, judgment, law, choice, power, honor.
domne, *s*, m., Lord.
dôn, *dêst*, *dêð*, imp. *dyde*, *dide*, pp. *dôn* (§ 213), do, make.
Dorceceaster, *e*, f., Dorchester.
Dorsǣte, plur. m., people of Dorsetshire.
dorst<*durran.*
draca, *n*, m., dragon.
dreâm, *es*, m., harmony, joy.
dreccan (6), afflict.
drenc, *es*, m., drink.
dreôgan (3), suffer, practise.
dreôrig-hleor, adj., dreary-faced.
drîfan (2), drive.
drihten (*y*>*i*), *es*, m., Lord.
driht-guma, *n*, m., nobleman.
driht-neâs, plur. m., slain in battle.
drincan (1), drink.
drohtnian (6), live.
dryhten (*y*>*i*), *es*, m., Lord.
dryht-guma, *n*, m., nobleman.
duguð, *e*, f., mankind, man, company.
durran, *dear*, imp. *dorste* (§ 212), dare.
duru, *e*, f., door.
dynt, *es*, m., blow, dint.
dŷre, adj., dear.
dyrne, adj., secret.
dyrstig, adj., daring.
dyrstignes, *se*, f., boldness.
dysig, adj., foolish.
dysignes, *se*, f., foolishness.

ð, see *þ*.

eâ, interj. with *lâ*, ah! oh!
eâ, f. (§ 100), river.
eâc, adv. conj., also.
eâcen, adj., august.
Eâdberh, *es*, m.
Eâdgâr, *es*, m., Edgar.
eâdig, adj., blessed.
eâdiglîc, adj., blessed.
eâdignes, *se*, blessedness.
eâdmôdlîce, adv., humbly.
Eâdmund, *es*, m., Edmund.
Eâdrêd, *es*, m.
Eâdrîc, *es*, m.
Eâdƿîg, *es*, m.
Eâdƿine, *s*, m., Edwin.
eâðe, adj., easy.
eâðmêdu, plur. n., humility.
eâg-e, *-an*, n., eye.
eahta, num., eight.
eahtoða, num., eighth.
eal, pron., all.
eâlâ, interj., ah! oh!
eâland, *es*, n., island.
eald, adj., old.
eald-gesegen, *e*, f., old saying.
eald-gestreôn, *es*, n., old treasure.
ealdian (6), grow old.
ealdor-bisceop, *es*, m., chief priest.
ealdor-dôm, *es*, m., first rank.
ealdor-man, *nes*, m., nobleman, senator.
ealdorscipe, *s*, m., first rank.
eald-riht, *es*, n., old custom.
Eald Seaxe, plur. m., Old Saxons.
eald-spel, *les*, n., old discourse.
Ealhstân, *es*, m.
eallunge, adv., altogether.
ealsƿâ, adv., just as.
ealu, *þes*, n. (§ 81), ale.
eal-ƿihte, plur. f., all things.
eam=*eom*, am.
Earcenbriht, *es*, m.
eard, *es*, m., earth.
eard-geard, *es*, m., land.
eardian (6), dwell.
eâr-e, *-an*, n., ear.
earfôð, *es*, n., toil.
earfôðlîc, adj., toilsome.
earm, *es*, m., arm.
earm, adj., poor.
earmlîce, adv., wretchedly.
eâst, adv., east.
eâsta, *n*, m., east.
eâstan, adv., from the east.
Eâst-Angle (*-Engle*), plur. m., East-Angles.
Eâst-Dene, plur. m., East-Danes.
Eâstran, plur. f., Easter.
Eâst-Seaxe, plur. m., East-Saxons.
êce, adj., eternal.
êcean, *êcere*<*êce.*
ecg, *e*, f., edge.
Ecgbriht, *es*, m.; *Ecgbrihting*, *es*, m., son of Ecgbriht.
Ecgbyrht, *es*, m.=*Ecgbriht.*
Ecgþeôƿ, *es*, m.
edor, *es*, m., hedge, fence.
êð, adv., easier.
Eðandûn, *e*, f.
êðel, *es*, m., home, country.
êðelƿeard, *es*, m., landlord.
efne, adv., even so; interj., well.
êfstan, (6), hasten.
eft, adv., after, again.
ege, *s*, m., fear.
egsian (6), be fearful.
ehta, num., eight.
êhtan (6), pursue.
ele, *s*, m., oil.
Eleutheri-us, *es* (§ 101), m.
ellen, *es*, m. n., might, heroism.
Ellendûn, *e*, f.
ellenƿeorc, *es*, n., mighty work.
ellenƿôdnes, *se*, f., fervor.
elles, adv., otherwise.
ende, *s*, m., end.
ende-byrdnes, *se*, f., order.
ende-dæg, *es*, m., last day.
ende-leân, *es*, n., retribution.
ende-sǣta, *n*, m., shore-guard.
endleofan, num., eleven.
engel, *es*, m., angel.
Englâ-land, *es*, n., England.
Engle, plur. m., Angles.
Englisc, adj., English.
ent, *es*, m., giant.
eode, *eôde*<*gân*, go.
eodor, *es*, m., prince.
eodorcan (6), ruminate.
eofor-lîc, *es*, n., boar's figure.
Eôforƿîc, *es*, n., York.
Eôforƿîc-ceaster, *e*, f., York town.
eom (§ 213), am.
eorð-bûende, plur. m., dwellers on earth.
eorð-e, *-an*, f., earth.
eorð-mægen, *es*, n., might of earth.
eorð-tilð, *e*, f., agriculture.
eorð-ƿeal, *les*, m., earth wall.
eôred, *es*, n., troop.
eorl, *es*, m., nobleman, earl, man.
eorlîc, adj., manly.
eorlscipe, *s*, m., nobility, manliness.
Eormanrîc, *es*, m.
eornostlîce, adv., earnestly.
eoten, *es*, m., giant.
eotenisc, adj., made by giants.
eôƿ, *eôƿic*, pron. plur., you.
eôƿer, pron. poss., your.
ercehâd, *es*, m., archiepiscopacy.
erian (6), plough.
esne, *s*, m., servant, man.
etan (1), eat.
Euridic-e, *-an*, f., Eurydice.

fâcen, *es*, n., fraud, crime.
fage, *es*, n., plaice.
fâh, *fâg*, adj., blent, stained.
fâh, *fâg*, adj., hostile.
fâh-mon, *nes*, m., foeman.
famig-heals, adj., foamy-necked.
fand<*findan.*
fârâ<*fâh.*
faran (4), go.
Faraôn, *es*, m., Pharaoh.
farôð, *es*, m., stream, flood.
fæc, *es*, n., space, time.
fæder, *es* (irreg., §§ 87, 100), m., father.
fǣge, adj., damned, deathlike.
fægen, adj., glad.
fægenian (6), fawn.
fæger, adj., fair.
fǣhð, *e*, f., feud.
fær, *es*, n., ship.
fǣr-bryne, *s*, m., fearful blaze.
fǣr-gripe, *s*, m., sudden gripe.
fǣrlîce, adv., suddenly.
færnes, *se*, f., transit, travel.
fæst, adj., fast; firm.
fæstan (6), fast.
fæste, adv., fast, firmly.
fæsten, *es*, n., fasting.
fæsten, *es*, n., fastness.
fæsthafel, adj., tenacious.
fæsthydig, adj., constant.
fæstlic, adj., firm.

fæstlîce, adj., firmly.
fæstnung, *e*, f., stability.
fæstræ̂d, adj., constant.
fæt, *es*, n., vessel.
fætels, *es*, m., pouch.
feallan (5), fall.
feâ-sceaft, adj., deserted.
feax, *es*, n., hair.
Februari-us, *-es* (§ 101), m., February.
fêdan (6), feed.
fêde, *es*, n., power to walk.
fefer-âdl, *e*, f., fever.
fêhst<*fôn*.
fel, *les*, n., leather.
fela, ind., many, much.
fela-hrôr, adj., very strenuous.
fela-meahtig, adj., very mighty.
feld, *es*, m., field.
feld-hûs, *es*, n., tent.
felgan (1), enter.
Fêlix, *es*, m. (§ 101).
fen, *nes*, m., fen.
fêng<*fôn*.
feô, *feôh*, *feôs*, n., flock, wealth.
feohtan (1), fight.
feônd, *es*, m., enemy, fiend.
feônd-grâp, *e*, f., foe's gripe.
feônd-scipe, *s*, m., hostility.
feor, adj., far.
feor, adv., far.
feor-bûend, adj., far-dwelling.
feor-cund, adj., foreign.
feôrd-a, *-e*, *-a*, num., fourth.
feorh, *feores*, m. n., life.
feormian (6), entertain.
feorran, adv., from far.
feorrancund, adj., from far.
feor-weg, *es*, m., far away.
feôper, num., four.
feôpertig, num., forty.
feôpertŷne, num., fourteen.
fêran (6), go.
fêr-clam, *mes*, m., sudden peril.
ferd, *es*, m. n., mind.
ferhd, *es*, m. n., mind, life.
ferian (6), bear.
fers, *es*, n., verse.
fetel-hilt, *es*, n., belted hilt.
fetor, *e*, f., fetter.
fîf, num., five.
fîfel-cyn, *nes*, n., race of fifels, sea-monsters.
fîfta, num., fifth.
fîftêna, num., fifteen.
fîftig, num., fifty.
findan (1), find.
finger, *es*, m., finger.
firâs, plur. m., men.
fisc, *es*, m., fish.
fiscere, *s*, m., fisher.
fiscian (6), fish.
flâ, *n*, f., dart.
flâh, adj., hostile.
flân-hred, adj., equipped with darts.
flax-e, *-an*, f., flask.
flæ̂sc, *es*, n., flesh.
flæ̂sc-mete, *s*, plur. *-mettâs*, m., meat.
fleâh<*fleôgan* or *fleôn*.
fleôgan (3), fly.
fleôhan, *fleôn* (3), flee.
flet, *tes*, n., hall.
flîtan (2), strive, fight.
flôc, *es*, n., flounder.
flôd, *es*, m., flood.
flota, *n*, m., ship.
flôpan (5), flow.
fôdor, *es*, n., fodder.
folc, *es*, n., folk.
folc-cwên, *e*, f., people's queen.
folc-gefeoht, *es*, n., great battle.
folcisc, adj., common.
folc-leâsung, *e*, f., false report.
folc-scaru, *e*, f., shire.
folc-stede, *s*, m., public place.
fold-bûend, *e*, plur. m., inhabitants.
fold-e, *-an*, f., earth, land.
fold-pela, *n*, m., wealth.
folgian (6), follow.
fôn, *fêng* (6), catch, take.
for, prep., for, before.
foran, adv., aforetime.
for-bærnan (6), burn.
for-beôdan (3), forbid.
for-beran (1), bear, forbear.
for-brecan (1), break.
for-bŷgean (6), depreciate, neglect.
for-dôn (irreg., 6), undo, destroy.
ford, adv., forth, afterward; *brengan*, utter; *fêran*, die; *gân*, succeed; *teôn*, conduct.
ford-fôr, *e*, f., departure.
ford-heald, adj., stooping.
ford-sîd, *es*, m., death.
ford-peg, *es*, m., departure.
fore, adv., for him.
fore, prep., before.
fore-bêcen, *es*, n., prodigy.
fore-gangan (5), precede.
fore-genga, *n*, m., forerunner.
fore-mæ̂re, adj., renowned.
fore-sprecen, adj., aforesaid.
forepeard, adj., early.
for-gifan (1), give, forgive.
for-gildan (*i*>, *ie*, *y*, *e*), give, pay.
for-gyrdan (6), gird.
for-gytol, adj., forgetful.
for-hæfednes, *se*, f., abstinence.
for-helan (1), conceal.
for-hergian (6), harry.
for-hogian (6), despise.
for-hôhnes, *se*, f., contempt.
forhtful, adj., timid.
for-hpon, adv., why.
for-læ̂tan (5), leave, neglect, permit, lose.
for-leôsan (3), destroy, lose.
for-lidenes, *se*, f., wreck.
forma, num., first.
for-niman (1), take away.
for-scrîfan (2), proscribe, doom.
for-seôn (1), despise.
for-sleân (1), break.
for-spannan (5), seduce.
forst, *es*, m., frost.
for-standan (4), withstand.
for-spelgan (1), devour.
for-pam, *-pan*, *-pæm*, *-pon*, *-pŷ*, because, for, therefore, wherefore.
for-pel, adv., very.
for-purdan (1), perish.
for-precan (1), drive.
for-pyrcan (6), obstruct.
fôt, *es* (§ 84), m., foot.
fracod, adj., mean.
fram, prep., from.
Francan, plur. m. (§ 101), Franks.
Franc-land, *es*, n., France.
frætpan (6), adorn.
frætpe, plur. f., ornaments.
freâ, *n*, m., lord.
freca, *n*, m., wolf (hero).
frêcne, adv., boldly.
frecnes, *se*, f., danger.
fremde, adj., foreign, strange.
fremian (6), aid, profit, exercise, perpetrate.
fremman (6)=*fremian*.
fremsumnes, *se*, f., kindness.
Frenciscan, plur. m., French.
freô, adj., free.
freôlîc, adj., free, noble.
freôlîce, adv., freely, nobly.
freôn (6), love.
freônd, *es*, m., friend.
freôndscipe, *s*, m., friendship.
freôsan (3), freeze.
frêum<*freô*.
frid, *es*, m. n., peace, protection.
frigman, *nes*, m., freeman.
Frîg, *e*, f., goddess of love.
frignan (1), ask.
frôd, adj., wise.
frôfor, *e*, f., solace, aid.
from=*fram*, prep.
fruma, *n*, m., beginning, maker, king.
frum-cyn, *es*, n., stock.
frum-sceaft, *e*, f., creation, birth.
frymd, *es*, *e*, m. f., beginning.
frŷnd=*freônd*.
frysan, *Frysan*, adj., Frisian(?).
Frysisc, adj., Friesic.
fugol, *es*, m., bird.
fugelere, *s*, m., fowler.
fuhton<*feôhtan*.
ful, *les*, n., goblet.
ful, adj., full.
ful-fremman (6), perform.
fulgon<*felgan*.
fullîce, adv., fully.
fulluht=*fulpiht*.
ful-neâh, adv., nearly, almost.
fultum, *es*, m., help.
fultumian (6), help.
fulpiht, *es*, m., baptism.
funden<*findan*.
furdon, adv., just, moreover.
furdor (*o*>*u*), adv., further.
furdra, adj., greater.
fûs, adj., prompt, ready.
fûslîc, adj., ready
fyl, *les*, m., slaughter.
fyligean, *fyligan* (6), follow.
fyllan (6), fill.
fylstan (6), aid.
fŷr, *es*, n., fire.
fyr, adv., far.
fyrd, *e*, f., army, expedition.
fyrd-getrum, *es*, n., battle array.
fyrd-hrægl, *es*, n., coat of mail.
fyrdian (6), make a campaign.
fyrd-searu, *pes*, n., equipment.
fyren, *e*, f., crime.
fŷren, adj., fiery.
fŷr-heard, adj., hardened with fire.
fyrhtan (6), conjure.

fyrhto, e, f., fright.
fyrlen, adj., remote.
fŷr-leoht, es, n., firelight.
fyrmest, adj., first.
fyrn-gepin, nes, n., old fight.
fŷr-spearca, n, m., spark.
fyrst, es, m., time, due time.
fyrpit (i, e, y), es, n., curiosity.
fyrpet-georn, adj., inquisitive.
fŷst, e, f., fist.

gaderian (6), gather.
gaderung, e, f., gathering.
gadîsen, es, n., gadiron.
gadu, e, f., gad, goad.
gafol, es, n., tribute, rent.
gafol-gelda, n, m., rent-payer.
Gai-us, -es, m., Caius.
galdor, es, n., incantation.
Galpalâs, plur. m., people of Gaul; France, § 101.
gamenian (6), game, pun.
gamol, adj., old.
gân (§ 208), imp. *eôde,* p. p. *gegân,* go.
gangan (5), go.
gang-dæg, es, m., Rogation day. Three days before Ascension were so called from processions.
gâr, es, m., dart, spear.
Gâr-Dene, plur. m., Danes of the Spear.
gâr-secg, es, m., ocean.
gâst (â>ǽ), es, m., ghost, spirit.
gærs, es, n., grass.
gæst, es, m., guest.
gæstlic, adj., hospitable.
ge, conj., and; both . . and.
gê, see *þû,* ye.
gea, particle, yea.
geaf<gifan.
ge-âhnian (6), appropriate.
ge-âhsian (6), inquire out.
geald<gildan.
gealdor-cræft, es, m., incantation.
ge-andettan (6), confess.
ge-andpyrdan (6), answer.
geâp, adj., vast.
geâr, es, n., year.
geara, adv., carefully.
gearcian (6), prepare.
geard, es, m., yard, home.
gearu (o), pes, adj., ready.
gearolîce, adv., clearly.
gearpian (6), prepare.
ge-ârpurdian (6), respect.
ge-âscian (6)=*ge-âhsian.*
geat, es, n., gate.
Geât, es, m.
Geâtâs, plur. m., Goths.
geatolic, adj., ornate.
geat-peard, es, m., gate-keeper.
ge-ærnan (6), run to, reach.
ge-bannan (5), order.
ge-bǽdan (6), attain.
ge-bǽru, e, f., action, means.
ge-bed, es, n., prayer.
ge-beôdan (3), bid.
ge-beorhlic, adj., safe.
ge-beôrscipe, s, m., beer-drinking.
ge-bêtan (6), pay.
ge-bicgan (i<y) (6), buy.
ge-bîdan (2), bide.
ge-biddan (1), pray.
ge-bîgan (î<ŷ) (6), convert.
ge-bindan (1), bind.
ge-bisnung, e, f., example.
ge-blôdgian (6), bloody.
ge-bôcian (6), enroll, give.
ge-bohte<ge-bycgan.
ge-bregdan (1), brandish.
ge-brengan (6), bring.
ge-bringan (1), bring.
ge-brôdor, irreg., § 87, brothers.
ge-brosnian (6), break.
ge-bûan (6), frequent.
ge-bûr, es, n., cottage.
ge-byre, s, m., occasion.
ge-bycgan (6), buy.
ge-cêlnes, se, f., refreshment.
ge-ceôsan, -ceâs, -curon, -coren (3), choose.
ge-cîdan (2), quarrel.
ge-cîgan (6), call.
ge-cneordlǽcan (6), study.
ge-cringan (1), fall.
ge-cpedan (1), say.
ge-cpylman (6), kill.
ge-cŷdan (6), proclaim, make known.
ge-cŷgan (6), call.
ge-cynd, es, n., kind, nature.
ge-cyrran (6), turn.
ge-cyrrednys, se, f., conversion.
ge-dafenian (6), become, fit.
ge-dǽlan (6), part.
ge-dêfe, adj., fit.
ge-dêman (6), judge, arrange.
ge-deorc, es, n., work.
ge-deorfan (1), work.
ge-dôn (6), do.
ge-dreccan (6) afflict.
ge-driht, e, f., throng.
ge-drŷme, adj., joyous.
ge-dpimor, es, n., conjuration.
ge-dyrnan (6), conceal.
ge-earnian (6), earn, merit.
ge-efenlǽcan (6), imitate.
ge-endian (6), end.
ge-endung, e, f., death.
ge-eôde<ge-gân.
ge-faran (4), depart, die.
ge-fægen, adj., glad.
ge-fæstnian (6), fasten.
ge-feohan, -feôn (1), rejoice.
ge-feoht, es, n., fight.
ge-feohtan (1), fight.
ge-feônde<ge-feohan.
ge-fêra, n, m., companion.
ge-fêran (6), go, reach, become.
ge-fêrscipe, s, m., society.
ge-fexôd, adj., provided with head of hair.
ge-flît, es, n., contention.
ge-flîtfullic, adj., contentious.
ge-flŷman (6), rout.
ge-fôn, -fêng, -fangen (5), catch, take.
ge-frætepian (6), adorn.
ge-frætpian (6), adorn.
ge-fremian (6), make, do.
ge-fremman (6), make, do.
ge-freôn (6), free.
ge-frignan (1), ask, learn.
ge-frinan (1), ask, hear of.
ge-fullian (6), baptize.
ge-fultumian (6), help.
ge-fylcan (6), collect.
ge-fyllan (6), fill, fulfill.
ge-fyrn, adv., formerly.
ge-fŷsan (6), hasten.
ge-gaderung, e, f., gathering.
ge-gân (see *gân*), go, travel, attain.
ge-gearpian (6), prepare.
ge-glengan, -glengde, -glencde (6), adorn.
gegnum, adv., in the way.
ge-grêtan (6), greet.
ge-grîpan (2), gripe.
ge-gyrpan (6), prepare.
ge-hâlgian (6), hallow.
ge-hâtan (5), name, promise.
gehât-land, es, n., promised land.
ge-hæftan (6), catch, bind.
ge-hǽgan (6), afflict.
ge-hǽlan (6), heal, save.
ge-hæp, adj., suitable.
ge-healdan (5), hold, keep, control.
ge-hêran (6), hear.
ge-herian (6), praise, laud.
ge-hêrnes, se, f., hearing.
ge-hleôtan (3), obtain.
ge-hnîgan (2), be humbled.
ge-hreôdan (3), load, adorn.
ge-hpâ, pron., each, whoever.
ge-hpæder, pron., either.
ge-hpǽr, every where.
ge-hpelc (e, i, y), pron., each.
ge-hpyrfan (6), convert.
ge-hŷdan (6), hide, bury.
ge-hŷran (6), hear.
ge-ladian (6), invite.
ge-ladung, e, f., church.
ge-læccan (6), catch.
ge-lǽdan (6), lead, bring.
ge-lǽran (6), teach.
ge-lǽred, adj., learned.
ge-lǽstan (6), follow, stand by.
ge-lǽte, an>on, f., meeting.
ge-leâfa, n, m., belief.
ge-leafful, adj., faithful.
ge-lênan (6), endow.
ge-leornian (6), learn.
ge-lîc, adj., like.
ge-lîca, n, m., like.
ge-lîce, adv., like.
ge-lîcian (6), please.
ge-lîhtan (6), approach.
ge-limpan (1), happen.
ge-limplic, adj., convenient.
ge-lomp=gelamp<gelimpan.
gelustfullian (6), delight.
ge-lustfullice, adv., earnestly.
ge-lŷfan (6), believe, trust.
ge-lŷfed, adj., infirm.
ge-man<gemunan.
ge-mǽran (6), celebrate.
ge-mǽre, s, n., boundary.
ge-mearcian (6), mark, plan.
ge-mêde, s, n., consent.
ge-met, es, n., manner.
ge-mêtan (6), meet.
ge-metlîce, adv., moderately.
gemon<gemunan.
ge-mong, -mang, es, n., crowd; *on gemong* (§ 341), amongst.
ge-munan (irreg., § 212), pres. *-man, -mon, -munon,* imp. *-munde,* remember.
ge-mund-byrdan (6), protect.
ge-mynd, e, es, f. n., memory.
ge-myndig, adj., mindful.
ge-myngian (6), remember.
ge-myntan (6), intend.
ge-nam<geniman.

ge-næ̂gan (6), supply.
ge-næglan (6), nail.
ge-neâdian (6), compel.
ge-neahhe, adv., enough.
ge-nemnan (6), name.
ge-nerian (6), save.
Genesis (§ 101), Genesis.
genge, adj., progressive.
ge-niman (1), take.
ge-nipian (6), renew.
ge-nŷdan (6), press; *nearu-ned*, captivity.
geô, adv., of yore.
geocian (6), yoke.
geofu=gifu.
geôgod, *e*, f., youth.
Geol, *es*, n., Yule, Christmas.
geômor, adj., sad.
geond, prep., through, beyond.
geond-styrian (6), move throughout.
geond-þencan (6), contemplate.
geong, adj., young.
geonglîc, adj., youthful.
ge-openian (6), open.
georne, adv., carefully, cheerfully.
geornfulnes, *se*, f., desire.
geornlîce, adv., gladly, diligently.
geôtan (5), pour.
ge-râd, adj., artful, skillful.
ge-ræ̂can (6), reach.
ge-ræ̂dan (6), read.
ge-ræ̂de, *s*, n., trappings.
geræ̂f, *es*, n., fate.
ge-rêfa, *n*, m., reeve, sheriff.
ge-reccan (6), compute.
ge-reord, *es*, n., speech.
ge-reordung, *e*, f., meal.
ge-resp, adj., established.
ge-rîdan (2), overrun.
ge-rîsan (2), suit, become.
ge-risenlîc, adj., fit.
ge-risenlîce, adv., fitly.
Germani-e, *-e*, f., Germany.
ge-samnian (6), assemble.
ge-samnung, *e*, f., assembly.
ge-sâpon<ge-seôn.
ge-sæ̂d<ge-secgan.
ge-sæ̂lig, adj., happy.
ge-sæ̂liglîce, adv., happily.
ge-scâd, *es*, n., difference.
ge-scæp-hpîl, *e*, f., the hour of fate.
ge-sceaft, *e*, f., creature, fate.
ge-sceap, *es*, n., creation, fate.
ge-sceppan (5), create, shape.
ge-sceran (1), shear, sever.
ge-scŷ, *es*, n., covering for the feet.
ge-scyldan (6), shield.
ge-scyrpan (6), clothe, deck.
ge-sêcan (6, § 209), seek.
ge-secgan (6, § 209), say, tell.
ge-sêdan (6), manifest.
ge-sellan (6, § 209), pay, give.
ge-sênian (6), cross, bless.
ge-seôn (1, § 199), *-seah*, *-sâpon*, *-sæ̂gon*, *sepen*, see.
ge-set, *es*, n., seat.
ge-settan (6, §§ 188, 190), set down, set up, people.
ge-sîd, *des*, m., comrade.
ge-sîd-mægen, *es*, n., band of comrades.
ge-sîgan (2), prostrate.
ge-sihd, *e*, f., sight.
ge-singan (1), sing.
ge-sittan (1), sit, settle on.
ge-sleân (1), slay, forge.
ge-spannan (5), fasten.
ge-spong, *es*, n., clasp.
ge-spræ̂c-e, *es*, n., conversation.
ge-stadelian (6), establish.
ge-stâh<gestîgan.
ge-standan, *-stôd* (4), attack.
ge-steal, *es*, n., space.
ge-stêd-hors, *es*, n., stallion, steed.
ge-stîgan (2), mount.
ge-stillan (6), cease.
ge-strangian (6), strengthen.
ge-streôn, *es*, n., wealth.
ge-stŷran (6), guide, stop.
ge-sund, adj., sound, safe.
ge-sundfullîce, adv., safely.
ge-sundrian (6), separate.
ge-speorc, *es*, n., gloom.
ge-speorcan (1), darken.
ge-spîcan (2), fail.
ge-sputelian (6), reveal.
ge-syllan (6), sell.
ge-synto, *o* (§ 88, *g*), success.
ge-tæ̂can (6), show.
ge-tæl, *es*, n., series.
ge-temian (6), tame.
ge-teôn, *-teâg*, *-teâh*, *-togen* (3), draw, educate.
ge-timber, *es*, plur. *getimbro*, building.
ge-trûpian (6), trust.
ge-trŷpe, adj., true.
ge-trymman (6), comfort.
ge-tpæ̂fan (6), distract.
ge-tŷan (6), instruct.
ge-tyhtan (6), teach.
ge-þafian (6), permit.
ge-þafung, *e*, f., assent.
ge-þah<ge-þicgan.
ge-þeaht, *e*, f. n., counsel.
ge-þeahta, *n*, m., counselor.
ge-þeahtend, *es*, m., counselor.
ge-þencan (6, § 209), think.
ge-þeôdan (6), join, devote.
ge-þeôde, *s*, n., speech.
ge-þeôdnes, *se*, f., desire.
ge-þeôfian (6), steal.
ge-þeôn (3), grow.
ge-þicgan, *-þeah*, *-þah* (1), receive.
ge-þincd, *es*, n., dignity.
ge-þingan (1), grow.
ge-þingian (6), compound.
ge-þoht, *es*, m. n., thought.
ge-þolian (6), suffer.
ge-þristian (6), dare.
ge-þuht<ge-þyncan, *pæs ge-þuht*, seemed.
ge-þpæ̂rian (6), accord.
ge-þpæ̂rnes, *se*, f., concord.
ge-þyld, *e*, f., patience.
ge-þyncan (6, § 211), seem.
gc-padan (4), go.
ge-pæ̂de, *s*, n., clothes, weeds.
ge-pæterian (6), water.
ge-peald, *e*, *es*, f. n., power.
ge-pealdan (5), be strong.
ge-peaxan (5), grow.
ge-pefan (1), weave.
ge-pemmedlîce, adv., corruptly.
ge-pendan (6), turn.
gê-peorc, *es*, n., work.
ge-peordan (1, § 204), become, be made, happen.
ge-peordian (6), adorn.
ge-peorpan (1), pass away.
ge-pîgan (*î<i*) (2), win.
ge-pilnian (6), wish.
ge-pinnan (1), fight.
ge-pin, *nes*, n., fighting.
ge-pislîce, adv., certainly.
ge-pita, *n*, m., witness.
ge-pîtan (2), depart, go.
ge-pitennes, *se*, f., departure.
ge-pitnes, *se*, f., knowledge.
ge-porden<ge-peordan, come to pass.
ge-porht<ge-pyrcan.
ge-prit, *es*, n., scripture, writing, letter.
ge-puna, *n*, m., custom.
ge-pundian (6), wound.
ge-punian (6), be wont.
ge-purdan=ge-peordan.
ge-pyldan (6), subdue.
ge-pyrcan(ean), *-porhte* (6, § 211), work, build, utter.
ge-pyrht, *es*, n., deed.
ge-pyrman (6), warm.
ge-ŷcan (6), add.
ge-yppan (6), disclose.
ge-yrnan (*y<i*) (1), run to.
gid, *des*, n., song.
giet, adv., yet.
gif, conj., if.
gifen, *geaf*, *gaf* (1), give.
gifen, *es*, n., sea, flood.
gifernes, *se*, f., greediness.
gifre, adj., greedy.
gif-u, *e*, f., gift.
gigant, *es*, m., giant.
gilp, *es*, m. n., glory.
gilp-hlæden, adj., vaunt-laden.
gim, *mes*, m., gem.
gîsel, *es*, m., hostage.
gist, *es*, m., guest.
git, adv., yet.
giu>geô, adv., of yore.
glædlîce, adv., gladly, cheerfully.
glæs, *es*, n., glass.
Glæstinga-burg, gen.dat.*-burge*, *-byrig*, f., Glastonbury.
gleâp, adj., clever.
Gleâpeceaster, *e*, f., Gloucester.
gleâplîc, adj., clever.
gleô-man, *nes*, m., glee-man.
gleôpian (6), jest, sing.
glîdan (2), glide.
gluto (Latin), glutton.
God, *es*, m., plur. *-as*, *-u*, m. n., God.
gôd, adj., good.
godcund, adj., divine, godly.
godcundlîce, adv., divinely.
godcundnes, *se*, f., godliness.
Godmundingahâm, *es*, m.
god-spel, *les*, n., Gospel, God's word.
god-spellian (6), preach.
gold, *es*, n., gold.
gold-fâh, adj., adorned with gold.
gold-finger, *es*, m., ring-finger.
gold-hroden, adj., adorned with gold.
gold-smid, *es*, m., goldsmith.
gomb-e, *-an*, f., tribute.
gongan=gangan, go, occur.

Gordian-us, es (§ 101), m.
Gotan, plur. m., Goths.
grafan (4), dig, grave.
gram, adj., fiendish.
grama, n, m., devil.
grǽdig, adj., greedy.
græf, es, n., grave.
græft, es, e, m. f. n., sculpture.
græs, es, n., grass.
greát, adj., great.
Grecisc, adj., Grecian.
Gregori-us, es, e, um, m., Gregory.
Grendel, es, m.
gréne, adj., green.
grétan (6), greet, approach.
grim, adj., grim.
grið, es, n., peace.
grím-helm, es, m., masked helm.
grimman (1), fret, hasten.
grin, e, f., net.
grindel, es, m., clog.
grôf<*grafan*.
grorn, es, n., grief.
grôpan (5), grow.
grund, es, m., ground.
grund-pyrgen, ne, f., wolf of the abyss.
gryre-síð, es, m., way of horror.
gûð, e, f., fight, war.
gûð-beorn, es, m., fighting man.
gûð-cræft, es, m., fighting force.
gûð-cyning, es, m., warrior-king.
gûð-fana, n, m., battle-flag.
gûð-fremmende, s, m., warriors.
gûð-gewǽde, s, n., war-weeds.
gûð-leóð, es, n., war-song.
gûð-môd, adj., battle-loving.
Guðrum, es, m.
gûð-searo, plur. n., equipment.
gûð-peard, es, m., general.
guma, n, m., man.
gyd=*gid*.
gyden, e, f., goddess.
gyddian (*y*<*i*) (6), say, sing.
gyfen<*gifan*.
gyld, es, n., tax.
gyldan (*y*<*i*) (1), pay.
gylt, es, m., guilt.
gyman (6), care, keep.
gym=*gim*.
gyrd, e, f., rod.
gyrla, n, m., clothes.
gystra, n, adj. *gystran*, adv., yesterday.
gyt=*git*, yet, again.

habban, hæfde (6), have.
hacod, es, m., pike.
hâdian (6), consecrate.
hâdre, adv., serenely.
hafela, n, m., head.
hafoc, es, m., hawk.
hâl, adj., whole, hale.
hâlettan (6), hail.
hâlgian (6), sanctify.
hâlig, adj., holy.
hâlignes, se, f., holiness.
hâl-pende, adj., sanctifying.
hâm, es, dat. *hâm, hâme*, m., home.
Hâmtûnscír, e, f., Hampshire.
hand, â, f., hand.
hâr, adj., hoar.
hara, n, m., hare.
Hardacnût, es, m.
Harold, es, m.
hâs, adj., hoarse.
hât, adj., hot.
hâtan, héht, hét, passive *hâtte* (5), order, call.
hât-pende, adj., torrid.
hæbbe<*habban*.
hǽð, e, f., heath.
hǽðen, adj. and subs., heathen.
hǽðen-scipe, s, m., heathenism.
hæft-méce, s, m., hafted sword.
hægel, es, m., hail.
hægl-far-u, -e, f., hail-shower.
hǽl, e, f., hail, safety.
hæled, es, m., man, hero.
Hǽlend, es, m., Saviour.
hælfter, e, f., halter.
hælu (*o*) (§ 88, *g*), hail, safety.
hærfest, es, m., harvest.
hæring, es, m., herring.
hǽs, e, f., hest, order.
hǽt-u, -e, -o, f., heat.
hé, pron., he.
heaðo-líðend, es, m., sailor.
heaðo-spât, es, m., battle-sweat, blood shed in battle.
heaðo-pǽd, e, f., battle dress.
heafod, es, m. n., head.
heafod-burh, e, f., capital.
heafod-man, nes, m., head-man.
heâh, heâ, héh (§ 118), adj., high.
heâh, adv., high.
heâh-cyning, es, m., high king.
heâh-deór, es, n, tall deer.
heâh-fæst, adj., changeless.
heal, le, f., hall.
heal-ærn, es, n. (§ 229), hall.
healdan (5), hold.
healf, adj., half.
healf, e, f., half, part, side.
Healfdene, s, m.
heal-reced, es, n., hall.
heals, es, m., neck.
heân, adj., humble, poor.
Heânríc, es, m., Henry.
heard, adj., hard.
heardlíce, adv., stoutly.
hearg (*h*), *e*, plur. *â, âs*, f. m., shrine, idol.
hearm, es, m., harm, distress.
hearp-e, -an, f., harp.
hearpere, s, m., harper.
hearpian (6), harp.
hearpung, e, f., harping.
hearra, n, m., Lord.
hebban, hôf, hafen (4), heave, move.
hédern, es, n., pantry.
hefigian (6), grieve, distress.
hefon=*heofon*.
hege, s, m., hedge, inclosure.
héhstan<*heâh*.
héht<*hâtan*.
hel, le, f., hell.
hel-dor, es, n., hell-gate.
helm, es, m., helmet, cover, protector.
Helmingâs, plur. m., descendants of Helm.
hel-paran, -pare, m. pl., dwellers in Hades.
hengen, ne, f., stocks.
Hengest, es, m.
heó<*hé*.
Heodeningâs, pl. m., descendants of Heoden.
heofon, es, m., heaven.
heofona, n, m., heaven.
heofon-beâcen, nes, n., sign from heaven.
heofon-candel, e, f., heafen-candle, fiery column.
heofon-col, les, n., coal of heaven.
heofon-líc, adj., heavenly.
heofon-ríce, s, n., heaven's kingdom.
heofon-torht, adj., heavenly bright.
heofon-peard, es, m., heaven's guardian.
heold<*healdan*.
heolster-sceadu (*o*), *e*, f., lurking-holed darkness.
heolstor, es, n., lurking-place.
heonan, adv., hence.
heord, e, f., keeping.
heorð-geneât, es, m., hearth-sharer.
heoro-grim, adj., fiercest (sword-grim).
heoro-pulf, es, m., warrior (sword-wolf).
Heorrenda, n, m.
heort (*heorot*), *es*, m., hart.
Heort (*Heorot*), *es*, m.
heort-e, an, f., heart.
hér, adv., here.
here, s, *heriges, herges* (§ 85), m., host.
here-cist, e, f., squadron.
here-fugol, es, m., army-bird.
here-gyld, es, n., army-tax.
herenes, se, f., praise.
here-reâf, es, n., spoil.
here-spéd, e, f., fortune of war.
here-toga, n, m., general, leader.
here-preât, es, m., squadron.
herges<*here*.
hergung, e, f., harrying.
herian (6), praise, laud.
herigendlíce, adv., so as to praise.
hét<*hâtan*.
hí, híe<*hé*.
híd, e, f., hide (of land).
hider, adv., hither.
híg<*hé*.
híg, interj., ha!
híg, es, n., hay.
hígdi-fæt, es, n., cunning bag.
hige, s, m., mind.
Higelâc, es, m.
hild, e, f., battle.
Hild, e, f.
hilde-bil, les, n., battle-axe.
hilde-deór, adj., fierce.
hilde-pǽpen, nes, n., weapon.
hilt, es, m. n., hilt.
hind, e, f., hind.
hinder, adv., back.
hió=*heó*.
hí-réd, es, m., family.
hip, es, n., shape, look.
híp-cûð, adj., well known.
hladan (4), imbibe.
hlâf, es, m., bread, loaf.
hlâf-æta, n, m., domestic.
hlâf-ord, es, m., lord.
hlæst, es, n., load.
hlǽp, es, m., tomb, cave.

hleahtor, es, m., laughter.
hleâpan (5), leap.
hleô, pes, m., cover, guardian.
hleôr-ber-e, -an, f., visor.
hlifian (6), rise.
hlîsa, n, m., fame.
hlûd, adj., loud.
hlutor, adj., loud, clear.
hlyn, nes, m., sound, music.
hlyt, es, m., lot.
hôciht, adj., hooked.
hof, es, n., house, court.
hogian (6), think.
hold, adj., kind, devoted.
holen, es, m., holly.
holm, es, m., billow, sea.
holm-clif, es, n., sea-cliff.
holmig, adj. *holmegum*, stormy.
homola, n, m., shaveling; i. e., fool, madman, or slave so punished for crime.
hond=hand.
hond-gemôt, es, n., battle.
Honori-us, -es, m. (§ 101).
horn, es, m., horn.
horn-geâp, adj., broad between the pinnacles.
hors, es, n., horse.
Horsa, n, m.
hraðe, adv., soon, quickly.
hran, es, m., whale.
hrædlice, adv., quickly.
hræðe=hraðe.
hræfen, es, m., raven.
hrægl, es, n., clothes.
hreâm, es, m., shouting.
hreâp, adj., raw.
hrefn=hræfen.
hrêmig, adj., exulting.
hreô, hreôh, adj., rough.
hreôpon<hrôpan.
hreôsan (3), rush.
hrîð, e, f., snow-squall.
hrîm, es, m., frost, rime.
hrînan (2), touch.
Hring-Dene, plur. m., Ring Danes.
hringed-stefna, n, m., the ring-prowed.
hring-mǣl, adj., ring-graced.
Hrôðgâr, es, m., Hrothgar.
hrôf, es, m., roof.
hrôf-sele, s, m., roofed hall.
hron-râd, e, f., whale-path, sea.
hrôpan (5), cry.
Hrunting, es, m.
hrus-e, -an, f., earth.
hrŷðig, adj., storm-beaten.
hrŷman (6), shout.
hrysian (6), clink.
hû, adv., how.
hûð, e, f., prey, spoil.
Humbr-e, -an, f., Humber.
Hunâs, plur. m., Huns.
hund, es, m., hound.
hund, es, n., hundred.
hund-nigon-tig, es, n. num. (§§ 139, 141), ninety.
hundred, es, n., hundred.
hund-tpelf-tig, es, n. num. (§§ 139, 141), twelve tens, 120.
hunig-spêt, adj., sweet as honey.
hunta, n, m., hunter.
huntian (6), hunt.
huntôð, es, m., hunting.
huntung, e, f., hunting.

hûs, es, n., house.
hûsel, es, n., housel, eucharist.
hpâ, pron. int., who.
hpanan, hpanon, adv., whence.
hpatung, e, f., divination.
hpæðer, pron., whether, which.
hpæðer, conj., whether.
hpæðere, adv. conj., yet.
hpæl, es, m., whale.
hpænne, adv. conj., when.
hpær, adv. conj., where.
hpæt, adv. interj., what, why.
hpæt-hpega, -hpegu, pron., somewhat.
hpætlîce, adv., promptly.
hpearfian (6), move.
hpelc=hpilc.
hpeôl, es, n., wheel.
hpeôp<hpôpan.
hpeorfan (1), wander.
hpîl, e, f., time, while.
hpilc, pron., of what kind, which, what, who, any one.
hpîlum, hpîlon, adv., sometimes, once.
hpistlung, e, f., whistling.
hpît, adj., white.
hpîtan (6), sharpen.
Hpîtern, es, n., Whitern.
hpon=hpam<hpâ, somewhat, a little; *nâ tô þæs hpon*, not to a little of that, not at all.
hpôn=hpon?
hponan=hpanan.
hpôpan (5), threaten.
hpurfe<hpeorfan.
hpŷ, adv., why.
hpylc=hpilc.
hvvyrfan=hpyrfan (6), tread the earth.
hŷ=heô<hê.
hycgan, hogôde (6, § 211), think, attend.
hŷd, e, f., hide.
hyð, e, f., port.
hyge, s, m., mind.
Hygelâc, es, m.
hyge-leâst, e, f., scurrility.
hyhtlîc, adj., delightful.
hŷnd, e, f., humiliation.
hŷran (6), hear.
hyrde, s, m., guard.
hŷrsumian (6), obey.

ic, pron. I.
îdel, adj., idle, vain, void, empty, deserted.
ides, e, f., woman, queen.
Ieopete, an, f., Judith.
ieted<etan, eat.
ig, e, f., island.
ig-land, es, n., island.
Iglea, indec., Iley.
Iî, indec., Iona.
ilca, m. *ilce*, f. n., pron., same.
in, prep., in, into, on.
inbry(r)dnes, se, f., inspiration, stimulation.
inca, n, m., complaint.
incund, adj., internal.
Ine, s, m.
infær, es, n., entrance.
in-gang, es, m., entrance.
innan, adv. prep., within, in.
inne, adv., within.
intinga, n, m., sake, cause.
intô, prep., into.

inpeard, adj., inward, inmost.
Iótan, plur. m., Jutes.
iôp=eôp, see *þû.*
îren, es, n., iron.
îren, adj., iron.
îren-bend, es, m., iron band.
irnan (1), run.
is, verb<*com.*
îsen, adj., iron.
îsene-smið, es, m., iron-smith.
îsig, adj., icy.
Israel, es, m., Israel.
itst<etan, eat.
Iuli-us, -es, -i (§ 101), m., Julius, July.
Ixion, es, m.

lâ, interj., lo! oh!
lâc, es, n., gift.
lâð, adj., baneful, hostile.
lâf, e, f., relic.
lag-u, -e, f., law.
lago-flôd, es, m., flood of waters.
lagu-cræftig, adj., knowing the sea.
lagu-strǣt, e, f., sea-road.
lâh<lîhan.
lampreda, n, m., lamprey.
land, es, n., land.
land-bûende, s, m., inhabitants.
land-fruma, n., m., prince.
land-gemyrcu, plur. n., landmarks, bounds.
land-man, nes, m., inhabitant.
land-scipe, s, m., landskip.
land-sittende, s, m., landholder.
lang, adj., long.
lange, adv., long.
lang-sum, adj., long-drawn.
lâr, e, f., lore, teaching, counsel, command.
lâreôp, es, m., teacher.
lâst, es, m., footprint, track.
Laurenti-us, -es (§ 101), m.
Lavitâ, plur. f., Lapithæ.
lǣdan (6), lead.
lǣfan (6), leave.
lǣgon<licgan.
lǣne, adj., transitory.
lǣran (6), teach.
læresta<læsesta<læs.
læs, adv., less; *þŷ læs*, lest.
læssa, adj., § 129, less.
læs-u, -e, f. leasow, pasture.
lǣtan, leôrt, lêt (5, § 208), let, order.
lǣped, adj., lay, lewd.
leâf, es, n., leaf.
leâf, e, f., leave, permission.
leâfnes-pord, es, n., leave.
leân, es, n., loan, pay.
leâs, adj., destitute, devoid.
leâs, adj., false, base.
leâsung, e, f., lying.
lecgan (6), lay.
Leden, adj., Latin.
leðer-hosa, n, leather stocking.
Legaceaster, e, f., Chester.
lencten, es, m., spring.
Lencten-fæsten, es, n., Lent.
lenge, adj., belonging.
lengest<lang.
Leo, n, nis (Latin), m., § 101.
leôd, e, f., people, men.

leôd, es, m., weregild, fine for killing a man.
leôd, es, m., prince.
leôd-gebyrgea, n, m., protector of the people.
leôd-mægen, es, n., host.
leôdon=leôdum<leôd.
leôd-perâs, pl. m., people.
leôd-perod, es, n., host.
leôđ, es, n., lay, poem.
leôđ-cræft, es, m., poet's art.
leôđ-cræftig, adj., skilled in poetry.
leôđ-sang (a>o), es, m., song.
leôđ-pyrht, e, f., poesy.
leôf, adj., dear; (a word of courtesy), my, sir.
leôfâđ, -ôde<lifian.
leôgan (3), lie, falsify.
leôht, es, n., light.
leôht, adj., light.
leôht-môd, adj., light-minded.
leôma, n, m., light, splendor.
leomum<lim.
leornere, s, m., learner, scholar.
leornian (6), learn.
leornung, e, f., learning.
lêt<lǣtan.
letani-e, an, f., litany.
libban, lifde (6), live.
lîc, es, n., body.
lîcetung, e, f., hypocrisy.
licgan (1), lie, wait.
lîc-hama, -homa, n, m., body.
lîcian (6), please.
lîcumlîc, adj., bodily.
lida, n, m., sailor.
liden<lîdan.
lid<licgan.
lîdan (5), sail.
lîf, es, n., life.
lifer, e, f., liver.
lifian, leofôde (6), live.
lîg, es, m., flame.
liged<licgan.
lîg-fŷr, es, n., flame.
lîg-ræsc, es, m., lightning.
lim, es, n., limb.
lîm, es, m., lime.
Lindesse, ind., Lindsey.
Lindisfarena-eâ, f. (§ 101), Lindisfarne island.
lind-hæbbende, pl. m., shield-bearers.
liodo-bend, es, e, m. f., limb-bonds, fetters.
Liofa, n, m.
lis, se, f., bliss, favor.
lixan (6), shine.
locc, ces, m., lock of hair.
loc, es, n., fold.
lôcian (6), look.
lof, es, n., praise.
lof-sang, es, m., hymn.
lond-ryht, es, n., land title.
longad, es, m., longing.
longe, adv., long.
longsum, adj., lasting.
lopystr-e, -an, f., lobster.
losian (6), be lost, escape.
lûcan (3), lock, close.
Luci-us, -es (§ 101), m.
luf-e, -an, f., love.
lufian (6), love, favor.
luflîce, adv., dearly, for a high price.
luf-tŷme, adj., benevolent.
luf-u, -e, f., love.
Lunden, es, m., London.
lust, es, m., pleasure, desire.
lustlîce, adv., willingly.
lutian (6), lurk.
lyft, es, e, m. n. f., air.
lyre, s, m., loss.
lystan (6), impers., please.
lytel, adj., little.
lytig, adj., cunning.
lytling, es, m., little one.

mâ, indec., more.
mâ, adv., more.
madelian (6), speak.
mâdum, es, m., precious gift, gem.
mâdum-, maddum-gifa, n, m., gem-giver.
magâs<mæg.
mâgon<mugan.
mag-u(o), -â, m., man.
mago-driht, e, f., crowd of youth.
mago-rinc, es, m., man.
mâh, adj., base.
man, nes, men, m., man.
mân, es, n., crime.
man-cpealm, es, m., death.
man-cyn, nes, n., mankind.
mân-dǣd, e, f., evil deed.
mangere, s, m., merchant.
manian (6), remind.
manig (i>e), adj., many.
manig-feald, adj., manifold.
mann-sliht, e, f., manslaughter.
mân-spara, n, m., perjurer.
mâra, mâre, adj., greater, more.
Marin-us, -es (§ 101), m.
Marti-us, -es (*-i*, Latin), m., March.
max, es, n., net.
mǣd, e, f., measure, age.
mæg<mugan.
mæg, es, plur. *magâs*, kinsman.
mǣg, es, plur. *mǣgâs*, kinsman.
mǣgđ, e, f., tribe, family.
mægen, es, n., might, strength, multitude.
mægen-fultum, es, m., strong support.
mægen-rǣs, es, m., strong assault.
mægen-pud-u, -â, m., strong wood, spear.
mǣl, es, n., time, meal, token; *Cristes mǣl*, cross.
Mælcolm, es, m., Malcolm.
mǣrđ, e, f., glory.
mǣre, adj., clear, illustrious.
mæsling, es, n., brass.
mæss-e, -an, f., mass.
mæsse-preôst, es, m., priest.
mæst, es, m., mast.
mǣst, adj., greatest, most.
mǣst, adv., most.
mǣte, adj., weak.
mǣton<metan.
mê, see *ic*, I, me.
meaht<mugan.
mearc, e, f., mark, border.
Mearce, plur. m., Mercians, Mercia.
mearc-stapa, n, m., treader of the marches.
mearc-preât, es, m., border host, crossing the border.
mearc-peard, es, m., watch of the border, wolf.
mearg, meares, m., horse.
med-micel (i<y), adj., not much, some.
medo-ærn, es, n., mead hall.
medo-ful, les, n., mead beaker.
mêde, adj., worn, sick.
medel-pord, es, n., formal word.
mehte<meahte<mugan.
melcan (1), milk.
melda, n, m., informer.
Mellit-us, -es, m.
meltan (1), melt.
menig-u(o), -o, -e, f., crowd.
mennisc, es, m., man.
menniscnes, se, f., incarnation.
meodo-rǣden, ne, f., treat of mead.
meodo-setl, es, n., mead seat.
meodu-heal, le, f., mead hall.
meolc, e, f., milk.
meord, e, f., reward.
meotud, es, m. (of God), creator, fate.
Merantûn, es, m., Merton.
mere, s, m., sea.
mere-lîdende, s, m., sailor.
mere-spîn, es, n., dolphin, porpoise.
mere-pîf, es, n., woman of the sea.
met>mettum, adj., painted.
metan (1), mete, pass through.
mêtan (6), meet, find.
mete, s, pl. *mettâs*, m., food, viands.
mete-þegen, es, m., table servants.
micel, adj., great, much.
miclum, adv., greatly.
mid, prep., with.
mid, adv., also.
mid, adj., mid, middle.
middan-eard, es, m., earth.
middan-eard-lîc, adj., earthly.
middan-geard, es, m., earth.
mid-dæg, es, m., midday service.
Middel-Angle, plur. m., Middle Angles.
middel-finger, es, m., middle finger.
midde-niht, e, f., midnight.
miht, mihte<mugan.
miht, e, f., might, power.
mihtig, adj., mighty.
mîl, e, f., mile.
mild-heôrt, adj., merciful.
mîl-pæđ, es, m., mile path, long road.
milts, e, f., pity, mercy.
mîn, pron., mine.
mis-dǣd, e, f., misdeed.
mis-lîc, adj., various.
môd, es, n., mind, spirit.
môd-gehygd, e, f., conjecture.
môd-geþonc, es, m. n., wisdom, thought.
môd-hpæt, adj., spirited.
môdig, adj., spirited.
mon<man.
môna, n, m., moon.
mon-cyn=man-cyn.

mônað, mônðes, m., month.
monig=*manig*.
monian=*manian*, exhort.
môr, es, m., moor, mountain.
morðor, es, n., murder.
morð-peorc, es, n., murder.
môr-fæsten, es, n., fastness in a moor.
morgen, es, m., morning.
morgen-gyf-u, -e, f., morning gift.
morgen-spêg, es, m., morning sound.
morne<*morgene*.
môtan, môste (§ 212), may, must.
Môyses, m., Moses.
mûð, es, m., mouth.
mugan, mæg, meahte, mihte (§ 212), may, can, be able.
Mûl, es, m.
mund, e, f., hand.
mund-bora, n, m., protector.
mund-byrd, e, f., protection.
mund-gripe, s, m., gripe.
munt, es, m., mount.
munuc, es, m., monk.
munuc-hâd, es, m., monk's condition.
murnan (6), mourn.
muscl-e, -an, f., muscle.
mycel=*micel*.
myne, s, m., minnow.
mynster, es, n., monastery.
myr-e, -an, f., mare.
myrgen, e, f., joy.

nâ, adv., never, not.
nabban, næfde (6), have not.
naca, n, m., ship.
naðor, conj., neither.
nâge=*ne-âge*.
nâht, adv., not.
nalæs, adv., not at all.
nalles, adv., not at all.
nam<*niman*.
nama, n, m., name.
nân, adj. subs., no, none, nothing.
nas-u(o), e, f., nose.
nât=*ne pât*.
nât-hpylc, pron., I know not who, some one.
nædr-e, -an, f., adder.
næfne=*nefne*.
nǽfre, adv., never.
nǽnig, pron., no one, not any.
nǽnne<*nân*.
nǽre=*ne pǽre*.
næs=*ne pæs*.
næs, adv. conj., not.
ne, adv. conj., not, nor, neither.
nê, adv. conj., nor.
neah, adv., enough.
neâh, adj. adv. prep., nigh.
neaht, e, f., night.
neâ(h)-lǽcan, lǽhte (6), approach.
nearpe, adv., narrowly.
neât, es, n., cattle.
neâ-pest, e, f. m., neighborhood.
nêd, e, f., need, necessity.
nefne, conj. prep., unless, except.
nêhstan<*neâh*.
nele<*ne pille*, § 212.
nellan<*ne pillan* (§ 212), will not.
nemðe, conj. prep., unless, except.
nemnan (6), name.
neôd, e, f., desire.
neôd-lîce, adv., eagerly.
neôd-pearf, adj., needful.
neôd-pearflîc, adj., needful.
neoðone, adv., beneath.
neom=*ne eom*, am not.
neôsan (6), visit.
neôsian (6), visit.
nergend, es, m., savior.
Nero, nes, m.
net, tes, n., net.
next<*neâh*.
nic=*ne ic*, not I.
nîcend, adj., new born.
Nîð-hâd, es, m.
nið-sele, s, m.
nîð-per, es, m., foe.
nigon, num., nine.
nigon-gylde, adv., nine-fold.
nigon-teôðe, num., nineteenth.
niht, e, f., night.
niht-helm, es, m., night's veil.
niht-sang, es, m., night song.
niht-scû-a, -an, -pan, m., night's shade.
niht-peard, es, m., night's guard.
niman (1), take.
Ninna, n, m.
nîpan (2), darken.
nis=*ne is*.
nipe, adj., new.
nô, adv., never, not.
nôht, f. n., nothing.
nôht=*nâht*, not.
nolde<*nellan*.
noma=*nama*.
nôn, e, f., noon, nones.
norð, adv., north.
norðan, adv., from the north.
Norðan-hymbre, pl. m., Northumbrians.
norðan-peard, adj., northward.
norð-dǽl, es, m., north.
Norð-hymbre, pl. m., Northumbrians.
Norð-men, pl. m., Northmen.
norð-peg, es, m., way to the north.
Norð-pegâs, pl. m., Norway.
Normandig, e, f., Normandy.
notian (6), use.
nû, adv. conj., now.
nŷd, e, f., need, necessity.
nŷd-grâp, e, f., resistless hand.
nŷhstan<*neâh*.
nymðe=*nemðe*.
nyt, adj., useful.
nytan=*ne pitan*, know not.
nŷten, es, n., cattle.
nytnes, se, f., use.
nytenys, se, f., ignorance, dulness.
nyt-peorð, adj., useful.
nyt-pyrðnes, se, f., utility.

ô, adv., ever, any where.
ôð, prep., even to.
ôð þæt, ôð þe, until, till this.
ôð-þæt-þe, until.
oððe, conj., or.
ôðer, pron., other, either.
ôð-standan (4), stop.
ôð-ŷpan (6), appear.
of, prep., from, of.
of-â-lǽdan (6), bring from.
of-âxian (6), learn from.
of-cuman (1), come from.
ofen, es, m., oven.
ofer, prep., over, against, after, by.
ofer-brǽdan (6), spread over.
ofer-cuman (1), overcome.
ofer-eâca, n, m., surplus.
ofer-eôde<*ofer-gân*, pass by.
ofer-gepeorc, es, n., upper-work.
ofer-holt, es, n., shield.
ofer-hrops, es, m., voracity.
ofer-met, tes, n., excess, pride.
ofer-spîðan (6), overpower.
ofer-teldan (1), cover.
ofer-pintran (6), winter.
Offa, n, m.
of-lyst, adj., very eager.
of-on<*of-unnan*.
ôfost, e, f., haste.
of-sleân (5), slay.
of-stician (6), stab, kill.
of-stingan (1), stab, kill.
oft, adv., often.
of-unnan, -ûðe, § 212, envy.
Ôlaf, es, m.
Olanîg, e, f., Olney isle.
oleccan (6), soothe.
ombeht, es, m., servant.
on, prep., on, upon.
on-ælan (6), kindle.
on-bærnan (6), enkindle.
on-be-lǽdan (6), inflict.
on-bryrdnes, se, f., instigation, inspiration.
on-cerran (6), turn, change.
on-cunnan, -cûðe, § 212, accuse.
on-drǽdan (5), dread, fear.
on-drysenlîc, adj., fearful, reverend.
onettan (6), hasten.
on-findan (1), find.
on-fôn, fêng, -fangen (5), receive, attain, take, find.
on-gangan (5), advance.
on-geân, prep., against.
ongeân, adv., again.
on-ginnan (1), begin.
on-gitan (*i, ie, y*) (1), perceive, know.
on-gitenes, se, f., knowledge.
on-hôn, -hêng (5), hang.
on-hyldan (6), rest, lay.
on-innan, adv., within.
on-lǽnan (6), loan, give.
on-lîhan, -lag (2), give.
on-lûcan (3), unlock, open.
on-rîdan (2), ride.
on-scûnian (6), shun.
on-secgan (6), sacrifice.
on-sendan (6), send.
on-seôn, -seah, -sêgon, etc. (1), see, look on.
on-slǽpan (6), sleep.
on-spîfan (2), sweep, swerve.
on-pacan (4), awake, is born.
on-pendan (6), change.
open, adj., open.
openlîce, adv., plainly.
ôr, es, n., origin.
orcne, s, pl. *âs*, sea-monster.
ord, es, n., beginning.

ord-fruma, n, m., prince.
Ordgâr, es, m.
ordian (6), aspire.
ôr-eald, adj., very old.
oretta, n, m., warrior.
Orfeus (§ 101), m., Orpheus.
or-gylde, adj., without were-gild.
or-mete, adj., immense.
or-trŷpe, adj., distrustful.
Osrîc, es, m.
ostr-e, -an, f., oyster.
Ospald, es, m., Oswald.
Ospio, m., Oswio.
oxa, n., m., ox.
oxan-hird, es, m., ox-herd.
Oxnâ-ford, es, m., Oxford.

pâpa, n, m., pope.
pâpan-hâd, es, m., office of pope.
Parcâs, pl. m., Parcæ, fates.
pater-noster, Latin, indec., m. n., our father, Lord's Prayer.
Paulin-us, es, m.
pællen, adj., purple.
pæl, les, m., purple cloth, pall.
Pedrid-e, -an, f.
Pefenasæ, indec., Pevensey.
Pelagi-us, es, acc. *-um*, § 101.
Penda, n, m.
Peortanea, indec., Parteney.
Petr-us, -es, § 101, Peter.
Pihtâs, pl. m., Picts.
Pihtisc, adj., Pictish.
pinepincl-e, -an, f., pinewincle.
plegian (6), play.
pliht, e, f., plight, danger.
pliht-lîc, adj., dangerous.
prætig, adj., deceitful.
preôst, es, m., priest.
prîm, e, f., prime, service for sunrise.
prôfian (6), prove, regard.
Puclan-cyrc-e, -an, f., Pucklechurch.
pund, es, n., pound.
pusa, n, m., purse.
Pyhtâs, pl. m., Picts.

racent-e, -an, f., chain.
râd, e, f., raid.
râd<*rîdan.*
rade, adv., quickly.
rand-piga, n, m., shielded warrior.
ræd, es, m., counsel.
ræding-e, f., reading.
Rædpald, es, m.
ræg-e, -an, f., roe.
ræst=*rest.*
reâd, adj., red.
Reâd, adj., Red.
reâf, es, n., robe, spoil.
reâf-lâc, es, n., rapine.
rêcan, rôhte (6), care.
reccan, reahte, rehte (6), reach, repeat.
reced, es, m. n., house, hall.
rêde, adj., fearful, truculent.
rên, es, m., rain.
reôc, adj., fierce.
regol-lîc, adj., regular.
rest (*e*>*æ*), *e*, f., rest.
restan (6), rest.
rêpet, es, n., voyage.

Rîcard, es, m., Richard.
rîce, adj., rich, mighty.
rîce, s, n., kingdom.
ricene, adv., straightway.
rîclîce, adv., royally.
rîcsian (6), rule.
rîdan (2), ride, oppress.
riht, adj., right, correct.
riht, es, n., right.
rihte, adv., rightly.
riht-lîce, adv., rightly.
riht-ryne, s, m., right course.
rîman (6), count, reckon.
rînan (6), rain, wet.
rinc, es, m., man, hero.
rinnan (1), run.
rîxian (6)=*rîcsian.*
Rodbeard, es, m., Robert.
rôd, e, f., cross, rood.
rôde-tâcen, es, n., sign of the cross.
rodor, es, m., sky.
rôf, adj., stout, illustrious.
rogian (6), prevail.
Rôm, e, f., Rome.
Rômânâ-burh, e, -byrig, f., § 101, Rome.
Rômâne, pl. m., Romans.
Rômânisc, adj., Roman.
Rôme-burh, e, f., Rome.
rômigan (6), strive for, use.
rôs-e, -an, f., rose.
rôt, adj., gay.
rôt-lîce, adv., cheerfully.
rôpan (6), sail, row.
rûm, adj., roomy, ample, vast.
rûm-heort, adj., great-hearted.
rûn, e, f., secret, reflection.
rûn-stæf, es, m., runic letter.
rycene=*ricene.*
ryht=*riht.*
ryne, s, m., course.

sâl, es, m., rope, net.
sâlum, 54, 19=*sælum.*
samod, adv., together, also.
sanct, adj., saint, holy.
sand, es, n., sand, shore.
sang, es, m., song.
sâr, adj., sorry.
sârig, adj., sorry, sad.
Satan, es, m.
sâp(o)l, e, f., soul.
sæ, s, m. f., sea, lake.
sæ-bât, es, m., sea-boat.
sæc, es, n., strife.
sæ-coc, ces, m., cockle.
sæd, p.p., *sæde, sægde*<*secgan.*
sæ-fæsten, es, n., fortress-sea.
sæl, es, n., hall.
sæl, es, e, m. f., time; *on sælum*, happy, safe.
sæ-lîc, adj., maritime.
sælan (6), tie, bind.
sæ-næs, ses, m., promontory.
sæ-rima, n, m., sea-shore.
sæ-pud-u, -â, -es, m., ship.
scacan (4), fly, flow.
scand-lîce, adv., slanderously.
scæd, es, n., shade, darkness.
scær-u, -e, f., tonsure.
scæt, tes, m., scat, 1-20th of a shilling.
scead-u(o), -e, f., shade, darkness.
sceada, n, m., enemy.

sceaft, es, m., shaft, spear.
Sceafles - burh, e, -byrig, f., Shaftesbury.
sceal<*sculan.*
sceam-u, -e, f., shame.
sceân<*scînan.*
sceâp, es, n., sheep.
sceâp-hirde, s, m., shepherd.
scear, e, f., (plow)-share.
scearn, es, n., dung, litter.
sceat, tes, m., the scat of Mercia; 30,000=£120.
sceât, es, m., lap, region.
sceât<*sceôtan.*
sceâpere, s, m., spy.
sceâpian (6), look at, observe.
sceddan (6), scathe, harm.
Scêfing, es, m., son of Scef.
scenn-e, -an, f., guard of a sword-hilt.
sceô, s, m., shoe.
sceôc<*scôc*<*scacan.*
sceolon<*sculan.*
sceôp-gereorde, s, n., poetry.
sceôta, n, m., trout.
sceôtan (3), shoot.
sceôtend, es, m., shooter.
sceô-pyrhta, n, m., shoemaker.
sceppan, scôp, sceôp (4), shape, create, build, give (name).
Sciddia, n, f., Scythia.
scild (*i*<*y*), *es*, m., shield.
scilling, es, m., shilling.
scîma, n, m., light.
scînan (2), shine.
scionon<*scinon*<*scînan.*
scip, es, n., ship.
scip-here, s, m., naval force.
scîr, adj., bright.
scîr, e, f., shire.
scîr-man, nes, m., man of a shire.
scolde<*sculan.*
scôl-u, -e, f., school.
scôp, es, m., poet, singer.
scotian (6), shoot.
Scottâs, pl. m., Scots.
Scottisc, adj., Scottish.
scrîdan (2), go, travel.
scrîfan (2), enjoin at confession, shrive.
scrûd, es, n., clothing.
scrŷdan (6), clothe.
scûfan (3), shove.
sculan, pres. *sceal, sculon, sceolon, scyle*; imperf. *sceolde, scolde*, § 212, shall, will, ought, should, would.
scyld, e, f., guilt, debt.
scyld, es, m.=*scild.*
Scyld, es, m.
scyld-hreôda, n, m., shield.
scyldig, adj., guilty, under penalty.
Scylding, es, m., descendant of Scyld.
scyld-piga, n, m., shielded warrior.
scyndan (6), haste, flee.
scypen, e, f., stable.
scyppend, es, m., creator.
scyte-finger, es, m., shooting finger, forefinger.
se, seô, þæt, (article) the; (demonstrative) that; (relative) who, that.
sealm, es, m., psalm.

sealt, es, n., salt.
sealtere, s, m., salter.
Sealpud-u, -â, m., Selwood.
seâmere, s, m., tailor.
sear-u(*o*), *-upes, -upe*, n. f., armor, contrivance, art.
searo-fear-u(*o*),*-upes*,n.,snares.
searo-hæbbend, es, m., one having arms.
Seax-burh, -burge, f.
Seaxan, pl. m.=*Seaxe*, Saxons.
sêcean, sêcan, sôhte (6), seek, approach.
secg, es, m., man, hero.
secgan, sægde>*sǽde* (6), say.
sefa, n, m., mind.
segel, es, m. n., sail.
segl-rôd, e, f., sail-yard.
segen, es, m. n., sign.
sêl, adj., good.
sel-cûđ, adj., rare.
seld-guma, n, m., house-man, man of low rank.
seldan (*a*>*o*), adv., seldom.
sele, s, m., hall, house.
sele-dreâm, es, m., joy in hall.
sele-ful, les, n., hall goblet.
sele-rǽdend, es, m., hall watcher.
sele-pegn, es, m., hall servant.
self, pron., self.
self-pil, les, n., self-will.
sellan, sealde (6), give.
sel-lîc, adj., sole, excellent.
semian (6), stay.
semningâ, adv., suddenly.
sendan (6), send.
sênian (6), sign, cross, bless.
seô<*se*; *seô*<*eom.*
seô, n, f., pupil (of the eye).
seôc, adj., sick.
seôđan (3), seethe, cook.
seofoda, num., seventh.
seofon (*o, a*), num., seven.
seofon-teôđa, seventeenth.
seofon-tig, seventy.
seofon-tŷne, seventeen.
seolfor-smiđ, es, m., silversmith.
seomian=semian.
seôn (1), see.
seono-ben, ne, f., wound of the sinews.
Sergi-us, -es, m.
setl, es, n., seat.
setl-gang, es, m., setting.
setl-râd, e, f., setting.
settan (6), set, put.
se-þeâh, adv., nevertheless.
se-þe, whoever.
Sevêr-us, -es, m.
si<*eom.*
sib, be, f., peace.
siccetung, e, f., sigh.
sîd, adj., great.
sîde, adv., far.
sîd-e, -an, f., silk.
sîdian, sîdeđ for *sîdađ* (6), extend.
sîd-fæđmed, adj., great-bosomed.
siđđan, adv. conj., afterward, after.
sîgan (2), sink, go.
sige, s, m., victory.
sige-eâdig, adj., blest with victory.
Sigebriht, es, m.
sige-cyning, es, m., victorious king.
sige-folc, es, n., victorious people.
sige-hrêđig, adj., glorious with success.
Sigel-parâs, pl. m.,Ethiopians.
Sigeric, es, m.
sige-rôf, adj., glorious with victory.
sige-sceorp, es, n., prize of victory.
sigor, es, m., triumph.
simle, adv., always.
sinc, es, n., treasure.
sinc-fæt, es, n., precious vessel, jewel.
sind, sindon, see *eom*, am.
sin-gal, adj., continual.
sin-gal-lîc, adj., continual.
singan (1), sing.
sin-niht, e, f., unbroken night.
siô=seô.
sittan (1), sit.
six, num., six.
sixta, num., sixth.
sixtig, num., sixty.
six-tŷne, num., sixteen.
slǽpan (5), sleep.
slǽp-ern, es, n., dormitory.
sleân, slæđ, imp. *slôg, slôh*, p.p. *slægen* (4), strike, slay.
slecge, s, m., sledge.
slege, s, m., blow.
slîđ-heard, adj., terrible.
slîtan (2), slit, tear.
smeâgan (6), examine, reflect.
smiđ, es, m., smith.
smiđđ-e, -an, f., smithy.
smîtan (2), smite.
smolte, adv., gently.
smylte, adj., gentle, pleasant.
snîpan (6), snow.
snottor, adj., wise, sage.
snyttr-u(*o*), *u*(*o*), f., sagacity.
sôđ, adj., true, sure, just.
sôđ, es, n., truth, justice.
sôđ-fæstnes, se, f., truth.
sôđ-lîce, adv., verily, truly.
sôhte<*sêcean.*
sôl=sâl.
solian (6), *sôlađ* for *solađ*, soil.
Somersǽte, pl. m., people of Somerset.
somod=samod.
sôna, adv., soon.
song, es, m., song.
song-cræft, es, m., poet's art.
sorh, sorg, e, f., care.
sorgian (6), be anxious, be cumbered.
spearpa, n, m., sparrow.
spêd, e, f., speed, power.
spel, les, n., story, tale.
spellian (6), repeat.
spere, s, n., spear.
sprǽc, e, f., conversation, argument, discourse.
sprecan (1), speak.
spur-leder, es, n., spur-leather.
spyrta, n, m., basket.
stacung, e, f., stabbing.
stalian (6), steal.
stân, es, m., stone, rock.
standan, stôd (4), stand, be, overhang, urge.
stân-hliđ, es, n., stone slope.
stapul, es, m., post.
stæđ, es, n., shore.
stæf, es, m., letter, Scripture.
stǽr, es, n., history.
steâp, es, m., cup, mug.
steâp, adj., steep.
stearc, adj., stiff, rough, severe.
stede, s, m., place.
stêda, n, m., stud, steed.
stefn, es, m., prow.
stelan (1), steal.
stenc, es, m., stench.
steorra, n, m., star.
steort, es, m., tail.
stician (6), stick.
stîđ, adj., stiff, firm.
stîđ-frihđ, adj., firm-minded.
stîđ-lîce, adv., severely.
stigan (2), mount.
stille, adj., still.
stille, adv., quietly.
stil-nes, se, f., stillness.
stôd<*standan.*
stôl, es, m., seat, throne.
stondan=standan.
storm, es, m., storm.
stôp, e, f., place.
strang, adj., strong.
strange, adv., strongly
strǽt, e, f., street, road.
streâm, es, m., stream.
strenge, adj., strong.
strong=strang.
strong-lîc, adj., firm, strong.
stunt, adj., dumb, stupid.
stŷl-ecg, adj., steel-edged.
styria, n, m., sturgeon.
styrian (6), stir, play, sing.
styrman (6), storm.
sûđ, adv. and indec. adj.,south.
sûđa, n, m., south.
sûđan, adv., to the south, from the south.
sûđan-eâstan, adv., indec. adj., lying to the southeast.
Sûđan-hymbre, pl. m., Southumbrians.
sûđan-peard, adj., lying to the south.
sûđ-healf, e, f., south half.
Sûđrige, pl. m., men of Surrey.
sûđ-rima, n, m., south coast.
Sûđ-Seaxan, -Seaxe, pl. m., South Saxons.
sûđ-peg, es, m., south way.
sulh, es, n., plow.
sulh-scear, e, f., plowshare.
sum, pron., a certain one, some, a;—adv.,with numerals, § 388.
sumor, es, m., summer.
sumur-hât, es, n., summer heat.
Sumor-sǽte, pl. m., people of Somersetshire.
sund, es, m., sea.
sundor, adv., apart.
sund-pud-u, -â, m., ship.
sunge<*singan.*
sunn-e, -an, f., sun.
sunne-beâm, es, m., sunbeam.
sun-u, -â, m., son.
spâ, adv. conj., so, as.
spâc<*spîcan.*
spâ-fela-spâ, adv., so many as.

spâ-hpâ-spâ, pron., whosoever.
spâ-hpæt-spâ, pron., whatsoever.
spâ-hpylce-spâ, pron., whatsoever.
span-râd, *e*, f., swan road, sea.
spâ-þeâh, adv., yet, however.
spæc, *ces*, m., taste.
spǣs, adj., kind, pleasant.
spǣsendu, pl. n., feast.
speart, adj., black, swart.
spefan (1), sleep.
spefel, *es*, m., sulphur.
spefen, *es*, n., sleep, dream.
spêg, *es*, m., sound.
spegel, *es*, n., sky, sun.
Spegen, *es*, m., Swain.
spêging, *e*, f., sound.
spegle, adv., glaringly.
spêigan (6), sound.
spelc=spilc.
spelgere, *s*, m., glutton.
speltan (1), die.
spencan (6), afflict.
speng, *es*, m., blow.
speord, *es*, n., sword.
speostor, indec. f., sister.
speot, *es*, n., crowd.
speotol, adj., clear.
speotole, adv., clearly.
spête, adj., sweet.
spêt-nes, *se*, f., sweetness.
spîð, adj., strong.
spîðe, adv., strongly, very; *spîðôst*, most.
spiðrian (6), vanish, cease.
spîfan (2), sweep.
spift, adj., swift.
spiftlere, *s*, m., slipper.
spilc (*i*, *y*, *e*), pron., such, as.
spilce, adv., as if, moreover, as it were, as.
spîn, *es*, n., swine, wild boar.
spingel, *e*, f., blow.
spinsung, *e*, f., melody.
sponcor, adj., weak, laming.
sputol=speotol.
spylce=spilce.
spynsian (6), sound (as music).
sŷ=sî, *seô*.
syddan=siddan.
sylf=self.
syllan=sellan.
syllîc=sellîc, wonderful.
symbel, *es*, n., feast, supper.
symle<symble<symbel.
symle, adv., always.
syn, *ne*, f., sin.
synderlîce, adv., peculiarly, individually.
syndrig, adj., sundry.
syn-gryn, *e*, f., sin's evil.
synoð, *es*, m., synod.
synt=sint<eom, am.
syrc-e, *-an*, f., sark, mail.

tâcen, *e*, f., token.
tam, adj., tame.
tân, *es*, m., rod, lot.
Tantal-us, *-es*, m.
Tâtpine, *s*, m., Tatwin.
tǣcan, *tǣhte* (6), teach.
tela, adv., well.
tellan, *tealde* (6), tell, reckon.
temian (6), tame.
tempel, *es*, n., temple.
teôða, num., tenth; *teôðe healf*, 9½, § 394.
teôn, *teâh*, *togen* (3), draw, withdraw.
teôn (6), make, fit out.
Teôlfinga-ceaster, *e*, f., Southwell.
thearfe=þearfe.
thonc-pord=þonc-pord.
tîd, *e*, f., time, day, hour.
tîhð<teôn, draw.
tihting, *e*, f., exhortation.
til, adj., good, fit.
tilian (6), till, treat.
tîma, *n*, m., time.
timbran (6), build.
tin, *es*, n., tin.
tintreg-lîc, adj., tormenting, infernal.
Tity-us, *-es*, m.
tô, prep., to, at, from, in, as, for.
tô, adv., too.
tô-, dis-, apart.
tô-brecan (1), break down, storm.
tôð, *es*, pl. *têð*, *tôðâs*, m., tooth.
tô-foran, prep., before.
tô-gædre, adv., together.
tô-geânes, prep., against.
tô-gelǣdan (6), bring to.
tô-genêdan (*ê*, *ŷ*) (6), compel.
tô-gepeôdan (6), unite.
tô-ge-ŷcan, *-ŷhte* (6), add.
torn, *es*, n., affliction.
tô-slîtan (2), tear.
tô-þon, adv., so.
tô-peard, adj., coming.
tô-peorpan (1), cast aside, overthrow, destroy.
tô-pidre, prep., against.
tredan (1), tread, pass over.
trendel, *es*, m., disk.
Trenta, *n*, m., Trent.
treô, *treôp*, *es*, n., tree.
treôp, *e*, f., truth, pledge.
treôp-pyrhta, *n*, m., carpenter.
trepp-e, *-an*, f., trap.
trimman (6), strengthen, are serried.
Tuda, *n*, m.
tûn, *es*, m., town.
tûng-e, *-an*, f., tongue.
tûn-gerêfa, *n*, m., town officer.
tpâ, num., two.
tpegen, num., twain, two.
tpelf, num., twelve.
tpelf-mônað, *es*, m., twelvemonth.
tpelfta, num., twelfth.
tpentig, num., twenty.
tpeôpa, num., twice.
tpŷ-bôte, adj., fined double.
tydran (6), produce.
tŷn, *tŷne*, num., ten.
tŷn-pintre, adj., ten-year-old.

þâ, art., <*se*.
þâ, adv. and conj., then, when.
þafian (6), like, assent to.
þâh<þîhan.
þancian (6), thank.
þancung, *e*, f., thanks.
þanne, adv., conj., then, than, when, yet, but.
þanon, adv., thence.
þâs<þes.
þâþâ, adv., conj., when, since.
þænne=þanne.
þǣr, adv., conj., there, where, if.
þǣr-rihte, adv., straightway.
þǣr-tô, adv., besides.
þǣr-tô-eâcan, adv., besides.
þǣr-pið, adv., therewith.
þæs<se.
þæs, adv., therefore, after, so; —*þæs þe*, because.
þæt<se.
þæt, conj., that, so that.
þætte, conj., that, so that, when.
þe, rel. pron., indecl., who, that, which; —with dem. or personal pron. making them relative, § 380+.
þe, conj., that, or, than.
þê<þû.
þeâh, adv., conj., though, yet.
þeâh-hpædere, adv., conj., yet.
þeahte<þeccan.
þeahtere, *s*, m., counselor.
þearf, *e*, f., need, use.
þearf<þurfan.
þearfa, *n*, m., needy one.
þearle, adv., very much, hard.
þeâp, *es*, m., custom.
þeâp-lîce, adv., mannerly.
þeccan, *þeahte* (6), cover.
þegen, *es*, m., thane, servant, soldier, knight.
þencan, *þohte* (6), think, ponder.
þenden, conj., while.
þengel, *es*, m., prince, lord.
þênian (6), supply, attend.
þênung, *e*, f., use, supply.
þeôd, *e*, f., people.
þeôdan (6), serve.
þeôd-cyning, *es*, m., people's king.
þeôden, *es*, m., lord.
þeôden-hold, adj., dear to the lord.
þeôd-gestreôn, *es*, people's treasure.
þeôd-scipe, *s*, m., discipline.
þeôf, *es*, m., thief.
þeôn, *þeâh*, *þûgon* (3), grow.
þeôs<þes.
þeôstor, *es*, n., darkness.
þeôstr-u(*o*), *-u*(*o*), f., darkness.
þeôp, *es*, m., servant.
þeôpa, *n*, m., servant.
þeôpan (6), serve.
þeôp-dôm, *es*, m., service.
þeôpian (6), serve.
þeôpot, *es*, m., servitude.
þes, *þeôs*, *þis*, pron., this, this one.
þicgan, *þeah*, *þêgon* (1), take.
þider, adv., thither.
þîhan, *þâh* (2), grow.
þîn, pron. adj., thine, thy.
þince<þyncan.
þing, *es*, n., thing.
þiossum<þes.
þis<þes.
þoden, *es*, m., whirlwind.
þohte<þencan.
þolian (6), suffer, lose, withstand.
þon<þam, adv., *nôht þon læs*, not the less.

þonc-ƿord, *es*, n., thanks.
þone<*se*.
þonne=*þanne*.
þonon=*þanon*.
þonon-ƿeard, adj., gone thence.
Þrâcia (Lat. indecl., § 101), Thrace.
þrag, *e*, f., time, state of things.
þræc-ƿîg, *es*, m., fierce fight.
þræl, *es*, m., thrall, slave.
þreât, *es*, m., company, band.
þreô<*þrî*, num., three.
þridda, num., third.
þrî-gylde, adv., threefold.
þrîste, adj., bold.
þrîste, adv., confidently.
þrîtig, *þrittig*, num., thirty.
þrittigôða, num., thirtieth.
þrôƿian (6), suffer.
þrôƿung, *e*, f., suffering.
þryð, *e*, f., strength, force.
þryð-ƿord, *es*, n., word of power.
þrym, *mes*, m., might, glory; —*þrymmum*, mightily.
þû, *þê*, *gê*, pron., thou, thee, ye.
þûf, *es*, m., standard.
þuhte<*þyncan*.
þûma, *n*, m., thumb; *þûman nægl*, *es*, m., thumb nail.
þunian (6), spread.
þunor, *es*, m., thunder; *þunres dæg*, Thursday.
þurfan, *þearf*, *þorfte*, irreg. (§ 212), need.
þurh, prep., through, by.
þurh-brûcan (3), enjoy.
þurh-fleôgan (3), fly through.
þurh-stingan (1), stab through.
þurh-ƿunian (6), continue.
þurstig, adj., thirsty.
þus, adv., thus.
þûsend, num., thousand.
þûsend-hîƿe, adj., of a thousand shapes.
þƿang, *es*, m., thong.
þƿîtan (2), cut off.
þŷ, instr. <*se*; adv., *þŷ lustlîcôr*, the more cheerfully; *þŷ læs*, lest; *for þŷ*, therefore, because, since.
þŷfð, *e*, f., theft.
þyhtig, adj. strong.
þylc, pron., the like, such.
þyle, *s*, m., orator, master of ceremonies.
þyncan, *þuhte* (6, § 211), seem.
þynne, adj., thin.
þyrel, *þyrl*, *es*, n., hole.
þyrel, adj., pierced.
þŷs, *þysses*<*þes*.
þŷƿan=*þeôƿan* (6), drive.

ûdon<*unnan*.
ûð-ƿita, *n*, m., philosopher.
ufan, adv., above.
uht-e, *-an*, time before light.
uht-sang, *es*, m., nocturn, hymn before light.
umbor, *es*, n., infant.
un-ârîmedlîc, adj., uncounted.
un-bunden, adj., unbound.
unc<*ic*.
un-câfscipe, *s*, m., inactivity.
un-clæ̂ne, adj., unclean.
under, prep., under, among.
under-bæc, adv. prep., behind.
under-fôn, *-fêng* (5), undertake, accept.
undern, *es*, m., third hour, 9 o'clock.
undern-tîd, *e*, f., third hour.
under-standan (4), understand.
under-þeôdan (6), addict, submit.
un-dyrne, adv., discovered.
un-eâðe, adv., hardly.
un-eâðelîce, adv., with difficulty.
un-foresceâƿodlîce, adv., unexpectedly.
un-forht, adj., fearless.
un-gedered, adj., unharmed.
un-gefræ̂glîce, adj., remarkably.
un-gelæ̂red, adj., untaught.
un-gelîc, adj., unlike.
un-gemetes, adv., immeasurably, very.
un-gemetlîc, adj., immeasurable.
un-gesæ̂lð, *e*, f., misfortune.
un-grêne, adj., not green.
un-hæ̂l-u(o), *-u(o)*, f., disaster.
un-heânlîce, adv., nobly.
un-hneâƿ, adj., liberal.
un-læd, adj., poor.
unnan, *an*, *ûde*, irreg., § 212, grant.
un-nyt, adj., useless.
un-ræ̂d, *es*, m., bad counsel.
un-riht, adj., wrong.
un-rîm, *es*, n., uncounted number.
un-scæððig, adj., innocent.
un-scennan (6), unfasten.
un-stille, adj., restless.
un-stilnes, *se*, f., disturbance.
un-synnig, adj., guiltless.
un-trum, adj., infirm.
un-trumnys, *-trymnes*, *se*, f., illness.
un-tyder, *es*, m., evil race.
un-ƿær, adj., unaware; *on unƿær*, unawares.
un-ƿealt, adj., steady.
up, adv., up.
up-âstîgnes, *se*, f., ascension.
up-lîc, adj., heavenly.
up-rodor, *es*, m., heaven.
ûre, pron. poss., our. See *ic*.
urnon<*irnan*.
ûs, see *ic*.
ût, adv., out.
ût-âdrîfan (2), drive out.
utan<*ƿutan*<*ƿîtan*, let us.
ûtan, adv., without.
ûte, adv., out, without.
ût-eôde<*ût-gân*, irreg., go out.
ût-fûs, adj., ready to go.
ût-gang, *es*, m., departure.
uton=*utan*.
ût-ræ̂san (6), rush out.

ƿâ, interj., woe, Oh.
ƿâc, adj., weak, poor.
ƿacian (6), watch.
ƿacol-lîce, adv., watchfully.
ƿacolre, comp. of *ƿacol*, very watchful.
ƿâfian (6), be astonished.
ƿagian (6), wag, be moved.
ƿâ-lâ-ƿâ, interj., alas.
ƿaldend, *es*, m., ruler, king.
ƿalenâ<*ƿealâs*.
ƿan<*ƿinnan*.
ƿand<*ƿindan*.
ƿang, *es*, m., plain.
ƿârig, adj., soiled.
ƿarôð, *es*, m., shore.
ƿar-u, *-e*, f., wares, goods.
ƿaru, *ƿære*, f., care.
ƿascan (4), wash.
ƿât<*ƿitan*.
ƿæcc-e, *-an*, f., watch.
ƿæ̂d, *e*, f., vestment, clothes.
ƿæ̂fels, *es*, m., robe.
ƿæ̂g, *es*, m., wave, ocean.
ƿæ̂g-holm, *es*, m., deep sea.
ƿæl, *es*, n., slaughter, death.
ƿæl-ceâsig, adj., slaughter-choosing.
ƿæl-fyll-u(o), *-e*, f., glut of slaughter.
ƿæl-gâr, *es*, m., death-bearing spear.
ƿæl-gîfre, adj., greedy for slaughter.
ƿæl-hlenc-e, *-an*, f. (slaughter link), coat of mail.
ƿæl-reôƿ, adj., cruel.
ƿæl-sleaht, *-sliht*, *es*, m., slaughter.
ƿæl-stôƿ, *e*, f., field of death.
ƿæ̂pen, *es*, n., weapon.
ƿæ̂re, *ƿæ̂ron*<*ƿesan*.
ƿær-lîce, adv., warily, carefully.
ƿærter, *es*, m., dweller.
ƿæs<*ƿesan*.
ƿæstm, *es*, *e*, m. f. n., fruit.
ƿæstm-bæ̂re, adj., fruitful.
ƿæter, *es*, n., water.
ƿæter-helm, *es*, m., (ice) water-helmet.
ƿæterian (6), water.
ƿæter-ƿyl, *les*, m., spring of water.
ƿê, pron. plur. of *þû*, we.
ƿeâ, *n*, m., woe.
ƿeal, *les*, m., wall, mound, shore.
ƿealâs, m. plur., (strangers) Welch, Britons.
ƿealdan (5), control, govern.
ƿealh-stôd, *es*, m., interpreter.
ƿealh-þeôƿ, *-þeôn*, m., Wealhtheow.
ƿeallan (5), gush; spring up.
ƿeal-steal, *les*, m., castle site.
ƿeard, *e*, f., guard.
ƿeard, *es*, m., watchman, warder.
ƿeardian (6), inhabit.
ƿeard<*ƿeordan*.
ƿearm, adj., warm.
ƿearp<*ƿeorpan*.
ƿeaxan (4), wax, grow.
ƿecta, n. m., *ƿecting*, *es*, m., son of Wecta.
ƿed, *es*, n., pledge.
ƿêdan (6), be mad.
ƿeddian (6), pledge.
ƿed-brôðer, plur. *-brôðru*, § 87, pledged brother, Christian brother.
ƿeder, *es*, n., weather, tempest.
ƿeder-ƿolcen, *es*, m. n., storm-cloud.
ƿedmor, *es*, m., Wedmore.

pefod, es, n., altar.
peg, es, m., way; *on peg*, away.
pegan (1), bear, march.
peg-fêrend, es, m., wayfarer.
peg-nest, es, n., provision for a journey.
pei, interj., alas.
pel, adv., well.
pêland, es, m., Weland.
pel-gehpǣr, adv., every where.
pel-hpylc, pron., each.
pelig, adj., rich.
pên, e, f., hope.
pêna, n, m., hope.
pênan (6), ween, hope.
pendan (6), turn, go.
pent<*pendan*.
peofed=*pefod*.
peoh, peôs, m., idol.
peôl<*peallan*.
peôp<*pêpan*.
peorc, es, n., work.
peord, adj., worth, esteemed.
peordan (*eo, u, y*); *peard, purdon; porden* (1), be, become.
peord-ful, adj., worshipful.
peord-georn, adj., eager for honor.
peordian (6), honor, worship, praise.
peord-mynd, es, n. f., honor.
peorpan (1), throw.
peoruld, e, f., world.
peoruld-hâd, es, m., secular condition.
peôx<*peaxan*.
per, es, m., man.
pêpan (5), weep, cry.
per-cyn, nes, n., mankind.
pered=*perod*.
pêrig, adj., weary.
per-leâs, adj., unmarried.
perod, es, n., crowd, company, folks.
pesan; pæs, pǣron; ge-pesen (1), be.
pestan, adv., from the west.
pêste, adj., waste.
pêsten, nes, m. n., waste.
pêsten-gryre, s, m., horror of the desert.
pest-Seaxan (*ea*>*e*), *-Seaxe*, plur. m., West-Saxons.
pîc, es, n., dwelling, village, camp.
picce-cræft, es, m., witchcraft.
piccian (6), use witchcraft.
pîc-freod-u, e, f., care of a village.
picg, es, n., horse.
pîcian (6), dwell, stop.
pîd, adj., wide.
pîde, adv., widely, afar.
pido-bân, es, n., collar-bone.
pid, prep., against, towards, with, for.
piderian (6), oppose.
pid-innan, adv., within.
pid-metenes, se, f., comparison.
pid-sacan (4), renounce, forsake.
pid-standan (4), withstand.
pid-stent<*pid-standan*.
pid-ûtan, adv., without.
pîf, es, n., woman, wife.
pîf-cŷd, de, f., visit to a woman.
pîf-man, nes, m. f., woman.
pîg, es, m., fight.
pîga, n, m., fighter, warrior.
pig-bed, es, n., altar.
pîgferd, es, m., Wigferth.
piht, e, f. n., wight, creature, whit.
piht, e, f., Wight.
pihtgils, es, m., Wihtgils.
piht-pare, plur. m., inhabitants of the Isle of Wight.
pi-lâ, interj., alas.
pil-cuma, n, m., welcome one.
pild-deôr, pildeôr, es, n., wild beast.
pile<*pillan*.
pilfrid, es, m., Wilfrith.
pilla, n, m., wish, purpose.
pillan, pile, pille, polde, irreg., § 212, will, would.
pilhelm, es, m., William.
pilnian (6), wish.
pilsǣte, plur. m., people of Wiltshire.
pil-sîd, es, m., chosen course.
piltûn, es, m., Wilton.
pîn, es, n., wine.
pind, es, m., wind.
pindan (1), wind, twist.
pine, s, m., friend, beloved lord.
pine-mæg, es, m., beloved kinsman.
pinnan (1), fight, strive.
pintanceaster, e, f., Winchester.
pinter, es, m. n., winter.
pinter-ceald, adj., cold as winter.
pinter-stund, e, f., winter hour.
pinter-tîd, e, f., winter time.
pîs, adj., wise.
pîsa, n, m., leader.
pîs-dôm, es, m., wisdom.
pîs-e, -an, f., manner, way.
pîs-fæst, adj., very wise.
pîsian (6), direct, rule.
pîs-lîc, adj., wise.
pisson, piste<*pitan*.
pist, e, f., food, prey.
pita, n, m., wise man, senator, counsellor.
pitan; pât, piton; piste, piston, pisson, irreg., § 212, know, observe.
pîtan (2), subj. *piton, putan, utan*, § 443, go, let us.
pîte, s, n., punishment, penalty.
pîtegung, e, f., prophecy.
pitig, adj., wise.
pîtnian (6), punish.
pitôdlîce, adv. conj., certainly, verily, but, for.
pitta, n, m.; *pitting, es*, m., son of Witta.
planc, adj., spirited, proud.
plîtan (2), look.
plite, s, m., look, beauty.
plite-beorht, adj., beautiful.
plitig, adj., beautiful.
plonc=*planc*.
pôden, es, m., Woden.
pôdening, es, m., son of Woden.
polcen, es, m. n., cloud.
polde, poldon<*pillan*.
pom=*pam, mes*, m. n., spot, sin.
pôma, n, m., noise.
pon, ponne (*o*<*a*), adj., dark.
pon-sǣlig, adj., unhappy.
pon-sceaft, e, f., misfortune.
pôp, es, m., cry, whoop.
porc=*peorc*.
pord, es, n., word.
pord-hord, es, n., word-hoard.
porhte<*pyrcan*.
pôrian (6), wander, go to waste.
porn, es, m., much, many.
porold-cræft, es, m., secular calling.
poruld=*peoruld*.
poruld-gesceaft, e, f., created world.
poruld-þing, es, n., thing of the world.
prâd, adj., hostile, bad.
prâd-lîc, adj., severe.
præcca, n, m., wretch.
præc-fæc, es, n., time of misery.
præt, te, f., decoration, jewel.
precan (1), punish.
preoden-hilt, adj., with a twisted hilt.
prîdan (2), wreathe, bind.
prîdan (6), grow; *prîted* for *prîdad* for the rhyme.
prîtan (2), write.
prixendlîce, adv., in turn.
puc-e, -an, f., week.
pud-u, â, m., wood, tree.
pudu-treôp, es, n., tree of the forest.
pudup-e, -an, f., widow.
pudu-pêsten, nes, m. n., uninhabited forest.
puldor, es, n., glory.
puldor-cyning, es, m., king of glory, God.
puldor-fæder, es, m., glorious father, God.
puldor-torht, adj., gloriously bright.
pulf, es, m., wolf.
pulf-heard, es, m., Wulfhard.
pultor, es, m., vulture.
punden-mǣl, adj., etched in curves, damaskeened.
punden-stefna, adj., having a curved prow.
pundon<*pindan*.
pundor, es, n., wonder.
pundor-lîc, adj., wonderful.
pundrian (6), wonder, admire.
punian (6), dwell, frequent, remain.
punnon<*pinnan*.
punung, e, f., dwelling.
purde<*peordan*.
purdian=*peordian*.
purd-mynt=*peord-mynd*.
putan, utan, uton<*pîtan*.
pylfen, adj., wolfish.
pyll-e, -an, f., spring.
pylm, es, m., flood, tide.
pyn, ne, f., joy, delight.
pyn-sum, adj., winsome.
pyrcan, pyrcean, porhte (6, § 211), work, make, do.
pyrd, e, f., fate.
pyrd, adj., worthy, guilty.
pyrde<*peordan*.
pyrhta, n, m., worker, maker.
pyrm, es, m., worm, serpent.
pyrm-fâh, adj., varicolored.
pyrm-lîc, es, n., body of a serpent.

pyrpan (6), turn, be refreshed.
pyrs-a, -e, adj. comp., worse.
pyrt, e, f., herb, plant.
pyrt-gemang, e, f., spices, perfume.
pyrtgeorn, es, m., Wyrtgeorn.
pŷscan (6), wish.

Ybernia, n, m., Ireland.
ŷd, e, f., water.
ŷdan (6), lay waste.
ŷd-lâd, e, f., watery way.
ŷd-lida, n, m., ship.
yfel, adj., evil.
yfel, es, n., evil.
yfele, adv., evilly.
ylca=ilca.
yld, e, f., age.
ylde, plur. m., men.
yldest<eald.
ylding, e, f., delay.
yld-u(o), e, f., age, old age.
ylf, e, f., elf, lamia.
ylp, es, m., elephant.
ymb, prep., about, after, according to.
ymbe, prep., about, after, next.
ymb-eôde<-gân, go around.
ymb-settan (6), set around.
ymb-sittan (1), >ymb-sittend, es, m., neighbor.
ymb-sprǣce, adj., whereof people talk.
ymb-ûtan, adv. prep., about.
yppan (6), open, disclose.
yppe, adj., detected.
yrdling, es, m., ploughman, farmer.
yrfe, s, n., inheritance.
yrfe-peard, es, m., inheritor.
irre, adj., wrathful.
ŷtemest, adj., sup. <ût, outmost, extreme.
ŷttra, adj. comp. <ût, outer.

APPENDIX TO VOCABULARY.

âdrincan (1), be quenched.
âgên, prep., towards.
âhafen<âhebban.
âhte, ought.
ald, age, 70, 3.
âlêde<âlecgan, lay, remit.
âlêh<âlêogan.
â-limpan (1), happen, come.
â-lŷfan (6), be permitted.
â-myrran (6), spend.
Angel, es, m. n., Angeln.
ângylde, adv., once.
anlîcnes, se, f., likeness.
ârôda, p. p. of ârian.
â-settan (6), set on.
â-springan (1), rise.
â-styrian (6), stir.

ǣ, f., law.
ǣfæst, adj., pious.
æfter, prep., among.
æfter-genga, n, m., successor.
ǣ-gleâp, adj., learned in the law.
ǣl, e, f., awl.
ælc, any.
ær, es, n., bronze.
æt-eôpan (6), appear.

be, prep., with, concerning.
beâh<bûgan.
beân-cod, des, m., husks.
be-clyppan (6), embrace.
be-eôde, beset.
be-fôn (5), clothe.
be-gŷman (6), take care.
be-healdan (5), take care.
behefe, convenient.
beheonan, this side of.
beôdan (3), demand.
beorgan (1), guard.
beôt, es, n., promise.
be-reâfian (6), strip.
bern, es, n., barn.
be-sceâpian (6), look at.
be-seôn (1), look around.
bêtan (6), repair.
be-tæcan, -tæhte (6), assign.
be-þencan (6), bethink.
bi-hroren<bihreôsan.
binna, n, m., bin.
bi-scerian (6), sever, free.
bi-perian (6), protect.
blâc, bright, pale.
blîde-môd=blid-môd.
blindnes, se, f., blindness.
blis, se, f., kindness.
blôtan (5), sacrifice.
borgian (6), borrow.
brecan (1), urge.
bûend, es, m., inhabitant.
bufan=bufon, above.
bûgan (3), submit.
burh-hlid, es, n., mountain slopes.
burh-sittend, adj., dwelling in town.
burh-paru, e, f., city, citizens.
bûtan, bûton, if only, except, but.

canon, es, m., canon.
cearian (6), care.
cû, cŷ, f., § 86, cow.
cuma, n, m., stranger.
cpehte<cpeccan.
cyn, nes, n., cynnâ, gen. plur., courtesies, etiquette.
cŷpan (6), keep.
cyrran (6), submit.
cyssan (6), kiss.

deôr-frid, es, m., deer-park.
driht, e, f., throng, company.
dugude and geogode, old and young.
dydrung, e, f., illusion.

eâc spilce, also.
eâcen, adj., pregnant.
ealdor, es, m., chief.
ealdorman, nes, m., governor.
eal-fela, adj., very many.
eallinga=eallunge.
ear, es, n., ear of corn.
earfod, e, f., tribulation.
êdel-peard, prince.
egesa, egsa, n, m., terror.
egeslic, adj., terrible.
ehtnes, se, f., persecution.
eln, e, f., ell.
eolet, es, m., bay.
eord-scræf, es, n., grave.

fandian (6), tempt, try.
fædm, es, m. f., expanse.
fæt, adj., fat.
feâ, feâpa, few.
feccan (6), fetch.
feor, prep., far from.
feorlen, adj., far.
ferd=fyrd.
ferh, es, m., swine.
findan (1), attend to.
floc-mǣlum, adv., in flocks.
flota, n, m., sailor, fleet.
folgad, es, m., service.
for-beôdan (3), restrain.
ford-bær(u), o, e, f., creation.
forgitan (1), forget.
for-gŷman (6), disobey.
for-nom<for-niman.
for-scrincan (1), wither.
for-spillan (6), waste.
for-peordan=for-purdan.
ful-fremed, perfect.
pâ . . . . furdum, as soon as.
fyr, farther.
fyrd-pîc, -es, n., camp.
fyrhto (undeclined), fear.

galan (4), sing.
gear-dæg, es, m., day of yore.
geare, adv., well.
gearpe, adv., well.
ge-bǣdan (6), constrain.
ge-belgan (1), gebealg hine, was angry.
ge-blissian (6), bless, rejoice.
ge-brocian (6), break.
gebûr, es, m., door.
ge-byrian (6), belong.
ge-ceôsan (3), decide.
ge-crong = gecrang < ge-cringan.
ge-dǣlan (6), allot.
ge-eâcnian (6), add.
ge-côde, subdue.
ge-fŷsed, stimulated, eager.
ge-gaderian (6), gather.
ge-gyrela, n, m., robe.
ge-herian (6), harry.
gehpǣde, adj., little.
ge-lyfed, adj., of advanced age.
ge-mêt, p. p. of gemêtan.
gemong, prep., among.
geneâ(h)-lǣcan (6), approach.

M

ge-nîpan (2), darken.
ge-nôh, enough.
ge-nŷt, *genŷdan*, compel.
geomore, adv., sadly.
ge-rǣdan (6), advise.
gesceaft, *e*, f., object, thing.
ge-seted, p. p., situated.
get=*git*.
ge-timbrian (6), build.
ge-þungen, p. p., great.
ge-unrêt, p. p., unhappy.
ge-pemman (6), profane.
gepilnung, *e*, f., wish, effort.
gepræc<*geprecan* (1), avenge.
gildan (1), pay.
gilp-cpide, *s*, m., boasting.
giô=*geô*.
gôl<*galan*.
grama, *n*, m. (Lat. ira), wrath.
grin, *e*, f., snare, noose.
grund, *es*, n., abyss.
gum-cyn, *nes*, n., tribe.
gylden, adj., golden.
gŷman (6), watch.

hâtian (6), hate.
hægelian (6), hail.
heâh, adj., right (hand), deep (sea).
Hereda-land, *es*, n., Norway.
hinder-geâp, adj., sly.
hring, *es*, m., ring (on the hand).
hunger, *es*, m., hunger, famine.
hpâ, any one.
hpæder þe, or.
hpæl, *es*, n., wheel, circuit.
hpeorfan (1), turn.

inælan (6), kindle.
inbindan (1), unbind.
îs, *es*, n., ice.

ladian (6), invite.
on lâste, forsaken.
lǣce, *s*, m., physician.
lǣce-hûs, *es*, n., doctor's house.
leahtor, *es*, m., reproach.
leâx, *es*, m., salmon.
leôd-geld, *es*, n., wergild.
leorning-cniht, *es*, m., disciple.
leornung, *e*, f., school.
licgan (1), lie dead.
lîhan, *lâh* (2), lend.
lili-e, *-an*, f., lily.
linden, adj., linden.
list, *es*, m. f., art.
lybbend<*lifian*.

man, *nes*, m., one.
mânful, adj., sinful.
manigfealdlice, adv., manifoldly.
manna, *n*, m., man.
mǣl, *es*, n., portion.
mǣnan (6), bemoan.
mænigo=*menigo*, multitude.
mæsse-reâf, *es*, n., mass-robe.
mǣst-râp, *es*, m., mast rope.
mêd, *e*, f., meed.
medume, adj., small.
meldian (6), speak, utter, display.

mergð, *e*, f., mirth, delight.
mete, *s*, m., dinner.
metod=*meotud*.
Metten, *e*, f., *Mettenâ*, plur., Fates.
mid þŷ, when.
mild-heortnys, *se*, f., mercy.
mon=*man*.

nâpiht, naught.
nǣdl, *e*, f., needle.
nægl, *es*, m., nail.
neôs-u, *-e*, f., nose.
neôpol, adj., deep, profound.
nîð, *es*, m., hostility.
nið-sele, *s*, m., hall beneath the sea.
nihtes, by night.
norðern, adj., northern.
æt nŷhstan, at last.
nŷten, *es*, n., beast.

ôð-beran (1), bear away.
ôðer, second.
of, prep., with.
ofer-prîgan (2), dress.
of-lyst, adj., desirous.
of-teôn, *-teâh* (3), draw off.
on, in; *on ân*, together; *on forð-peg*, for departure.
on-gemong, prep., among.
on-gên=*on-geân*.
on-stellan, *-stealde* (6), establish.

pallium=*pæl*.
peneg, *es*, m., penny.
pluccian (6), pluck.

râ, *n*, m., roe-buck.
rand, *es*, m., shield.
rǣdan (6), read.
ræft, *es*, m., mold.
rǣran (6), raise.
reâfere, *s*, m., robber.
reliquiâs (Latin), relics.
Reste-dæg, *es*, m., Sabbath.
rîce, *s*, n., reign.
rihtpîsnes, *se*, f., righteousness.
rîpan, *râp* (2), reap.
rŷpan (6), ravage.

sacerd, *es*, m., priest.
sâpan (5), sow (seed).
scacan (4), shake.
sceaða, *n*, m., robber.
sceaðenes, *se*, f., robbery, injury.
sceard, adj., p. p., mutilated.
scearp, adj., sharp, keen, wise.
sceat, *tes*, m., money.
se, whoever.
sîð, *es*, m., adventure, departure, time, § 145.
sîð-fæt, *es*, m., course.
siððan, as soon as.
snyttrum, adv., skillfully.
sôð-cpide, *s*, m., true word.
sôn, *es*, m., sound.
spêd, *e*, f., living, property.
spêdig, adj., rich.
staca, *n*, m. f., stake, pin.
styric, *es*, m., steer, calf.

sunna, *n*, m., son.
spâ, which.
spîcan (2), fail.
spimman (1), swim.
spincan (1), toil.
spŷðre, comp. of *spîð*, right (hand).
sŷfernes, *se*, f., soberness.
syllan (6), sell.
syxtig-feald, adj., sixty-fold.

tǣlan (6), slander.
timbrian (6), build.
tô ricene, too quickly.
tô pel, so well.
torht, adj., bright.
tunec-e, *-an*, f., tunic.
tpâ, twice, 31, 29.
tpelfta niht, Twelfth night, Epiphany.

þâ, since.
þane=*þone*<*se*.
þanon, whence.
þæs þe, after.
þæslîce, adv., fitly.
þrimilce, *s*, m., May, *on þam mônde þripa on dæg meolcôdon heorâ neât*.
þrot-e, *-an*, f., throat.
þryccan (6), oppress.
þŷslic, such.

ultor, *es*, m., vulture.
un-dyrne, adv., unmistakably.
un-rihtpîs, adj., unrighteous.

pax-georn, adj., voracious.
pæl-ceasega, *n.*, slaughter-chooser, raven.
pǣr, *e*, f., promise, faith.
pederâs, pl. m., Weder-Goths.
pel, very.
penge, *s*, n., cheek.
peordian (6), present.
peorod=*perod*.
pered, adj., sweet.
perian (6), wear, defend.
pið, opposite to.
pigend, *es*, m., warrior.
piht; *mid pihte*, by any means.
pilcumian (6), welcome.
pilsumnes, *se*, f., devotion.
pîn-sǣl, *es*, n., wine hall.
pîs-e, *-an*, f., business, affair.
pitad=*piton*, know.
plǣtta, *n*, m., nausea.
plite-pam, *mes*, m., disfigurement of looks.
præce, *s*, m., exile.
præc-sîð, *es*, m., exile.
precan (1), sing.
prixlan (6), exchange, sing.
pundrum, adv., wondrously.
purman=*pyrmum*?

ŷðlâd, *e*, f., voyage.
yldo, undeclined; age.
yldesta, *n*, m., prince.
ymb-hŷdig, adj., anxious.
yrre, *s*, n., wrath.
ŷst, *e*, f., storm.

THE END.

VALUABLE STANDARD WORKS

FOR PUBLIC AND PRIVATE LIBRARIES,

PUBLISHED BY HARPER & BROTHERS, NEW YORK.

☞ *For a full List of Books suitable for Libraries, see* HARPER & BROTHERS' TRADE-LIST *and* CATALOGUE, *which may be had gratuitously on application to the Publishers personally, or by letter enclosing Five Cents.*

☞ HARPER & BROTHERS *will send any of the following works by mail, postage prepaid, to any part of the United States, on receipt of the price.*

MOTLEY'S DUTCH REPUBLIC. The Rise of the Dutch Republic. By JOHN LOTHROP MOTLEY, LL.D., D.C.L. With a Portrait of William of Orange. 3 vols., 8vo, Cloth, $10 50.

MOTLEY'S UNITED NETHERLANDS. History of the United Netherlands: from the Death of William the Silent to the Twelve Years' Truce—1609. With a full View of the English-Dutch Struggle against Spain, and of the Origin and Destruction of the Spanish Armada. By JOHN LOTHROP MOTLEY, LL.D., D.C.L. Portraits. 4 vols., 8vo, Cloth, $14 00.

NAPOLEON'S LIFE OF CÆSAR. The History of Julius Cæsar. By His Imperial Majesty NAPOLEON III. Two Volumes ready. Library Edition, 8vo, Cloth, $3 50 per vol.

Maps to Vols. I. and II. sold separately. Price $1 50 *each,* NET.

HAYDN'S DICTIONARY OF DATES, relating to all Ages and Nations. For Universal Reference. Edited by BENJAMIN VINCENT, Assistant Secretary and Keeper of the Library of the Royal Institution of Great Britain; and Revised for the Use of American Readers. 8vo, Cloth, $5 00; Sheep, $6 00.

MACGREGOR'S ROB ROY ON THE JORDAN. The Rob Roy on the Jordan, Nile, Red Sea, and Gennesareth, &c. A Canoe Cruise in Palestine and Egypt, and the Waters of Damascus. By J. MACGREGOR, M.A. With Maps and Illustrations. Crown 8vo, Cloth, $2 50.

WALLACE'S MALAY ARCHIPELAGO. The Malay Archipelago: the Land of the Orang-Utan and the Bird of Paradise. A Narrative of Travel, 1854–1862. With Studies of Man and Nature. By ALFRED RUSSEL WALLACE. With Ten Maps and Fifty-one Elegant Illustrations. Crown 8vo, Cloth, $3 50.

WHYMPER'S ALASKA. Travel and Adventure in the Territory of Alaska, formerly Russian America—now Ceded to the United States—and in various other parts of the North Pacific. By FREDERICK WHYMPER. With Map and Illustrations. Crown 8vo, Cloth, $2 50.

ORTON'S ANDES AND THE AMAZON. The Andes and the Amazon; or, Across the Continent of South America. By JAMES ORTON, M.A., Professor of Natural History in Vassar College, Poughkeepsie, N. Y., and Corresponding Member of the Academy of Natural Sciences, Philadelphia. With a New Map of Equatorial America and numerous Illustrations. Crown 8vo, Cloth, $2 00.

WINCHELL'S SKETCHES OF CREATION. Sketches of Creation: a Popular View of some of the Grand Conclusions of the Sciences in reference to the History of Matter and of Life. Together with a Statement of the Intimations of Science respecting the Primordial Condition and the Ultimate Destiny of the Earth and the Solar System. By ALEXANDER WINCHELL, LL.D., Professor of Geology, Zoology, and Botany in the University of Michigan, and Director of the State Geological Survey. With Illustrations. 12mo, Cloth, $2 00.

WHITE'S MASSACRE OF ST. BARTHOLOMEW. The Massacre of St. Bartholomew: Preceded by a History of the Religious Wars in the Reign of Charles IX. By HENRY WHITE, M.A. With Illustrations. 8vo, Cloth, $1 75.

LOSSING'S FIELD-BOOK OF THE REVOLUTION. Pictorial Field-Book of the Revolution; or, Illustrations, by Pen and Pencil, of the History, Biography, Scenery, Relics, and Traditions of the War for Independence. By BENSON J. LOSSING. 2 vols., 8vo, Cloth, $14 00; Sheep, $15 00; Half Calf, $18 00; Full Turkey Morocco, $22 00.

LOSSING'S FIELD-BOOK OF THE WAR OF 1812. Pictorial Field-Book of the War of 1812; or, Illustrations, by Pen and Pencil, of the History, Biography, Scenery, Relics, and Traditions of the Last War for American Independence. By BENSON J. LOSSING. With several hundred Engravings on Wood, by Lossing and Barritt, chiefly from Original Sketches by the Author. 1088 pages, 8vo, Cloth, $7 00; Sheep, $8 50; Half Calf, $10 00.

ALFORD'S GREEK TESTAMENT. The Greek Testament: with a critically revised Text; a Digest of Various Readings; Marginal References to Verbal and Idiomatic Usage; Prolegomena; and a Critical and Exegetical Commentary. For the Use of Theological Students and Ministers. By HENRY ALFORD, D.D., Dean of Canterbury. Vol. I., containing the Four Gospels. 944 pages, 8vo, Cloth, $6 00; Sheep, $6 50.

ABBOTT'S FREDERICK THE GREAT. The History of Frederick the Second, called Frederick the Great. By JOHN S. C. ABBOTT. Elegantly Illustrated. 8vo, Cloth, $5 00.

ABBOTT'S HISTORY OF THE FRENCH REVOLUTION. The French Revolution of 1789, as viewed in the Light of Republican Institutions. By JOHN S. C. ABBOTT. With 100 Engravings. 8vo, Cloth, $5 00.

ABBOTT'S NAPOLEON BONAPARTE. The History of Napoleon Bonaparte. By JOHN S. C. ABBOTT. With Maps, Woodcuts, and Portraits on Steel. 2 vols., 8vo, Cloth, $10 00.

ABBOTT'S NAPOLEON AT ST. HELENA; or, Interesting Anecdotes and Remarkable Conversations of the Emperor during the Five and a Half Years of his Captivity. Collected from the Memorials of Las Casas, O'Meara, Montholon, Antommarchi, and others. By JOHN S. C. ABBOTT. With Illustrations. 8vo, Cloth, $5 00.

ADDISON'S COMPLETE WORKS. The Works of Joseph Addison, embracing the whole of the "Spectator." Complete in 3 vols., 8vo, Cloth, $6 00.

ALCOCK'S JAPAN. The Capital of the Tycoon: a Narrative of a Three Years' Residence in Japan. By Sir RUTHERFORD ALCOCK, K.C.B., Her Majesty's Envoy Extraordinary and Minister Plenipotentiary in Japan. With Maps and Engravings. 2 vols., 12mo, Cloth, $3 50.

ALISON'S HISTORY OF EUROPE. FIRST SERIES: From the Commencement of the French Revolution, in 1789, to the Restoration of the Bourbons, in 1815. [In addition to the Notes on Chapter LXXVI., which correct the errors of the original work concerning the United States, a copious Analytical Index has been appended to this American edition.] SECOND SERIES: From the Fall of Napoleon, in 1815, to the Accession of Louis Napoleon, in 1852. 8 vols., 8vo, Cloth, $16 00.

BALDWIN'S PRE-HISTORIC NATIONS. Pre-Historic Nations; or, Inquiries concerning some of the Great Peoples and Civilizations of Antiquity, and their Probable Relation to a still Older Civilization of the Ethiopians or Cushites of Arabia. By JOHN D. BALDWIN, Member of the American Oriental Society. 12mo, Cloth, $1 75.

BARTH'S NORTH AND CENTRAL AFRICA. Travels and Discoveries in North and Central Africa: being a Journal of an Expedition undertaken under the Auspices of H. B. M.'s Government, in the Years 1849–1855. By HENRY BARTH, Ph.D., D.C.L. Illustrated. 3 vols., 8vo, Cloth, $12 00.

HENRY WARD BEECHER'S SERMONS. Sermons by HENRY WARD BEECHER, Plymouth Church, Brooklyn. Selected from Published and Unpublished Discourses, and Revised by their Author. With Steel Portrait. Complete in 2 vols., 8vo, Cloth, $5 00.

LYMAN BEECHER'S AUTOBIOGRAPHY, &c. Autobiography, Correspondence, &c., of Lyman Beecher, D.D. Edited by his Son, CHARLES BEECHER. With Three Steel Portraits, and Engravings on Wood. In 2 vols., 12mo, Cloth, $5 00.

BOSWELL'S JOHNSON. The Life of Samuel Johnson, LL.D. Including a Journey to the Hebrides. By JAMES BOSWELL, Esq. A New Edition, with numerous Additions and Notes. By JOHN WILSON CROKER, LL.D., F.R.S. Portrait of Boswell. 2 vols., 8vo, Cloth, $4 00.

www.ingramcontent.com/pod-product-compliance
Lightning Source LLC
LaVergne TN
LVHW011225110826
845150LV00006B/1551

9781425516062